RACERS APART

DEDICATION

To Donald Campbell and Lee Taylor, on account...

At his memorial service Lee's family chose the John Denver song
The Eagle and The Hawk. Its words summarize so well the freedom
of those who reach beyond the norms of everyday life:

> I am the eagle, I live in high country
> In rocky cathedrals that reach to the sky
> I am the hawk and there's blood on my feathers
> But time is still turning, they soon will be dry
> And all those who see me, and all who
> Believe in me,
> Share in the freedom I feel when I fly.
>
> Come dance with the west wind
> And touch on the mountain tops;
> Sail o'er the canyons and up to the stars;
> And reach for the heavens,
> And hope for the future;
> And all that we can be;
> And not what we are.

RACERS APART

Memories of motorsport heroes

David Tremayne

MRP

MOTOR RACING PUBLICATIONS LTD
Unit 6, The Pilton Estate, 46 Pitlake, Croydon CRO 3RA, England

First Published 1991

British Library Cataloguing in Publication Data

Tremayne, David
  Racers apart
  I. Title
  796.72092

ISBN 0-947981-58-6

Typeset by Ryburn Typesetting Ltd; origination by Ryburn Reprographics, Halifax, West Yorkshire

Printed in Great Britain by
The Amadeus Press Limited, Huddersfield, West Yorkshire

PHOTO CREDITS

All photographs within this book (other than promotional material) were taken by LAT Photographic with the following exceptions: Front cover: Donald Campbell, © The Press Association; Chris Amon: portrait © Gerhart Brinkmann, in March 701 © Trevor B. Morgan; Mario Andretti: Indy Lola © Art Flores; Donald Campbell: portrait, in *Bluebird K4* and *K7* boats © The Press Association, *Bluebird CN7* car photograph by British Petroleum; Jim Clark: Indy 1964 courtesy of Indianapolis Motor Speedway, Jim Clark Room © David Tremayne; Graham Hill: portrait © Toni Temburg; Ray Keech, Frank Lockhart and Lee Bible: Lockhart portrait and in *Stutz*, Keech in *Triplex* and Lee Bible courtesy of Bob Constanzo at Daytona International Speedway, Keech in Simplex courtesy of Indianapolis Motor Speedway and Cyril Posthumus; Rick Mears: in Brabham courtesy of Nigel Roebuck, at Indianapolis 1991 courtesy of Indianapolis Motor Speedway; Ron Musson, Bill Muncey and Dean Chenoweth: Muncey portrait, Atlas Van Lines, Chenoweth portrait and *Miss Budweiser* courtesy of Kevin Desmond, *Nitrogen Too* courtesy of Roger Newton, Musson portrait and *Bardahl* action courtesy of Ken Muscatel, Antique Raceboat Foundation; David Purley: portrait © Peter Tempest; Jochen Rindt: portrait with Chapman © Toni Temburg; Pedro Rodriguez: portrait © Peter Tempest, in BRM P160 © Diana Burnett; Eddie Sachs: portrait, in 1961 Watson roadster and in 1964 Shrike courtesy of Indianapolis Motor Speedway; Raymond Sommer: photographs courtesy of Cyril Posthumus; Jackie Stewart: 1973 portrait © Trevor B. Morgan; Roger Williamson: portrait © Trevor B. Morgan.

Contents

INTRODUCTION

What makes a hero? It's a concept I've always found a little difficult to define concisely, but my dog-eared *Collins English Dictionary* makes a pretty good stab. 'A man distinguished by exceptional courage, nobility, fortitude; a man who is idealized for possessing superior qualities in any field'.

I like that. Somebody who arouses feelings of admiration, awe, respect, call them what you may. To that you might add: 'someone who is prepared to risk everything in his pursuit of a goal, who never gives up, nor gives less than his all. A man with whom one might converse pleasantly, yet from whom one feels totally separated when he climbs into the cockpit of a racing car or boat and prepares to demonstrate the unusual talent by which he lives. Somebody rendered different from normal people by his willingness to live on the outer edge of skill and luck, no matter what the possible consequences or cost'.

I have met, and liked, a lot of second-rate racing drivers over the years, but you will not read of them here. Instead, within these pages are stories of those who have exposed them for what they are. Not all of the people I have chosen to write about possess, or possessed, all of the aforementioned qualities; indeed, rare are those so blessed. Some I never met, others I knew, or know well and like. Still more I admired as drivers, yet disliked as people. I don't pretend that this is a comprehensive list; it certainly isn't. There are many drivers worthy of the description who don't appear here, simply because this is a personal selection, based on what the individuals have meant to me.

Each of the drivers in this book is in his own way a little light in the aurora of my ardour for racing. Some were extinguished along the way, in some cases well before I came on the scene, but each can be rekindled in those private moments when the rest of the world can go to hell, or when I get together with other racing enthusiasts.

With each rekindling comes such pleasure, tinged with sadness though it may be, that at times I have experienced a sort of breathless exhilaration in recalling their exploits, and gone back about my business with stronger heart and fresh motivation.

I love reading. One of the few things I seriously resent about the sinecure of motorsport writing is that it leaves so little time to indulge in that simple passion. You can't read and write at the same time. Well, I can't, anyway. Yet there have been times when I have sat, eyes occasionally moist if the writer is good enough, just reading about racers. Many of my heroes have been underdogs, and I have always been moved by poignancy.

I felt it reading about Denny Hulme's courage in dealing with his Indy burns in the aftermath of Bruce McLaren's death. There was the iron man upon whom everyone was relying to hold the shattered team together, going through pure hell as his weakened skin would blister and split every time he held a race car's steering wheel. What touched me most was the fact that he said barely a word about his plight, nor will he to this day. Yet what agony he must have endured.

Or there was Neville Duke's courage at Farnborough in 1952 when he took his Hawker Hunter up immediately after John Derry's awful accident, and smashed the Sound Barrier. It wasn't bravado, it wasn't callous, but a kind of soul-purging, for Derry had been a good friend.

Or there was the time when Innes Ireland explained to writer Michael Cooper-Evans how he felt when his friend and team-mate Alan Stacey had been killed at Spa in 1960. Though it was years later, Michael felt a deep embarrassment to have intruded into Innes' personal life when he realized that that lovely, colourful Scot was crying as he retold the tale.

Ah, therein lies the fascination of the people within a wonderful sport, those who by their exploits enrich the lives of others around them. At a time when the sport's image is frequently tarnished, it is heartening to know such people still walk among us, if only we have the eyes and sensitivity to see them.

They need not always be drivers. One of my favourites, who very definitely is not, nor ever could have been, is an outwardly blunt individual who can be ruder than I would ever dare be, the kind of man who will stick to you like glue when you are his only companion at an airport or wherever, but who will abandon you without compunction at the delayed check-in if a third party is free. Yet somewhere within his rotund frame beats a heart whose components are like those of a gold watch. One day he learned of the death of a close friend's adult son. The close friend was a successful driver already mentioned. My friend's wife discovered him, alone, this hardened, untouchable, cynical man, crying his eyes out in the back garden.

These are the stories of racing people that so fascinate me, not always of derring-do on the tracks, but of the human background to the characters involved and their accomplishments.

I hope I have done the right thing by the racers in this book, and maybe even settled some sort of subconscious debt owed them for the enjoyment they have given. I hope you enjoy reading it, too, and can accept the omission of personal favourites. God knows, there are enough of them. But most of all, I hope at times that it grabs you by the heart and re-ignites a familiar spark within all who admire those who are prepared to lay everything on the line in pursuit of their ambitions and personal credos. They may have enriched their own lives in doing so, but they have also enriched countless others.

DAVID TREMAYNE
Harrow and Stapleton, 1991.

ACKNOWLEDGEMENTS

Quite the nicest part of writing this book, the pure self-indulgence aside, has been the unstinting help and encouragement I have received from a number of sources. Countless racing people have given freely of their time and anecdotes, and for that I am deeply grateful.

Besides all those extant racers who appear within these covers, I have to thank many others: Ken Anderson; Dorothy Taylor Arevalos; John Baldwin; Herbie Blash; Sir Jack Brabham; Ross Brawn; Nick Brittan; Bob Burd; Eddie Cheever; Peter Collins; Bob Constanzo; Mike Cotton; Jabby Crombac; Jim Deist; Ron Dennis; Frank Dernie; Kevin Desmond; Mike Earle; Chris Economaki; Art Flores; Trevor Foster; Barrie Gill; Alex Hawkridge; Alan Henry; Mark Hughes; Jeff Hutchinson; Eddie Jordan; Gordon Kirby; LAT Photographic (Steven Tee, Bob McCaffrey, Charles Coates, Malcolm Griffiths); Bruce McCaw; Chris Mears; Pat Mennem; Louie Meyer; Maureen Mitchell; Ronan Morgan; Gordon Murray; Ken Muscatel; Steve Nichols; Ken Norris; Jack Oliver; Tim Parnell; Ian Phillips; Christine Philpott; Dave Price; Heinz Pruller; Bobby Rahal; Jo Ramirez; Alan Rees; Nigel Roebuck; Keke Rosberg; Dennis Rushen; Dick Scammell; Sally Swart (nee Stokes); Patrick Tambay; Steven Tee; Trish Tremayne; Ken Tyrrell; Dick Wallen; Prof Sid Watkins; Kathy Weida; Tom Wheatcroft; Bob Williams; Frank Williams; Peter Windsor; and Eoin Young.

1

CHRIS AMON

Whatever did he do to Lady Luck?

"On the track he was brilliant, off the track he was a disaster!" – Eoin Young

I don't think anyone ever did really figure it out, least of all Chris Amon. He was, is, a charming bloke, personable, fun at parties, of easygoing temperament. Hell, he even liked a drink and a smoke. He didn't have two heads, wear funny clothes, or squeeze the toothpaste at the wrong end.

But whatever it was he did to Lady Luck, and whenever he did it, it was bad. Whatever wounds she felt, they went deep. With Reg Parnell (at that time running the Bowmaker Lola team) she took him from New Zealand to Europe as a teenager, ready to race Formula One in 1963, and then with Reg's unexpected death early the following year she cast him off. In 1968 and '69 she tantalized him with the sight of Formula One victories for Ferrari, only to snatch them away. Even in 1971 and '72 she denied him again. In 1974, cruellest of all, she led him into the fiasco that was building his own, disastrous Formula One car, when he could have sat in the very Ferrari that so nearly took Niki Lauda to his first World Championship. At every turn, it seemed, lay frustration. If Chris wasn't retiring from the lead he was moving from the right team at the wrong time, snatching defeat from the very jaws of victory.

Could he ever outrun his bad luck? He had been the golden boy as early as 1963, yet through his career he endured more misfortune and disappointment than most of his contemporaries put together. Even that unlucky American Dan Gurney managed four Grand Prix wins and three non-championship Formula One races. In the end, all Chris had to look back on in terms of concrete results were two non-championship Formula One wins, a Le Mans victory and the 1969 Tasman Championship. Yet this was the man who had raced Jimmy Clark – at the time recognized without question as the best driver in the world – wheel-to-wheel in the 1968 Tasman.

Like Jimmy, Chris was a quiet man with strangers, and like him, too, he could warm up at parties. They shared comfortable upbringings and farming backgrounds, and that same detestation of self-aggrandizement. In Chris that was particularly noteworthy, given the silver spoon that had early been slipped into his mouth. Both were hopelessly disorganized in their private lives away from motor racing, too.

If anyone had been pitched back into Formula One in the deepest section of water, it was Amon. He was taken on as a fourth driver by Ferrari at the beginning of 1967, and by the midpoint of the season he was leading the team

after Lorenzo Bandini had been killed, Mike Parkes severely injured and Ludovico Scarfiotti temporarily discouraged. It was quite a gamble for Enzo, because Chris had had only a few good CanAm runs with Bruce McLaren by then, plus the victory at Le Mans with him in 1966, when Lady Luck must have been on vacation.

The two New Zealanders and their team-mates Denny Hulme and Ken Miles lined up for Ford's *coup de grace*, the dead-heat finish, but the organizers were not so keen. Because Chris and Bruce had started further down the line-up – had actually qualified *slower* – they gave them first place on the basis that they had covered the greater distance in the 24 hours. Poor Ken and Denny were thus robbed of their victory, on one of the few occasions when the luck really ran with Chris.

Ferrari himself had been impressed, and an approach was made. As he would later with Villeneuve, he had a feeling about Chris. It was the lifeline the Amon career needed.

Back home in New Zealand he had learned to fly at the age of 16 on his father's sheep farm. He had also done enough with the ex-Owen Organisation Maserati 250F, and then with a brace of Coopers, to attract attention, even if his races tended to end prematurely even then. At Sandown Park in 1963 he was preparing to go back to sheep farming when Reg Parnell whispered a few sweet nothings in his teenaged ear before departing for England. Days later he called again, summoning Chris to Goodwood to test his Formula One Lola-Climax.

Amon took to the car instantly, taking a fifth in the Glover Trophy at Goodwood and then a sixth a fortnight later at the Aintree 200. People began to take notice of the cheerful kid who drove with such confidence, and over the following two seasons he learned about Grand Prix racing in a variety of machinery: the Lola, a Lotus-Climax, a BRM-engined version and then another Lotus-Climax. The results weren't desperately encouraging, though; fifth in Holland in 1964 had given him his only championship points. But when Reg died he struck lucky and went to work with McLaren, the man who would so influence his early career.

A brief outing in a works Cooper-Maserati at the 1966 French GP at Reims led nowhere, and first time out in the Ferrari at Monaco in 1967 he was forced to drive lap after lap past the burnt wreckage of team-mate Bandini's car after the Italian's fatal accident. He finished third, placed fourth in the Dutch GP at Zandvoort, and then third again at Spa-Francorchamps. That time it was team-mate Mike Parkes who lay in hospital, with multiple leg fractures after crashing on the first lap of the Belgian GP on oil spilt from Stewart's BRM.

A lesser man might have weighed the odds and chosen an easier living, but Chris persisted and fought some mighty battles with the Repco Brabhams, and by the end of the year a season's development had taken the by now 48-valve Ferrari closer to the dominant Lotus-Fords of Clark and Hill. At Watkins Glen Chris was running them both down during the United States GP. Hill had a baulky clutch, and Clark would later break his rear suspension and limp to victory. Had Chris been around by then he would have won. Instead, his engine had long since lost its oil pressure. It was a similar story in Mexico, where he qualified alongside Clark, chased him valiantly, and then ran out of fuel in the closing laps. The pattern was emerging.

When a Ferrari *did* win a Grand Prix, in France in 1968, it was new team-mate Jacky Ickx's, at Rouen. Chris chose the wrong tyres, but in any case was honest about his performances in wet races.

"A new young driver is quick in the wet... it doesn't bother him. I never liked the wet, although it depends on the circuit. Honestly, I can go out on a wet day and I've got no idea before the race whether I'll go well or not. In the dry I've got a pretty fair idea, but I can get in the car under wet conditions and be absolutely hopeless. I can't get going at all. Yet another day I can throw it all over the place and not be bothered."

By then he had lost the Spanish GP at Jarama after starting from pole and leading until lap 58 when his fuel pump blew a fuse. At Spa he led John Surtees comfortably on the opening lap, but was baulked by a slower car making its way back to the pits – "bloody Jo Bonnier!" – and fell behind the Honda. It promptly threw a stone through the Ferrari's radiator before retiring itself. Another pole, another victory lost. He was on the pole again at Zandvoort, but was an unhappy Firestone-shod sixth in rain that favoured Dunlop. Rouen brought only 10th, and then at Silverstone he fought tooth-and-nail with Jo Siffert's Lotus, briefly getting ahead, but having to settle for an honourable second. "They were a bit pissed-off about that until they saw the state of my tyres."

In the awful conditions at the Nurburgring he was running a strong third in the German GP when the differential failed, and at Monza, in Italy, he was running second when he slid off on oil and had the grandparents of a shunt, which threw the Ferrari into the trees. "That was a big one," he recalled years later. "In fact, I had an 8-millimetre movie of the whole thing. *Autosprint* used a perfect shot of me upside-down 30ft in the air, with my hands still on the wheel. I stayed in the car the whole time, because that was only the second time we were using seat belts. I'd had them fitted at the Nurburgring to keep me in my seat over the bumps. But for them, well... it was exactly the same thing that had happened to Mike Parkes at Spa the year before, except that he was half-in and half-out of the car. That's the fastest accident I ever want to have."

At St Jovite in Canada it seemed, finally, that his luck had turned. After sharing joint fastest practice time with Rindt, he set joint fastest lap with Siffert and was leading by a country mile on the 73rd of 90 laps when his transmission expired. Somewhere, it seemed, Lady Luck had a wax effigy of his car and delighted in sticking pins in it. "That was the biggest disappointment. A minute ahead, and it just stopped. I was just sick. It was a very hard one to lose. You know, I may not have shown it at the time, but as it went on it got more and more frustrating. I didn't give the impression, but it got to me." His sense of irony is finely honed, and he added: "That certainly stimulated some decisions which I made which were less than good..."

"He was", said Ferrari designer Mauro Forghieri, "a tremendous driver. The one I believe could really fight with Clark. But perhaps he didn't believe he was as good as he really was..." And Chris *didn't* believe he was as good as Jimmy. "I always said that Jimmy was the one man I felt I could go with only on my day. I never felt confident of beating him. He had this ability to draw on that little bit more each time. In a straight dogfight he maybe wasn't at his best, and he made one or two mistakes when we raced against each other in the 1968 Tasman series which let me lead a lap or two, but when he was out front, where he liked to be, he didn't make mistakes. I always felt more pressure when I was leading than I did when I was trying to lead. I think that's the more normal way."

Equipped with a 2.4-litre Dino V6-engined Ferrari he won the Tasman-opening New Zealand GP at Pukekohe, and then won again at Levin, but as Clark's Lotus 49 came on song the championship swung the way of the Scot. Nobody who watched them race in the Australian GP at Sandown Park, however, had any doubt about Amon's ability. He and Clark were literally glued together throughout the 55 laps, and as he crossed the line Jimmy's eyes were everywhere as he watched for the Ferrari in his mirrors. It was there alright, a mere tenth of a second behind.

"We'd been together the whole race and I'd observed early on (and I'm sure Jimmy had, too) that if I led I couldn't pull away. We'd both come to the conclusion that all that mattered would be the last corner on the last lap. I spent most of the race right behind and I had a bit of a plan, but I outfoxed myself. I had to see if it would work three and then two laps from the end, and each time I had my car ahead as we crossed the line.

"He had a lot better brakes on the Lotus, as I recall, because we only had Formula Two brakes on our cars, and each time I led he passed me into Turn One the following lap. On that final lap I tried exactly the same thing, but he kept it in fourth and didn't change up to fifth; he held on to the gear just that much longer. That's what did it. I'm sure he'd worked it all out earlier, but if I hadn't shown my hand..."

In 1969, with Clark dead, Jochen Rindt provided his principal opposition, but with four victories Chris was untouchable, taking a richly deserved title success. If he thought it was an omen of things to come, he was soon to be disabused. Lady Luck was just getting ready to twist the knife.

The Ferrari 312 again flattered to deceive, and he was always convinced that the latest version of the V12 was less powerful than the old, which itself had been no match for a good Cosworth V8. Third at Zandvoort was to be his sole reward, and behind lay lost victories yet again. After Rindt's Lotus had crashed at Montjuich Park in the Spanish GP, Chris had built up another commanding lead, nursing the V12 with only 10,200 of its permissible 10,900rpm. Still it blew on lap 57, and Stewart never had a luckier win. At Monaco he shadowed the Scot's Matra until his differential failed, and when Jackie retired only six laps later, Graham Hill came through for his fifth and final Monaco success. By the British GP there was simply no point in continuing, and Ferrari withdrew to test and develop a new car, the 312B, with its Forghieri-designed flat-12 power unit. Here, again, the story was agonizingly typical. Whenever Chris drove it, it broke. His patience broke with it.

"I'd been driving Ferraris which handled well but had nothing like the power of their rivals. I told Ferrari, which didn't make me popular, but it was true. Then I tried the flat-12 and I knew immediately that it was a different matter. It

Jarama 1968 was so typical of the Amon Luck. Once Jean-Pierre Beltoise had retired in Ken Tyrrell's Matra-Ford, Chris kept Rodriguez' BRM at bay and was headed for victory when a fuel pump fuse blew on his 59th lap.

had power, alright. But every time I tested it, the thing flew to bits. That was the final straw. I'd had a really demoralizing year and the flat-12 was going to be the saviour, the bright hope. When I first tested it it did three laps before the crank broke. The next time it was five laps before something fairly major went wrong. I thought 'God, this is going to be the same as 1969'. I really didn't think I could cope."

He quit to join the newly formed March team, adamant that he must have one of Cosworth's Ford DFVs behind him. "That was the other thing. The people I considered my main rivals – Stewart and Rindt – were winning with the Cosworth DFV, and I thought it would be best to compete on equal terms, so it was a combination of both things, plus the faith I had at that time in Robin Herd, whom I'd known well in my McLaren days." It was to be the biggest mistake of his career, and history was to be denied what would have been a Rindt/Amon battle for the World Championship. Truly, it was one of racing's great Might Have Beens.

The Ferraris went from strength to strength, with Ickx running the Austrian close for the title. The March, ultimately, flattered early only to deceive in the cruellest manner. There were few bright spots, although in April he did win the *Daily Express*/GKN International Trophy race at Silverstone, where he beat Stewart's similar March fair and square.

For once it was a fairy tale. He took pole in his Firestone-shod 701, and led the first heat for an easy triumph. In the second Stewart won in his Dunlop-shod version after getting a better start, but Chris set fastest lap and was right on his tail when he was baulked. Overall, he won by a comfortable 10 seconds. Momentarily, it looked as if, after all, moving from Ferrari hadn't been such a dumb idea.

There were seconds, too, two of them. At Spa he finished behind Rodriguez, and at Clermont-Ferrand, in France, behind Rindt. Spa was the real tantalizer.

11

"I saw this white thing just coming like a rocket behind us, after I'd led the first lap and then retaken the lead from Stewart on the third. I couldn't figure out who it was at first, then I saw it was Rodriguez. I sat right behind him then, and all I could think was, 'It won't last. It's a BRM. It won't last'." It did. Of all days, that was the one the V12 held together, to beat Chris by a mere 1.1 seconds after nearly 100 minutes of racing. Chris smashed the lap record, and his average speed was only three-hundredths of a mile an hour slower than the Mexican's, but second was not first. By the end of the season he had lost faith in March, and it in him, a brilliant drive in Austria and an excellent third behind the Ferraris in Canada notwithstanding. The best thing he could have done was bury the hatchet and sort himself out with the team for 1971, so he left to join Matra. Had he stayed, with the slippery 711, he might finally have cracked it. After all, Ronnie Peterson finished second in the World Championship that year to Stewart, and he was still a novice.

Perhaps his most satisfying day came at Silverstone early in 1970. He'd switched from Ferrari because he wanted similar equipment to Stewart, and in the International Trophy race he beat the Scot fair and square for the first of his two F1 triumphs.

That was Chris' problem. He was totally disorganized outside the car. He made even Clark look decisive. Whatever advice he took, invariably it seemed to be wrong.

OTHER VOICES

Eoin Young – a close friend

"We used to drink at this pub called the *Gloucester Arms*, in Kingston, when we worked for McLarens. That was when he was with Reg Parnell. We used to knock off work at 5 o'clock, 5.30, and we'd always be in the pub, Tyler Alexander, Wally Wilmott and me, Chris, Peter Revson, anybody of that lot who lived in the Surbiton area. We'd all be in there by 6 o'clock and we wouldn't go out till 9, 9.30, 10 o'clock for dinner. If Amon wasn't singing *Danny Boy* by 8 o'clock there was something wrong! He drank gin and tonic. We always used to say, when sponsorship came in, it was a pity Chris was too late because Gilbey's would have sponsored him like a shot!

"He thoroughly enjoyed life, but it's amazing when you think that when Reg Parnell brought him over he was only 19. When you think of 19-year-olds now, and there he was getting dropped straight into Formula One. It was just amazing.

"When Reg died Chris was really cast off, and then in 1965 he was working with Bruce because he had nothing else to do. All he had was the promise of a CanAm drive as soon as Bruce made two cars. But to begin with there was only one. And so, all he had to do was the testing. We were running Firestones then, so he did a lot of Firestone testing, and they soon found that he was a brilliant test driver. I mean, nobody knew why.

"I think it was when he was still with McLarens, it was at Silverstone. He came in and they were fiddling about, nothing much going on, and Bruce Harre, Firestone's race engineer, had said, 'When he comes in we'll play a joke on him. We'll make a big performance of switching all the tyres around, but we'll actually send him out on the same set'. So they did that and he went out and they all of a sudden thought, 'Christ, what have we done? If he comes back in and says, 'Oh, they're much better', we've ruined the guy's career'. There was no way out of it, and so they were terrified when he did come in and he sat there. And then suddenly he said, 'Look, I don't know quite what to say, these tyres feel just like the ones you took off. Could there have been some mistake?'. They were all so relieved!

"I'm sure it was either that incident, or an incident very similar, that got back to Ferrari, because they were on Firestones then as well, and that's how he got the Ferrari drive, through his testing.

"Reg dying really upset the plans. If Reg had lived Chris was his ace card, and he would have got the good Lotuses, he would have got the good engines. But when Reg died that was all the driving force gone. And Chris was literally cast adrift.

"Then he had the drive with Bruce with the Fords. Bruce got him that drive and helped him a lot. Bruce got him opportunities he might otherwise, almost certainly wouldn't otherwise have got if he'd been knocking around on his own. He was certainly a brilliant driver, but as good a driver as you are, if you don't get the opportunities you're never going to be able to show it. At that time, being a New Zealander and a friend of McLaren's was probably the best thing that happened to him.

"The trouble was, I don't know whether he felt he always needed a manager, but he had a succession of them and they just led him astray. I'm sure Chris would say the same thing. What happened with one thing was that he got into flying, and he was very enthusiastic about it. He'd learned at school, when they had an airfield about 10 minutes away from home. Here in England he had a Cessna dealership based at Fairoaks, and Chris was then getting the Matra drives and he didn't have time to run it, so a friend, Bill Bryce, was helping him out. Then they decided they'd form a company called Brymon Airways, which was Bryce and Amon, and it's still going.

"At this point Amon's manager said, 'Oh look, this whole airline thing isn't going well, we've got to get out of it. Sack Bryce and let's just close the whole thing down'. Bryce got to hear about it, went to his local bank manager and said, 'I think I can buy this company, will you back me?', and the guy said 'Yes'. The way I hear the story, Bryce went back to Fairoaks and Amon's manager comes in and says, 'You're fired', and Bryce says, 'I'm sorry about that, *you* are. I've just bought the company!'. So they were within an ace of closing the whole thing down and Bryce bought it and took it on. So, I mean, I know there's been a lot of stories about that, but I'm sure they never came from Chris.

"The John Dalton Amon deal was just another of Chris' disastrous moves. Then he was into buying old MkII 3.8 Jags and fettling them up and selling them to the colonies about the time the market went tits-up and nobody needed them. He used to have sort of six or seven old MkII Jags on the lawn outside his house when they were all living in Surbiton.

"The story of Chris' life was getting it wrong. He had a brilliant natural talent. On the track he was brilliant, off the track he was a disaster!"

■ ■ ■

With Matra it was almost Ferrari all over again, with a gutless engine allied to an excellent chassis, possibly the best of the crop. He actually won a Grand Prix that year, in Argentina, but it was non-championship and, in truth, it was a slightly lucky win. Not that, with his own ill-luck in the past, anyone would ever hold that against him. Unusually for him, a couple of his rivals had fallen by the wayside after coming off second-best to the hard-driven Matra as he triumphed over Henri Pescarolo and Carlos Reutemann.

"The trouble was, that 1971 engine was dreadful. Seriously, it was laughable, and the situation just got worse. I was third in Barcelona and then Monaco was OK, but from then on the engines were pathetic and we got to some circuits where we just didn't have a hope. After Germany they decided to give Austria a miss and just try and concentrate on developments for a month."

They came back at Monza, where he put the car on the pole. From lap 36 onwards it appeared he had worked himself into position for victory, and until lap 46 he was only headed once. Then he tore away one of his visors, and ended up losing them all. With his eyes exposed to the 170mph slipstream he fell to the back of the five-car bunch battling for second in his wake, finally finishing sixth. Perhaps he would have finished in that position anyway, for on the final lap the V12 hiccoughed with serious fuel starvation... Amon luck yet again.

This time he stayed for another season, but really 1972 was precious little better, that wonderful day at Clermont aside. "The Monza engine was OK, as good as a Cosworth, but it was only OK on the fast tracks. In places like Mosport it was awful. And the problem in '72 was that they were so inconsistent. Where you needed torque, the engines just didn't want to know. At some places it was as good as a Cossie, at others simply dreadful."

At Monaco, where it rained, he was again in visor trouble, but apart from the need to stop every three laps for a new one, he was lapping as fast as Beltoise, who won... At Clermont he qualified fastest and took an immediate lead, driving with brilliant precision. For exactly the first half he kept the blue car ahead of Hulme and Stewart, and then on the 20th lap he picked up a puncture. He was already second to Stewart when he pitted, then he rejoined in eighth place with a new tyre. Thereafter he drove like the wind, smashing the lap record as he recovered to third place. It was the drive of the year, but yet again victory had been denied. It was to be the last major disappointment. In October, Matra finally let him know it wouldn't be continuing in Formula One, and after another brief flirtation with March, Chris was stymied when Max Mosley decided he could save money by not hiring him; he was left high and dry.

"That race at Clermont was a hard one to lose, too. An enormous disappointment. And possibly it was the one that really changed my career, because if I'd won I think Matra would have decided to stay on for 1973..."

In a car he was sublime, with an intuitive touch that very few drivers are granted. His talent and precious little else brought the dreadful Martini Tecno to sixth place at Zolder in 1973, but by his own admission, later in the year in the wet at Mosport he was "absolutely pathetic" in a one-off drive for Tyrrell. He was his own toughest critic.

By then a die was firmly set in his mind. The only way ahead was to build his own car. Businessman friend John Dalton agreed to help him, and Gordon Fowell, who had designed the alternative Tecno that year, was entrusted with creating an advanced machine to be powered by the Cosworth DFV.

"Most people will think we've copied the Lotus 72", Chris said at the launch of the pale blue Amon AF1 at Goodwood in March 1974, "but the only similarities are the torsion bars and the inboard front brakes. But we feel that the basic concept of the car is different, really a lot more like the new JPS than the 72. If you opt for a relatively simple car you can build it pretty quickly, sort it out fairly easily and probably be more successful more or less immediately." He was thinking of the March 701 and the Tyrrell 001. "It may take some time to get our car fully competitive, but I'm sure it will be worth it in the long run."

Once again he had made a catastrophic decision. The Amon was of advanced concept, siting all its fuel in one tank behind the driver to centralize its weight distribution long before that became *de rigeur*, but it was hopelessly uncompetitive.

"The big trap is to get so involved with the whole thing that you never stop thinking about it. You've got to concentrate on the driving", he said. "Previously I got far too involved in far too many controversial things, and I've been with teams where there's been too much in the way of politics. Now when you start thinking about that side you think about it more than the driving side. You just get stale."

There was precious little driving to think about. By Jarama the experimental aerodynamics had been abandoned and the car started from the penultimate row of the grid. Chris retired when a front brake shaft snapped. At Monaco he qualified it 20th, but the handling was so spooky he withdrew. He tried again in Germany, where he had sinusitis and Larry Perkins took over and crashed in practice, and then Chris ran off for a couple of inconclusive outings for BRM. The one good decision he made was not doing a deal with Bourne for 1975.

The whole situation was a total fiasco, made worse by the knowledge that he had turned down not only Ferrari in the middle of 1973 but, midway through 1974 when Rikki von Opel quit, the second Brabham.

"Ferrari was having problems in 1973, when I was supposed to be driving the Tecno. That was either late or wasn't working. Ferrari called me and David

Yorke and I went to see him. He asked if I could do some races until the Tecno was ready, but Martini, or I think it was probably the Pederzani brothers, weren't keen. I had to say, 'No'." Again, that sense of ironic humour. "Had I taken the Ferrari drive, it's extremely unlikely that I'd have wanted to go back to Tecno..."

There had been rumours, too, of the Yardley McLaren drive that year. "No, the only contact I had with Teddy Mayer was at the Nurburgring in 1976 when he asked me what my plans were for 1977. I told him I was having my house built in New Zealand and that I was going home. Hindsight is a marvellous thing, but that was probably a good decision."

On the Brabham occasion it was not stupidity that prevented him taking a decent ride. It was old-fashioned integrity. "Without John Dalton we couldn't have done anything. He was an old friend I met when I arrived in Europe to drive for Reg. He had always taken a great interest in my racing, and when I asked him to come in to help, he did. He had been very patient and he spent one hell of a lot of money on our own car. The cost of building a car of that sort of configuration is an absolute fortune."

And therein lay the rub. Chris was too loyal to Dalton to take the other opportunities that could have revitalized his career. In the light of what he was to achieve with Mo Nunn's little Ensign team in 1976, they certainly would have.

"I said 'No' to Bernie on the basis that we were doing our own thing. If I'd gone off to drive the Brabham it would have knocked the morale of our team. It wouldn't have been fair to John or to the guys who were working all hours. Once again, if I'd got into the BT44 I'd never have gone back to my own thing. But it was very hard to turn down, very tempting; Brabham was very good that year.

"Our own car was very complicated, far too complicated for our resources in hindsight. The big problem was that things kept falling off. In the initial outings I'd do a few laps and something would drop off. We ditched a lot of the good features, beefed it all up, and then it became overweight. As things began to hold together, it couldn't be competitive because it weighed too much. And it had some fundamental geometry faults in the suspension."

A chance invitation from Mo Nunn took him to the tiny Ensign team in Walsall late in 1975, for what was really intended to be a one-off drive in the Austrian GP. During practice he stunned Nunn by detecting when the designer/builder had fiddled secretly with the rear wing. After telling him to leave the car as it was, Chris returned to the track and felt a change as small as one notch in the rear wing adjustment, and he came in to query it.

"When Mo had called me, I had really agreed to do the race simply because I hadn't done a GP that year and I wasn't doing anything else that weekend. I had a quick think and thought, 'Why not?'. I did it out of interest more than anything.

"Well, Mo told me that the guy they had – Roelof Wunderink – wasn't really getting the job done, but that they weren't looking for a test driver. 'We'll come up with the ideas, you drive', was his attitude. That lasted five minutes by the time I got there! After that wing test I think I convinced him to listen to me and we'd see what could be done."

The following year it proved a brilliant little partnership. In Spain his debut in Mo's updated car reaped fifth place after a fight with Reutemann and Pace in the Brabham-Alfas. In Belgium he qualified eighth and was pushing Scheckter for fourth place behind the Ferraris and Laffite's Ligier when the left rear wheel fell off and threw the car upside-down into a bank. At Anderstorp, in Sweden, he was sensational. All the old flair was evident as he qualified the little N176 an amazing third, and was headed only by Andretti's Lotus and the Tyrrell six-wheelers until he crashed with steering failure. He was quick, too, at Brands Hatch as he proved beyond question during the British GP that his ability was undimmed, but after the recent failures and then Lauda's accident, he decided enough was enough at the German GP. A great Formula One career had ended.

"I did 1976 very much for pleasure," he said, a strange remark for a Grand Prix driver to make at the best of times. "I knew I was intending to come back to New Zealand, and I enjoyed the challenge. We had no money, Brabham's 1972 engines, and very few resources. I wasn't paid a cent."

The atmosphere allayed the cynicism that had been building within him for the modern racing scene, but the accidents became worrying. "I must admit that it ceased to be fun after a while. In Belgium there wasn't so much time to think before the car crashed, but at Anderstorp it seemed like three weeks as the catchfencing got closer and closer. It was a reflection of our lack of resources. The design was alright, but there was so much pressure on the guys. In Sweden the steering arm had pulled out of the upright because it wasn't put in properly. But it had been put in at 4 o'clock one morning as the car was being rebuilt after the Zolder shunt, when they were struggling to get the job done.

"It became a bit frustrating. We were so far down on power. It was fun to be up there in the first few races, but then it became an exercise in frustration. There was no light on the horizon."

The one thing I never understood was why he failed at Indianapolis, if he could run so fast and so smoothly elsewhere. Perhaps it was the sustained nature of the speed, the proximity of the wall. To this day, he doesn't really know the answer himself. You sense that he'd like to.

In 1976 with Mo Nunn's underfinanced little Ensign Amon's star was ascendant once again as he produced a stunning series of drives that embarrassed far more affluent operations. He drove for nothing, for the love of it, and only when its fragility reached worrying proportions did he finally decide to hang up his helmet.

"Of course, I first went there in 1967 with this BRP-built thing that was then owned by an American, and initially it seemed to go not too badly. Prior to qualification, though, there had been Monaco and we'd just lost Bandini. When I went back to Indy Monaco was very much on my mind. Then, when I was warming this car up a rear upright broke and I had a monumental spin and brushed the wall. They fixed it for the second day or week of qualifying, but they didn't fix it properly. It was still spooky, and I began to lose confidence. With McLaren in 1970, well, the cars weren't very good. They were very difficult to

drive. Denny said that at the time, and so did the other guys they got to drive them. It wasn't just me. I really just couldn't get with it, either the car or its turbocharged engine. There was a half a day's response to the throttle, which meant you had to get your foot back in it at the same time as you braked. I just couldn't get it together. The track seemed so narrow, as if there was nothing to go into."

Only days later he went to Spa, where he lapped fast enough for pole and would have won but for Pedro Rodriguez's sensational drive for BRM. Spa, with its trees and banks and funny weather, and the Masta kink which he managed – "once and never again!" – to take flat.

"Yeah, that was funny. Spa was much more difficult, much more dangerous. I never really knew in my own mind why I didn't make Indy work. I suppose there was a bit of a sense that it was too easy to get involved in somebody else's accident. But I was absolutely miles off the pace. Six to eight miles an hour off Denny, and his burns didn't help. I've no excuses for that, really. I never felt happy there, and the days dragged on so long. You'd say the same thing to the same people day after day, and you'd do but two laps before there'd be another yellow flag. It just ground on."

Typical Amon. No attempt to excuse himself, nor to cover things up. Just a genuine interest in why he hadn't been able to handle a situation. In a racing career far better than its results ever suggested, it was the one thing he didn't make work.

OTHER VOICES

Nigel Roebuck – journalist and close friend

"I first met Chris at Barcelona in 1971, my first Grand Prix. I was covering it for *Car and Driver*. It was a curious thing, one of those very few times in life when you meet someone and you just know they are going to be a close friend for life. He was certainly my favourite driver of the time, after his Ferrari years. He was such an artist with a car. As soon as I got involved in Formula One, such as I was then, he was the guy I wanted to know, if that were possible. Nobody knew me at all, but we hit it off instantly. He was very much a star then, but he was so friendly, helpful and open.

"My first proper interview with him was between Clermont and Brands in 1972 for *Competition Car*. It was down at Chris Amon Engines, his company that built Formula Two BDA engines. He had Aubrey Woods from BRM working there. Of course, the whole thing was a disaster! He lost a fortune. When I went there it was virtually going down the pan. We spent the first 40 minutes trying to get the coffee machine working, and in the end he hit it with a hammer! When Woods walked in, Chris got him to go to the pub for some meat pies for lunch. I thought, '*I* have meat pies for lunch, but he's a superstar'. I couldn't believe how down-to-earth he was.

"That winter, Justin Haler of *Competition Car* said, 'Let's do a book on Chris'. I just believed him, then, and Chris thought it was a great idea. He believed it, too, and on the strength of that we did 37 hours of tape. Chris had no contract, didn't ask about money. Nothing. Despite everything that had happened in his life, he hadn't become cynical.

"Well, Haler disappeared and the book never happened. It shattered me, and I thought breaking it to him would be very difficult. I rang him and said I couldn't believe it, but there it was. He just said, 'Oh well, it was quite therapeutic just talking it all through. Are you still coming down for lunch on Sunday?'. It wasn't my fault, but I felt like just another one in the list of people who'd let him down. Anyone else would have cut me dead, but he couldn't see that. He was an immensely kind bloke, and all the things that I thought were important in life were the sort of things he thought were important, too.

"I once did a sort of *Desert Island Discs* thing with him, and asked him what luxury he would take, and he said it would be a Ferrari, a dog or a gin and tonic. You couldn't have anything animate, so he said, 'It'd have to be the Ferrari or the gin and tonic, then. I couldn't have a Ferrari because it would need gas, so it would have to be an everlasting supply of gin and tonic...'"

■ ■ ■

As a racing driver Chris Amon had it all, speed, flair, and that uncanny ability to understand what the car was telling him. He could win in sportscars as well as single-seaters, but never quite in a full-blown Grand Prix. History will record that as a ludicrous paradox. Some said he lacked the will to win, the mean streak. It didn't look that way at Watkins Glen in '67, Jarama, Spa, Brands Hatch, Monza, St Jovite or Mexico City in '68. Or at Monza in '71, or Clermont in '72. Or at a host of other venues. But perhaps he was just too nice a guy to be a super-successful racing driver, or maybe, unlike Clark, who was so similar, he just never found his Chapman figure.

Today he farms his sheep and maintains his ties with his old life via a deal with Toyota. "I'd like to win the World Championship, sure!", he said once, "but I don't want to be doing this for the next 10 years." He says he has no regrets, and he and Tish are very happy.

But what might he have achieved had he stayed with Ferrari for 1970, or returned in 1973 to enjoy the same machinery Niki Lauda subsequently exploited so well in '74 and '75? Or if he had granted Gerard Ducarouge's wish and gone to Ligier in 1979 after Patrick Depailler had broken his legs hang-gliding... The thoughts are tormenting enough for enthusiasts, let alone for the man himself.

In 1990 the Amons came over to England to look up old friends. A group of us met up for lunch at the *Barley Mow*, in East Horsley, an establishment rendered infamous by E S Young in his *Autocar & Motor* columns. Partway through, Roger Hill, the long-serving Tyrrell mechanic, wandered in and was re-introduced to Chris, whom he couldn't have seen for at least 13 years. He barely noticed, grunted something and moved on. I wanted to grab him, shake him, remind him all over again of that big blue Matra wailing through the climbs and descents of Clermont-Ferrand that day when not one of the world's best could hold a candle to him until Lady Luck intervened. But then these things take different people different ways.

Our conversation got around to that race as the afternoon went on, and one of our number teased him again as they reminded him of Jackie Stewart's comment, "I was the only one who avoided the stones that day, that's why I didn't get a puncture."

"Balls", said Chris succinctly. "The bloody road was littered with them. That race was a little hard to cope with. I lost 90 seconds and threw caution to the wind. I was all over the place. Anywhere there was available track, I was on it, and I didn't get another puncture." He laughed heartily. "I don't altogether follow Jackie's logic on that one!" That was the other thing about Amon; he never had time for hyperbole, and could send it up beautifully in that soft ironic tone.

During that trip he and Tish went back to Clermont for a reunion, and he was due once again to be reunited with the Ferrari 312B that he never raced, in an historic demonstration. With incredible *deja vu* it broke its engine in England the week before, and he had to make do with a Formula Two Lotus with a 1-litre BRM engine. That broke, too, dropping a valve while he was at the wheel. Whatever he had done to the old bawd, Lady Luck's wounds really had gone *deep*.

2
MARIO ANDRETTI
Stand on the gas

"It's incredible. Anything he shows you, he has to start the engine. Motorcycles, karts, snowmobiles, you name it. And as soon as it bursts into life his face goes into this great beam." – Nigel Roebuck

ANDRETTI. It rhymes with confetti, as one magazine feature assured its readers back in 1966 when they were still having trouble winding their tongues round the name of the skinny little Italian guy who had just stolen the pole at Indianapolis after walking away with the previous year's USAC Championship at his first attempt.

Today there is no need for rhymes. The name Andretti has become a part of American folklore, synonymous with charisma. Mario has it in spades. He is more laconic than a whole repeat series of *M.A.S.H.*, the man who thrilled schoolboy readers of motoring magazines in early 1977 with pre-unveiling descriptions of the Lotus 78 such as, "You wait until you see Colin's new car. Man, it feels like it's painted to the road!".

Andretti turned 50 in 1990, yet races on with the vigour of a man half his age. There is no sign whatsoever that he's ready to hang up that silver crash helmet with its red stripe. Such suggestions are not welcomed. Some men race cars because it seems like fun, some just for the money. Some, a precious few, are literally *born* to race them. Mario Andretti is one of them. He was put on earth to race cars, and it comes so naturally to him that he has no thought of quitting. Far from it. As recently as 1989 he was even considering an offer to return to Formula One, the arena that made him only the second World Champion to come from Uncle Sam's shores.

When Gerhard Berger was sidelined for the Monaco GP with burnt hands after his horrific accident at Imola, Ferrari turned to Andretti. If it had asked former drivers Carlos Reutemann or Jody Scheckter you would have been amazed. Even Lauda. But Andretti? Somehow it seemed logical. A lot of drivers would have given their right arm for the chance, but for a guy approaching 50 it maybe wasn't the best option. Mario, the racer, thought otherwise.

"There was a certain approach", he smiled, "but the biggest problem was that there would have been no time at all to test. If the car'd had a conventional gearbox it would have been something to go for, but without that, and being a street circuit, it would just have been a folly. But had it had a conventional gearbox? A good car in a one-off race? Why not? I would've given it a serious go, sure." No worries about his own ability, about the dangers of one-offs to fragile reputations, just a racer's pragmatism. Pure Andretti.

The trick had worked once before, when Ferrari gave him the call for Monza

Mario Andretti doesn't just sound like a racing driver; he looks every bit like the layman's image of one, too. Some race because of the glamour, some for the financial rewards, but Mario is one of that select band literally born to race.

in 1982, that awful year in which it lost Gilles Villeneuve and Didier Pironi. It had worked like a charm.

Mario is open, honest, a man not afraid to show feelings. "It was an emotional situation. Yes, it was. Because one of the reasons, not the main one but one of them, that I'd left Formula One at that point was I was with an uncompetitive car and it left such a sort of a sour taste with me. I wasn't going to go through another year like that, and it was getting pretty much time for me to go back home. It was an easy decision to go back, if you will, because of the uncompetitiveness of the Alfa Romeo.

"But then to go back to Formula One and at least have a good go at it, a good car, was very satisfying. I tested at Fiorano (Ferrari's private test track) just a couple of days before. I came in early and did a day and a half, which was very, very useful."

In typical Andretti style he stepped off the plane wearing a Ferrari cap. Just as he had in a one-off with Williams at Long Beach earlier in the year, he wore pukka overalls. No stitching patches on an old set. "I figure if they hire me, I give them the most professional show I can." He did that alright, when he put the red car on the pole in the dying moments of qualifying and then raced it home to third place. The tifosi was orgasmic.

"The transition to a turbocharged Formula One car was never a problem. It just shows that when you have some experience under you in an Indycar and you get into a good Formula One, the transition can be a very pleasant one", he said, almost irritated that there should be any suggestion that acclimatization would take long. The bridge between the two disciplines is something he has always felt about strongly, the more so in recent years as son Michael has come to consider crossing it more and more. Nothing burns the elder Andretti up more than hearing disparaging remarks about Indycar drivers made by Formula One people.

His own experience of making the move was bitter sweet, ironically with suggestions that it was tainted initially by a team he'd end up winning for.

"Before I went to the Glen in 1968 Monza was supposed to be my debut, and we tested there before the Italian GP and we ran very quick. As a matter of fact, it was my first time ever in Formula One and the Lotus 49 was a very competitive car." His voice softened, like that of a man recalling an old love. "It was worth waiting for the opportunity. It didn't disappoint. Just the opposite... It was something waiting for me because Colin Chapman had promised me back at Indianapolis in 1965, in my rookie year, that if I ever wanted to get into a Formula One car, I just had to call him when I was ready. Typical Colin. And I called him in '68 and he didn't blink an eye. He said, 'We'll do the last two races'."

That time at Indy both Chapman and Jim Clark had been quick to see the potential of the little Italian-born rookie. Jimmy was a confirmed Andretti fan. "Jimmy really rated Mario", said the Scot's former girlfriend Sally Swart. "He was really impressed with his driving, and had admired it since day one when Mario went to Indy. I had a nice opportunity of telling Mario that years later, after Jimmy died, and you should have seen his face. I think he gave me a big hug, because it meant so much to him." It is pleasing that Andretti should then, and in later years, become the man to get the closest with Chapman to the relationship Colin had had with Jimmy.

"At Monza it felt so good right away. Of course, the rest is history. We qualified the car and they wouldn't let us run in the race because of the Hoosier 100, which was a Champcar race, one of the traditional races, which we'd done the day before. The lucky thing in a way was that it was a Saturday event – they usually had the championship races on a Sunday – but the unlucky part was that it was within the 24-hour rule, falling technically within the period during which you couldn't do another race before a GP.

"It's not that we went into it blind, however. The organizers at Monza had a lot of political pull with the FIA at the time, and also Count Giovanni Lurani was an influential speaker in Italy, and they promised that they would waive the rule so we could do both races. Well, what happened is that we were running good, and it's a matter of record that in testing I ran quicker than the Ferraris had tested previously.

"I ran the first 20 minutes of practice, and of course I had to really get on with it. I picked up a couple of tows because at the time it was very important to pick one up. Matter of fact, who gave me the tow was Bobby Unser with the BRM. He was my pal and I'd brought him over and got Louis Stanley to give him a drive. It was not a good car, but it was good enough for a tow, I can tell you that. In fact, I tried to tow him, but he couldn't keep up!

"So we could only do the first 20 minutes of practice, and I was quickest then, and we left for the airport. That time stood for seventh quickest of the weekend, so we were seventh on the grid. When we came back from the Hoosier 100" – (Mario had finished second in it to Foyt) – "it was well organized because Firestone was footing the bill for this whole thing. They had a synchronized private aircraft to pick me up and do everything properly. In fact they'd laid on two cots – Formula One, first class! – for us to sleep in on our way back. I think it was fantastic. I got enough sleep. So what happens is that we arrive there and apparently there was a protest. You don't know, but I think it was Ferrari. I never knew. So they wouldn't let me run, but they held the car on the grid to make it look like I never arrived. So I'm the one that looked bad.

"I was so pissed-off we took it out on our hire cars!" He laughed, a teenager's laugh. "Bobby and I just destroyed those cars!

"Anyhow, that meant my debut was to be the Glen. For me it was a very happy time. There was no time to test beforehand, and honestly I'd never seen the track. Everyone thought it was home track, but I'd never been up there at that time. In all fairness, however, the Glen was a fairly simple layout, which helped for a first timer, and the car was good. That's when I worked very closely for the first time with designer Maurice Phillippe, because he was on the third car. And he actually got his hands dirty, just to help out, because it looked like we had a shot at really doing well. You know, we were up with the times and we just got on pole. Squeaked it past Stewart by seven-hundredths. It was very close, but a satisfying feeling, you know?

"The fact it was a third car showed in the race itself. It had a split nose design, and the bottom half which held the wing collapsed, so it was dragging, but that wasn't the worst. The clutch started slipping. In fact the clutch started slipping like, right after the start. I led off the line, and as I was going through the gears it was going eeeyagh, eeeyagh, you know, just picking up, and Stewart got me down the straightaway. I held on for three or four laps and it just got worse and worse." Nonetheless, it was a stunning debut. Surprisingly, however, it didn't lead to a full season in 1969. His commitments to Firestone were simply too tight.

"Firestone was embarking really on a head-to-head with Goodyear. It was sort of a market where they were competing for drivers who could get the job done. So they were totally counting on me to be in the States."

He stayed there for two more seasons, occasionally dabbling with an uncompetitive STP March 701 in 1970 before joining Ferrari in 1971 with a deal woven round his USAC commitments. He kicked off that season perfectly with his first Formula One victory when he passed Denny Hulme's ailing McLaren M19A to snatch the South African GP. Then he followed that with a rousing success in the non-championship event at Ontario Motor Speedway, the Questor GP. The skinny kid who had burst on to the USAC scene was now shaking up the Formula One establishment.

"At the Nurburgring I finished fourth, and I think Mauro Forghieri was more interested in me when I did that than when I'd won in South Africa! After that they offered me a regular drive. They offered to buy me a house in Italy,

By 1966 the rookie had won the USAC Championship title and proudly wore number one on the Brawner Hawk at Indianapolis, where his driving had already drawn praise from Jimmy Clark. Twenty five years later 'The Fonz' is still looking hard for his second victory at the Brickyard to back up his 1969 success.

whatever I needed." It seemed like every racer's dream. Andretti was certainly interested. "I pondered that and I went to Akron, and Firestone just begged me not to do it. They said they'd try to arrange it so I had whatever drive could fit in. They offered a lot of money." Mario laughed, an honest laugh. "You can't always be motivated by that, but you can't overlook it, either. It was a lot of money for those days. So I just had to do it, and I still don't have any regrets." Road racing opportunities in America were rare in those days, and a Ferrari sportscar programme kept his hand in nicely. "In spirit, though, I was always in Formula One."

A keen assessment of all the angles of his profession has always been one of Mario's traits. Even in the early days, when Al Dean's chief mechanic Clint Brawner was looking for a new driver and started checking him out, it was obvious he was a cut above the norm. Just before he drove Brawner's roadster at Trenton in 1964, the impetuous Andretti had taken out Don Branson in a sprintcar encounter at Williams Grove. Branson wasn't the kind of driver who took kindly to rookies doing that to him. Having chewed out Andretti he started on Brawner. As Mario said, it didn't seem like the ideal way to impress a man who held your future in his hands.

Brawner liked the way Andretti worked his way through selection of tyres, though, the way he spoke his mind when necessary, but listened at others. As the two of them worked together, so the legend of Andretti's car sorting abilities grew its roots.

That ability to see all angles extends to the media. Victory in the USA GP West at Long Beach in 1977 helped him on his way to the 1978 World Championship, but where the Europeans were already sold on the talents of the quotable American, his home media only finally became convinced he could do the Formula One job at that race. It hurt. After Monza and Watkins Glen in 1968, and South Africa and Ontario three years later, it really hurt. What's more, Andretti isn't so thick skinned that he won't admit it.

"For some reason or other, the press... well. Today you have expert press that really takes you right through it. When there's a story of any kind, they sorta follow it. In those days they didn't. As a matter of fact there was a lot of scepticism. There is today, but if you can dispel that they'll pick it up. In those days it was there, and it was there because nobody would do anything about it. Nobody would focus and say, 'Hey, let's have a look at it', or whatever. You were forever in this crusade, defending certain positions. That's the way it was.

"It's fair enough, because I'd never fault one side or the other. Everybody seems to have their own little world. The Europeans, obviously, they focus on Formula One. That's where it starts and that's where it ends. Americans are the same with Indycars. And very few are the ones who look at the bigger picture and assess it properly. You have that today, as well.

"So it was a matter then of increasing the fire to prove it. Let's face it, when Colin and I joined in '76 at Long Beach, Sam Moses of *Sports Illustrated* said, 'Here's a has-been constructor getting together with a has-been driver in Formula One'. I'll never forget that. I said to myself, 'I've been smoked here, but they can swallow those'. There's a certain satisfaction in that, in a certain sense, since it's put that way."

As history relates, Chapman and Andretti were far from spent forces. Moses did swallow his own words. They ended that season with a victory in Japan that was overshadowed somewhat by the drama surrounding James Hunt's World Championship victory, but which nonetheless laid the final groundwork for what was to follow. A series of blown engines and the odd driving error or incident lost them the 1977 title, but with the Lotus 79 the following year Mario finally took the Formula One crown. Chapman let it be known he felt closer to Mario than to any driver since Clark, yet Andretti himself is now cautious in his assessment of their relationship.

At Monza in 1968 he was startling when he practised the spare Lotus 49 for the Italian GP. He was fastest by the time he had to leave for America, and his time remained seventh fastest overall. By any standards it was a dramatic debut.

"Working with Colin was no trip to Paris, you know?", he'll point out. As he worked with Brawner he learned the minutae of chassis set-up, and would later be the man to introduce buzzwords such as corner weighting and tyre stagger to Formula One, not that he himself treated them as such. At Long Beach in

1978 he introduced the now fashionable idea of hand-cutting tyres, drawing on his midget experience. Undoubtedly, his ability to get the very best from his chassis was instrumental in helping to pull Lotus round in 1976. And yet he and Chapman had plenty of clashes.

In South Africa, in his championship year, for example, he lost the race after Chapman had insisted on drawing out one gallon of fuel to save precious weight. The Lotus 78 ran out before the end.

"I think if you look historically at Lotus, it had tremendous high peaks, but also the deepest valleys, and I think it goes back to Colin being the moody genius that he was. He would create something and it was good, it was different, a new toy, and then he'd either get bored or just go way over and reach for the stars on his next project. Like the 80. There I think he was on the right road, but only halfway.

"He and I had mon-u-men-tous arguments. He was getting more and more downforce out of the car, because obviously we were learning more and more, and in those days we were in the infancy of ground effects, so there were *big* gains to be had. But he would do *no-thing* about the stiffness of the car. So, to be able to take advantage of the downforce, you had to run very stiff springs, but to be able to feel the stiff springs you had to have a good, stiff car. The torsional stiffness in that car was probably only 2,000 pounds per degree. Which is ridiculous. Everything would pop! We used to go to some small track in France to test before Monte Carlo, a very Mickey Mouse type of circuit. We go there with the 80, and obviously the car was just craving to be stiffer and stiffer. We put a set of very stiff springs on there and as soon as I went out I said, 'RIGHT! This has got it'. And three laps later the car started just going off. Doing weird things. It would take a set, you'd have cross weight for the next corner...

"I proved it to him in Spain with the 81. I'd jacked the car up at a corner and just taped two strings across the cockpit, and as I jacked the car up all you had to do was just bounce it on the other side and the spring was going. Alright, I wanted just to show it to him. And he hit the ceiling! He just did not accept the driver having any kind of an engineering input.

"All I wanted to do was sort of point out what was happening. I don't ever want to be the one to dictate, in any way, on the technical side. All I want to be is just part of it, that's all. Not a mechanic, not an engineer, but I'm interested because it helps me to help the team by knowing what's going on. And the way I arrived at this in Spain was because in practice in the morning we finally got the car going pretty good, but in fact we were struggling. The car is up on the first platform jack, they only had one, and we found the car had a cracked rear wishbone and they were changing it, jacking it up at one corner. And the car up to that point had second quick time. I went out again with exactly the same tyres, and I knew it wouldn't be good enough for pole, but would be competitive, and then I'd go to new tyres and try to see if we could get a bit more. But at least try to get that. And so I go out and qualify, but could not come within half a second of that time. The car felt just cross weighted. So finally I started really riding the kerbs and the car felt just diabolical. Just remember there had been this jacking about for about an hour and a half. So I took Bob Dance to one side and said, 'We've just got to go through this. We gotta prove a point'. That's when we did the wire thing. But Colin, as soon as I said, 'Let's look at this', he just hit the ceiling.

"When you go back, Nigel Bennett was along, and Nigel was in total agreement, but his hands were tied. He just couldn't make those decisions himself. So we sat down the week after the race and talked over what we were going to do, and Colin's gone to some Greek islands on holiday, and we didn't get a collar around the cockpit until the British GP in July. And at the British we were right in there and the car was really competitive, but we broke the engine. But that was as competitive as we had been. But then everything else started going, it started popping rivets on the bulkheads, so the car just needed

25

to be totally redone...

"This is what Patrick Head had done with his Williams, and we were looking at it in Spain, and he was one that really understood what it needed. He had a very stiff car, which was just paramount. Just the right mentality. Nigel Bennett, when he saw the Williams, he said, 'There's the way our car should be'."

OTHER VOICES

John Baldwin – Parnelli engineer 1971–'75

"Mario is a *driver*. Once he has the bit between his teeth, he really flies. He's a very good test driver, and on the race side he's good, too, when he's really motivated and happy. When I worked with him he always drove a bit better when he was a bit upset. His feedback was very good, but he did have a tendency to have things figured in his mind about what he wanted done to the car. But when the car was going quickly, it was difficult to argue with him...

"Things got a bit political at Parnelli's; they wanted to use Eagles in USAC. We first ran them at Ontario, but when Al (Unser Snr) had his, Mario outqualified him and outraced him in the Parnelli. We found out later that Bobby Unser had an advantage in the turbocharger with *his* Eagle, which was super-quick...

"Mario could pinpoint what the car was doing. He was an easy guy to sort a car with."

■ ■ ■

Few fathers ever get to race wheel-to-wheel with their sons. I wondered if Mario finally found a point when he raced with Michael, at which he decided he needn't worry any more?

"Well, I'll tellya, at the beginning there's a lot of apprehension because you're concerned about a lot of things, mainly safety, and then you want him to do well, you want him to feel good. Yeah, it's mixed emotions there, it really is. Something totally new to me. You know, the first race he went out there, and I think he did very well in a sense that he was really trying. He was not just wanking, accepting to be lapped, nothing like that. That's the thing I noticed right away, he would not accept not being competitive. You could always see that he was trying hard, just pushing. I figured just as soon as he gets his perspective together here, he's gonna go. And almost immediately he just became one that you knew you had to race.

"He was determined to turn the team around, and this he did on his own. He just put personal feelings aside and suggested a total regrouping which helped the entire team to really come together. And as soon as he got Barry Green as team manager, I tellya, things started happening. I became envious of the way that his team looked really together. They had Adrian Newey as their aerodynamics technician, who I rate really high, and they were a force really to be reckoned with, no question.

"The very good thing that we have here in the team now is that it's very special to have a team-mate that you know is completely honest with you. And we share right up to race day. Share everything. It's an open book. And it's increased the dimension of the team. I've always operated well as a number one, *alone*. Historically I have not been good, I've been distracted and disrupted, when it's equal number one, or whatever. I don't know what it is. I wish I could pinpoint it." He laughed. "Maybe it's my character! I was not myself in the first year, in '89. In '90 I started really accepting it a lot better and really maximizing it. Hopefully we'll do even better in '91."

"Time to go, Bobby." Mario consults his watch as he and Unser (in sunglasses, with BRM boss Louis Stanley to his left), prepare to dash to the airport en route to the Hoosier 100 race that ultimately prevented either of them participating at Monza.

1989, of course, brought that very nasty shunt on the streets of Toronto when he ducked out from behind another car to find that Roberto Guerrero's wrecked car had been left on the track even though the flags had been withdrawn. He ploughed straight into it.

"Yeah, I know. It could have been rough if I'd been a couple of inches further over." He sounded bored, slightly tetchy, to be reminded of it, as though many use it as a suggestion that he should think of quitting. "I realize all that. But you can bring that up and it's not that I don't have a conscience, if you will. I'm aware of all the aspects there. I took a peek because I didn't see the flag any more, and I assumed the car had gone. But it was still there. I could not believe that they would do that. Especially as you're in a sort of radius in that corner, it's like a sort of tunnel, and so at least where the flag was I had a sort of idea where the car was. Now, with no flag, I kinda do this", he indicates jinking slightly to the right, "and the car is there. I could not believe that they would do that."

Predictably, he didn't let the incident that could well have brought his career to a permanent halt rest there. "I got to the bottom of it and there were marshals trying to defend themselves and everything, you know, but bullshit. The policy in effect is that if the car remains for whatever reason, in any area, whether it's dangerous or not, as long as it's on the track the flag shall remain static. The marshal was saying that if they held the flag there they had no more ammunition if something else happened, so I said, 'Have you ever heard of standing and waving?'."

It was his first big accident since Pocono in 1985, the year after he had again won the CART Championship.

"I got hurt at Michigan with eight laps to go in a 500. The right front wheel just sheared when the stub-axle broke and I went straight in. The wheel and brake came right in. I had a broken pelvis, three cracked ribs, and a collarbone. I missed the next race – first time I ever missed a race through injury – and the following race two and a half weeks later was a 500, and I aimed to make that. I gotta give the doctors so much credit for trying to deal with our emotions, trying to help. Normal doctors say, 'Hey, you'll be laid up for six months, and I don't want to hear anything else. That's it, end of story'. These guys, young guys, the orthopaedics that follow the circuit, they know how we think. And

27

they also know that because of that we're good healers, because we do whatever. You know, they have this unit that stimulates blood flow, and if they said keep that on 10 hours a day, do it, then I used to just do everything to the tee, all the therapy. I think I was back in shape two weeks, three weeks before normal.

"The Pocono race was not a good choice for a comeback. It's just so bumpy. Jesus Christ! When the car would bottom it was just like an electric shock going through my pelvis. I had a company, Spanco Corporation, which makes very specialized impact pads, had them come up there and fit up the car with all these super-duper things. And, you know, it was some degree of help. I think once I was in the car it wasn't so bad. The problem was getting in and out of it. Once I was in it and could take a set, I could deal with it a lot better. But it was tough. One helluva race. A really traumatic day all through because that morning Michael had had a helicopter crash. So it was a day like you never saw! Unbelievable!" He finished sixth, the seat belt helping to keep his collarbone together. It was one of the few times he ever had to be helped out of a race car.

If time heals his rare injuries, it certainly hasn't healed the hurt at being rowed out of his second victory at Indianapolis, in 1981. Even now, 10 years later, the nerve is still very raw.

"I'll tellya, I could never, ever accept the way it was dealt. They went through hearings, all sorts of motions, for six months, and the bottom line is that USAC and the Speedway got totally intimidated by Roger Penske's lawyers, and he had a very powerful sports lawyer that's always in the limelight with boxers and so forth. The truth is beyond a shadow of doubt that he did exactly what he was penalized for, and then they had a panel of three judges; one abstained, the other two said that under these circumstances – whatever circumstances they meant I don't know – the penalty was too severe. Yes, he did pass under the yellow, and yes, he deserves a penalty. However, he will not be assessed the lap penalty, he'll only be assessed a $40,000 fine, or something like that.

"To me, I thought that was totally ludicrous. I mean, it was pathetic to change the rules just because it was at Indy. And it's not that precedents hadn't been set. There were guys like Jerry Grant who committed infractions similar to that and were penalized and went from second to sixth. You know what I mean? But only because he was second, obviously, the penalty stood. But at Indy, because you were first it almost seemed like you were immune from anything. So then, to add insult to injury, the following year at the drivers' meeting the chief steward, Tom Binford, who, to be fair, did not agree with the decision, but was powerless because we did not protest, he said, 'Now it's gonna stick! Now be warned.'

"What's the difference between now and then? To me, sure, it's not the type of thing where you wanna win a race under protest, and so on and so forth. But I would have taken it, mainly because I've had so much shit there and bad luck that I'd take it any way. I think that would have made up for the ones I deserved. I felt that, within the rulebook, I won that race, because Bobby Unser and I were running together that day, close enough, and whether I would have beaten him or not, obviously fair-and-square, we'll never know, because I didn't get that opportunity. But all I know is we went out of the pits together late in the race after our last stops and he was in front and I was right on his gearbox, and he joined the pack 11 cars in front of me. So I had to go by 11 cars to even hope to get by him. I finished second on the track anyway, so chances are I could've possibly won that race. He passed 11 cars under the yellow flag, and that's still a penalty today. I would have accepted it easier if they would have said regardless of all the evidence we can't prove beyond a shadow of a doubt that he did that. I could've accepted that line, as hypocritical as it would have been, but to say, yes, you did commit the infraction, but we're gonna bend the rules to accommodate it? No way. I guarantee that if that would have been at Milwaukee, that's it, there would have been no question.

"I said I'll go out there and commit these atrocities to my advantage and win a race for a $40,000 fine *any* day! Especially at Indy. *Any* day. I tellya what, I'll never accept that one. Never ever." The way he was treated during the 1991 500, 10 years on, when he was at the centre of a black-flag controversy, suggests that USAC's bruised feelings have yet to heal.

Mario tends to play down his achievements in sprintcars, although when I showed him and Michael a poster shot at Trenton, he instantly identified the track and the meeting despite the huge dust cloud that obscured most of the detail. "The last time I was in one was I think about '66/'67. Do I miss them? Let's put it this way. I enjoyed it, driving those cars. I was always in a good car, I mean at least when I was in USAC, and I think I did pretty well, you know, I won some races, was always up front. I didn't run sprintcars as much as Foyt, some of those guys. Because it was sorta getting to the point that it didn't make that much sense. The risk you were taking, there were many that hurt themselves there and hurt their chances in a Championship car."

He doesn't often look backwards, anyway. "I think there's enough to look forward to. I think the only people who are nostalgic are those who are bored at the time and they say, 'Ah gee, remember the good times, remember the days?', and they're sad about the moment. I'm not. I'm happy about the moment. Very honestly I look forward to tomorrow, and what it has to offer, and what I have to do to progress and to do better than I did yesterday. I look back with fondness on a lot of moments in my career, but I'm not nostalgic at all. Really, I'm not. Even Formula One. It was a great period in my career. A great sense of satisfaction, just what I really wanted, and so valuable to me. And yet I'm very happy where I am, with what I'm doing, and I'm only there because of the way the Indycar series is and what it has to offer. Right now I'm happy enough to see that maybe Michael is going to carry on that side of it, you know, get his licks in there."

Total synergy: Mario Andretti was instrumental in helping Colin Chapman develop the Lotus 78 and the 79, with which he is seen on his way to victory at Jarama in 1978 during his triumphant World Championship year.

What completes Andretti, both as a racer and as a man, is his compassion. He felt deeply when friends such as Billy Foster, Lucien Bianchi, Ronnie Peterson and Gunnar Nilsson succumbed. Less warm was Wally Meskowski, at one time his USAC crew chief. When he was asked for time off to bury a dead colleague, Meskowski simply replied, "Whaddya wanta go to his funeral for? He ain't coming to yours". Andretti laughs at the recollection. "Yeah! I think he was the coldest man I've ever known. But I liked the guy. I really liked the guy. There

was something about him. Just like, say, Colin, he was one that was going to give you a good car. Certain guys just seem to strive for that, just to give you everything possible. Wally gave you that impression. It's a different world, sprintcars and Formula One, but it's the same thing, isn't it?

"It's funny, he kinda warmed up to me because I think I gave him a couple of trophies! He won a lot of races, with some of the best drivers out there, and I shared a couple of trophies with him. God, you'd think I'd given him the world. That's the first time I ever got any reaction out of the guy."

One time, off Long Beach, his willingness to try any kind of machinery took him aboard Mary Rife's dragboat. "I was just a passenger, like an idiot." His voice dropped. "Just scared to Jesus. I tellya what, I drove one during that intermission, and I forget the class, but it was fast enough to frighten the hell out of me. The guy gives me some instructions. 'Just line yourself up on the rope at the starting line, and I don't think you'll need to press the nitrous pedal', he says. 'It'll be quick enough.' So I thought, 'Hell, I'm gonna do it'." He broke into a deep laugh. "So I pressed down on that thing. He tells me there's gonna be a torque steer. He says, 'But don't correct for it. It'll look like its headed for the buoys, but it'll straighten itself out'. I don't know. My intuition was to correct." He laughed again. "I shouldn't have, because then it goes this way! I still crossed the traps at, I think it was, 120-some miles an hour. I think I must have got it up to at least 150 or 160 because at one stage I was carrying a lot of speed.

"Then Mary took me on and we ran through the traps about 174. Top time of the day was 194, I remember that! Those things are so quick it's like an explosion."

OTHER VOICES

Dick Scammell – former Lotus mechanic

"He's a real racer. He really wants to drive racing cars. He knows what he wants and he gets it. He goes out and does his utmost with what he's been given, and he's not one to choose his days.

"When we were testing the Indy turbine Lotus in 1968 Mario wanted a ride, so Granatelli put him in Graham Hill's car. We had to stuff six pullovers behind him to make him fit the seat. But he went out and ran close to 170 in 10 or 12 laps. He obviously had a *lot* of talent, and he did that through pure curiosity."

■ ■ ■

Mario Andretti has never lost sight of his early dreams when, as boys in a displaced persons camp in Trieste, he and his brother Aldo had imagined themselves as racing drivers. When they had gazed wide-eyed at photographs of Alberto Ascari in action.

"In my eyes Ascari was the big idol. He was the catalyst that made me decide what I wanted to do. I've been influenced so much by him. There were moments when I'd say, 'I wonder what Ascari would do under these circumstances?' Yeah, he meant a lot to me." Just as Mario has himself, perhaps, meant much to many a newcomer.

Nor has he lost his pure love of racing, which embraces every aspect and has made him the perfect ambassador for the sport. He looks every inch a racer, sounds it, too, with that laconic nasal drawl. And the name is perfect. But Mario also *thinks* like a racer, every moment of the day. At 53 Victory Lane – for years his home in Nazareth, Pennsylvania – the garage is littered with adult mechanical toys. "It's incredible. Anything he shows you, he has to start the engine. Motorcycles, karts, snowmobiles, you name it", said Nigel Roebuck.

"And as soon as it bursts into life his face goes into this great beam."

Nor has he realized all his ambitions, despite his successes in midgets, sprintcars, Indianapolis, sportscars, NASCAR or his Championships in USAC, CART and Formula One. Le Mans, the race so fashionably disliked by many topliners, still exerts a pull. In 1967 he crashed his Ford MkIV there when a tired mechanic put one of the new brake pads in the wrong way round, and he wiped out three other works cars. In 1969 his close friend Bianchi was killed testing there. In 1982 he and Michael were prevented from racing their Mirage by petty rulefogging. In 1983 they were third, and in 1988 sixth, sharing with Mario's nephew John. And still he wants to go back, as if failure to have won the French classic is eating away at him.

Age and experience might not have eradicated the streak of impetuosity that has characterized his style ever since his sprintcar racing, and which occasionally resulted in first-lap incidents in his Formula One days. But then neither have the years blunted his speed, his commitment or the incredible smoothness that has always been his driving hallmark. And as the vision time at Indianapolis – the time it takes to arrive at what you can see – has reduced from the 5.8 seconds it was when he started there in the Sixties to around 1.5 seconds in the Nineties, so has he adjusted to keep ahead of the game.

"Nobody will ever do what my Old Man has done", says Michael proudly as he stands on the threshold of his own Formula One career, and he's probably right. The most telling tribute that one can pay his father is that watching them in their Newman Haas Lolas, it is frequently impossible to tell the charismatic 51-year-old legend from the 28-year-old. The Old Man still drives with all the fire of Clint Brawner's rookie back in 1965.

Perhaps his greatest quality, though, is his charisma. When you've met Mario Andretti, even if you have no interest whatsoever in motor racing, you leave knowing that you've just met Somebody.

3
TONY BRISE

There but for fortune

"Tony was good, he showed that. He would have been a force to be reckoned with, no question." – Mario Andretti

Some said he was arrogant, too cocky by far. They'd said the same thing years before about Jochen Rindt, and first impressions had been wrong there, too. Tony Brise had it all. Temperament, flair, car control, and the brain of a thinking race driver.

He was highly intelligent, not only when he was racing cars and in the way he worked around them, but also in his relationships with people. What his detractors mistook for arrogance was supreme self-confidence. He was good, and he knew it. He had that confidence youth has when it knows it is correct to be confident. Some people just interpreted it the wrong way.

He started racing his father's karts when he was seven and stayed with the category for 10 years, and in 1969 he was joint British Champion. "At one stage", he recalled, "the other drivers used to get very angry being beaten all the time due to such a favourable weight distribution as I had, and they made me start from the back of the grid." Eventually, he went into Formula Ford with Elden, towards the end of 1970, learned the hard way about bad cars, but won 25 or so races with a Merlyn in 1971. At the end of the year Bernie Ecclestone offered him a drive in Colin Vandervell's Brabham BT35 Formula Three car, and in his first pukka outing he finished third behind Roger Williamson and David Purley. He was already in good company. The Brise family worked out a deal on a BT38 for 1972, but it was a big disappointment. The GRD 372 was the car to have that season, as Williamson was proving so effectively.

It took a long time to secure a sound engine deal, and for a while he was rated as a bit of a whinger as he constantly bemoaned lack of power. It was the oldest Formula Three excuse. "Unfortunately, the Holbay engines I was using were reliable old plodders, the quick engines being reserved for the front runners. But as soon as I got a GRD things improved, and I started to get engines as good as the quick boys, who included Roger and Andy Sutcliffe." It had only been after an argument with Holbay that he suddenly got another unit that allowed him to start pushing the leaders, however. By season's end GRD's Mike Warner saw Tony as Roger's logical replacement, and the two of them fought a brilliant duel at Snetterton which Roger won by a nose. It was like the Stewart/Rindt battle at Silverstone in 1969: finishing second on such a day was no disgrace.

Brise's acumen was evident even then in the manner in which he approached BBC Radio Medway and the *Kent Messenger* newspaper, offering to broadcast

A partnership lost: Tony Brise and Graham Hill formed the basis of something very special during 1975, and at last the double champion saw in his young protege a star who could carry his team's name with honour as he himself finally retired from driving to concentrate on management.

and write for them about his racing exploits, and both were impressed enough not only to accept his offer, but to sponsor him, too.

But when the GRD didn't work as well in 1973 things became desperate. By mid-season he hadn't won a thing and was 40 points adrift of Alan Jones' GRD. Then they bought a March 733 and suddenly things clicked. On July 29, the day that Williamson was killed at Zandvoort, Tony finally won at Brands Hatch, following up with another victory there at the end of the year that narrowly clinched him the John Player Championship with 123 points to Jones' 121 and early pacesetter Russell Wood's 119. He also took the Lombard Championship. Things looked perfect for 1974, except that the offers just weren't there.

"I thought I had the perfect credentials", he said, "but nobody seemed remotely interested." It was a ridiculous situation, given that his latent talent had been obvious right from the outset. Oh, Max Mosley had offered him a deal for Formula Two, but it required money, and the Brises just didn't have the sort of cash Max had in mind. "That was the trouble. Everybody assumed the deal was firm, and by the time they realized it wasn't, other opportunities had gone." Not for Brise the good fortune Roger had had to get involved with Tom Wheatcroft.

He was quite open in his self-assessment at that time, and in quantifying his relative lack of popularity in certain areas of the media around this point. "I suppose it's because they don't like somebody rich and they don't like me winning at 21. And probably because the English temperament demands adulation for the underdog. Also, a lot of journalists are bigoted, and if I say that I am not in favour of baulking or something, they tend to think that I'm a big ****. As far as the drivers are concerned I think that is because I am successful and on the way up; after all, nobody has shown such consistency as me this season in Formula Three." Tony Brise's light was not tucked away beneath anyone's bushel. Even then, he was imbued with the sort of self confidence we saw at a similar stage in Ayrton Senna's career.

He still had the March, but yet another season of Formula Three was unattractive, for many reasons. Then, after a possible Formula One drive in the Hesketh Surtees TS9B that had catapulted James Hunt to the fore had fallen through, he fitted the March with a Formula Atlantic engine and, narrow wheels and all, entered the race that supported the International Trophy race at Silverstone. He won with dramatic ease, despite qualifying only eighth and having clutch trouble at the start. That one race proved to be a turning point, and sparked all manner of offers that his double Formula Three titles had simply failed to do. He opted to run for Teddy Savory's Modus concern in Formula Atlantic.

It was another year spent learning the hard way, but it paid off in the long-term and they were ready to dominate in 1975. He did exactly that. And yet he had come so close to giving it all up.

"I had one Formula Ford title, two Formula Three championships, a Grovewood Award and was third in Atlantic, even though I missed a load of races. I had a reputation for being inconsistent, which I honestly didn't think I rated. I decided that 1975 would be it, succeed or quit. It was a thin line between climbing up the racing ladder and staying around too long, bumming off people." He was far too proud to spend his time doing that.

The season began shakily with a spin in his first race en route to victory, but then his new calm approach reaped dividends and brought him six wins in succession. Things were about to happen with dramatic speed. He received a call from Frank Williams, and tested an FW03 at Goodwood as a result. "I was really pleased, because I didn't feel daunted in any way by the car. The step from Atlantic to Formula One didn't feel as bad as the move up from Formula Three to Atlantic, to be honest. It felt very good. I could tell what it was doing, and better still, I could tell the team. It felt just like a big kart; you had to drive it hard on the throttle, in a big drift, to kill the understeer. I loved it."

Frank was impressed, and invited him to race at the Spanish GP at Barcelona as Jacques Laffite had a prior commitment to the Formula Two race at the Nurburgring. Tony agreed, but only after consulting Teddy Savory. The last thing he wanted to do was to play anything but straight with the man who'd given him his fresh chance. Suddenly, it was all coming right. He qualified a very good 18th in what was recognized to be a mediocre car, and was quicker than the experienced Arturo Merzario. He finished a splendid seventh. Tony Brise, Grand Prix star, was on his way.

OTHER VOICES

Frank Williams

"He'd been pretty devastating in Formula Atlantic and it was obvious to me the guy was a little bit special. He was different to everyone else around him. He did a bit of testing for us at Goodwood and we had an oil problem and lost an engine. It wasn't his fault, it was a Williams lack of knowledge problem, but he was very quick. At home, immediately. Good communication, he understood the car. He was ahead of the game, he wasn't flustered.

"He finished seventh for us at Barcelona, and it was obvious that he was a man who, if we'd got him, he'd have done a lot for Williams and would have pulled us right up, but Graham beat us to it. He had a better deal to offer, quite

By Zandvoort in 1975, his one year of racing at the highest level, Brise had already done sufficient to confirm his potential in Hill's Embassy racer, and comfortably eclipsed team-mate Alan Jones who would go on to win the 1980 world title.

obviously. It was a very short-lived possibility.

"But the guy was very talented, would have been an English Great. To be honest, I'd been keeping an eye on him for a year or two beforehand in Atlantic. He was very easy to get on with and this arrogance thing never came to me. I do not recall that about him. I'm not being charitable, I never had a problem with him in the brief time we worked together.

"Yes, he would have been an English Great, the talent was certainly there."

■ ■ ■

He kept studying, even while he was racing, as Jonathan Palmer later would, and he came out of Aston University with a BSc degree in Business Studies. He knew which way up things were meant to be. He didn't let his Grand Prix debut go to his head, and he prepared calmly to return to Formula Three for the Monaco support race at Savory's behest. Teddy hoped Tony would repeat Tom Pryce's fantastic success of the previous season, especially as he had finished second then to the Welshman. Though he had to make a pit stop in his heat for attention to a loose plug lead, Tony stormed back into contention to qualify for the final. The Swede Conny Andersson threw away his chances by jumping the start of it and getting penalized a minute, then Larry Perkins appeared to have everything under control when he crashed out of a handsome lead.

Thus it boiled down to the Brazilian Alex Ribiero trying everything he knew to keep Brise at bay after Tony had literally ripped through the field in stunning style. It was almost inevitable that they should ultimately collide at Mirabeau when Alex slammed the door as Tony dived for the inside, and the race was left to the unknown Pirelli tyre tester Renzo Zorzi, who would play such a fateful role during the South African GP at Kyalami two years later.

If Tony was disappointed, his discontent didn't last long. Graham Hill, 'Mr Monaco', had been impressed with what he had seen, and offered him the drive in his Hill GH1 in Rolf Stommelen's enforced absence following his accident in the Spanish GP.

His debut for Hill in the Belgian GP at Zolder was little short of sensational as he qualified the bulky car seventh on the grid, ahead of World Champion

35

Emerson Fittipaldi and his McLaren. He spun after three laps and later retired with engine trouble, but after an appalling time in qualifying in Sweden, where he ran into all manner of mechanical trouble, he was running fifth with only seven laps to go when he lost fifth gear. Mark Donohue passed him, but he hung on to take a championship point at only his third attempt. He qualified and finished seventh at Zandvoort, where he lapped new team-mate and old Formula Three sparring partner Alan Jones, and he was seventh again at Paul Ricard, where he pushed Scheckter hard for sixth before gear selection problems intervened.

His fluid style impressed everyone, as did his ability to provide lucid information on the car's behaviour. "He was relatively easy on his cars, he didn't brutalize them", said Nick Brittan, by then his manager. "He just extended his machinery and made it work."

He crashed in both England and Germany, having looked forward to racing at the Nurburgring with almost childish excitement. At Silverstone he had dealt with Mario Andretti and Carlos Reutemann with the panache of a veteran and had been taking a second a lap off the gaggle comprising Regazzoni, Pryce, Lauda, Scheckter, Fittipaldi and Hunt as they battled for second place. His joint seventh fastest lap was set as early as the ninth, at a time when only Pryce was pushing as hard. In qualifying at Monza he was simply staggering as he lined the Hill up in sixth place. Sadly, that race, too, ended prematurely when he was knocked off in the first chicane.

"I watched him out the back of the circuit and I honestly felt that each time he came through would be the last", said Nick. "But he got it back like Jean Alesi does today. There was no proper suspension or tyres on that thing, and it wasn't a brilliant car. It was just stretched on tiptoe. It was a colossal demonstration of car control and balls. Graham was impressed!"

The remainder of his Formula One season petered out in a series of silly incidents, but he did three Formula 5000 races in the States in Teddy Yip's Sid Taylor-run Lola T330. He had been second with it at Brands Hatch in August before it was shipped Stateside, but he'd been dominating the race until he sustained a slow puncture five laps from the end and consequently was pipped by Jones. At Long Beach in September he was simply awesome. As Mario

Later that season he took on Mario Andretti in a straight fight round the streets of Long Beach, and came so close to victory in the inaugural F5000 race that paved the way for the Grand Prix that would follow. By then, Tony Brise's talent had been lost.

Andretti set the early qualifying pace in Parnelli Jones' Lola, Tony dogged him all the way, driving with a style and precision that drew praise from all the regulars. "The car really feels right", he beamed as he continued lapping very quickly until a driveshaft broke. Sadly, it was to be a bad omen.

He started the first heat alongside poleman Andretti, and as Mario made an uncharacteristic error on the run down to the first right-hander at the end of Shoreline Drive, Tony darted into the lead. He stayed there confidently as the recovering Mario went by Tom Pryce for second place on lap four, and try as he might, the Italian-American simply couldn't make up the deficit by the end of the 12 laps. It was a brilliant performance from Brise, all the more so after forcing Andretti to fluff his entry to that first corner.

For the final, heat two victor Al Unser Snr was alongside Tony, with Mario and Brian Redman behind, and again Tony outdragged the field into the first turn. As he battled to keep Andretti's Lola behind, Brise looked completely unruffled as he threaded his way round the downtown streets. Eventually experience told and Mario overtook, but when his engine broke shortly afterwards, Tony looked set for a brilliant victory. During the course of his battle with Mario he had lowered the lap record to 1 minute 19.9 seconds, a second and a half faster than Andretti's pole time. However, it was not to be, and a broken driveshaft robbed him of the win virtually within sight of the flag.

Later he would finish fourth at Laguna Seca and sixth at Riverside, and when he clinched the John Player Formula Atlantic Championship his moral debt to Savory was fully repaid.

OTHER VOICES

Mario Andretti

"Tony did a couple of our Formula 5000 races. He was strong. Long Beach was the only place where we hurt tremendously. There was a thing about a Weismann diff, and for some reason we were kind of stuck on that. I'd never run a 5000 on a circuit like that, and we should have had a cam and pawl in there. What happens with a Weismann diff when you put power on is that both wheels are driving. It's like a spool. The car just had a terrific amount of understeer through the hairpin. It was probably the only race where in qualifying I felt like I was giving away tremendously.

"Brise came on with Sid Taylor and they had it right. Fact I think Brian Redman did, too. I felt kinda screwed there, didn't feel competitive. But Tony had a lot of talent. Yeah, I rated him. Tony was good, he showed that. He would have been a force to be reckoned with, no question. It was a shame, such a big waste."

■ ■ ■

In October, just after Tony had flown back from Laguna, Graham Hill launched his new lowline GH2, which had been designed by the unassuming Andy Smallman. It was smaller and lighter than the GH1, and in a brief test with it at Silverstone Tony was immediately impressed. "It's got a lot of bite at the front end", he told Hill. "It feels very good, and considering how cold it is today there's a great deal of grip all round. And it doesn't kick back through the wheel when you go over bumps, like the old car did." He was bubbling with enthusiasm when he returned to America for the Riverside race, confident that he had a tool that would let him win races in 1976. The feeling grew when the team went to Paul Ricard in November to give it its first serious development testing.

He was feeling settled with his place in Formula One, the category in which

37

he had expected to race long before he finally did. He had worried that the Formula Three type of rockape driving would still be a feature, and had been pleasantly surprised to find that the more experienced drivers believed, as he did, in giving rivals racing room. "It's clean, and that's the way I like it to be", he said.

What he didn't like was the Grand Prix Drivers Association, and he wanted to resign from the organization. However, on Hill's advice, for which he had the greatest respect, he didn't. It troubled him that, as he saw it, each member of the GPDA was more interested in his own situation than in the overall good of the sport, and he was not the sort to remain too silent when he felt strongly about anything. He was keeping a lid on his feelings, biding his time, aware that he was still a new boy.

It was during the return flight from the Ricard tests, on November 29, that Hill's Piper Aztec crashed while he was attempting to land in fog at Elstree aerodrome, in Hertfordshire. Hill, Brise, Smallman, team manager Ray Brimble and mechanics Terry Richards and Tony Alcock were all on board and were killed instantly.

OTHER VOICES

Nick Brittan – manager

"I used to race karts with John Brise, Tony's father. He built the Brise kart I used when I won the European Championship in about 1902. John and I were good mates. At home at the time he had two kids, Tony and Tim, rushing around doing what two kids do at that age. Basically I knew Tony before he even began to register me.

"I gave up karting, and John and I went in different directions. John went on to race an Arnolt-Bristol and Cooper 500s, as well as stock cars a bit later on. Once he was at this Formula Three/500 race at Montlhéry and he filled out the entry form. Name: John Brise. Driver: As above. He appeared in the French press, and was mentioned as such by the commentator, as Asa Bove...

"When Tony went Formula Three we had a little chat, a family yarn, and I pointed out this and that and left them to get on with it. Tony was a stunning success. Meantime, I was managing Jody Scheckter. John and Co said to me, 'Tony's a bit of a star, a colossal talent, where do we go from here?'

"Graham Hill was still establishing his Embassy team, and somewhere down the line, probably the Spanish GP when he drove for Williams, he had seen Tony. Probably it was also the Formula Three race at Monaco, and he'd taken note. I spoke to Graham about Tony and it all came together. They got on really well. The bottom line was that Graham agreed to give Tony a crack.

"It was obvious to everyone that he was a goer, a worthwhile commodity. He wasn't particularly athletic, but he was a good chess player; he weighed people up well. And he was plenty brave; he knew exactly what his car control ability was. We entered into a sensible management deal and did the usual bit.

"One time we were up at my cottage in Norfolk, seeing Teddy Savory of Modus on a bit of business. For some reason Graham was up at Hethel seeing Colin Chapman, and said if we wanted a lift down to London to meet him at Shipton aerodrome. It was a tiny strip, and as soon as we slammed the plane door we went straight up. I thought, 'Aren't we meant to check instruments or whatever?'.

"Tony was learning to fly and was up in the front seat with Graham, doing the apprentice flier bit. There was a security zone over Mildenhall, the American Airforce base. It was called the Strategic Air Command triangle. The SAC triangle. Everything went up when the four-minute warning went, that sort of thing. You couldn't fly through it, you had to negotiate two legs of the triangle and go around it. Tony told Graham that and Graham just smiled. He switched all the radio off and gave it full throttle and just flew straight through it. He said it would save 20 minutes. He thought it was tremendously good fun, and nobody ever found out, although the radio their end was going bloody mad!

"We landed at Elstree where he had his car, and he just went straight in, without a word to the control tower. He taxied straight up to the hangar, and as we turned into it this guy ran up like Ben Johnson and jumped up on the wing. I'd never seen a man black in the face before. He actually punched the window. He yelled, 'Graham Hill, you think you own this place!'. Graham just shrugged and laughed, and eventually the guy left him to it. It must have been four or five weeks before the big business.

"A week or so after that we did the Embassy deal, a three-year contract with Graham Hill, the whole thing. It was a beautiful contract, with serious money for a young promising guy. And there was a clause where Embassy could place him elsewhere if things didn't work out with Graham.

"One time Tony and I came back from Switzerland on a Swiss plane, after doing some business for Embassy. We were playing chess on my travelling set when the plane hit a clear air pocket and suddenly, without any warning, dropped 200 feet. It was most unnerving. I distinctly remember two things about it. One was me panicking and all the chess pieces on the ceiling, the other was Brise sitting there in total control. It was a real do, there were a couple of broken arms where people hadn't been wearing their belts.

"The thing that was in my mind is, 'I'm dead!'. And Tony was as cool as a cucumber, no sign of panic whatsoever. Ten minutes later the same thing happened again, exactly the same. Tony was again in absolute control, not even flinching... I thought, 'So this is how racers are meant to be'. Three weeks later it was all over...

"Graham had been told to divert to Luton when he crashed at Elstree. The whole thing was ghastly. Everything was blown apart. Poor Janet, Tony's wife, was just blown apart. They were very close, they'd not long been married. She was a very level-headed girl. It broke my bloody heart. We'd put such a lot in, and he would have gone all the way, no question. It got to me quite badly.

"Tony had that magical thing, there was no question in his mind, no second thoughts. He could screw the arse off the car, and if the car could win, then he'd win. There were no jitters, no silly comments before a race. He was totally, quietly confident. He was quite capable of standing up on his hind legs and talking. A year down the track Tony Brise would have been an eloquent after-dinner speaker. He impressed people in boardrooms, too. He was smart, with a good sense of humour."

■ ■ ■

Graham Hill had resisted retiring from active driving for years, but in Tony Brise he saw that he had a fine successor, and Tony's very talent eased the older man's pain at giving up the thing he loved doing best. He recognized that his young protege had the potential to uphold the team's honour on the track in a manner he himself no longer could. They had a very strong bond, founded on mutual respect, and were shaping up into a potentially formidable partnership.

All the indications are that Tony Brise would have matured not only into a Grand Prix winner and a World Champion, but also into an eloquent, assured spokesman with strong views on the sport. Of the three of the generation that British motor racing lost in the Seventies – Roger Williamson and Tom Pryce being the other two – he would probably have become the most rounded superstar.

4

DONALD CAMPBELL

The man in the shadow

"What hurts, what really hurts, is when you go down the side of life's last mountain."

At 8.47am on January 4, 1967, Donald Campbell's luck finally ran out. A haggard, besieged man, he fought his last great joust with the unknown, took what amounted to a desperate, bloody-minded gamble, and lost. In one of the most spectacular accidents ever captured on film, Britain's speed king of the Fifties and Sixties died in a dramatic somersault that sent his beloved *Bluebird* boat crashing to the depths of Coniston Water. He was only yards short of achieving his goal of becoming the first man ever to set a Water Speed Record in excess of 300mph.

He was born Donald Malcolm Campbell on March 23, 1921, but spent much of his life wondering if the Donald should have been there. Life pitched him into an extraordinary background that forever shaped his entire character. He was, for the first 28 years of his existence, The Son of Sir Malcolm Campbell. Even when the grand old man of record-breaking died on the last day of 1948, Donald still saw himself that way. His father cast a long shadow from which he never truly emerged.

Throughout his career, first as a racing driver and then as a record-breaker, Sir Malcolm had been big news. In the era after the First World War, when all of Europe was counting the cost of the bodies which had been left broken on the battlefields of France, Britain lionized its newly emergent heroes. And as the Twenties moved into the Thirties, far from waning, such practice grew more intense, as if record-breaking was a means of proving the country's strength and technical superiority to any future aggressors.

In those days, those who were not of diamond merchant and insurance broker Sir Malcolm's breeding knew their place. Then, it was the deeds of the heroes that were newsworthy, not their sexual predilections or their private lives. There was none of the popular media's current penchant for picking them to pieces whenever they stumbled from grace, or for raking up scandal. Today's newshounds would have had a field day with Campbell.

Of course, you had to deliver before you were certified a hero, but thereafter the heroics themselves were sufficient. Campbell, cocksure, arrogant and possessed of stop-at-nothing determination, won the Land Speed Record a unique nine times, the one on water four. Even when he failed occasionally, as he did trying to break Sir Henry Segrave's record at Verneuk Pan in 1929, the press was benign. It revered him; it feared him, too. In those days, rubbishing a

"Donald was twice the man his father ever was," said his mother, Lady Dorothy, but he never escaped from the long shadow of Sir Malcolm. Throughout his own illustrious career of record breaking, the small boy within the man still aspired to accomplishments that he believed might have won his late father's approval.

national hero was tantamount to treason.

While the Old Man was still alive, there was only room for one record-breaker in the family, and Sir Malcolm always made that abundantly clear. If it emasculated the boy, that was just too bad. His wish was that his only son should find something less strenuous as a career, and it was so strong that he didn't even leave his *Bluebird* car or hydroplane to him when he died. He once speculated that Donald was so accident prone he would kill himself if he ever drove a speedboat. If Donald wanted any of his record memorabilia or equipment he had to buy it at an auction intended to raise money which would go into a trust for Sir Malcolm's grandchildren. It was typical of his cruel meanness.

Early in 1949, as the younger Campbell brooded over the death of his father, record-breaker Goldie Gardner casually mentioned that American industrialist Henry Kaiser was building a boat called *Aluminum First* to break the record. The news seared into Donald, and he made an instant decision to carry on. He sought out his father's faithful chief mechanic Leo Villa, who had known him since he was an infant, and a die was cast. He parted with the 1935 *Bluebird* car to buy back the Rolls-Royce piston engines Sir Malcolm had discarded in favour of jet power after the war, had the *Bluebird K4* converted back to propeller drive, and embarked on the record-breaking trail that would end so spectacularly.

Once he thought he had broken his father's mark, only to find the timekeepers had been mistaken. So he chipped steadily away, and simply became more determined when the American Stanley Sayres stole it at 160.32mph. He was lucky to survive when *K4* hit a submerged railway sleeper at 170mph in 1951. The boat was wrecked, and to make matters worse, Sayres

41

upped the record to 178.497mph in his revolutionary *Slo-Mo-Shun IV* the following year. Then Britain's other top contender, John Cobb, was killed on Loch Ness that September. Despite that tragedy, however, Donald decided to keep going, and he sank all the money he'd made from his engineering business to have Ken and Lewis Norris design and build him his own jet-powered craft, *Bluebird K7*. It was a courageous decision worthy of his father, and after months of problems he finally squeezed past 200 with 202.32mph on Ullswater in July 1955.

The Fifties were his best years, when he made an income from the record by nudging it up a little each time out to earn the Butlin Trophy and the £5,000 put up annually by holiday camp magnate Sir Billy for the Briton breaking it. He was young, successful, at the peak. The fire that drove him to continue after Cobb's death took him to 216.20mph on Nevada's Lake Mead in November '55, then to 225.63, 239.07, 248.62 and 260.33mph on Coniston in the years up to 1959. He was every schoolboy's hero, the consummate record-breaker. Yet while the world now saw him as a success in his own right, Campbell was still trapped in his father's shadow, forever seeking greater success as if driven by the need to prove to himself that he was capable of the sort of feats that would have met with paternal approval.

At Lake Mead he had discovered call girls in a big way, and spent time diligently dialling and entertaining in his hotel. Even now the locals remember him, "and the way he just had to have girls like kids have to have candy". At the man-made lake had also come the dream to build the ultimate car, to smash past Cobb's long-standing 394.19mph record.

It wasn't enough just to build something similar. Like all of his projects, the *Bluebird CN7* would be the biggest and best of its type. Designed by the Norris brothers, it was powered by a Bristol-Siddeley Proteus gas turbine, which drove all four wheels. The record was a foregone conclusion when the mighty car was shipped out to Utah's Bonneville Salt Flats in August 1960 for the Great Confrontation, yet Campbell ended up doing just what Athol Graham did in his backyard special, City of Salt Lake. Nervous of opposition which included Dr Nathan Ostich's jetcar, Mickey Thompson and Art Arfons, both Campbell and Graham accelerated too fast, too soon, and flipped. Graham was killed; only *Bluebird*'s superior constructional integrity saved Campbell's life in the 360mph accident, which he liked to claim was a product of hyperventilation caused by breathing excessive oxygen.

Despite a fractured skull, he was determined to have another try, and such courage persuaded BRM owner Sir Alfred Owen to sponsor the construction of a second car. The whole thing was to prove a ghastly mistake. Campbell turned his back on Utah and headed for Australia's Lake Eyre, where reportedly it hadn't rained for nine years. As soon as he arrived it did, and weather problems forced postponements until 1963, and then caused some more. At one stage he had to drive the car off the salt under its own power. The attempt was cancelled, and to make the situation worse Craig Breedlove managed 407.45mph in August in his pure-jet *Spirit of America*. It was a pointer to future form, prophetic writing in the salt.

Campbell returned to Australia in 1964, enduring further bouts of poor weather and acrimony as his nominated stand-in accused him of cowardice. The situation was bad for a number of reasons. The weather was still malignant, and money was short. The press continued to give him a hard time. Worse, the surface of the only track available – designer Ken Norris called it Hobson's Choice – was not good enough to allow *Bluebird* anywhere near the 475mph for which she was geared. A salt island had had to be milled away in the middle of it, and the salt had refused to reconstitute properly. On every run Campbell knew he would hit that slushy part near maximum speed.

"Even just to get to Lake Eyre we had to drive for 30 miles on an unmade track, which was winding and boggy", explained Norris, "and then go over the

In his early days, stung by American challenges, he took over his father's old boat, Bluebird K4. Under full power acceleration it was a brute, as this Coniston shot from 1950 reveals. By then faithful friend and advisor Leo Villa had become a regular passenger as they worked tirelessly towards 170mph.

causeway the Army built, and finally another 11 miles out on the lake itself. With all those problems Donald was still under great stress, and I think when he got into the cockpit he tended just to go for it. He was the one who had to make the decision. He must have been bloody-minded on the two record runs."

Campbell carried on until he finally squeezed them in, each, amazingly enough, at 403.1mph, to grab what was still the official Land Speed Record. Breedlove's mark hadn't been recognized by the FIA. Eyre's surface was treacherously fragile and *Bluebird*'s 52-inch diameter wheels and Dunlop tyres punched ruts throughout the course's length. Matchbox-size chunks of rubber littered it. His success was the act of a supremely courageous man, yet few really cared. Hadn't Breedlove gone faster? And why did Campbell's efforts always seem to be surrounded by so much drama?

Within three months Tom Green's *Wingfoot Express* had officially erased his hard-won glory. Within 18 the record had been punched to a pure-thrust 600mph. *Bluebird*, the multi-million pound pride of British industry, was a White Elephant. Even the wheel-driven record succumbed to the American Summers brothers in 1965.

At the end of 1964 he became the only man in history to break both the Land and Water Speed Records in the same year when he took *K7* to 276.33mph on Lake Dumbleyung in Australia on December 31. Then in 1965 he invited the British press and industrial contacts to a grand reception at his house, Roundwood, to see the *CN7* and *K7* and to unveil the mock-up of the rocket car – *Bluebird Mach 1.1* – which the Norris brothers were designing in readiness for another attack on the Land Speed Record. Several companies expressed interest, but he was to be bitterly disappointed with the low-key press reaction.

While the Fifties may have been a muted echo of the Thirties, the Sixties were very different. Popular interest centred less on man's earthbound exploits, even if he aimed for the Sound Barrier, as Campbell did, and more on the conquest of space. The lunar launches may have been a giant step for mankind, but they were a massive setback for men such as Campbell. Who cared about a man who wanted to go over 750mph on land when others were heading for the moon?

The final film interviews with him at Coniston reveal an understandable bitterness. He wasn't a newcomer to the record game, but a proven contender, yet apart from the *Daily Sketch*, nobody really showed any interest in supporting the project. Campbell was mainly financing the venture himself, and his brief to Ken Norris was simply to adapt the old boat to take the more powerful Bristol-Siddeley Orpheus engine in place of the Metropolitan-Vickers Beryl with which it had won all its previous successes. Of course, it shouldn't have been necessary to adopt the Heath Robinson tactic of lashing sandbags to the transom to cure the nose-heaviness that arose from the difference in weight between the two power units. Of course, calculations should have been made beforehand to ensure that the air intakes were strong enough to withstand the Orpheus' extra demand for air. Instead, there was embarrassment when *Bluebird* – the fastest boat in the world – couldn't initially drag itself from the water and start planing properly; then near disaster when the engine sucked in the rivets from the air intakes during a static test and wrecked its turbine blades.

On film Campbell appeared with his jaw stuck out defensively, a stag at bay. His tone was clipped and impersonal as he made lame excuses about going into the unknown and exploring new technology as they progressed. His pride would never have allowed him to admit publicly that he'd had to take financial shortcuts.

"There is no form of advanced engineering, no form of record-breaking", he said, "where you get it smooth. It just doesn't happen. It wouldn't be record-breaking if it did happen that way. World's records today are broken, but very seldom, which is perhaps one of the reasons why you don't get away with them easily. This is one of the misfortunes that befall you if you decide to try and follow this rather stony path. But it doesn't matter if you're playing with a world's record-breaking car, a high-speed aircraft, or a high-speed boat, or any form of advanced engineering, rocketry, or what have you." As the pressure mounted inexorably through such technical setbacks, poor weather and then a fuel feed problem, he became more withdrawn, his attitude during interviews more go-to-hell. Asked the age-old question, 'Why do it?', he would reply in a petulant fashion that suggested he didn't give a damn what anyone else thought of his endeavours. "A lot of people like to sit on their behinds, don't they, in the comfort of their own armchairs and watch television, but what do they know?"

In truth he was edgy, and expressed himself badly in response to something he'd been answering throughout his career. He cared very much about what others thought, about upholding national honour, for that was a cornerstone of his entire approach to record-breaking. It wasn't for Britain and for the hell of it, as Richard Noble's effort would be. It was for Britain and to prove it to himself, to appease the shadow of his father, just as it always had been. What nobody realized at the time, until it was too late, was that they were witnessing the slow, inexorable destruction of the man.

He'd been through it all before, of course, never more so than at the spiteful Lake Eyre. Yet somehow, in his own backyard it assumed a new dimension, with representatives of the daily press and television networks on site continuously, awaiting something newsworthy. "When you start something like this, you pass the point of no return", he said. "There is no going back in life. Once you start something you've got to finish it. You see, this is not done as a public appeal or a public entertainment, but to achieve a goal, which is to see a British boat first past the magic 300." As December moved into January at Coniston, and winter edged him closer to his destiny, the point of no return was already a very long way behind him. There would be no stopping the treadmill.

January 4 was dark and still as the *Bluebird* team assembled at dawn, readying for what everyone was certain would be the all-out attempt. Across the lake in the darkness, the surface of the water was flat calm. Conditions were ideal. Campbell, anxious to get the whole business over and done with, strode down to the boathouse, spoke in a terse, preoccupied tone to Villa, and was out on the lake in *K7* as first light enhanced the beauty of Grisedale forest. At

8.42am he was away, skimming through the measured kilometre at 297mph. It was a fraction short of his target, but nothing he couldn't make up on the mandatory return run.

There was a radio communication glitch that prevented him actually speaking to Villa, who listened with astonishment as he announced that he was returning less than 4 minutes after he had stopped, without bothering to refuel. At 8.46 he sped back up the lake, but without a full fuel load *Bluebird* was a different creature, more skittish, considerably lighter. His wash from the first run hadn't died down, either, but was rolling back in from the shore. The seeds of disaster had been sown.

He was 150 yards – less than a second – short of the end of the kilometre when, after a period of violent tramping from sponson to sponson, *K7* lifted gracefully from the water. His radio commentary was blurred and indistinct, but there was no falter in his crackling voice. *"Nose up... Pitching a bit down here, probably from my own wash... Straightening up now in my track... Passing close to Peel Island... Tramping like mad... Full power... Tramping like hell here... I can't see much and the water's very bad indeed... I can't get over the top... I'm getting a lot of bloody row in here... I can't see anything... I've got the bows up... I'm going... Oh..."*

After turning a complete somersault, *Bluebird* broke into pieces and sank. The wreckage of the boat was located 140 feet down, but though a team of naval divers led by the experienced Lieutenant-Commander Futcher tried again and again to locate his body, it was never found.

Twenty years later the newspapers made much of contentions that Donald Campbell was driven by a death wish, and had simply decided he'd had enough. It was true he often brooded about advancing age – "There's too much time to grow up and grow old" – and was fearful of suffering debilitating illness in the way his father had in the final months of his life. He was terrified of cancer, although there was never any evidence he was suffering from it. But the suggestions were nonsense, a sad product of sensationalism at its factual worst, and ignorance of what drove him.

His behaviour had been unusual on the final day, but after nine weeks of tribulation that, too, was understandable. From his own experience he knew only too well the risk involved in making a return run immediately after the first. In September 1956, on the first leg of his 225mph record, he achieved 286 on the way down, but was so badly shaken about on an immediate return that he couldn't better 164. In 1967, *Bluebird* was fitted with a special rod which protruded into the water when actuated, to act as a brake. It made his wash even rougher...

He was also aware of the risk of failing to refuel. Not only would there be less weight over the front planing points, but if the Orpheus actually ran short of fuel on a faster return run, the lack of thrust would have the dramatically destabilizing effect of further reducing downloading on them.

So why, after seven water records and one on land, did such an experienced pilot make such an error? Why, with his fastest ever speed in the bag from the first run, didn't he simply wait for conditions to return to perfection? The questions would torment Villa until his death.

"I think he just wanted to get it over with", said Norris. "He didn't want to commit suicide or any of that rubbish. He just wanted to get to the Boat Show with his *Jetstar* project. I think he decided to take the chance to try and catch that calm spell before the wash from the first run came back, to get it done. We'd put on those new spray deflectors, which now I always liken to 'Dame Edna's spectacles', and I called John Stollery at Imperial College; we worked out their lift and found that it was only marginally worse. The difference in weight between the two engines was also only marginal. We had to trim it again, but again it was only marginally worse. They were all only little things. We worked out the moment about the centre of gravity with the ballasted transom, and a

lift margin of 4 degrees, which in practice was quite a lot of movement for such a long boat, and the safety margin was still thought to be enough. It would have been OK if he hadn't run into that wash."

The answers also lay in the length of time the team had been at Coniston, and Campbell's desire to finish the job, and in the continual financial problems of his final years. "The old meter's ticking over all the time", he acknowledged. He knew too well that the media didn't possess infinite patience and, while that wouldn't normally have swayed him unduly, the added financial strain made things intolerable. He was also acutely aware that another drawn-out saga would harm his chances of raising the finance for the rocket car, which after all was the reason why he was pushing a 12-year-old boat 50mph beyond its original design limit. His reasoning was sound enough for he'd gambled in similar fashion when time was against him at Dumbleyung, in Australia, when he literally beat the advance of the clock to set his 276mph record on the very last day of 1964. But even Donald knew he was playing Russian Roulette with more than one loaded chamber this time.

At 8.42am on January 4 he went out in a bloody-minded mood to confront his destiny, a weary George ready at last to slay the final dragon. At 8.47 the risk ceased to be calculated and became a gamble, and he paid the price.

He was an extraordinary character, often genuinely afraid, especially after the harrowing accident at Utah and the number of times he relived it mentally during the ghastly ordeal at Lake Eyre. His daughter Gina recognized many occasions when he simply didn't *want* to go ahead, yet every time he did, for though he often admitted to being frightened, the fear of ultimate failure to achieve a goal was far stronger than any he might experience during its attainment. He had made a brace of runs over Christmas, when the team had gone home for the holiday and he had only local assistance, and he claimed to have reached 286mph, his best speed to date. There was something reactionary in the decision to risk so much then, when the timekeepers' clocks were stilled, but he proved to himself that he could still do it.

If he was frightened during those final moments at Coniston, he gave no indication of it. Instead, he spiralled to his death still going for it, still maintaining his commentary. It was not the act of a frightened man, nor one bent on a death wish, but the act of an Abnormally Brave individual, a fatalist totally committed to his beliefs and ideals. Across the world, in New Zealand for the Tasman series, Jim Clark went missing for two hours after he was handed a newspaper bearing the news of Donald's death. It was the Scot's way of getting over things that affected him deeply.

What drove Campbell on? Single-handedly he had fought off three major jetboat attacks from the Americans (one, Lee Taylor, was incapacitated for 18 months after an accident in 1964, but was building up to a fresh attack while *Bluebird* was at Coniston). "It's something I feel *has* to be done", he said, as he stressed how much the Americans were investing. "The way to beat them is to bump it out of their reach." Few really believed him, taking it as his excuse for another go. A little research would have revealed Alcoa's massive investment in the unsuccessful *Tempo Alcoa* and *Miss Stars & Stripes II*, and Harvey Aluminum's association with Taylor's *Hustler*, but Campbell was all they wanted to know about. As it turned out, his sense of urgency was justified less than six months after his death, when Taylor finally managed 285mph to win the record back for America.

Campbell was the kind one either loved or loathed, capable of tremendous charm or off-putting prickliness. Tom Fink, the engineer who trained Ken Norris and helped Australian Ken Warby to his own water records, worked with Campbell in the early Fifties. Once asked the difference in working with Warby, he replied, "It's nice to work with someone who is prepared to take advice..."

OTHER VOICES

Ken Norris – *Bluebird* designer

"I think that was a little harsh. He was always asking my advice. 'What do I do on this run, Ken?' Whether he always emulated that when he got in the cockpit differed, because he always said, 'When I get in the boat it's my decision', but he would talk to me about it.

"When he made that acceleration run at Bonneville, he asked me what he should do. I told him not to boot it down straight away, but to get the acceleration run we needed and to build it up gradually. I think he booted it straight away. Mind you, the oxygen thing could have been some of it, but he put his foot down too hard and swung it. He lost all of the wheels on the four-wheel drive. He says he watched it in a detached manner and he never ever said,

'Well, I think I booted it too hard'. Maybe, yes, he had to rationalize things that way to himself. The Dunlop man just thought he lost it.

"You should bear in mind that Donald cracked his skull in his helmet, and yet he only had a small amount of head movement in the cockpit, so it must have been quite a blow. I don't think he was quite the same after that. He was always conscious of that. He was more serious after Bonneville. And unlike Richard Noble, he always admitted to fear. Fear was his survival kit.

"My guess is that in 1966 he was shorter of money than ever after three years of non-activity in record-breaking. He'd originally mortgaged his house for the land record. The film *Across the Lake* maybe made more of it, because he wouldn't have behaved that extremely, but...

"He wasn't the type to bear grudges. With Donald it was a flash fire, then it was all forgotten. He didn't get mad with me at all; he'd call me Prof, or something, or You Old Bugger, and he was certainly full of fun. Not as remote from the team as Richard Noble was from the *Thrust* team. Donald was there with the team up to his elbows. He'd stand on the table and dance at Christmas, that sort of thing. He was one of the boys.

"On his own he could be pretty quiet and severe, as if he was thinking some of the thoughts he didn't express when he was talking to you. I think he was more of a showman in company. He liked an audience. He wouldn't have got where he did if he hadn't. He wouldn't have gone to sponsors' meetings the way he did. Brother Lew and I would arrive, and the sponsors would come in, grumbling about the project and bad press reports, that sort of thing, what's he after now? And he'd come in all kitted out in his London togs, you know, and in about 2 minutes they were saying, 'Yes Donald, no Donald, whatever you like Donald'. Terrific!

"Happy go lucky? Yes, he was always jolly and chatty. And he always joined in on the engineering. He made the release pin for launching the boat, for example. He was always very conscious of what the engineering was. When we went to Saunders Roe for the boat he appreciated what was happening with the towing tests in the water tank. He was a good engineer.

"He preferred the water, no doubt to it, but he would have been OK with the rocket car, even though he would have preferred to do a new boat.

"Donald was a friend, and with friends you tend to worry a hell of a lot. You spend a lot of time worrying about that when you design something. We also had a job to do, though, when *Bluebird* was finished, and had to keep our business going, so we couldn't be with him all the time. I was at Coniston just the night before and I didn't expect him to run the day he did, even though he told me on the 3rd that it would all be over by next morning, certainly by the weekend, when we intended to come back. As it turned out, the 4th was the only good day with suitable weather.

"I motored home through the night, then I heard the news the next day, so I turned straight round and drove back to Coniston. I had to make an official report on the accident. An awful thing to have to do."

■ ■ ■

Campbell also had an intensely superstitious character. The teddy bear Mr Whoppit had to travel with him whenever he ran *Bluebird*, and was reunited with his love Whacko after each run. He once had his flat number changed because its product was 13. He hated the colour green. He said he had seen the face of his father reflected in the open cockpit canopy of the *Bluebird* car on Lake Eyre as he steeled himself to make the return run that he believed would kill him during his successful Land Speed Record attempt. "Well boy", he claimed Sir Malcolm had said. "Now you know how I felt that time at Utah when the wheel caught fire in 1935. But don't worry, it'll be all right, boy."

On the evening of January 3 he played a form of Russian patience with

On a cold Wednesday morning early in January, Donald Campbell took the Bluebird K7 hydroplane out on to Coniston Water for the last time, desperate to win his eighth Water Speed Record and to generate interest and support for the supersonic jetcar he planned. After a first run at 297mph, he was estimated to have been travelling at well over 320mph when the boat somersaulted. Those who had accused him of nervous exhaustion were humbled as he maintained his radio commentary to the very end.

friends. When he turned up the ace and then straight afterwards the queen of spades, his immediate comment was, "Mary Queen of Scots drew the same two cards the night before she was beheaded. One of my family is going to get the chop. I pray to God it isn't me." It was the kind of thing that drove the down-to-earth Villa to distraction.

The following day he took *Bluebird* out for the last time. The night before he'd told a friend, "If the chop does come, I hope I'm going ruddy fast at the time". He was. Estimates varied from 310 to 328mph. Even now, only Taylor, Warby and Craig Arfons have gone as fast or faster.

"It is sad and distressing to know that the supremacy this country once held in the realm of high speeds on land and water is now a thing of the past after the endeavours of the two courageous persons who strived so hard to keep this country on top", Leo Villa told me in 1973. As Donald received the Queen's Commendation for Gallantry posthumously in 1967, so Leo received an OBE. He died in 1979.

To Donald Campbell, life was a series of mountain tops. "What hurts", he confided, "what really hurts, is when you go down the side of life's last mountain."

He was still ascendant when the light went out.

5

JIM CLARK

The gentle giant

"Even now I can't imagine just how good Jimmy was..." – Peter Windsor

There are times when it seems we have almost become conditioned to accept bad grace in sports heroes. Witness recent events in the world of Formula One; the disgrace of the Tyson/Edwards fight. The message is clear. In the late Eighties or early Nineties a result wasn't enough if sufficiently powerful parties felt so inclined to question it. Today, if you don't like the outcome, you protest. You might not get what you want, just as Tyson and promoter Don King eventually didn't, but with luck you'll so smear the success of a rival that mud will stick, and there will be some people out there who believe you when you say you lost unfairly.

It's a sorry comment on the state of sport today, and one that was thrown into harsh focus during the Mechanics Grand Prix Challenge, the charity clay pigeon shoot, at Gleneagles one snowy February weekend in 1990. It was, of course, impossible to overlook John Young Stewart, the mastermind behind the whole thing. As I watched Jackie weaving his consummate spell that weekend, I found myself wondering what Jim Clark would have become had he enjoyed a kinder fate. It was my journey of rediscovery of Clark that effectively led to the concept for this book.

There were plenty of reminders of the quiet Scot at Gleneagles, the man in whose shadow Jackie once bounced. His biographer and friend Graham Gauld lunched at the hotel on Sunday, at Stewart's invitation. Innes Ireland's booming bass recalled that Scotland had three, not two, doughty contenders back in the early Sixties. Even Jack Oliver, best non-mechanic shot with an impressive sixth overall in the individual rankings, had a Clark connection. The Romford racer, of course, was Jimmy's replacement at Gold Leaf Team Lotus in the dark days that followed April 7, 1968.

On the way back from Gleneagles we stopped off at Duns to visit the Jim Clark Room in Newtown Street. We hadn't been there since our honeymoon nearly 11 years earlier. It was closed for the winter, although its guardians were working hard to have it open all year round, but opening it up for us was no hardship to them. We were greeted with the same sort of courtesy that used to be taken for granted when Jimmy was racing; nothing was too much trouble. It was rather touching.

Stepping in among the glittering trophies, which make McLaren International's foyer look like Camden Lock market, is to step back to a bygone

Prince and king: Jackie Stewart stood at Jim Clark's shoulder during the older Scot's greatest year in 1965, but their personalities could not have differed more.

era when sportsmanship was king, when the *manner* in which one competed was every bit as important as the results one achieved. The respect in which Jimmy was held in life still wreathes around the glass cabinets and the photo board, and they still speak with amused affection of his daredevil antics with Colin Chapman's Ford Galaxie in which he pounded around the local lanes.

Clark had become something of a man about town near the end and had mixed emotions about his life sharing a flat in Paris with the French motoring doyen Jabby Crombac, but still he loved nothing more than to return to his cattle and sheep, or to immerse himself in curing the mechanical ills of one of the Edington Main tractors.

His Eddie Sachs Scholarship Trophy, which he won at Indianapolis, struck a chord. "My Indy", was how Sachs used to describe the 'Brickyard'. The Clown Prince of the American scene, they called him when he was out of his car, for that was when his self-deprecating laughter hid his acute awareness of the dangers of his profession. When he was in the cockpit he was a different man, calculating, fearless, quick, one whose tragedy was to be killed at the oval circuit. He had loved it so much, even though it had always treated him so unkindly; it did so right to the end, as he died in somebody else's accident.

Clark, highly strung though he was, didn't hide his neuroses with laughter. Sometimes he seemed a bundle of nerves out of the car, and would chew his finger ends incessantly. But like Sachs, he was calm whenever he was in it. In a race car, Jimmy Clark was a giant. His GP record says it all: he won 25 races from 72 starts, started from pole 33 times (a record only beaten in 1990 by Ayrton Senna) and set fastest lap in 28 races. He was only ever beaten into second place once, when John Surtees headed him home at the Nurburgring in 1964. Usually he either won or failed to finish.

After team-mate Alan Stacey was killed there in June 1960 (poor Jimmy refused to believe that he had a wooden leg, which he did), Clark hated Spa, yet how he went there! He won his first GP there in 1962, and then triumphed each year until he became a first-lap retirement in the 1966 monsoon race. The 1964 event had been lucky, after Gurney and Hill had run out of fuel and McLaren out of sparks, but in 1965 he won by a country mile.

Occasionally, there have been suggestions that Clark won because he always had the best cars, that the 1½-litre Formula One machines were not proper racing cars, that the gladiators of that era fought with plastic swords. They overlook certain truths. A lot of the time Clark, like Ayrton Senna and Alain Prost, *did* have the best equipment, and as they would, so he used it to the full. In so doing he called upon an unequalled ability to bring together his talents for smoothness, precision, consistency and, above all, sheer speed, to produce a flowing style that was the envy of all his rivals. Nothing troubled him in a race car, and while he could pinpoint problems, he was just as adept at adjusting that style to cope with them.

At Monaco, in 1964, his rear anti-roll bar broke while he was leading. Former Team Lotus mechanic Dick Scammell, now Racing Director of Cosworth Engineering, recalled, "Jimmy was very easy on the car, able to adapt extremely quickly to any changes, in either conditions or the machinery. That year at Monaco his lap times went up a little while he sorted it out, but then he went back to his old times.

"Of course, we weren't sure immediately what the problem was, and I was detailed to go down to the hairpin to see if I could see any obvious damage. Well, the second time Jimmy came round after I'd arrived there, he'd picked me out and gave me the thumbs up! He could adjust himself not only to the changed car condition, but also to that sort of change, within a lap! He carried on as if nothing had happened. It made you almost wonder why we had fitted the roll bar in the first place!"

With the change to the 3-litre formula in 1966, Formula One got back its power, yet ironically, one of Clark's greatest races was at Zandvoort that year in the 2-litre Climax-engined 33. There he hounded the 3-litre Repco Brabhams of Brabham and Hulme without mercy, leading until he was delayed by overheating. Clark the underdog was every bit as skilled as Clark the superior. At Monza he had the 3-litre BRM H16-engined Lotus, and electrified the crowd after a spectacular recovery from a slow start. He persuaded the bulky machine on to the front row in the finale at Mexico. In between the two, he had even persuaded it home first in the US GP at Watkins Glen. True, it was a success that owed something to fortune, but it showcased perfectly his uncanny ability to pace a race and spare his machinery. And he was adaptable. In 1967, at Riverside, California, he drove an unfamiliar Vollstedt USAC car, one of his rare single-seater outings in something other than a Lotus, and he duelled for the lead with Gurney before it dropped a valve. In those days Dan *was* the Californian orange grove track.

In the Lotus 49, in his final full year, he had the machine to demonstrate his prowess to the full, and he was great. Though he made it seem so, the 49 was not a meek car. It had initial handling anomalies, and the power curve was abrupt and peaky, even if the Ford Cosworth DFV was the most powerful engine of the year. He won first time out with it at Zandvoort, and he drove mightily on his way to sixth after plug problems at Spa. He led every race he started with it, adding the British, US and Mexican GPs to his tally. Again at the Glen, his uncanny mechanical sympathy helped him bring the car home despite broken rear suspension. Tyre fitters for both Dunlop and Firestone always reckoned they could tell Clark's tyres apart after a race, they were so relatively little used.

At Monza that year he was magic, turning in a performance that matched Fangio's 1957 German GP victory. After sustaining a puncture while racing for the lead with Hill, Brabham and Hulme, he pulled back a complete lap deficit –

at Monza! – to retake the lead from Brabham and Surtees, only to have the Lotus stammer on the final lap with fuel starvation that dropped him to third. His fastest race lap equalled his pole time. The kudos he got for that race irritated him, however, for he always thought the 1962 German GP had been his greatest race. There he had qualified third to Gurney and Hill, but he forgot to switch on his fuel pumps at the start, was left on the grid, and had to tiger through from last place, driving flat-out in the dreadful conditions, to finish fourth.

He so very rarely made mistakes. In 1961, he was involved in a racing accident with Ferrari driver 'Taffy' von Trips, at Monza, in which the German World Champion-elect was killed, along with nine spectators. He was deeply affected by it. At Brands Hatch, in 1965, he crashed along Bottom Straight while under pressure from Dan Gurney in the Brabham. He was, however, a gentleman who unfailingly gave his rivals room.

"You always knew with him that if at all possible he'd bring the car home, like he did at Watkins Glen in 1967", said Scammell. "And if Jimmy went into the last lap third in a bunch, you'd have no doubt he'd be first at the end."

He was very even tempered and rarely got upset – apart from the celebrated punch-up with a marshal at Zandvoort one year after being man-handled away from a corner where he had been spectating – and the only thing that made him edgy was inexcusable problems on the car, but then he just let his point be known. That time at Monza in '67, when he had been given insufficient fuel, he cut down Chapman with a few words, quietly spoken, but well-chosen.

He was versatile, too. In 1960 and '61 he put the Border Reivers Aston Martin into the lead on the first lap at Le Mans, and he and Roy Salvadori were third that first year. His antics in the Lotus Cortina are still talked about today whenever photographs of him two or three-wheeling through Bottom Bend at Brands Hatch surface, and when he ran one in the RAC Rally his performance was electrifying. He tried his hand at NASCAR, too, and impressed in a Ford

Jimmy could drive anything quickly, as witnessed by him drifting his Zagato Aston Martin round Goodwood. Out of the cockpit he was indecisive, yet within it his greatness took him beyond his rivals. As his performances often showed, though, within the quiet man there was a frequent desire to show off when he was at the wheel.

Fairlane at Rockingham in 1967. Whatever the discipline, he was an absolute natural, genuinely curious to try something new, and sufficiently possessed of that inner confidence, no matter what external appearances might have suggested to the contrary, to indulge that curiosity. In a car, Jimmy liked to show off.

He was the sort of driver whose entire mind was not taken up with what he was doing in race car. Others might get saturated and need to concentrate all their faculties to do the job, but Jimmy always had a bit left over to think about it all, to study the wider picture of a race. At Monza in 1965, for example, he and Gurney were embroiled in a heady battle when they came up to lap Innes Ireland, still perhaps smarting a little after being replaced at Lotus by Clark at the end of 1961. Innes gave Jimmy several hefty chops each time he attempted to pass. In the end Clark backed off a little going into the Lesmo corners, and let Gurney by. Innes thought Dan was Jimmy, and as he slammed the door again on the American, giving him a big moment, Jimmy ran round the outside of the pair of them. It was a champion's thinking...

His greatness wasn't confined to driving. In 1963, at the behest of British reporters, he took to visiting the press box after each GP to relay his views to the journalists. He detested sloppy reporting, but was quick to praise accuracy, and for the rest of his career he remained faithful to this practice. Today we take post-race conferences for granted, but it was Jimmy who helped set the pattern that led to them. And now we look at glum lesser drivers, being paid many times what he earned, and see them having to be coerced into attending post-practice sessions or post-race conferences...

To me, Indianapolis was the greatest index to his true genius. There, in the backyard of American racing, he was every bit as great as he was in Europe. Five times he raced there, and with better fortune he could have added three more wins to his crushing 1965 triumph. Indeed, seasoned insiders at the Brickyard still insist that it was *he* who won the 1966 event, not Graham Hill.

From the moment he drove there, he was quick. Scammell: "After Watkins Glen in 1962 we went up to Indianapolis with the Lotus 25, just as it was, because Colin wanted to find out something about the Speedway. We just turned up one morning and said, 'We want to run our car'. Typical European attitude, ignoring all the folklore!

"We were told about the rookie test, and Colin was most unimpressed. They had some hot drivers out there to watch him – I think Foyt was one of them – and Colin said, 'Tell us what it is, and Jimmy will do it'. He was mad when he was told they'd need to talk to Jimmy between each stage! He said, 'We haven't got all day'.

"Anyhow, the Yanks were amazed. Jimmy went straight out and hit the required speeds instantly, doing exactly what he had to do at each stage. His only problem was when the car seemed to wobble a bit exiting Turn Four just before he completed his final run. They all thought he'd lost it, but he just came calmly into the pits, and when they made a fuss about it he just said, 'Didn't you see that rabbit that ran across the track? I didn't want to hit it.'

"He was quite remarkable. It's difficult to compare sportsmen over the ages, but for sure he would have been the very top whatever era he'd raced in."

He ran well over 140mph in a 1½-litre car with its tyres pumped up, on a track he'd never seen before, and which would later spook such talented Formula One drivers as Chris Amon and Alan Jones...

Had he understood a little better the liberal interpretations of the rulebook pertaining to yellow light periods, he would have taken the 1963 race when Lotus returned with its Ford V8-powered 29s, but rather than rail against the manner in which Parnelli Jones and J.C. Agajanian had won (one contemporary report cited Clerk of the Course Harlan Fengler as Jones' co-driver when he refused to black flag him during the Great Oil Leak Controversy), Jimmy merely congratulated Parnelli politely and filed the lesson away for future reference.

He never made the same mistake twice.

Despite his performances there, he hated Indianapolis, all the razzmatazz and ballyhoo. It was all totally foreign to the nature of the quiet farm boy from Duns who was still only just beginning to realize and appreciate the awesome talent that had taken him to the top of the world. He hated the Americans' over-familiar way of stopping him to shake hands and say, 'Hiya Jimmy, nice to knowya'. "But they *don't* know me, and they probably never will", he used to say to friends. He was not an unfriendly person, but his innate shyness meant that it took him some time to relax in the company of newcomers to his circle.

Indianapolis is an American tradition, but in most ways he was the last person to transplant from Scotland into Hoosier country. Yet he charmed them over there. They treated him very poorly to begin with because The Establishment was afraid of his car. They came up with a microphone after he'd won in 1965 and demanded to know when he was coming back, and he said, "I don't know if I *am* coming back next year". That absolutely floored them. He told them that he had to think about it. He never signed a contract more than a year ahead, because he simply didn't know what he was going to be doing. He wanted to be able to decide that, and although he had difficulty with decisions, he didn't want other people making them for him.

He was a very generous person who really didn't make much of a fuss about money. Perhaps he should have. After participating and winning at Indy he realized he had the potential to earn a lot more racing in America, and he did some racing there he would rather not have done. He realized that however much he disliked the Brickyard, he couldn't really afford not to race at Indy. He once said, "Every lap I was in the lead I could see dollar signs in front of my eyes".

Despite his hatred of Spa, where he had seen Alan Stacey and Chris Bristow perish, Clark dominated the Belgian GP in the early Sixties. He won four times in a row, starting with the 1962 race here in the beautiful Lotus 25.

OTHER VOICES

Pat Mennem – journalist

"It was in 1966, or possibly 1967, that he called me from Heathrow, where he was bound for a US flight. He had got into financial trouble and was having to live in France at that time, which depressed him. I think, so the story I was told goes, that somebody had been careless talking about the money he had in the Cayman Islands when they were out in a restaurant, and they'd had somebody from the Inland Revenue sitting beside them!

"Anyhow, he was bound for Indianapolis, and he didn't like it very much, one way or another. He rang me and asked me to come along for a drink. He'd had a few noggins, actually. He would occasionally, but it was very rare. What I couldn't get into his head was that I couldn't get through to his side of the airport lounge without a ticket, and he couldn't come back through to where I was because that would have counted as another trip to Britain!

"He was very highly strung. A Border farmer transformed into this glamorous world of motor racing. He was still a little bit wary of it, and still a Border farmer at heart. I once went to market with him in Edinburgh and they were all farmers there. He'd won both his World Championships, but nobody ever mentioned motor racing at all. All they talked about was sheep. He told me that was what he wanted to go back to. He was much more interested in whether parking meters were being installed in Duns Mains, things like that, when he was living in France."

■ ■ ■

He finished second in the 1963 race, won the USAC qualifier at Milwaukee later that year, led comfortably at Indy in 1964 until the rear suspension was shattered when his left rear Dunlop threw its tread, and then beat Foyt conclusively to win in 1965. In 1966, he astounded locals by spinning through two complete 360s, not once but twice, in the treacherously slippery Turn 4, and keeping the engine running so that he could neatly snick back into the race when he had the flame red STP Lotus 38 pointing back in the right direction. The Americans weren't quite used to seeing that kind of talent deployed in recovering from an error, let alone seeing it twice!

At the end of that race Jimmy confidently headed for Victory Lane, only to find Graham Hill's Lola already there. Almost certainly there had been a bungle in lap scoring, when the timers confused Clark's car with team-mate Al Unser's, and when Jimmy ventured to suggest later to Graham that he might have scored his second successive triumph, the Englishman simply replied, "No way, mate, I drank the milk!", referring to the time-honoured liquid reward for the winner. Had that happened to almost any current day driver, the consequences don't bear thinking about...

Jimmy's latent curiosity put him into the STP Paxton turbine during tyre testing in 1967 – he had been dying to try it when his long-standing friend Andy Granatelli wheeled it out, and needed no second bidding when the beefy STP boss invited him to hop aboard – and he returned to Pau's Formula Two race in France to tell Jabby Crombac, "I have just tested the car which is going to win Indy this year!". He was so nearly right. He tried it later to the revised regulations, and the following year also tested the dramatic Lotus 56 turbine which he would have driven in the 1968 500. Ah, what a combination they would have made! He was fast from the outset, and the 56 was tailormade for his impeccably smooth style...

What would Jim Clark have become? He would have been 54 on March 4, 1990, just after our Gleneagles trip, while Stewart would be 51 on June 11 that year. It's impossible to imagine him assuming the sort of publicity mantle that

As a further index of his talent, Indianapolis succumbed to his skill. At the start of the 1964 race he led Parnelli Jones, Bobby Marshman and A.J. Foyt and was leading when a thrown tyre tread smashed the rear suspension. In 1965 he went one better than his second place in the controversial 1963 event, winning comfortably in the Lotus 38.

rests so easily on Jackie's shoulders. The limelight never drew him, and even though he was becoming more relaxed within it just prior to his death, he retained his farmer's reserve to the end. Even after winning the 1968 South African GP he was still questioning whether he *really* wanted to become World Champion again and have to put up with all the inevitable publicity that went with it. Motor racing was his sport, but it was always farming that he regarded as his occupation.

Once, flying out to Pau, he simply handed his girlfriend Sally Stokes a map and said, "Get me over the Channel, and then we'll follow the railway". "He was happier to have found the way to Pau than he was to have won the race", she recalled. Towards the end of his life, however, the indications were that he was taking a fresh approach to risks.

Just before his death he spoke with Gauld and pondered the possibility of marrying and settling down on the farm, cutting all his racing ties. At the same time, though, his life as a tax exile in Paris had given him a taste for town life. He also talked of putting something back into the sport, of flag marshalling or taking up racing photography. The subject so fascinated him that he would often help trackside snappers to achieve better pictures by beckoning them into a better position as he drove past one lap, then putting on a special display just for them the next. How times change...

"Maybe partly he'd have gone back to farming," said Sally. "He really loved the life and the friends. Maybe he'd have gone back partly, but I can't believe he'd have done it entirely. It would have seemed too quiet for him. But he had a great respect for farming and farming people, he called them the salt of the earth.

"How long would he have gone on? We had a telephone conversation shortly before he died, and he was probably talking about retiring and I can't remember what I was saying, but then he said, 'Well, what if I died? What if I got killed on the track?'. And I was so surprised and so jolted, because he'd never even mentioned it before in all the years. And I was wondering if he actually thought about it and *was* considering retiring at the time."

He told the writer/photographer Max le Grand in October 1967, when discussing the waywardness of the Lotus 49 for *CAR* magazine, "People say I have a lot of luck when it comes to shunts. I must say I seem to have got away with it. But what do you say? Is it luck?"

Perhaps he would have retired at the end of 1968. Stewart doesn't think he would have stopped then – imagine what he could have done with the Lotus 72. "I think he would have gone on. He didn't have anything else to go to. That was his most comfortable life. For Jimmy, the easiest thing he did in life was sitting in a racing car. He was becoming more rounded, able to stand and talk in front of people. He was never really comfortable with that, but it was a lot easier for him than it had ever been.

"He was happy with what he'd achieved, but he was still insecure with his life because he didn't know whether he wanted to be a farmer or a racing driver. He knew he was a racing driver, he knew his skill was in racing, but he still wanted to be that farmer, he was still a country border farmer. And he was headstrong. He didn't want to get married, he didn't think it was right to be married and be a racing driver. But he had lots of girlfriends and a couple of serious relationships."

Others suggest he was planning to marry a girl called Diane and to retire at the end of 1969 to split his time between sheep farming in New Zealand and Scotland.

OTHER VOICES

Sally Swart (nee Stokes) – Jimmy's girlfriend, 1963 to '66

"He could never really understand his power behind the wheel, it came so naturally. No matter where he was, even from the beginning. I first saw him race at Mallory Park in 1958, as I lived in Leicestershire and went along with a whole lot of friends who were enthusiasts. In the five races of the day, three were won by this stranger from Scotland, I think in a Lister-Jag. He really impressed everyone with his driving. He was always very unassuming about it, but when you spoke to other people about it he was always the person to beat. That little bit quicker, that little bit neater in the corners. I think that's what other drivers admired about him. He was in supreme control of both himself and the car in all circumstances and in an awful lot of cars.

"We first met in 1963 through Gunella Whitmore. John and Gunella were good friends of mine in London, and when I came down I often used to stay with them. They had a house near Grosvenor Square. There was a whole gang of friends. Jimmy invited me to the premiere of *Cleopatra* – he was very shy doing that!

"Gunella said afterwards that it was highly organized by her because Jimmy didn't dare ask me out. I thought that was very sweet and very flattering, really. She invited me to lunch and Jimmy just happened to be there, but it was all carefully planned.`She left us to do the washing up. I don't know why he needed courage. Gosh! That evening at the cinema was two or three nights later. John came and I met Stirling there. I was so thrilled. We all travelled on the tube together – in our evening dresses! It was really great fun.

"Jimmy was very quiet and retiring in those days. He was reserved with new people until he felt comfortable. He would talk when other people asked him questions. Sometimes he would get going. But he opened up much more with people he knew, and he liked to talk about the racing and all the hairy moments, as if he was on safe ground.

"He really loved driving, even in road cars. Often we used to drive up from London to Scotland, and he was setting up the car and going so smoothly through the corners. He was very safe.

"Yes, I know about the story of him crashing several times at the Y-junction near his farm. Making up his mind was his big problem, all the time. Always. 'Where shall we go and eat?', I'd say. 'I don't mind. Where do you want to go?', he'd respond. 'I don't mind. Where do you want to go?', I'd say again. Ah, it was terrible!

"I said, 'However do you make up your mind to turn a corner?', and he said, 'I don't have to make it up, that's automatic. That's natural. That's no problem for me'. And I knew then, and I know doubly now, that he became a different person when he entered the cockpit. And he also, sadly in a way, became a different person when he left that car. He seemed almost an incomplete person. He was such a genius in a car, but he was like a lot of geniuses. They have flaws in the rest of their personality because so much goes into that part of them which is the super talent. He became more of a complete person the longer he was in racing because he did get used to it, to the glare of everything. And I know he enjoyed the glare later on, but he certainly didn't in the beginning. This agony of decisions that he had, still that remained. He got a bit better, and I think it made it easier for him when he'd become World Champion, and maybe proved something to himself.

"Once, in 1964, one of my girlfriends and I went to the Horse of the Year Show and Jimmy came along. He enjoyed the jumping, and jumped out of his seat in sympathy each time a horse went over a fence! In the interval he came back from the gents giggling. He'd been washing his hands when the guy next to him had looked up at him in the mirror and just goggled as he recognized him. He looked at Jimmy and said, 'Aren't you at the wrong show, mate?'. Jimmy thought that was very funny.

"I thought it was wonderful the way the towns honoured him. I'm afraid it's a Biblical quote, but you're never honoured in your own town, just everywhere else. Even Christ wasn't honoured in Nazareth. But Jimmy was honoured in his home town of Duns. They gave him the freedom of the city, and made a big fuss and celebration. I know he was really touched by that. And they put up 'memorials' in other villages. For him, when he was still alive. He opened things, things were done in his name. He became more at ease with the public.

"He never lost sight of his roots, just became a fuller person as the years went by. He got quite boisterous! He would start things off and he could be quite mischievous, quite a party animal in the end.

"Now we know that to die at 32 was desperately young.

"I never did see him lose his temper. He would be upset at excessive press coverage; he hated exaggeration. In fact I think very few people really did know him very well. Just a handful of us. Because of his natural reserve he wanted to keep it that way. He was close to Graham Gauld, close to Colin, of course, closest to Jabby of the journalists. And Ian Scott-Watson, whose cars he drove, to begin with. He liked it that way. He wasn't very open in his character. And I don't think that changed, he just became more at ease with the situation later. But it didn't mean to say that he didn't enjoy things that went on; he did. He enjoyed a party with friends, and danced with the rest of us. When people befriended him that meant really that he had let them become his friends. He also didn't have much time. It wasn't that he wanted to be unfriendly. He was off at different places *every* weekend and it takes time to be really good friends.

"Jimmy never really sold himself like Jackie did. His character was totally different. His talent wasn't in that way. He was just a quieter, more reserved character. I don't know Prost, but he sounds very much like Jimmy. He sounds a gentleman on the track, which Jimmy was, too. He cared for the safety of other people.

"I do think he settled into the form of being a racer in the later years, although I didn't see him so much then – we were together from '63 to '66. But then we always kept up a nice contact after that, talked together on the phone. I spoke to him just before Hockenheim...

59

"Jimmy could cut off, he really could. There were somehow two totally different parts of his life, the driving and the rest of it. It seemed like that to me, anyway. His total concentration; I suppose that went into the nail-biting. My nails were never anything to write home about, but his were really yukky. He'd bite them right down. But otherwise he didn't show much sign of nerves, it was amazing. Perhaps it was because he kept himself busy. Just before a race he used to be taping up his goggles, or fiddling with his helmet, or biting his nails, or pacing up and down. He had a very springy walk. You could tell him a mile away walking across a paddock. A bit of spring heel! He didn't really seem very nervous at race time, and I admired that. And he was totally relaxed around the car, he obviously felt so much at home in it.

"When he was out of the car again he wasn't visibly different to anyone else. This is just my own theory, but he went back to his indecisions as soon as he stepped out. As soon as he sat in it he was the total master and he never even thought of decisions. He drove the car with his head and the seat of his pants. Some even said he wasn't all that good as a test driver because he adapted so well to any faults to get the best out of it. He could win races in very lame cars. But he could go round in test mode when he needed to. In a race it was amazing how he could adapt.

"Marriage? I think he was frightened of commitments like that, but maybe he could have settled down. Yeah. I think he would have preferred to live in Scotland, even though he liked to be the man about town in Paris. I don't know how good his French was. I think he left that to Jabby!

"He loved children. He had lots of nieces and nephews in Scotland, and got on fine with them. I still see them. His younger sister is godmother to my daughter.

"Often he had to present the prizes at Scottish car club dances, so we often went back up to Scotland. Places like Ingliston. He would still do that, even after winning the championships. Scotland and his family and friends were always very important to him."

■ ■ ■

In Stewart's early days with Tyrrell in Formula Three, and then with BRM in Formula One, Clark was a source of great help. Jackie admired him and drew on him as his own career developed.

And in turn, as Clark watched the maturation of Stewart, and the manner in which the younger Scot capitalized on his potential, it taught him a lot about the business side of the profession. Jimmy might have been shy, but he had a farmer's natural shrewdness, bred while selling his pedigree Border Leicester, Suffolk Downs and Oxford Downs rams at the Kelso market. He wasn't long in catching up.

"He was a highly introverted man", Jackie said. "He ate his fingers, not just the nails, but the skin around them as well. But living in Paris changed his life quite a lot. He became a more liberated man, more worldly and rounded.

"Colin had protected Jimmy from almost everything. He could depend on Colin to do everything for him, to fix his racing cars, to do his travel, because Lotus did that. When he went to Paris he had Jabby and a fellow called Michel Fanquel, who was a great friend of his. Jabby was more his racing and his Chapman link, but Michel was a totally different animal, more social. He opened the world to Jimmy. And Jimmy was suddenly not the border farmer depending on Colin Chapman, Jimmy Line and Chris Weir, who were his accountant and his lawyer in Duns. Suddenly he was living in Paris, the most sophisticated city in the world, probably.

"And you know, I saw it, the change. I mean, he was a different man. And we had spent a lot of time together. I mean, Jimmy in 1964, when we shared an apartment – John Whitmore's apartment in London, the West End, Mayfair – to

the man I would go to Paris to see when I was there on business with Elf, was just totally different.

"He was more independent, more vocal about what he wanted. And I think Colin was going to have more and more trouble with him, if you know what I mean. Because until then Jimmy asked Colin about everything, and Colin told Jimmy how it was going to be, because Jimmy needed that leadership, he needed that figure there."

Besides 25 GP wins, they shared the ability to inspire. When he dedicated a memorial plaque to Clark at Loretto School in 1969, the Very Reverend R Leonard Small, MA, DD, said: "Jim Clark was not only a World Champion racing driver, he leaves the memory of a champion of the individual in an increasingly impersonal age, an age in which we are all of us continually pressurized into the mould of the group, slowly but surely, if subtly forced to conform to the dull pattern of the average and the ordinary of the crowd".

Stewart, meanwhile, forged on. Behind him he leaves not just those 27 GP wins and three World Championships, but his legacy of enhanced safety on the circuits of the world. The diehards to whom racing had to be a blood sport pilloried him as a 'milk and water' driver as he campaigned for sensible safety precautions, but history relates that the Armco rash for which he was directly responsible was instrumental in preserving life. Lack of popularity was a small price to pay. Ironically, had there been suitable barriers at Hockenheim in 1968 Clark might not have perished.

Jackie Stewart, the outgoing, consummate pro; Jimmy Clark, the very private racer who loved his farm but was just entering a period of fresh enlightenment when he died.

With Clark, as with all true champions, his successes were of course something far more than mere luck, the product of the ultimately indefinable innate talent. It made him the greatest of his era, possibly of all time. But on April 7, 1968, what luck he did enjoy finally ran out.

He didn't even want to go to Hockenheim. Initially he had been scheduled to drive the new Ford F3L at Brands Hatch in the BOAC 500 held that same weekend, but the engagement to drive the tricky Lotus 48 in the Formula Two race took precedence. The car was uncompetitive, and Jimmy took any topliner's attitude to such a vehicle: he didn't like it. He was used to better. Derek Bell, then a novice making a name in single-seaters, was amazed over breakfast that morning when Clark warned him to give the 48 a wide berth when he came up to lap it. "Me, lap it? This was Jim Clark!"

Chris Amon noticed that the Scot was in preoccupied mood all weekend, and Sally Stokes had been disquietened about what would be their final telephone conversation. "He was a bit worried that he'd been rear-ended in Spain by Jacky Ickx the previous weekend. The car had gone straight from Barcelona to Hockenheim. Colin thought the crash was due to a flat tyre, but it could have been a combination of both things. If there had been a deflating tyre it could have put a strain on the rear suspension that could have been damaged by the crash in Barcelona." Clark, it seemed, had been greatly irritated by Ickx's driving in Spain.

He had struggled with the car all weekend at Hockenheim. In a damp, miserable first heat he was lying eighth when it spun into the trees on the outward leg from the stadium. Many theories were put forward, but a slow puncture which then led to the tyre suddenly pulling into the wheel well and destabilizing the car was the most plausible. The 48 hit a stout tree sideways-on at 140mph. Jim Clark, for all his greatness, stood no chance.

At Brands Hatch, Crombac walked the paddock in a daze, tears streaming down his face. "Jimmy has been killed at Hockenheim", he told others. They would not believe him. I was 15, watching the BOAC 500 on television. Motor racing on the box was a rare treat in those days. Over the regular commentary – I think it was Raymond Baxter if memory serves correctly – I heard someone say in the background, quite quietly, 'Jim Clark's been killed at Hockenheim'. Nobody said anything, and it was as if I had imagined it. But I knew I hadn't. Then somebody else said, 'Don't be ridiculous'. Moments later the news was confirmed officially. I'd never met Clark, but that afternoon I went straight out on my bike and pedalled its wheels off in an impotent juvenile rage. That week's issue of *Motoring News* was the only one ever produced with a black border. The staff were so shocked, the full obituary didn't appear until the following week.

OTHER VOICES

Peter Windsor – Williams team manager

"When I was a kid at school, Jimmy Clark was my life. I worked with Geoff Sykes, who ran the Warwick Farm track, near Sydney, addressing envelopes, that kind of thing. Jimmy came out in 1965 for the Tasman series, and through Geoff I found out what flight he was on from South Africa and I rang Qantas and got the list of passengers – Mr J Clark, Mr P Rodriguez, Mr J Stewart! – and went to meet them at the airport.

"In 1968, after Longford, where Piers Courage won, Jimmy was due to fly back to London, and I went to see him off. The plane taxied off and then stopped. Everyone else left, but I hung around just to see it take off, but it didn't. I forget what was wrong, but they came back in, and there I was, alone with Jim Clark! We had coffee together and talked for half an hour. About all

sorts of things, although funnily enough I felt like I already knew so much about him I nearly had nothing to say.

"I asked him all sorts of minutae, like why did he use a dark blue peak on his helmet in Mexico in 1966, instead of the usual white one, and he told me he'd broken the white one the race before and Buco only made dark blue peaks. After a while he had to go, and that was the last time I saw him. Four months later he was killed.

"He opened a bank account in Sydney for his prize money, and I was in charge of it. Later, I bought Ian Scott-Watson's old Lotus Elan when I came to England, and drove up to Duns and met Jimmy's mother.

"Jimmy was my whole life. I was physically ill when he was killed. It took me a long, long time to get over it."

■ ■ ■

Jimmy and Jackie. Two great Scots. Two legends. Two so very different destinies decreed by Fate. The violence of Clark's passing left his contemporaries feeling utterly naked and frighteningly vulnerable. "If it could happen to Jimmy, what chance had we?", asked Chris Amon, and his question spoke for them all. "His death was to motor racing what the atomic bomb had been to the world", said Stewart.

The sport had not only lost a gentleman and a gentle man, but the man many still believe to be the greatest driver ever. He never forgot his basic enthusiasm for racing, nor that so many others shared it. Perhaps that explained his popularity. The fans had a genuine affection for him, even those like myself who had never met him. He was able to accept the losses of the 1962 and '64 World Championships at the final races – the latter on the penultimate lap! – with grace and equanimity, as he did 'losing' the 1966 Indy 500. He was a sportsman whose like has not been seen again. His death coincided with the end of the era of pure trade support, and came just at the dawn of the new commercialism. His last GP was won, perhaps fittingly, in the old Team Lotus green-and-yellow colours, and though he had won Tasman races since in the new John Player Gold Leaf livery, one senses he would have come to hate the pressures and demands of the new age of sponsorship.

The King had gone, and as racing struggled to find meaning and direction in the aftermath, Graham Hill was asked what he would miss most about Jim Clark. "I was quite touched by Graham's answer", said Sally Swart. "He said, 'I'll miss his smile'. I thought that was awfully nice. He had a very little-boy smile, a kind of three-cornered big grin, and I thought that was very nice of a team-mate to say that. I'll miss his smile..."

Today they still remember the gentle Scot with reverence in his home town of Duns, and the Jim Clark Room is tended with the dignity and enthusiasm that were so much a part of his makeup.

6

DAN GURNEY

America's finest?

"To me he was one of the greatest drivers we have ever seen – one of the best drivers America had." – Jo Ramirez

Nature has always been good to Dan Gurney. It gave him the looks of a matinee idol, driving talent similar to Jim Clark's and an easygoing temperament that was the envy of his rivals.

At 60 he still looks good. His 6ft 3in frame carries the expansion of age well. The sparkle has never left the clear blue eyes, around which the laughter lines still crinkle with youthful zest. In his heyday he looked like the archetypal Sixties beach boy, cool, lean, laidback. He needed to be with all the disappointments racing threw at him. After Chris Amon he was surely the unluckiest Grand Prix driver of them all, but invariably he took the knocks without rancour, accepted them as part of the game, and came back for more.

When you meet him you are instantly reminded that this is the face that looked down on the delighted spectators, his right hand waving, at Spa-Francorchamps that day in June 1967 when finally the luck *did* go his way and he won the Belgian GP in that glorious Eagle-Weslake. Somehow, it always seemed to me, that car was made to win that sort of race, so rakishly elegant was its beak and metallic dark blue paint. Let the others win the Mickey Mouse stuff. This was a real racing car, made to win on real Grand Prix circuits.

"That was a real high point", Dan recalls today with that slow, easy smile. "I didn't realize it at the time, of course. Jimmy went faster in practice in the Lotus, but I had the lap record in the race, and that meant something to me because that car also had fastest lap at the Nurburgring. In the race the engine had a high-speed miss, and I didn't know what it was. I thought it was too lean and was gonna burn a piston. I was trying to figure out a way not to let that happen, but there wasn't much you could do outside of quitting. So, at that time, while I was trying to figure out what options I had, Jackie Stewart came past me in the BRM. I remember when Jackie was coming up on me that I was trying to figure out this engine thing. At high speed it was going eeee-be-be-be-eee. And as he came up I was sitting way down in the car, and he came on the left up the straightaway. As he came alongside I kinda sat up in the car and waved him by, like that!" He made a sweeping gesture. "Go on, *quick!* Just to show him. When he went by, next thing I could see was a little spiral of lubricant of some sort coming out of the gearbox, and I thought, 'Whoa, hey, maybe that's going to turn into something worse'.

"By then I'd decided that this engine doesn't seem to be getting any worse,

The son of an opera singer, Dan Gurney has the looks of a matinee idol and the temperament of Job. Ferrari's north American farm system took him to F1 within as few as 22 races, but despite the pressures on him during a career at the top level his benign character never changed.

it's just continuing this way, so I just thought I might as well run the risk of doing something and went after him. Next thing I know he started having some trouble, and that was it. He was not just having to hold it in gear, there was some other problem because there was something coming out of it. It was the sort of thing when you say, 'Hey, that doesn't look as if it's going to last very long'."

It was one of those fantastic fortnights a driver is sometimes lucky enough to experience. For Dan it meant even more, for they didn't come along very often for him. A week before Spa he was winning at Le Mans for Ford, sharing with A J Foyt. "The great thing there is that we were the hares nobody expected to last. And old A J was really underrated in Europe. A good race for us!"

Daniel Sexton Gurney, the Long Island-born son of an opera-singing father and a musical, artistic mother, was a former hot rodder who became the product of the Ferrari farm system. He cut his teeth in as few as 22 races in Southern California, in his own Triumph and then in a Porsche, but later in Frank Arciero's brutish 4.9-litre Ferrari, before Ferrari importer Luigi Chinetti did some fast talking to Italy.

"There were relatively few Ferraris around the world at that stage and they were aware of what was happening to their cars each weekend. I was able to draw some attention through Chinetti that led to me being asked to try out for the Ferrari factory. I'm wading through what seemed like a long time when it seemed nothing was going to happen, and finally, when the big break did come, it came very rapidly. My first Formula One race I was sitting there at Reims with no more than 22 races completed, and those were the most minor races because there weren't many events at that time!"

He impressed immediately, finishing second to team-mate Tony Brooks and ahead of friendly Californian rival and team-mate Phil Hill in his second race, the German GP at Avus. He was third in Portugal and fourth in Italy. Later, he and Brooks drove together at the nine-hour race at Goodwood, also sharing the fastest lap. "That was a big thrill for me. If you were able to drive with a Tony Brooks or a Jean Behra or a Stirling Moss you felt, hey, that you couldn't ask for a better team-mate and you were going to whip any combo out there. That's a great feeling, and it was a mutual thing. That was terrific."

At the end of the year he established what would come to be the Gurney pattern, leaving a team at just about the wrong time. For many drivers Ferrari is the peak; for Dan it was just the beginning. He went to BRM. He grinned when I asked why! "Aside from ignorance, a miscalculation on my part. Probably an inability or reluctance – or a combination of both – to communicate with Enzo Ferrari, even though he treated me very well for that particular time. He was understanding, he even probably gave me opportunities other people on the team didn't get. He liked me. Only it was one of those things you find out by the way things evolve, as opposed to actually talking to him.

"I was green, an American that grew up on Long Island and then moved to California. I didn't know how to do it. I was in awe of him. Generally he could give his drivers the needle through the press or through comments and various kinds of rumours. I never was subjected to that myself, but there was no doubt in my mind that a great deal of that went on. I'm sure I *could* have been in a position where I would have been subjected to it, but I wasn't."

He also felt he was underpaid, and was keen to embrace the growing rear-engined revolution. BRM looked good from the technical standpoint. It proved an awful season. In nine starts apiece, he, Graham Hill and Jo Bonnier had a finish each. Dan also had a nasty shunt at Zandvoort which broke his arm and killed a spectating boy. "That was one of the earth-shattering revelations, to find out that not all Formula One cars were as strong as the Ferraris were." The accident was caused by mechanical failure, when a road-car brake hose proved unequal to its job and burst going into Tarzan at the very moment he was trying to develop the late braking skills of Moss. He remembers the moment vividly.

"It was terribly unfortunate that the boy was killed. But it was as though I had nothing to do with it. I didn't have a choice in my own mind. He was on the other side of a good size hill, in a lane for spectators that had barbed wire on both sides of it, so he was in the right place. But that was maybe 100 yards from the race track. I arrived there in the air, having been pretty doggone high, and there was no way to see it. It was one of those things where you don't want to go off into deep sand going sideways because you'll roll, so I went off straight and there wasn't anyone in sight. I went through an advertising sign, everything. It was an interesting thing to realize that, hey, this is part of this business, also."

He won his last race for the team at Ballarat, in Australia, before switching to Porsche. In 1961 Ferrari won the championship, in 1962 BRM. He was aware he might be moving at the wrong times. "I went to Porsche and vowed at the time that I'm not going to leave no matter what happens, of course not knowing that they were going to quit at the end of '62...!"

At Reims, in 1961, the race became a battle between himself and rookie Giancarlo Baghetti in the Ferrari. He missed winning his first GP by a tenth of a second. Had he been a little more ruthless he could have won, but that was never his style.

"I *could* have moved over on him, but it was one of those things I was honour-bound not to do." He paused to laugh about modern-day tactics. "I don't know where that stops. You either do it or you don't do it. Some people won't do it. Once it starts, why then, hey, the sky's the limit. Katy bar the door. You can do whatever you want to do. It was dangerous enough then that if somebody did that, somebody definitely was going to get hurt in a big way. And these people that did sort of take that approach usually weeded themselves out in a big hurry.

"I got a lot of static for letting this unknown guy beat us, generally outside Porsche, not from the team. It was interesting, you know. I felt it took a lot just to *be* there in a position just to get beaten. I had plenty of time to try and do it either way. If I would slipstream, come off the last time behind him, I couldn't get by him till quite a ways past the start/finish line. If I came off ahead of him, he could get by before we got there!" He laughed again. "So I was divided. I hoped if he made a little oo-oo and I got into the last turn first, which is what I

"Afterwards I figured that if the plane taking us home were to crash, at least I'd won a Grand Prix." Dan's first success came at Rouen in the Porsche flat-eight in 1962, and with typical modesty he was quick to point out that Clark and Hill had fallen by the wayside before he could reach the chequered flag first.

did on the last lap, that he might just make a little bit of an error or a bigger one. But he didn't!"

He won his first GP at Rouen the following year, and remains as modest about it now as he was then. "I wasn't really a big factor. Graham and Jimmy both had problems. Although I felt I drove the wheels off that thing, it was done most on reliability. It was very close on weight with the Lotus and the BRM, but the biggest problem I would think was low and mid-range power. It was weak. It had a relatively narrow range of what in those days was good power; it was probably making 185bhp.

"You know, in those days we did a lot of flying, as we do today. But there was a little more concern that the planes were not quite as reliable as they ought to be! I remember thinking, 'Well, if this plane goes down now, I will at least have won a GP race!'. It was a great feeling, of course."

He loved the Nurburgring, and felt his best race with Porsche was that year's German GP. "I did do a fair amount of testing there after our first race with that new car. I managed to beat the lap record there to take pole for the race. Had it been dry I was able to go really quick. With that same dry set-up in the rain I was able to go very quick compared to the leaders, Hill and Surtees. Now I don't know where Jimmy was at that time", [he'd forgotten to switch on his fuel pumps at the start] "but Graham ended up winning. I could run them down, both he and John Surtees, in the rain, but I couldn't get by them. I came awfully close to hitting them several times in an attempt, many attempts, but it was that mid-range power and their rain set-up; they could put the power down better than I could. But I was still able to go faster had I been able to get by them, because the balance on that car was excellent. And I knew where the track went. So that was a bitter disappointment, to be in a position to do well and the way the weather goes. It was still a terrific race. Those were both very good boys, I think." He laughed heartily at his understatement.

The 1967 race also belonged to him until the Eagle broke a drive-shaft. Typically, he bore the disappointment well. "Of all the places I would have liked to have won, I'd say that was the one. It was a universal joint that failed. Tim Wall, my chief mechanic, always blamed himself for that. I don't feel that was fair to him at all, but he wanted to blame himself. You know how a lot of times the mechanics put the shafts at the maximum angle and then give them a little clearance? Well, he said he hadn't had a chance to do that, or something. He was a great mechanic. I think the mechanics in those days were nigh on to supermen, you know. Team managers, mechanics, hands-on doers, engineers that worked on gearbox lube systems, these guys did this in a way where a lot of engineering was involved. They just gave so much. These guys just worked such punishing hours and sustained long times there with little if any recognition and virtually no money, but they were extraordinary men. The sort of guys who'd still be there in Formula One even if all the money pulled out."

By 1968 the Eagle's wings were clipped, yet in the rain at the Ring he was again mighty. "I was actually third, kind of like 1-2-3, that close, after moving up from fifth the previous lap. It was on the furthest part of the circuit and the highest part, a quarter-mile after the Karussel. There's a little right-hand turn at the top with a little bank maybe that high, it's pretty sheer. And there was a little sharp rock sticking out and I just clipped it. Never made a mark on the wheel, but it blew the tyre. I limped back and it took a long time with a handbrace to change the wheel.

"One of the things which was very satisfying is that I remember going through the South Curve in a big opposite-lock slide after the finish, waving at the crowd, and they were all jumping up and down with their umbrellas. The car was right on the money and so that was a very memorable event. It was just one of those things that was just too damn bad. I think I finished ninth or something." Mistakes like that were very, very rare from Gurney, rarer even than his good fortune.

OTHER VOICES

Jo Ramirez – Eagle mechanic

"He was one of the best drivers I ever worked with and one of the best bosses and the best friends. In every way he was terrific. I had a lot of time for him. To me, he was one of the greatest drivers we have ever seen – one of the best drivers America had.

"He had a tremendous style. He would win from the beginning, he didn't have to work himself up to it. He was fantastic, like Prost. He wouldn't go off the road. But his biggest problem was that he was a great fiddler. He fiddled with the car all the time, and at times we used to laugh about it. He would come in and say he wanted to change this, change that, and then he'd say, 'Terrific', and it would all be the same! Sometimes the car wasn't improved, but he'd try so hard just to show the guys that he was quicker. Then later he'd say, 'I think we'll go back to what we had'.

"Dan used to do a lot of travelling. I think it was not good for him. It used up a lot of his energy. He did a lot himself, but he could delegate. I wouldn't have thought he was a great manager, but probably a lot of drivers who end up managing their teams are good drivers, but not such good managers. But he had a lot of way with people. He knew how to treat people and he knew how to motivate them. Everyone loved to work with him because of that.

"When things went wrong he bounced back quickly. He always had this very nice smile, and he'd say, 'Oh well, another race'. He was better than all the other drivers of his time, except perhaps Jim Clark."

■ ■ ■

Mostly, it was the machinery that let him down. That and, perhaps, that penchant for fiddling with the car. He was the greatest technical fidget. "He was another good one", remembered Jack Brabham, for whom he drove and led and won races once Porsche had withdrawn. "Not quite as committed, perhaps, as Jochen, but very quick on his day. But he tended to mess with the car too much."

With Brabham he emerged as a truly great driver, frequently the one man able to carry a challenge to Clark. He won the team its first ever Grand Prix, at Rouen in 1964. Money was tight – "The way Jack ran, he was squeezing every farthing, I think. Not because he was basically that way, but because there wasn't any money." – but he was often a leader only to have the car break. At Spa in 1964 he was totally dominant from pole position, only to run short of fuel right at the end. Lost opportunity followed lost opportunity. "I was kinda philosophical about it", he admitted with a shrug and that wide grin that lights up his handsome face. "I realized that it didn't do any good to go around whining about it. It was just against my principles in a way! I still enjoyed the racing a great deal and felt that there was always a good opportunity. One can dwell on the negative aspects, and the positive. You're still gonna go through the same life, looking at it one way or another." I showed him a photograph of himself and Clark at that Spa race, sitting together on their cars smiling after both had run short of fuel. He laughed heartily, without a trace of bitterness.

We talked of the 1965 Race of Champions, where he had pressured Clark into one of his very rare mistakes, but Dan refused to take any pleasure from that memory. Instead, he almost came to Jimmy's defence.

"I had managed to do some tyre testing for Goodyear at Riverside, including some rain tyres where they set up sprinklers, all that sort of stuff. So when I arrived there I was pretty doggone hot, in mid-season form. Tyre testing was a new thing then, right at the pioneering edge of it. I always thought, incidentally, that that was one reason why Stewart did so well.

The art of the racing driver. Gurney balances the Eagle-Climax in a beautiful four-wheel drift as he negotiates the dunes at Zandvoort in 1966, his first year as a Grand Prix constructor.

"So Jimmy just tried, you know, and managed to overdo it a little bit. I was surprised. No, I didn't think I had him handled, even though I was catching him. I think you have to wait and see. Under those situations you don't really know. A driver like Jimmy is going to be very resourceful. Of course, you can't be mesmerized by watching what he's doing, you have to concentrate on what you're doing, also, so it's a matter of concentrating on all these things. All of us are much better in hindsight. If you're running him down and he's getting a little more ragged, a little more ragged, why that's encouraging, but who knows?

"That's one of the things about Stirling Moss. On one or two occasions where I was able to run him down, he might wave you by, so you wouldn't see him coming unravelled. And next thing he'd be all over you. It was an interesting way of trying to deal with that situation."

Predictably, at the end of 1965 he left Brabham at precisely the wrong moment. The following year Jack took his third title with the Repco-powered car, and the year after that Denny Hulme kept the ball rolling. Surely, with his speed and the car's inherent reliability, Dan would have been very strong had he stayed...

The chance to do his own Eagle project proved irresistible, however, as Goodyear agreed to finance both Indianapolis and Formula One cars designed by Len Terry. The former would use the Ford V8, the latter Harry Weslake's neat V12.

"I thought of the Eagle name", affirms Gurney with pride. "Wonderful? Yeah! I was surprised nobody else had used it. I liked its connotations with the American flag, too. Len and I worked on that little sort of suggestion of the beak and it came out beautifully."

Indy in 1966 was a great moment for him as his new car made its debut, but it became one of the few times when he really did struggle to maintain his even temperament following the startline shunt which wrecked it. Dan chuckled at the recollection. "I was plenty mad because the ordeal of getting ready for the Indy 500, which is still one bloody race, at that time just consumed so much time and you had your neck stuck out. I never went to Indy with a car I'd raced before going there, you know?. Only realized that recently. When you look back on it and realize just how important all that testing is, it was just a *dumb* way to do it!" He laughed yet again, at himself. "But that's the way we did things then!

"I do remember saying that you'd think that 33 of the world's supposedly best drivers would be able to drive down a piece of straight road for 100 yards without running into each other."

Gurney has never really been given the credit he deserves for influencing so much the changes that have taken place at the Brickyard. Brabham started the mid-engined revolution in 1961, but it was surely Dan who really got things rolling by interesting Colin Chapman and Ford and cueing up the success Jim Clark was to enjoy there. That came about through his 1962 experiences as a rookie in Mickey Thompson's mid-engined Buick-powered car designed by Englishman John Crossthwaite. Mention Thompson's name at Indy even today and it stirs controversy, for memories of the 1964 holocaust remain vivid, but Gurney is adamant that Mickey's first Indy contender was his best.

"That first one I drove was an excellent car. Crossthwaite never achieved great fame, but that was an excellent car, good looking, handled well. Unfortunately, Mickey's mind set was more quarter-mile and not 500 miles" – again, the Gurney chuckle – "but it was a very good car. The cars that came after that, the one that claimed the lives of Dave MacDonald and Eddie Sachs, sure, that was not very good. It had small, very wide and flat tyres, used with a suspension camber curve that was meant for the old-fashioned skinnier tyres, and those two things were not compatible. When they put a whole load of fuel in it for the first time, why, there wasn't that much rubber on the track. And that was a huge amount of fuel that that thing could carry. They put a huge weight difference in that and they'd never done that before the race. MacDonald was talented and brave, but that's what killed him.

"But that first year's car, I'm sure, was a much better car than what they came back with the following year.

"I'd driven that, seen what Cooper did in '61, and also the way Formula One had gone to mid-mounted engines. I went to Indy with John Zink's turbine car in 1962, but did my driver's test in a front-engined Offy roadster. The turbine car just wasn't going to get it done because it was short on power, so I swapped over, but didn't get into Mickey's car until the day before qualifying. I qualified

"Left-hand down a bit, A.J." Dan lets partner A.J. Foyt do the chores as they celebrate winning the 1967 Le Mans in the Ford MkIV. Popular legend has it that Dan stuck religiously to a time four seconds a lap off his best, knowing that Foyt would be determined to match whatever time he did. Had they both driven to their maximum, the car might not have lasted...

eighth. It was capable. If that thing had run properly it could have won the race. It was that good."

For the next three years he would contest the 500 in the Ford-engined Lotuses that completed the great revolution, and the reason they did was because Dan had brought together the genius of Colin Chapman and the might of Ford. In that move he laid the basic groundwork for the new pattern Champcar and set in trend the concepts that still hold good today.

"Chapman was the acknowledged genius of European auto sport at that time, I would say, and having watched how Cooper did and having seen the mid-engined car make the front-engined one obsolete, it became very obvious that this was going to happen whether I liked it or not at Indianapolis. Therefore, why not acknowledge that the top guy right now is Colin Chapman? I invited him to come to that race in '62 as a spectator, just to get a feel for it. I was also establishing a relationship with Ford through a stock car drive that I had, so that's how that came about.

"Colin was impressed. He had to be. Not necessarily with the machinery, but with the size of the crowd, the spectacle, and all the goings on and tradition. And that sign 'The Capital of World Motor Sport', or whatever it is that they have outside the Speedway! That really got him wound up! I also introduced him to the Ford people and was sort of standing alongside Colin when we went through the strategy sessions with Ford. 'How much power do we need to make?', all that sort of stuff, as they tried to see whether they could make it with what they already had."

As a driver in USAC he was always one of the best. He placed second at Indy in 1968 when Bobby Unser won in one of his cars, and seemed to have a permanent lock on the Rex Mays 300 at his beloved Riverside, where he also triumphed in NASCAR machinery. In the CanAm, too, he was the scourge of the McLarens with his Ford-powered Lola, but always the Gurney luck stopped him at crucial points. Throughout, he was a true champion of the stock-block engine.

"What started me thinking of something with stock-block Ford V8s in 1964 was that, among others things, I noticed that Keith Duckworth was doing great things with Ford Anglias. I thought, well, maybe we can do something like that with a Ford. Or a Chevrolet for that matter, but I happen to be from the old flathead days a Ford fan as opposed to a stove bolt, which is a Chevy fan. Not a very complimentary name! I went to the Weslakes and asked them would they do that?"

Why was he so attracted to very individual paths in life, I wondered? It brought forth another grin and another chuckle. "It's true I have gone my own way and I know you didn't mean it to sound like criticism. It's alright if it is! But it's just the way it's been. I think the challenge has always been something that means a lot, and you like to try and do things in a way that's a little bit out of the ordinary. I still have remnants of that today! It's a lot of fun."

His cars have triumphed three times at the Brickyard, in '68, '73 and '75, and in 1972 Bobby Unser set nine track records and seven poles. The last CART win came in 1981 courtesy of Mike Mosley at Milwaukee. But perhaps the greatest legacy and the least appreciated is the Gurney Flap, developed by Dan and Bobby.

"It was at the end of a very frustrating bunch of days at Phoenix International Raceway in 1970. We had been there for two or three days, trying everything, changing bars and springs and tyres and wings and everything. We were flat out of ideas. Bobby said, 'Hey, boss, you're supposed to able to be creative or innovative, can't you come up with something?' It was a real challenge put like that.

"We didn't have much time, we didn't have much equipment. But I had spent a lot of time dabbling with various spoilers and things on the back of CanAm cars. I said, 'Let's bend up a little bit of 90-degree aluminum like this, and we'll

71

pop rivet it on', and we did that. That was the way it happened. A spoiler that'll work on a body, why wouldn't it work on a wing? Hell, let's try it!

"We did that and Bobby went out and ran and came back in, kinda pulled up, engine off. Just sat there and didn't say anything. Then he said, 'Look around and see if anybody's watching us. Don't say anything! This thing is so *strong*, it's stuck the back on this car so much that I don't want anybody to know how really terrific this thing is!'. So that was really it! There wasn't anyone there, anyway, but he was worried that some spy would see what we had done.

"So we kept it for a long time and people would look at it and say, 'What the hell have you got that damn thing on there for?', and we'd have some story, 'Well, it's a little weak back there and we're trying to strengthen it', something like that! Took them half a season to figure it out. Took them a long time.

"We went down one day to a small wind-tunnel, with maybe a 5ft square test section, and in it was a NACA standard airfoil, with maybe a chord of 36 inches. You could change the angle on it as it was running and it had a lot of little ports all the way from the leading edge across the top and then on the bottom. Each one of these was attached to a little capillary tube that came out through the airfoil, through the side of the wind-tunnel and up to a big sight gauge manometer on the wall. It was huge, probably 8ft high, and there were maybe 40 of these things. It took up a whole wall. Well, we ran this in the tunnel and with the standard airfoil on there you could see on the manometer's sight gauge where you had attached flow or where you had turbulent separation, and you could also listen to it. Well, when we realized we had done something interesting was when we put the flap on that same airfoil after we'd done the baseline; it blew a bunch of ink out of the sight gauge, and all the aerodynamicists that were there looked at that and they didn't know what to say! It was a major thing!

"The very fact that it's still there, and here we are in 1991, 21 years later, couldn't be a better testimony. You walk down any pit lane and there they are. And that's how it happened."

Back in the Sixties, *Car and Driver* editor David E Davis started a spoof 'Gurney for President' campaign that actually gained a little momentum, with a lot of hot rodders and the like wearing bumper stickers proclaiming allegiance. Dan's first brush with politics was to prove a lot happier than his second...

After Mosley's victory in the Milwaukee 150 things began to go awry after Dan entered into a partnership with Mike Curb, who had a long association with the sport, but was also a former Lieutenant Governor of California and chairman of the committee to help re-elect President Reagan, himself a former Governor of the state. Gurney goes very quiet whenever the subject comes up. What went wrong? Was it a personality clash? "You could say that!", he said eventually. "But it was much more than that. Much more diabolical. I don't want to get into it too much, but let's say I received an education I wasn't intending to get. I found out, I'm trying to be careful here, all the undesirable accusations you might hear about politicians. Mike made a run at taking this away from me". He gestured around the All American Racers headquarters in Anaheim.

"It was a very shattering experience for me because I found out that this system of justice that I thought was very fair, where the good guys weren't going to get taken advantage of, or weren't gonna lose their shirts, well, I found out that in fact if you have deep pockets and a glib tongue and believe everything you say whether it's true or not, a civil lawsuit at that time, the backlog, was between four and six years before you were going to get a hearing. If you were somehow sued and your business was tied up, you were going to have to hold your breath for four to six years, and some people could do that and some people couldn't.

"Well, there was a small window because Mike was running for Lieutenant

Typical in so many ways of the Gurney character was his 1968 'McLeagle', an Eagle-modified McLaren M6A. Predictably, Dan ploughed a lone furrow as he tried to make the Gurney-Weslake headed Ford V8 competitive with the Chevrolets. Equally predictably, the combination heads for retirement here at Riverside in 1968.

Governor again, where he really didn't want to get a lot of negative publicity, and I got with an excellent attorney. We took on Mike and I ended up losing a position in CART, but saving my company and coming away with an education. It was really something. A real eye-opener."

Today he has strong links with Toyota, and having moved All American Racers through the IMSA GTU and GTO categories, his Eagles are leading contenders in the popular and competitive GTP sportscar series. 1990 brought four victories. "I did some commercials for Toyota and sounded them out about competition plans", he said happily. "They hadn't decided to come back in yet, but they shortly did, and they have gradually been turning up the wick. They work like a glacial approach, they don't really make any blindingly fast moves, but the moves they do make seem to have enormous momentum, and they just keep on coming. We won the GTO Championship in 1987 and then won more races in that area than anyone in 1988."

He is still the archetypal racer, always looking for that extra tenth or more saving. As a driver Dan Gurney was a brilliant all-rounder. He won in NASCAR, USAC, Formula One and sportscars. In 1967 he became the first driver to triumph in all those disciplines. Perhaps curiously, though, he never raced a sprintcar, "But I drove one round the block here!", he points out quickly. It belonged to his parts man, and his hot rod racing on the streets background came out again.

He keeps in touch with the current Formula One scene, but regrets many of the changes that have taken place since his heydays. "It's a shame that the spectacle has gone. I've often felt that the powers that be kinda got it backwards because they've made these cars so fast they've had to modify all the old circuits, and that just seems wrong. What is it: they've thrown the baby out with the dishwater? They killed an awful lot of nostalgia and history, and that's a doggone shame.

"I see some of the circuits today and I think to myself, 'I don't like the way it's going'. I don't want to say anything to belittle what the guys can achieve, but somehow the circuits are so artificial and they almost invite what you saw in Japan. I'm a fan of both of those fellows, they're both terrific. While I feel that Ayrton Senna has an edge on Alain Prost" – he pronounces it Proast – "the minute I say that I realize that Prost can probably beat him the next time they try, you know? It's that close."

Harking back to that gripping dice at Reims with Baghetti, he continued, "Nowadays the attitude seems to be if we touch, we touch. It's the argument whether you give a guy racing room. Perhaps it's because of the danger, the lessening of the danger.

"The breaking of links with the way it was saddens me, and yet I'd probably have to go along with it. The reduction in the number of fires is certainly terrific. The incredible increase in cornering speed isn't. I think that's an artificial thing. To me you've got an aeroplane with wheels on it. It'll go round the corners much faster because it's got a lot more traction. Big deal, right? I think that has hurt the sport. People are not stopping to think that they're gonna damage motorsports. Either way, that's a lack of vision by the quote 'leadership' unquote, and the problem then becomes one of advocating danger against safety." He gave a short laugh. "And that you can't win!"

As far as his own career is concerned, Dan Gurney is, typically, a man of few regrets, and there is still much pride at what he achieved in Europe with his own Formula One project.

"If I look at it today, I realize that we didn't care that people said that you couldn't do it for the amount of money that we had, or the number of people that we had. We wanted to have a go at it, and we did, and at least we got one Grand Prix race under our belt, which was no small achievement, and we got the Race of Champions at Brands, and we had these other lap records. So we were really close a lot of the time. It was a terrific time and I generally look back on it with very good feelings.

"Yeah, it was enormously difficult running Formula One and Indy projects, I'm sure it was, and I don't know where all the energy and the ability came from. But in that era more people did it that way even though it was all in all probably an inefficient way of doing it. You hoped that your inefficiency was more efficient than the other guys'!

"Money was the problem in the end. We'd taken over doing the engines, but Goodyear pulled the plug. What actually happened was that the Goodyear people decided they needed more help back home. That really was a very difficult situation. But that's why in the end I had to make the decision, do I continue in Europe and probably lose what you see here, or not, and I chose to try and come back here."

He stayed in Europe in 1968 to race with a borrowed McLaren M7A and did enough to show the old fire was still there, and he did another three Grands Prix in 1970 in the immediate aftermath of Bruce McLaren's death. He even won the two opening CanAms with the M8D until contractual problems arose.

"Teddy Mayer and I never really hit it off that well, although some of the CanAm drives I got to do, specifically the one after Mosport, were among the better ones I ever did. That generally wasn't a very satisfactory relationship. It was too bad. I won't say it was their fault any more'n it was mine, but I did it mostly out of feeling for Bruce, not because I was really trying to get back into it.

"I did those last Grands Prix out of respect for Bruce and because of Denny's burns. Also, in looking back, I made some bum calls on the set-up of the car just through ignorance. I was not happy with the results, but I felt good about my own driving ability. But I also felt as though I was in a position where I was really not going to be involved any more. So it was a strange combination. But I certainly didn't feel like I was going to quit driving any more, but I felt as though in order to be satisfied with how well you did you're going to have to spend sufficient time doing it. In the end, if you don't have a 100% desire to do that, say you only have 99 or 98, that's a good enough reason to stop. That's what happened to me in Formula One.

"Part of it was being lonely, because a lot of people that I had great respect for weren't there any more, and life was just becoming more and more complicated, having to make some decisions even though I didn't want to. All those things. But in the end it boils down to desire. If sufficient desire is there it's a pleasure to have to concentrate on all the various elements that you need to have a grip on in order to do really well and to win. Whereas if that ever becomes a job, it's not the same."

He retired on October 4, 1970 with 37 major wins under his belt, but was tempted back once, in 1980, when he was partnered with Dale Earnhardt's Mercury team for the Riverside NASCAR race. He was as fast and smooth as ever, qualifying seventh and running as high as second when the input shaft broke. "You know", he said, with a twinkle in his eye, "the mind plays fascinating tricks. You forget all the things you'd rather not remember, and just remember all the good things." Why had he done it? "Oh, curiosity. Just curiosity..."

OTHER VOICES

Mario Andretti

"Besides Alberto Ascari, the other guy that I really looked up to was Dan Gurney. I really, really liked Dan's style. There was something about his driving, what he was doing, the fact that he went boom! Here's an American kid. Boom! Formula One. And right away he's with Ferrari.

"I don't know. There were many others along the way, but to me he was a stand-out. He was an inspiration to me. There was something about him that really was a spark for me. Sure you had the Fangios and Mosses, whom I admired tremendously, but it was Ascari and Gurney somehow that were motivating factors for me."

■　■　■

Dan Gurney was a brilliant driver, a quiet, calm, gentle sportsman who never let himself nor his team down. Not surprisingly, he felt a strong affinity with Jim Clark, with whom he was teamed at Indianapolis in the Lotus-Ford years. "I would say he was the best I ran against", he said quietly. "And Jochen, too, although he wasn't in a really good car when I was racing there. But I could tell there was an enormous amount of talent there. He was another sort of gifted driver, but the best was probably Jimmy.

"He and I had a doggone good relationship, even though it was difficult because we were competing with each other, even on the Lotus team during all the Indy stuff. But still we had a very good relationship. I held him in the highest regard. There was no side to him. He was what he was. I liked it because he was one of the few that was seemingly confident enough to go venture out into other areas. He enjoyed that, and he was good enough to do it, so he won an enormous number of fans on this side of the world just because of that. He didn't spend a whole lot of time trying to convince people he was good; he just got out there and did it."

At Clark's funeral his father spoke quietly to the tall American, and told him that he had been the only driver his son feared. Gurney never forgot that

remark, the highest accolade anyone could have received.

"It destroyed me, really, in terms of my self control. I was drowned in tears. To hear that from someone whose son had been killed and wasn't there any more, it was more than I could cope with. For a long time I didn't say anything about it because I felt it was a private thing, and I didn't want to utilize it to sort of glorify my driving ability or reputation, but it certainly was the biggest compliment I ever received." He continued, almost shyly, "For someone who raced in a lot of what was acknowledged as being the top rank of racing, at the time I was driving, why, it became very precious to me. I also managed not to win a World Championship and I didn't win the Indy 500, or a few other things, so something like that means a great deal to me. And I also know that I was held in good esteem, and I was considered pretty doggone good by the guys that were running at that time. When someone says something like that, it's pretty much like they're saying to others, 'Well, put that in your pipe and smoke it'. Mr Clark was even kind enough to send me a tape of that, a year later."

After his retirement, it mattered more to him that he had enjoyed the respect of his peers than that he hadn't won the World Championship or Indianapolis. He ploughed a lone furrow when the mood took him, and he was never afraid to experiment. That was what made Dan Gurney what he was. Succeed or fail, his trademarks were always that even temperament and the wide grin that brought his face alive. All who raced against him thought he was an ace, quite possibly America's finest.

7

GRAHAM HILL

The perfect ambassador

"I think that as a character, he was an example of what is best in a professional racing driver, he really worked at it." – Colin Chapman

The profile everyone in Britain knew. When he was in pensive pre-race mood like this, Graham Hill was best left alone. When the business of the day was over, a different man emerged.

The trick was always to try and take him out of Jim Clark's shadow before you tried to assess his achievements. "He didn't have Jimmy's natural flair," they said. "He really had to work at everything he did."

Years later they would say the same thing about Nigel Mansell in comparison with Ayrton Senna or Alain Prost. As if the endeavour of putting effort into something in order to achieve it was somehow belittling.

Who *did* have Jimmy's flair and natural ability? Perhaps a handful of drivers since motor racing began? Having to work bloody hard to match him was no slight. If anyone took themselves to the very top by sheer persistence, guts and application, it was Norman Graham Hill.

To enthusiasts in their hundred thousands the world over he was Mr Motor Racing. With his erect bearing, clipped manner of speech and that bristling military moustache, he was the perfect ambassador for British motorsport. Much loved is a term that falls easily into overuse, but it applied totally to Hill. He enjoyed genuine affection wherever he went, even in the short months left to him after his eventual retirement from the cockpit. He loved motor racing wholeheartedly, and motor racing in turn loved him, recognizing just how much he had put back into the sport.

There were two Graham Hills. One was that popular figure with the Oxford blue helmet and its famous eight vertical white flashes which represented the oar blades of the London Rowing Club. He said he liked a sport that let him sit down. Now the colours are carried again into battle by son Damon, who at the time of writing is on the fringe of Formula One as the Williams team's test driver.

The other was a very withdrawn, formidable figure, wound up tight before a race. Then, Hill was Mr Hyde, dangerously unapproachable. Journalists and autograph hunters alike ventured into his environment distinctly at their peril.

OTHER VOICES

Ian Phillips – former journalist

"My first meeting with Graham Hill was at Rouen, in 1971, when I was travelling in Europe for the first time. I was a raw recruit, just out of British club racing. Graham had won the first Formula One race I ever saw, at Goodwood in Easter 1962. He was still a hero in my eyes, and I was over-awed to say the least.

"I hung around the team for hours while he went through tyre selection and studied his gear ratio chart. At last he folded it away and I saw my chance. I was nervous and I introduced myself hesitatingly. He gave me a real grilling.

"'Who do you work for? How long have you been with them? Where are you from?' I told him everything, and then he said, 'OK, now what do you want from me?'.

"He could not have been more helpful, either then or at any time subsequently. He was very sensitive to criticism, though. You had better be able to defend your position when next you met.

"He was a hard man, hard on himself most of all, and he expected the same of others. He had no time for wankers."

■ ■ ■

A fellow *Autosport* scribe who, ironically, would work later with Hill in his Embassy days, fared less well on his initial meeting at Oulton Park. Hill uttered a terse two-word Anglo-Saxon expression indicating that he should go away, but relented as the name *Autosport* sank in.

As he prepared for the final battle in the 1962 World Championship at East

London, in South Africa, commentator Chris Economaki made two mistakes. He approached at the wrong time, and led with his chin. "What is it that bothers you most on a day like this?", he asked. "People like you coming up and asking me questions like that", was Graham's reply. Truly, one needed to choose one's moment with great care... And yet his mood lasted only as long as he concentrated for the coming battle. Afterwards, that stern mien would give way to a ready grin, and an exaggerated wink as he threw out a risqué remark. His repartee in particular was brilliant, the equal of professional showbiz friends such as Eric Morecambe and Bruce Forsyth. But sometimes it was not quite to everyone's taste. On the 1973 Tour of Britain, as he completed a run at a circuit, he was asked what it had been like. "It's as slippery as snail snot", came the reply.

He *had* made it to the top on his own efforts. In those early days nobody gave him anything. It all came through sheer persistence, hard work and blatant opportunism.

As Damon would later, he began his career on motorbikes, taking part in scrambles and rallies, and it was during a trip up to Oxford that he was involved in the road accident that smashed his left thigh and left that leg half an inch shorter than the right.

He was always in a rush to bypass accepted means of doing things, and he taught himself to drive after he'd actually bought his first car, a 1934 Morris Eight four-seater. Just as Jackie Stewart had trap shooting before he discovered motor racing, so Hill had rowing. The colours on his helmet had been earned the hard way. He stroked the London Rowing Club's first eight to victory in the Grand Challenge Cup at Henley in 1953, having rowed there for the second eight the previous year. It was while 'resting' during the rowing off-season that he saw a magazine advertisement offering membership of the Universal Motor Racing Club and the chance to drive a racing car for five guineas. He made the journey to Brands Hatch, and then returned there regularly, often taking illicit time off from his engineering apprenticeship with Smiths. It was wholly typical of him that he began to help prepare the driving school car in order to offset his costs, also that when the school business went bust he elected to quit Smiths and concentrate full-time on finding a way into motor racing.

Those early days were littered with examples of his opportunism. He talked his way into another driving school job on the strength of his four-lap experience at the first. He signed on the dole and travelled to the circuit from North London every day while his father thought he had a 'proper' job. He became such a regular at the Steering Wheel Club that nobody ever thought to question whether he had actually paid a membership fee.

He had his first race in a Cooper 500 in April 1954, and was second in his heat and fourth in the final. He never looked back, and relentlessly he parlayed his services as a mechanic into regular drives in other people's cars.

Later that year the opportunism really paid off when he met Colin Chapman at Brands at the August Bank Holiday event and literally attached himself to the nascent Team Lotus. He was beached, completely out of money, unable even to afford the fare back to London. Without a second thought he hitched a ride back in the Team Lotus van, and to his benefit Chapman immediately assumed he was a friend of partner Mike Costin's, as Mike was assuming he must be a friend of Colin's. Neither found out at the time, and by the time he arrived back home Hill had enjoyed a free meal and talked himself into a mechanic's role with the team. It was to be the beginning of a great relationship.

"He really was a penniless, out-of-work apprentice", recalled Chapman. "He started helping us prepare the race cars, so I thought we'd better give him something, so we paid him a pound every day he turned up."

The sport has changed irrevocably since those carefree days. Perry McCarthy (a latter-day Eddie Sachs) is one of the few drivers possessed now of that cheeky but grimly determined streak at a time when the majority of aspiring racers seem to want all expenses paid. Hill continued scrounging rides as his career began to flourish. He left Lotus to join Speedwell Conversions, the North London-based tuning company, but then Chapman summoned him to drive the new works Lotus in the 1958 Monaco Grand Prix. It was apposite that his Formula One career should start there in view of the enviable record he would establish round the streets of the Principality. He ran as high as fourth before a halfshaft broke and the car shed a wheel.

By 1962 he had climbed the mountain and was Champion of the World with BRM. The British team had great cause to be thankful for his contribution, for not only was he a tireless 'worker', but probably only Jack Brabham and Bruce McLaren knew more about setting up Formula One cars at that time. Hill had a penchant for fiddling, experimenting endlessly with his equipment as he sought an advantage. He was an absolute stickler for detail, but he drove himself as hard as he did his mechanics. One year, when he was out in Australia and New Zealand for the Tasman series with BRM, he persuaded the team's chief designer Tony Rudd to make up a rear anti-roll bar whose characteristics fell exactly between those of the only two available. "There was only about one per cent in it, and I didn't think it could possibly make any difference", said Rudd, "but he thought he'd go faster – and he did." During his time with Team Lotus, Herbie Blash remembered: "After a session Jochen would just bounce in and bounce out again. But Graham would sit down and make a job list from one to 20. He'd sit for hours thinking about set-ups."

The 'worker' approach reaped him many dividends. He was not Jim Clark, but when they shared equal equipment, as in 1967, the year Graham returned to Team Lotus when he finally began to believe he would be painted British Racing Green if he stayed any longer with BRM, he was far from outclassed.

His greatest years were those in the early Sixties when he was with the Bourne team. The 1960 P48 rear-engined car was desperately unreliable, and he and team-mates Dan Gurney and Jo Bonnier had but a handful of results between them. And yet he came so close to victory in the British Grand Prix at Silverstone that year. One of the reasons he was so loved by spectators was his impish sense of humour. Before the Grand Prix there was a Mini race, and for a laugh, Hill conspired with his fellow drivers for them all to start in reverse when the flag fell... "It was hilarious", he chuckled. "But you were always a bit worried that all the other buggers would stick to the game plan."

He won that race, but enjoyed a crueller fate in the big event. Jack Brabham had dominated qualifying in his Cooper-Climax, but Hill was in brilliant form all weekend and had wrestled the BRM to a surprise second place on the grid. Then he so nearly threw it all away by stalling at the start. He had already had magneto trouble when they warmed the engine that morning, but this time he was lucky, and after Tony Brooks' Cooper-Climax had rammed him from behind he was able to get under way with a push-start. The military moustache was bristling!

He drove that race in a blind rage. Carving his way through the field, he had recovered to sixth place by lap 20, and six laps later he took Bruce McLaren for fifth. Then, on lap 37, having just disposed of Jim Clark and John Surtees, he found a way past Innes Ireland into second place and was now only five seconds behind Brabham. He then set about reducing the gap with a commitment that induced the sort of alarm amongst spectators that Ayrton Senna generates today. He made them gasp.

There was nothing in it by lap 52, the BRM frequently alongside the Cooper, and a lap later Hill was in the lead. The crowd went berserk, screaming itself hoarse, just as years later it would again, first for John Watson and later for Nigel Mansell. Graham Hill was going to win the British GP, his home race, and his first Grande Epreuve. The tension reached fever pitch as the Englishman and the Australian fought it out wheel-to-wheel, Jack continuously maintaining the pressure.

Nobody has won as many times at Monaco. After leading but retiring in 1962, Hill put a stranglehold on the event for the next three years, and then won back-to-back again in 1968 and 1969. Here in 1965 he tigers back in his BRM after shooting down the escape road avoiding another car.

Then, with less than five laps to go, Graham slid off. He was mortified, furious with himself. Keen to increase his cushion over Brabham, who by then had resigned himself to second place, he had passed two other cars on the approach to Copse Corner, but had arrived too quickly for his spongey brakes and left the track. "I was worried about the feel in the brake pedal. Dan had had a rear hose burst at Zandvoort just before. I was coping with that when I came up to lap Phil Hill's Ferrari and another car at Copse. I had to decide; did I try to pass, or just sit behind them and let Jack get closer? I tried to go past them, arrived a bit quicker than normal, and the brakes just weren't up to it." His race ended in the ditch, but the crowd cheered him to the echo as he walked back. The legend was born that day.

Perhaps his greatest race came two years later at the Nurburgring, his first Championship year. In qualifying he had wrecked the latest BRM when he came unexpectedly upon the camera which had been shaken loose from Carel Godin de Beaufort's Porsche and had fallen into the road. At 130mph down the tricky ziz-zag section known as the Foxhole, he didn't have much room for manoeuvre and the BRM skated into a ditch at very high speed. Winded but unharmed, he clambered out just before Tony Maggs' Cooper arrived and finished off the BRM, but Hill the gentleman managed to flag down Maurice Trintignant before the Frenchman suffered a similar fate.

Against that background, his raceday drive stands out even more. It was wet, and when Jim Clark momentarily forgot to switch on his fuel pumps at the start, the race became a three-way fight between Hill, Surtees and Gurney. Graham had strained his neck and bruised his shoulders, but he took the lead from Dan passing the pits on the second lap, and thereafter the trio was never more than five seconds apart. Hill won that one the hard way, with just 4.4 seconds covering the three of them at the finish. It was not the success of a second-rater...

During those years Monaco simply surrendered to him, and from 1963 to 1965 nobody else got a look in as he scored his hat-trick. The last of the three was another outstanding drive. Baulked from a comfortable lead by Bob Anderson's troubled Brabham at the chicane on lap 24, he had slid up the escape road. By the time he rejoined the race he was fifth, 33 seconds behind Stewart, but he tigered back and passed Surtees, Jackie, Brabham and Bandini to win by more than a minute. Clark and Gurney might have been absent competing at Indy, but nothing could detract from his performance. At that Monaco race he insisted on hosting a party at Pirates, where he celebrated not only his own triumph, but also the fact that Jimmy had just won Indy. Similarly, Watkins Glen was a happy hunting ground, until 1969...

Stewart was open in his praise for Graham's manner when he joined BRM as the new boy in 1965. Just as Jackie would later be totally open with team-mate Francois Cevert, so Graham was with him. There were no secrets. When Graham ran wide at Parabolica on the last lap of the Italian GP and Jackie nipped through to take his first GP victory, there were no recriminations. Graham was the first to congratulate him.

For all that his critics might denigrate him as a grafter, he could match Jimmy at times during 1967. First time out in the tricky Lotus 49 he took the pole and was leading comfortably when his new Ford Cosworth DFV engine broke, and at Le Mans he again ran ahead of the Scot. He looked a comfortable winner at that great Monza epic until his engine broke again, and at Watkins Glen he took the pole and should have won but for the intervention of mechanical problems and the challenge from Amon's Ferrari, which obliged Clark to abandon team plans to let Hill win and to move ahead of him.

Where Jimmy seemed able to nurse his equipment, however, Graham's speed sometimes came at the expense of reliability. If there was bad luck going, he seemed to get it. While Clark took four wins, a third and a sixth from that year, Graham had to be content with just a second place at Monaco, a fourth in Canada and another second at Watkins Glen.

That he *could* beat Clark he had proven on other occasions, not the least of which was the *Daily Express* International Trophy race at Silverstone in 1962. There, as the stacked exhaust pipes fell one by one from his new BRM, he made the most of Masten Gregory baulking Clark on the last wet lap to storm alongside the Scot as they exited Woodcote. Off line on the outside, he slithered sideways, but pipped the surprised Jimmy by mere inches, and he was never a man to be beaten easily.

The Lotus twins started 1968 with another one-two in South Africa, but that was to be Jimmy's last victory. Hill was at Hockenheim the day he died, and to him fell that mountainous task of pulling together the shattered team.

He was approaching 40 at a time when motor racing was increasingly becoming a younger man's sport. Young lions such as Jackie Stewart and Jochen Rindt would soon be snapping at his heels. He himself was deeply affected by the tragedy. Yet somehow Graham Hill found the reserves to lead Lotus back into the battle at Jarama, even though, just days earlier, the team had been dealt another hammer blow by the death of Mike Spence at Indianapolis. At that awful time motor racing staggered from one tragedy to another, and Hill emerged as the figure to give it direction.

He won that race in Spain. True, Amon, Beltoise and Rodriguez had all led until they struck trouble, but Graham's was a worthy victory, won despite intense pressure as Denny Hulme frequently drew his bright orange McLaren to within half a car's length until his transmission gave trouble. It was Hill's first win since Watkins Glen in 1965, and his first for Lotus. He joked that he had worried about being able to recognize the chequered flag when it was finally waved at him.

It was also a deeply emotional success, one that could not have come at a more beneficial moment for Colin Chapman. Clark *was* Team Lotus, and with his death its heart had been torn out. That win was instrumental in helping the Lotus founder to muster the strength to carry on.

At Monaco, too, Graham triumphed, and when Stewart returned to the fray at Spa, having missed two races through wrist injury, they fought out the World Championship until the final race of the year. Stewart lost at Spa, but won at Zandvoort, the Nurburgring and Watkins Glen. Interloper Hulme won at Monza and Canada to threaten for a second successive title. Graham retired from the British GP at Brands Hatch after leading the race with ease, but in Mexico he fought fair and square with Stewart and Jo Siffert, the winner of the British race, to take his third GP victory of the season and with it his second World Championship. For the sport, it was the best possible result. Even Stewart agreed. "Graham was the right man to win", he conceded charitably. "I could not then have done the title the justice it deserved when it came to things like public speaking."

OTHER VOICES

Colin Chapman

"I think Graham was always a little disappointed that he couldn't go as quick as Jimmy in the same car, but he never showed it, and he worked so hard. He was always very magnanimous. And then when Jimmy had his accident Graham was superb, because the team was on the point of going to pieces. I felt I didn't want to go racing any more, but anyway Graham went to Spain and won the race. It was hard to believe, and this was just what we wanted to pull us round.

"It was then that I thought, 'Well, we're going to try to win the World Championship without Jimmy'. Everyone responded tremendously because of Graham, and we did."

■　■　■

Graham and Jimmy had been good friends. Rivals, but *friends*. With today's drivers, such are the stakes, the two terms are more often than not mutually exclusive. Their friendship was based on respect, and when they fought, they did so cleanly. "When I got back to the pits that day at Hockenheim", he said, "I reacted oddly, I suppose. I didn't really take anything in. I'd seen where somebody had gone off, and mentally I hadn't given anything for their chances, but I never thought for a moment it was Jimmy. It took me a long while before it finally sank in."

In his rookie year at Indianapolis, he came home the winner for John Mecom after team-mate Stewart's late retirement, although the issue is still clouded as many insiders still believe he was handed Jim Clark's second win. When Jimmy himself ventured such an opinion afterwards, Graham replied dismissively: "No way, mate, I drank the milk..." in reference to the winner's traditional refreshment.

What happened at Indianapolis in 1966 and at Watkins Glen in 1967 might have strained weaker relationships. Certainly today the Indy affair would have been enough to set drivers at one another's throats. The regulars at the Brickyard still smile knowingly when that race is mentioned, and nod. "Jim Clark won that one", they will tell you. "The lap scorers mistook Jimmy's car once for Al Unser's and missed one of his laps."

Ford desperately wanted a 1-2 on home ground at Watkins Glen in 1967, and Walter Hayes asked Graham and Jimmy not to indulge in a fight. They agreed to toss a coin for the victory, for such was the dominance of the Lotus-Fords that they were the most likely contenders on such a quick track. Whoever lost would be 'given' the Mexican GP. Graham won the toss, and Jimmy readily agreed to support him. The arrangement has a strange sound today.

Graham duly led, but began to experience difficulty changing gear as his clutch was malfunctioning and the ZF gearbox's synchromesh made clutchless shifts more difficult. Chris Amon in the Ferrari was beginning to pressure Clark, and as Graham slowed Jimmy had little option but to obey fresh pit signals and move into the lead. Later in the race Jimmy's rear suspension broke and he just made it to the line. If the pit crew had signalled Graham about the problem, he could have won after all, but afterwards, he accepted the quirks of fate stoically.

In 1968, too, he fought honourably at Indianapolis and was a potential victor in his Lotus turbine on his last appearance at the Brickyard.

In 1969 he was teamed with Jochen Rindt, and though they shared joint number one status, Jochen was the faster. Graham was second at Kyalami, but both of them suffered major accidents when their wings broke in the Spanish GP at Barcelona. Hill, indeed, whose car had crashed first, was instrumental in helping to rescue Jochen from his battered Lotus 49B. With the Austrian sidelined, he upheld the team's honour at Monaco with his fifth and final victory, achieved in style after Stewart and Amon had retired, but thereafter he very much played second fiddle.

As Rindt refused to drive the four-wheel-drive Lotus 63, Graham diligently supported Chapman and accepted his lot. The fire still burned fiercely, though, and at Monza in particular he drove superbly. He started a long way down the grid, caught up to the leading group, lost touch with it, and then staged a tremendous recovery, despite a broken exhaust, to move back into the bunch.

He was vying with Stewart, Rindt, Beltoise and McLaren when a driveshaft broke with five laps to go. Less than a month later came the shunt at Watkins Glen that signalled the end to his real Grand Prix career.

His 49B had been handling badly throughout the race, consuming its experimental rear Firestone tyres rapidly. After a spin he had had to jump out and push the car before it would restart, and it was while preparing to stop for fresh rubber, and with his seat belts still unfastened since he needed assistance to secure them, that a rear tyre deflated and flipped him into a spectacular series of rolls. He was thrown out and he suffered serious leg injuries.

Perhaps he should have retired there and then, but that was not Graham Hill's way. He loved racing, and was not prepared to give it up, especially under such circumstances. He promised he would be on the grid at Kyalami, in South Africa, when the 1970 season began, and he was. Yet this was not a young man at the peak of his recuperative powers. He was over 40 years old.

The same grim determination that had won him so many hearts now won him the battle to recover from a broken right knee and a dislocated left knee and badly torn ligaments. Even in hospital and awaiting an operation, his sense of humour surfaced. "Tell Bette I won't be dancing for a while", he joked. He was surprised when people thought he had done anything remarkable, and commented: "I enjoy racing so much it's hardly surprising I've put a bit of effort into getting back to it, is it?"

He received an ovation when he started his Lotus 49B in the South African GP, only five months after his accident, and there were tears as he brought it home a gallant sixth. He had to be lifted from the car. Circumstances had changed, however. He was no longer part of Team Lotus, but running for privateer Rob Walker.

"He was such a character, you know, that if he'd got hurt again it would all have seemed rather pointless", said Chapman. "I don't mind saying that I didn't want to encourage him to drive again. I even went to the extent of offering him the job as team manager and paying him the same money if he wouldn't drive.

"But Graham didn't want to retire from his hospital bed, so he fixed up that drive with Rob and forced himself back to good health."

It was a patchy year without any major success, and when it finally arrived, his Lotus 72 was less than perfect, even if he did get it going very quickly for a while at Watkins Glen. The one victory had been getting back into a racing car at all.

He moved to Brabham in 1971, and though he crashed at his beloved Monaco, he surprised everyone but himself by taking the lobster claw BT34 to victory in the International Trophy at Silverstone and then by winning the Easter Monday Formula Two event at Thruxton, beating Ronnie Peterson. By now, however, such results were the exception rather than the norm. He stayed with Brabham for 1972, but also started up his own Formula Two operation, Graham Hill Racing. Le Mans that year brought him the final component of the Triple Crown – the World Championship, Indianapolis and Le Mans – and an achievement no other man could match. With Henri Pescarolo he steered his Matra MS670 to success over team-mates Francois Cevert and Howden Ganley. It afforded him immense pleasure. And at Monza's Lottery came his final race win in the Brabham BT38.

His fans still adored him, but privately his friends worried about him and wished he would hang up his helmet. When the offers of drives began to run out in 1972, they secretly hoped he would quit, but instead he set up his own Formula One team with Embassy support and a Shadow DN1 for 1973. "People have always said I'm an ambassador", he joked, "so I thought it was about time I had an Embassy." Like Donald Campbell, Graham Hill was a man who always needed fresh mountains to climb.

It was an awful year, but he could still joke. "You meet a nicer class of people at the back of the grid", he said. 1974 was little better, but by 1975 Graham Hill

Racing with Embassy was making serious progress. Rolf Stommelen even led the Spanish GP at Barcelona until his terrible accident when the rear wing broke off. Still the questions about retirement persisted. That year's Brazilian race had been his 176th, a record that Riccardo Patrese would finally surpass only in 1989. His friends were beginning to despair.

With Clark gone and Colin Chapman still in shock, Hill rose superbly to the occasion to win the 1968 Spanish GP at Jarama. The victory, his first since 1965, came at a critical moment and gave Team Lotus the confidence that it could carry on without the legendary Scot.

The 1971 International Trophy would have been the perfect result on which to end, or Le Mans the following year. He had mellowed immensely from the intense persona of his early days, but whenever anyone was foolish enough to raise the subject, the moustache would bristle, the jaw would thrust out and he would reply with a withering look: "The only time I think about it is when idiots like you come up and ask me that bloody silly question."

At Monaco he failed to qualify, and those who cared for him were deeply saddened at the disappointment that etched itself across his face. The writing had been on the wall for some time, but he had carried on out of sheer enjoyment, as A J Foyt later would in Indycars. Neither cared that their fans might feel let down or embarrassed on their behalf by their reduced performances, such was the narcotic effect of driving fast. Graham was also a late starter. He didn't hold a driving licence until he was 24, he first raced at 25, and he won his first Grand Prix when he was 33.

At that Monaco meeting 23-year-old Tony Brise drove beautifully from the back of the Formula Three grid to challenge for victory. Hill saw his potential and signed him for the rest of the year. Together they began to make serious progress and on the way established a very strong bond of mutual respect. It was very difficult, but Hill had finally found a means of standing down with dignity.

At that year's British Grand Prix at Silverstone he made the official announcement and was cheered wildly as he strolled down the pit lane, and he admitted there was a lump in his throat and tears in his eyes as he drove a final demonstration lap. As ever, he hid his emotions well behind that poker face. Walking away from that side of things was so difficult for the man who, when once asked his motivation for race driving, had given a succinct reply. "When I do a very quick lap in practice it is amazingly satisfying. You come in and you just want to shout: 'Beat that, you buggers!'"

He was a hard taskmaster, hardest of all on himself. He was intensely self-critical. He was a man of courage, too. At Sebring, in 1962, he slipped a disc while lifting a crate of spares, but he refused to be daunted by it and contested several races in that Championship year shrugging off the discomfort of a steel corset. His greatest assets were his fantastic ability to concentrate wholly on the job in hand, his single-mindedness and his refusal to give up. Like Clark, he excelled in other categories, winning races in Austin A35s, Ferrari GT0s, Jaguar E-Types and Mk2s, Lotus Cortinas and big banger sportscars such as the Lola T70.

Unlike Jimmy, he thrived in the limelight, was drawn to it like a magnet. He was the life and soul of parties and thought nothing of dancing on table tops, even though he once ended up spearing his calf with a broken wine glass stem. At times he seemed like motor racing's answer to that delightful showbiz character Terry-Thomas. Away from the pressure before a race, he was charming and witty, the perfect after-dinner speaker, and on one occasion in 1960, when he was in New Zealand, he enlivened a dull party at Pukekohe by streaking round the swimming pool!

When Lorenzo Bandini ran into the back of his BRM in Mexico in 1964 and lost him his second World Championship, he accepted it as a motor racing accident. Later, in good humour, he sent the Italian a book on driving techniques.

He was also a compassionate man. After his accident he campaigned strongly in Britain to have the pale blue invalid tricycles replaced by proper cars, and he visited the saloon car driver Peter Procter many times as he recovered from the serious burns he sustained from his accident at Goodwood. Behind the scenes in 1962 he was instrumental, with Jonathan Sieff, Charles Lucas, Anthony Marsh and Brian Essendon, in rebuilding a boys' club in Clapton, in the East End of London. He threw vast energies into the project over the years as he became President of the Springfield Boys' Club, inspiring hundreds of youngsters by his example, and using his name ruthlessly to raise funds. When they needed a new building, he told Marsh, "You go ahead with the planning, I will find the money". And he did. He also found the time, despite all the pressures of business and racing, and on one occasion, when he worried he had

As his F1 career faded, Hill showed from time to time that he could still win races. At Le Mans in 1972 he shared this Matra with Henri Pescarolo, and his success there made him the only man ever to complete the Triple Crown – victories in the World Championship, Le Mans and Indianapolis.

not spent as much time with the boys as he felt he should have, he asked 'Bunter' Marsh to bring the mountain to Mohammed. He threw open the facilities of his house in Shenley to the boys for a day instead.

As President he would write personal letters to the influential, and he gave the club a motto it retained long after he had gone. "We are in the business of growing *people*", he said.

OTHER VOICES

Barrie Gill – former journalist/commentator

"I owe everything that's happened to me in motor racing to Graham Hill. I was a reporter on the now defunct *Daily Herald*, which became *The Sun*, and I was sitting in the office one day when the editor walked in and said, 'Tommy Wisdom's leaving, you're the new motor racing correspondent'. He might just as well have said I was the new ice hockey reporter, for all I knew about either. My first race was that International Trophy at Silverstone in 1962 when Graham won going sideways across the line. Armed with all this incredible knowledge of the sport I went back to the office and said, 'I've just seen the next World Champion, we need to sign him for a column'. The editor said, 'OK, we'll sign him, but if he doesn't win you're out of a job!'.

"And, of course, it went all the way down to the South African GP on December 29, and just before the start Graham said to me, 'Sorry, but there's no way I can win this. Jimmy's car's just too good. Don't worry, we'll find you something to do'. And when this plug fell out of the Lotus on lap 62 there's this dervish dancing in the pits! Graham's first words to me as World Champion were, 'I think I'm getting a cold'! Then he spent his second night as Champion in jail in India because he hadn't had the right injections...

"He was an inspiration. He would never give up. He always said you could do anything if you put your mind to it. He, Jack Brabham and I once had to speak in Birmingham about the dipped headlight campaign, and when it came to his turn Graham stood up and said, 'If all the Minis that were built in Birmingham were laid end to end on the M1, some fool in a Ford Anglia would try to overtake them'. That was his speech!

"After that he really worked on that, and he became the best after-dinner speaker there was. But he really sweated over it. He hated being asked at very short notice. But he taught himself to do it.

"Practice in the old days went on for hours, and he was always flogging round. He'd probably driven five Grand Prix distances before the proper event started.

"He was a great sportsman, and corny though it may sound, he was an example to everyone. He was finicky, and he'd drive the mechanics mad, but he was a bit special. After all, he was the first Englishman to win the World Championship in a British car. People tend to ignore him when they look at history, but he won five Monaco Grands Prix, Indianapolis and Le Mans. He also did the RAC Rally. He'd just have a go at anything. He used to joke about getting paid for his hobby.

"There were three secrets to Graham Hill. One was his total commitment. Whether it was working with the Springfield Boys' Club or winning for BRM or Lotus, he would never give less than his best. We did a column together and he'd often change his mind afterwards when he read it. Once in a race preview it said something like, 'Wish me luck', and he said, 'I didn't say that. Take it out next time. They all deserve luck, not just me'. And it went in three times, even though we told the subs. It turned out it was a printer who was a Graham Hill fan, putting it in each time in hot metal just before it went to press... Graham had a great sense of fair play.

"He would check every word and we'd argue, but it never affected our friendship. In my first column my tape didn't work and I spent all night trying to remember what he'd said. Later he put in his book: 'To Barrie, in memory of the time when the tape broke and a friendship began'.

"Two, there was his sense of humour, and three was the fact that he genuinely enjoyed it all. He would be wrapped up in concentration on the grid, but behind it all was an unbelievably wicked sense of humour. At Monaco after he'd won he would see Prince Rainier at the Cafe de Paris and then excuse himself and go down to the Tip Top for hours, singing with the mechanics, dancing on the tables. Inevitably, his trousers would come off at some stage...

"Once I had peritonitis, and he flew back from Monaco. There he suddenly was, striding into my ward. He stayed for ages signing autographs for everyone as he walked round the beds. When he won Le Mans Jo Bonnier had been killed during the race, and he insisted on coming all the way up to the roof to do a tribute to his friend for the BBC. He was always aware as a World Champion that you had a responsibility to put a lot back into the sport.

"Had he lived I think he would have become the Chairman of the Board. Look at that show we had at the Albert Hall before the 1976 British GP. That was all planned with him, me, John Webb of Brands Hatch and Walter Hayes of Ford, just before Graham's death, and it still went ahead in front of 5,000 people and the television cameras. Stewart and Bruce Forsyth did a double act, Shirley Bassey sang, I did a dance routine with Lena Zavaroni and Henry Cooper. All the drivers were there and were interviewed. Can you imagine it now, Alain Prost and Ayrton Senna dancing on stage? He was the only driver who could have been the catalyst for that; that was the sort of thing Graham inspired. All the proceeds went to children's charities."

■ ■ ■

Apart from his achievements on the race track and his roguish television persona that made him equal to any interviewer and a source of great amusement to audiences, he appealed as a family man with his devoted wife Bette and children Damon, Brigitte and Samantha.

Without the physical side of motor racing, flying assumed an even greater importance to him, but the test programme of his new Embassy Hill GH2 was still uppermost in his mind as he and his team headed home from Paul Ricard, in the South of France, in his Piper Aztec. On November 29, 1975, a cold, foggy Saturday night in England, it all came to an end.

There were disquietening aspects about the accident. He was trying to get his mechanics back in time for an official dinner in London, and he refused to divert to Luton. Instead, he elected to land at Elstree where their cars had been left, taking a route that Chapman had taught him. In the conditions he was very slightly off target and it cost him his life, and those of Tony Brise, designer Andy Smallman, team manager Ray Brimble, and mechanics Tony Alcock and Terry Richards. His family lost almost everything in the horrible aftermath of grief and legal actions.

Above it all stood Graham Hill the way the public and the sport remembered and revered him. He could be intolerant, and he was not a saint, but his sense of humour and fun, his big heart and sheer personality had literally made him a legend even while he lived. He was much more than just the archetypal *Boys' Own* racing driver. Bigger, even, than a household name. With his death, even the man in the street who cared little or nothing for motor racing felt a sense of sadness and loss at the passing of a man who had become a national institution. No other British racing driver ever inspired such genuine affection in the hearts of laymen and aficionados alike.

8

PARNELLI JONES

Why did he walk away?

"You know, when I left the Speedway a couple of days later I felt bad. It was like I'd left home and knew I'd forgotten something, but couldn't remember what it was."

Losing the 1970 British Open at St Andrew's was something that golfer Doug Saunders never really got over. On the last hole of the tournament he missed a simple 18-inch putt. Could he ever forget it?, he was asked, some 20 years later. "Sure", he replied easily. "Sure I can forget it. Sometimes I can forget it for a whole hour at a time."

Rufus Parnell Jones can sympathize with him. Few other drivers have ever got so close to triumph in the Indianapolis 500 as he did in 1967, only to have the great prize snatched away. He literally ran away with the Memorial Day classic in Andy Granatelli's controversial STP Paxton turbocar until bearing failure sidelined him with only three of the 200 laps left.

"Yeah", he says even now. "It was kinda hard to believe..."

Granatelli had always been one to thumb his nose at the Establishment at Indy, where for years he had tried to win the 500 with a succession of supercharged Novis which made more noise than speed, but were loved for it nonetheless by everyone but the men who had to drive them. It was when he tried one of them for the portly STP oil treatment magnate that Parnelli really got Andy fired up. Jones drove one during a Firestone test at Indy and got it round faster than anyone else had. "Andy was real impressed. After that he was constantly hounding me to drive for him, but I had a good ride anyway with Agajanian. I never wanted to race the Novi because it was so unreliable!

"When Andy put together the turbine, mine was the first door he came knocking on. I never thought it would work, but I told him if he wanted me to drive it, to have it at Phoenix, where I was testing my own car in readiness for the 1967 season, and I'd have a look. I took a ride and I became more impressed. I thought of the publicity it could bring and figured I could stir up the racing organization. And I'd get well paid."

Jones always had a fair idea of the value of a dollar – "He was a money driver. He always won when the money was there", said historian Dick Wallen – and Granatelli was offering $50,000 and half the race purse. The more he looked at it and drove it, the more the turbine intrigued Parnelli. Others had tried to make axial compressor engines work at the Speedway, but none had ever done anything worthwhile. The shrewd Granatelli, however, had employed aircraft designer Ken Wallis to create something radical in the form of an X-shaped aluminium chassis that forked at each end to accommodate the suspension.

A man of the people. Parnelli Jones' ebullient style won him countless fans, on both the USAC sprintcar and champcar trails. In the crew-cut racer they recognized the talent of one of the few men who could take on Foyt on either dirt or pavement.

The driver was located in the right-hand side, and a Pratt & Whitney ST-6 turbine engine from a snowplough, rated at a conservative 550bhp, was in the other. Allied to four-wheel drive, it was an unconventional concept that promised much. Parnelli was quick to realize that, and to appreciate that there was as much Establishment anger at its appearance as there had been when the first rear-engined 'funny cars' really began to hit the 'Brickyard' five years earlier. He found himself in an ironic situation, having been the darling of that very Establishment four years earlier when he had fended off Jim Clark's 'new fangled' Lotus to win with the old-fashioned roadster of yesteryear. It afforded him much amusement.

"Sure, there was lots of animosity, but I didn't mind all that. The other guys hated the car, complained of all sorts of things, from the smell to the heatwaves, but they respected my ability."

Mario Andretti said he could barely drive around it on the track, it was so big. Foyt said its air brake flap obscured his vision. Joe Leonard (who would nearly win the 1968 race in a Lotus turbine!) said the smell of its kerosene diet made him feel ill, that he could barely see through the turbine's exhaust heat haze. What amused Jones so much was that he knew full well all the shortcomings of a machine that all of his rivals immediately began to dub the car that would finish the piston engine.

"You gotta understand that I only ran Indy of the 1967 Champcar races, and where I qualified, sixth, was the furthest back I'd ever been in my seven starts in the 500. I knew I'd run away from them on race day. I'd been accused of sandbagging in qualifying, but that wasn't it. That thing had tremendous torque, which got it out of corners real fast, but halfway down the straightaways it would just fall flat on its face and peter out. Why, some of the guys were actually repassing me at the end of them!

"It was like a model airplane, you know? You wind up a rubber band on the propeller and the moment you release it you get the maximum thrust, but then it begins to falter.

"We could change the gears to make it run faster at the end of the straightaways, but then it would just take longer to get to them. I knew, though, that in qualifying a lot of the guys had 10, 15% nitro in their methanol, so I knew I'd be OK in the race, when they had to run straight methanol, especially when they had 70 gallons aboard. With that turbine it didn't seem to matter to it whether I had full or nearly empty tanks. Didn't seem to bother it at all."

Parnelli the proud racer was rankled to start only sixth. "So at the start I went right up in the grey on the outside, to show them all what four-wheel drive and I could do." By Turn Three he was in the lead, and running away, just as those rivals had feared. That, it seemed, was all she wrote. If only the ink hadn't run out.

The turbine had been plagued with transmission failures in practice and qualifying, but in the race, 'Samson', 'Silent Sam', 'The Vacuum Cleaner' or 'The Whooshmobile', as the Dayglo red car variously became known, was in a class of its own. So was Jones, exploiting his advantage to the full. He'd said before he wouldn't run the 500 again unless he had a lock on it, but this was more like a death grip. He ran his first lap at a record 154mph, and just kept going. Even when rain caused the race to be stopped after 18 laps, he and the turbine were unfazed. When it was re-run the following day, they simply took up where they'd left off. The opposition was annihilated. Three laps from the end Parnelli could see Foyt's Coyote-Ford ahead of him as he came up to lap it, and he wasn't even using the maximum thrust. Along the way he'd given the record book typesetters a week's overtime.

"For the last 10 laps I was just holding the throttle at a steady pace. I had nearly a lap on Foyt, but I was hanging back. I didn't want to lap him, to rub it in. They were giving me a countdown on the laps to go and a yellow came out right near the end. I backed off and let it trickle round for a few laps, then the green came back on. I mashed the gas, there was a grating noise, and that was that..." The outer race of a $5 bearing in the gearcase had broken, destroying the gears. With seven and a half of the 500 miles remaining, he was out.

"I had no warning. It just went. It was fortunate for me that I'd won the thing once before. It would have been much harder to take if I hadn't won in 1963. It hurt Andy more than it hurt me. But even so I just couldn't believe it. You know, when I left the Speedway a couple of days later I felt bad. It was like I'd left home and knew I'd forgotten something, but couldn't remember what it was."

As Granatelli's tears flowed, Foyt lost no time telling the world how illegal the turbine was as he quaffed the victory milk. It was a controversial way to end his last Indy, but Jones had been no stranger to controversy all his life. Born on August 12, 1933 in Texarkana, Arkansas, he was the son of a labourer who learned at an early age that life could be tough. He became tough with it. When the family moved to Torrance, in California, he grew up in a hard little gang. "I reckoned I was the hardest bastard in the whole damned world, and I figured that racing drivers always had more guts than anyone else. I made up my mind early that I wanted to be one."

He began in 1950, around his 17th birthday, in early model stock cars, running with the name Parnelli Jones. A kid called Rufus got a lot of heat in his neighbourhood, and after an aunt had started calling him Parnellie he took a liking to his second name, kept the added i, dropped the e, and had a little less fighting to do. "Stockers were about as low as you could get at the time. I'd got an old early model 1934 Ford jalopy which we carted from dirt track to dirt track."

In those heady days of American racing they used to have a lot of cars show up for qualifying, usually more than 100 every week. The organizers would only take the fastest 16 for the main feature, the second fastest 16 for the semi-final and then another 16 for the consolation. There were a lot of disappointed drivers, but Parnelli went a whole year like that without missing a feature. It was dog eat dog, and he had the sharpest set of teeth. He had a pair of hardened fists, too. Along the way he earned a reputation as a ruthless competitor, utterly without fear, the bravest of the brave, a man prepared to push his opposition out of the way if the necessity arose. There were a lot of fights, but his upbringing

The controversial victor at Indianapolis in 1963, Jones fought the rearguard battle for the roadster in the tragic 1964 event, battling hard with early leader Bobby Marshman but retiring dramatically when the faithful Ol' Calhoun caught fire during a pit stop.

had prepared him for that. Those fists saw a lot of action. But bit by bit the brash kid worked his way out of his own cars and into other people's. By 1954 he was racing in the modified stock car category, and learning fast.

"It was in the modifieds that I really began to realize just what you could get away with in an automobile. And what you couldn't. They were really open-wheelers, and if you reckoned you were going to put the wheel in somewhere then you'd better be damned sure where you could put it in and where you couldn't."

But if he was brash on the track, he had his moments of reservation off it. In 1956 he met Vel Miletich, the Los Angeles businessman whose partner he would become in a whole series of ventures. Back then, Vel and partner Oscar Maples had the best stock cars around, and Parnelli was keen to let them know he was available if they needed fresh talent. He spent an afternoon agonizing about calling them, then his own phone rang. It was Miletich offering him a ride. It was a gamble both would have cause to celebrate.

The Jones legend began to take tangible shape in 1958 when he and Miletich took their Ford down to South Carolina to join the NASCAR boys. "We went down to Darlington, which was as important then as Daytona is now, and started to run right with them. I managed to get up to the lead by the first pit stop after starting 44th on the grid, and that shook them a bit. Then the engine blew while I was trying to make up time later in the race." The following season they went into sprint cars in the IMCA series. He was unfamiliar with the cars, joined in halfway through the season, but finished fifth in the championship. First time out at Houston, in 1960, as a member of the USAC Championship, he set a new lap record. That championship was his and it remained his property for the next three years, even though he was running stock-block 5-litre Chevrolet engines against the superior Offenhausers. He wasn't just dominant; the opposition went to the slaughterhouse.

"When you were a kid brought up in America you didn't dream of Formula One", he said, "but of Indy. That was my thinking. I wanted to go there real bad." The Brickyard beckoned, but he was shrewd and had no intention of wasting his hard-won reputation by failing first time round in a bad car. He'd seen too many young hopefuls rebound off their dream that way. So he missed racing in the 1960 500, but he went to watch, particularly down in Turn One, and he put the information he gleaned to good use for the rest of the season on the USAC Champcar trail.

"I was lucky, too. Firestone just took a liking to me right off and they let me take this car out and run it around Indianapolis. I ran 135mph with no problem. I was just stroking it because I wasn't really supposed to run over 100. Then I wound it up to 140 in the end when a real quick lap was around 147. Man, I couldn't believe it. I thought, 'Gee, just wait 'til this deal comes off, we're really gonna show these guys how the cow eats the candy!'"

His plans went a little awry when his sponsor began prevaricating at the start of 1961 and mechanic Johnnie Pouelsen asked Tony Bettenhausen to try the car instead. He fell in love with it so much he had backer Lindsey Hopkins buy it. By a quirk of fate, having turned down Hopkins' offer to be Bettenhausen's back-up, Parnelli was invited to drive for one of the most prestigious and colourful owners ever to run at Indy: the white-suited, white-stetsoned J.C. Agajanian, the Armenian immigrant who had made millions from hog farming and garbage disposal. Jones and Aggie's Watson roadster, 'Number 98' or 'Ol' Calhoun', would become one of the Speedway's most famous partnerships.

The association began badly when Jones had to take his rookie test. "I couldn't run fast enough! It was a tricky little deal. I managed to get through the first two stages of the four-stage test and on the third one I reckoned I was travelling 'bout as hard as I could. You had to jack up about five miles an hour on each run. I just couldn't do it over four laps. I could get one in and three out, you know, but I couldn't put it all together. So Harlan Fengler, the Chief Steward, told me to take it very easy and not to worry the next day. That night I drove round the track with several other drivers and they asked me where I was turning in and backing off. One of them said, 'Are you using the brakes?', and I replied, 'You're darned right I'm using the brakes!', and he said, 'Well, that's your problem!'

"Apparently the technique was to back off early and blind it through the corner. 'Jeez', I thought, 'these old guys must have been round here too long, it all sounds too much like hell raising to me'. But I took their advice the next day and ran right up with the leaders. Then I found myself thinking: 'If I could only run a little deeper into the corners and a little faster...'" Parnelli Jones had arrived.

The art of avoiding the brakes wasn't all that he learned, for his homework down in Turn One the previous year had paid off in another unexpected way.

"When I was down in there watching qualifying, Jim Hurtubise qualified fastest. He had this tyre thing all worked out and would get the car sideways. It wasn't until 1961, my rookie year, that I realized what he'd been doing. As the car drifted in the turn its rear tyres, being tall, tucked under very slightly. As he straightened up coming out of the turn the tyre popped back up and acted as a catapult mechanism. I almost hit the wall when I tried it, it was one of them squeakers! I'd done a lot more tyre testing for Firestone and I tried it during them, and I got to know what to expect when the car got sideways, and what I should be doing when it came back. I knew when to catch it. I was comfortable with that, and I could set the car up to run with less understeer, even with a little bit of oversteer, so it would come off the turns quicker."

He kept quiet about his little secret, just as Hurtubise did, and suspected that Eddie Sachs was the only other racer to latch on to it. Others discovered it unwittingly, but they were the only three able to exploit it. Sachs, predictably, couldn't keep quiet about it. "I've learned more from that young rookie in qualifying", he said, "than from anyone else all the time I've been at Indy."

Fittingly, Jones battled for that 1961 race with Sachs and Foyt, and led 27 of the laps. He only succumbed when his engine went sick, but for much of the distance he had driven with one hand, wiping the blood from his goggles with the other after he had been hit in the face by a chunk of metal thrown up by another car. Jones wasn't just smart, he was tough, too.

In 1962 he had the race in the bag with 'Ol' Calhoun', and had lapped eventual victor Rodger Ward, when a brake line failed. Brakes were useful for racing, if not in qualifying. "I came into the pits while I was leading and almost quit. But I was earning $150 a lap for leading so I figured it would be a good idea to stay out as long as I could!" He wound up seventh. When he came back in 1963 it would all be different as he fought his rearguard action against the 'funny cars'.

"I wasn't suspicious of the rear-engined cars when they began appearing at Indy", he is quick to point out. "I was sort of in awe of them. They looked fragile, but were in a lot of ways safer than what we had, though in some ways they weren't. The cars we drove were heavier – antiquated as I look at it now! – but more durable."

He nevertheless became the darling of the diehards as that race culminated in a tense battle between 'Ol' Calhoun' and Jimmy Clark's little Lotus 29, Jones exploiting the former's power, the latter the Lotus' handling and fuel and tyre economy. As it drew to its climax Clark lost time under the yellow flags, and then the roadster began leaking oil like a sieve and Clark was slithering all over the track in his efforts to stay on terms. Colin Chapman stormed down to see Clerk of the Course Harlan Fengler, demanding that Jones be black-flagged. Agajanian, equally incensed, argued against it. Jones, after all, had started from the pole and was the sole American in a position to stem the floodtide of the European invasion. His stonewalling went on long enough for him to be able to convince Fengler that the leak had stopped, and the black flags didn't flutter. Jones won his first and only 500 to a mixture of jeers and cheers. In the eyes of many, the Establishment had deliberately cheated Clark and Lotus out of a justified victory.

Jones and colourful STP boss Andy Granatelli had the 1967 Indy 500 sewn up after paralysing their opposition with the Paxton turbocar, only to be let down with three of the 200 laps remaining by a gearbox bearing failure. "It was kinda hard to believe..." he recalled in 1991.

Sachs, the flap-jawed Clown Prince, was one of the loudest in his criticism. At the victory banquet he told Jones he blamed him for a spin that had robbed him of *his* chance of winning. That he should have been black-flagged. Then he started in on Agajanian before coming back for another go at Jones.

"It's not right that he said he spun on my oil", said Parnelli. "In 1963 the thing that really got me was that the track was oily all day, especially in the second half. Jim Hurtubise in the Novi and Dempsey Wilson in the Vita Orange Juice Special, for example, ran right out of oil! My leak came only 10 laps from

95

the end and it all came out in a hurry. I could see puffs of smoke off the car, and I almost spun out! When my car started leaking it was more obvious, I guess, and I got all the blame! One of Mickey Thompson's cars had blown its engine and left a huge oil drift right through the turn. That's where Sachs had spun out. Also, a nut on one of his rear wheels had come loose, irritating his spin. They finally got him pushed away after it, he got going and spun at the end of the next straight when the wheel came off.

"Anyhow, he keeps saying he spun on my oil. So I tell him he's full of shit. So he says I'm full of shit. So I say, 'I'm gonna bust you in the mouth', so he says, 'Go right ahead'. So I hit him!"

Jones roars with laughter about the incident now, and is generous in his praise of his temporary adversary. "He was a character, anyway. He was a beautiful guy. I really admired him a lot. I always liked him, and we stayed on terms after that victory banquet. Sure I had to slug him; he called me a liar. But like I said, he was a good guy. We need more like him in racing, even today."

Did he ever feel in his heart of hearts that he should have been black-flagged?

"Well", he smiles, "this is how I feel about it. First of all, you can't add oil at Indy, and that's why they all had fairly large tanks. It was roughly a five or six-gallon tank. It was mounted with two tubes running through it, one taking the oil into the engine compartment and one taking it back out. We built a special aluminum tank for 1963. It slipped right over them tubes and there was a bolt that held it on. But it cracked at the point where these tubes went into it. Now, although it was a six-gallon tank, we only ran four and a half gallons or so to allow for expansion. I'm running around leading the race, not running hard at all.

"Then all of a sudden, with no warning, I start getting sideways in the runs. It's frightening. I've no idea what it is except I can see a puff of smoke from under the exhaust. For about two laps, I'm telling you it was unbearable; I damn nearly spun out. In the meantime, the oil level drops below the crack and I suddenly found myself picking up speed again. As soon as the oil dropped down below the crack it was alright. And *nobody spun during that particular spell...*

"After that I had no problems at all. In fact the next to last lap I ran one of the fastest laps of the race. I didn't know they were thinking of black-flagging me, but if they had I wouldn't have come in anyway! I'd have let them argue about it afterwards!"

The following year he had Indy sewn up again when Clark's Lotus went out early with tyre trouble, but then 'Calhoun' caught fire in the pits and he was captured forever in a dramatic photograph as he departed from the still rolling roadster in a perfect backward-roll.

For 1965 he made the switch to the 'funny cars', and was quick. In Clark's Indy-winning 38 he underlined his own versatility by taking the chequered flag at Milwaukee, and then again at Trenton. Those who knew what they were talking about had no hesitation in naming Rufus Parnelli Jones as the best driver on the Champcar scene. Bobby and Al Unser thought he was the best oval pavement racer they'd ever seen (and that Foyt was the best on dirt). Jackie Stewart concurred. The reputation sat well with him, yet by 1966 he was virtually set to walk away from it all.

Why?

"What happened with my 'retirement' was that by 1966 I was running two cars that I had built, I had one at Indy and Dick Atkins had the other. We were at Milwaukee and Dick's literally blew its side off in the garage. It must have caught a spark or something. Dick didn't have a drive, so I thought, 'Why not let him drive my car?'. So I did. It didn't seem so important by then to be driving all the time, and I didn't care whether I had my full diet of racing. I drove that car at the end of the year at Phoenix and was leading when the engine blew, spewed oil on to the rear tyres, and spun me into the wall.

"Firestone gave me the distribution rights for all of its race tyres on the West

In a sportscar, just as in anything else, Jones was a hard racer, as Jim Hall discovered during their battle at Riverside in the 1968 CanAm series. He adopted an intimidatory style, and wasn't afraid to sacrifice a little glassfibre bodywork if the occasion demanded it...

Coast in 1964, and we grew with it. They kept hounding me to open a retail store, so I did, and it was a booming success. We opened another, and so was that. My first I opened in 1966. I also had 25% of a Ford dealership. I had a lot of business interests to keep track of."

To somebody raised the way he had been, financial considerations were always important. Parnelli took them very seriously. But there was something else, too. Romance had hit him, as hard as he had once hit his dirt track rivals. After he married Judy he changed fundamentally. It was as if he felt he had lived long enough on the edge. The bravest of the brave walked away for love.

"I had made a lot of sacrifices for my career. I had no kids and no family because of it. I loved kids and wanted to have some, and my wife and I thought my real future lay with quitting Champcars. I didn't retire as such – I'm not even retired today – but I thought I'd do some racing with a rollbar over my head, like stockers and TransAm. And that's how I've done it. I've never gone backwards."

The turbine apart, he stayed true to that plan, but the versatility was there again in 1970 when five wins with his TransAm Mustang secured the championship for Ford. There were no regrets. He formed an organization with Bill Stroppe and they won more races. Along the way he took in California's Baja classic, a blind across brush deserts that broke weak contenders. Jones himself once likened it to a 24-hour plane crash. Today, he still runs there.

OTHER VOICES

John Baldwin – Parnelli engineer 1971–'75

"He was really into his off-road Bronco. I did it in my spare time, and he threatened to thump me if I couldn't work on it! He wasn't interested in the business side; Vel did all that. Parnelli would just play with the Bronco.

"He was very successful with it, too. He rolled it five times once, and still won by a couple of hours. He spent a lot of time recceing, seeing where he could pass. He was controversial, and they banned him for a time. All the other guys were in it for the endurance, but he was always going for it, a real racer. The Mint 400 was two 200-mile laps. One time he lapped the field!

"He was a good bloke to work for, a bit of a rough diamond."

■ ■ ■

"I liked all forms of racing, road racing, sprint cars, ovals. More of each at different times. I'd race cars, anything, with four wheels. I always liked the challenge of the Baja. I was down there this year, not competing this time, but fooling around, doing a little bit of work. The equipment is better there these days, but it's still tough physically. And it's very gratifying to win. I won the 1000 twice, the 500 twice and the Mint 400 once, all in a modified Ford Bronco. Real fun."

His activities with Miletich took them into the USAC Indycar Championship by 1972 with a radical new car with distinctive dihedral wings. It performed badly, initially, but the Vel's Parnelli team went on to take victories for Joe Leonard, Mario Andretti and Al Unser Snr before the dramatic announcement that the Californians were going to take on the Europeans in Formula One with Andretti driving.

OTHER VOICES

Mario Andretti

"Parnelli was definitely one of the tough, tough competitors. I won the '65 National Championship in my first full year, and the only reason I did it was that Parnelli retired. Had he remained in that series – equipmentwise pretty much I felt I had the others covered enough, the car was good and the team was good and Foyt, strong as he was, I felt I had him covered – but Parnelli? I think he was just too strong for me to handle at the time, especially that first year. So him retiring was just great for me!

"You gotta respect that in many ways each man has to make his own decisions. He was not happy with it, but I think it was really an intelligent decision from his standpoint. Vel Miletich *loved* Parnelli Jones and he cut him in on the business as a 50% partner. This guy had a multi-million dollar business. So Parnelli at the time – we're talking about the Sixties – became a millionaire overnight. Why the hell should he keep going and bust his butt the way he was going? There was sure a chance it would happen. He made a wise decision, sure, for his life, but you could tell for sure that he was never satisfied with that, because there was so much fire left in him. When he was doing TransAm it was between him and Mark Donohue, but he was so far superior as a driver in my opinion.

"Parnelli had his own type of finesse, if you will. He was rough and tough and just loved to lean on guys. Even in sportscars. He'd never *ever* wind up a race without busted fibreglass all over the place. You know, at times he'd just go in the corner and just lean and intimidate guys that way. He was a great intimidator. But he knew what he was doing. It wasn't that he was going in out of control; he was very much in control. He did it while he could get away with it. He was smart. A strong driver. You look at his exploits, even against Foyt, stuff like that, he had Foyt covered.

"Parnelli couldn't finish races. He just couldn't finish races. He had a lot of the same problems. He'd go and be really competitive and then, boom!, some crappy thing, an oil leak or whatever, would put him out. With Agajanian's car he was the class of the field, but he only won one race. He shoulda won every race he entered at Indy, including that one with the turbine."

■ ■ ■

It was not the first time Jones' name had been linked to Formula One. Lotus had offered him a ride as far back as 1965.

"After I won for Chapman at Milwaukee and Trenton in 1964 I was impressed by the handling of the Lotus, but I didn't like the fact that it ran gasoline, or that it was all wrapped around you." Everyone, Parnelli in particular, was by then very safety-conscious after Sachs' fiery death at Indianapolis. "The fuel cells we had back then weren't anything like as good as the ones we have today.

"He offered me a ride in Formula One, but at the time I didn't really believe in it. It didn't seem as professional to me then as Champcar racing was. Don't get me wrong, I'm not knocking Formula One, or what it has become, but our racing was on a roll at that time. As a kid, I thought if I was ever fortunate enough to win at Indy, I'd quit. And I nearly did. I promised a friend that I would. But winning Indy opened so many doors in so many ways.

"Firestone encouraged us to set up the Formula One programme in 1974, but after we'd built the cars it quit and pulled out of Formula One and USAC. That left us with the cars all ready to go, but Firestone had been our major sponsor. When it went we had enough funds just to run that one year, in '75, then we got out. We had to run the car on Goodyears!" The Parnelli-Ford VPJ4 was a very neat little chassis engineered by Maurice Phillippe, and Mario even led the Spanish GP with it at Montjuich Park, having inadvertently nudged Lauda's Ferrari into a spin when Brambilla ran into the back of the American car. But it was a tough year, with insufficient finance, and that hurt development. Mario placed only fourth in Sweden and fifth in France. Vel's Parnelli Jones Racing struggled into 1976 before killing the project after Long Beach.

OTHER VOICES

Mario Andretti

"Parnelli never had a feel for Formula One. No-one did, except me. I'm the only one that pushed that. Oh, and the people we hired, because a lot were ex-Lotus.

"John Barnard was the one who really fixed up Maurice Phillippe's car. He was brought in by Parnelli right when we were doing Formula 5000, and then we were embarking on this Formula One thing. It was a beautiful car, but Maurice did not have a good feel for the suspension settings and all that sort of thing. He was the worst one to take you on the track in the ballpark with the wheel rates. He had no idea. Huh. It's amazing with all of his experience! When John Barnard came on it's just amazing what he did, and just *now*!, like *this*! He was such a practical type of engineer. For instance, we were preparing for South Africa and testing at Riverside. I had a record there of 1m 11.55s in the Formula 5000 Lola. The quickest I could do was a 15.7s in the Formula One, and we were going to South Africa? John came on and put that car on the bench and put the scales on it and started jacking it up, just quickly, figuring the wheel rates and changing this and that, and we went out there, and *bang*!, into a 12 almost immediately. He was that kind of guy, and you could tell he could go right to the beat of things, even then.

"'76 was a terrible way of handling the situation. Obviously I think I was the only force that really wanted that programme to go. We had a good budget, really a good one, and somehow they were never gung-ho. So we had some problems, changed the engine, and we had, right on the grid or something, a water leak or something. Water all over the place. All that stuff. Big panic again. And Vel, he was a typical, you know, wealthy, successful American boy! And he didn't like what he saw. He went and told Chris Economaki, and he said, 'That's it. This is my last race in Formula One'. And that was that. And Economaki, after the race, says, 'Well, Mario, it's too bad this looks like being your last race'. And I said, 'What?', and he says, 'That's what Vel told me. This is the team's last race, he says, and you'll continue in Indy Cars'. I said, '*He* will, but *I* won't', and left it at that. Vel tried to hold me to the contract, but I said, 'Vel, do whatever. Take me to the Supreme Court if you want. I'm gonna do Formula One and I'm gonna drive Indy Cars for Penske. Take that one to the judge!"

■ ■ ■

The redundant Formula One car provided the basis for a highly successful USAC Champcar programme that would introduce the Cosworth DFX as the engine for Indycar racing. The wheel had come full-circle.

"I'd have liked to have carried on", said Jones, "but we had a good car for the USAC Championships, and we went back there. Formula One was challenging, and I like to think that we did a lot for it. We taught Maurice Phillippe some new ways of fabricating, and John Barnard saw some good things, too, when he came over here. Our Formula One car amazed our UK mechanics, because they could bolt our American-made parts on without having to change them to fit. We had good tolerances, and it wasn't the usual situation where no two pieces were alike."

Today, Rufus Parnelli Jones has come a long way since those brawling stock car days, even from his days as the yardstick of Champcar racing. The highly successful businessman, urbane and articulate, is a marked contrast to the deep-etched, Sachs-punching image of his younger days.

When he wanted to be, as he weaned himself off racing, he could still be as fast as anyone. The same year he won Indy he conquered Pikes Peak, the notorious hillclimb course that snakes up 4,707 feet in 12.5 tortuous miles. That year, and the next, nobody got close to him in stock cars, and as replacement for the late Dave MacDonald in the King Cobra sportscar, he dusted the opposition at Riverside. His drives in CanAm showcased his uncompromising nature perfectly. At Laguna Seca, in 1966, he moved from 23rd on the grid to 13th on the first lap in the first heat before retiring, then burst into the lead of the second by lap 41 after passing John Surtees, Phil Hill and Jim Hall on the same lap. The fact that Surtees spun off after they made contact was just too bad in Parnelli's view. "But boy, Surtees was *hot!*" In 1967 he ran the dominant McLarens hard at Riverside, Laguna and Vegas. The following year there were rumours that Ferrari was talking to him about Formula One. Yet when he felt his time had come, he accomplished that rare feat of walking away with dignity.

"I do have to say that in my own opinion I was a natural road-racer", he says without a trace of bragging today, going against the opinion of the Unsers by adding, "and probably not a natural on the ovals. There I didn't know where I was going to begin with. But I took to road racing like a duck to water..."

What else might he have achieved had he raced longer, let alone had he accepted Colin Chapman's offer of Formula One?

9

RAY KEECH, FRANK LOCKHART and LEE BIBLE

Soldiers of speed

"Doing something well is so worthwhile that to die trying to do it better cannot be foolhardy." – Bruce McLaren

Always there were contrasts in the story, enacted at a time when the world was in the grip of Land Speed Record fever. At a time when 200mph on land had only just been broken, and was regarded with the same awe as the first lunar landing. On the one hand, there was Ray Keech, brawny, towering, a no-nonsense sprintcar driver with a temper most were advised to avoid arousing. Then there was Frank Lockhart, slim, small, almost frail-looking, the cerebral genius who'd been dubbed a dunce at school. And between them, in the background – always in the background – lurked the shadow of Lee Bible, the mechanic, the ultimate underdog.

The contrasts weren't confined to the men. No two machines ever illustrated more graphically the disparate approaches to the pursuit of ultimate speed during the Roaring Twenties than the *White Triplex* and the *Black Hawk Stutz*. It wasn't just the colour connotations associated with each that were opposites. The engineering philosophies themselves were further apart than Ronald Reagan and Colonel Gaddafi, too. While one ushered in the application of cold science that would become mandatory in much later years, the other was a little short of a saurian throwback, Tyrannosaurus Rex on four wheels.

Lockhart was a difficult kid, who could just about read, but only spell phonetically. In his early life in Dayton, Ohio, he struck up a friendship with Milton Wright, the bishop in the United Brethren Church whose sons Wilbur and Orville would teach the world to fly at Kitty Hawk in 1903, the year after Frank was born. In the absence of his father, the Wright family's intense practicality influenced him profoundly. Even when his mother moved him to California when he was six, that love of mechanics endured.

Lockhart was often petulant, filed small talk in the waste bin and would stop at nothing to bend others to his will. But put him in a race car and his touch had a brilliant intuitiveness. He could charm out the maximum a car had to give just by driving it better than the next man. Then put him in a workshop and his engineering talents and visions bore the hallmarks of genius, and served to further the racing advantage nature had already bestowed upon him.

At school in California his teachers had been unable to perceive any merit within him, and thought he was illiterate. Yet despite his apparent academic shortcomings, while still in his teens he drew streamlined cars that were way ahead of their time and later he would refine the products of the greatest

technical brains in American racing.

Few paid him any attention when he turned up at Indianapolis in 1926. Those who did know anything about him were perhaps aware of his background of successful sprint racing. He might have embarrassed the drivers of Millers and Duesenbergs on Californian tracks with his antics in a modified Fronty Ford, but hey!, this was Indy. And this was his first visit. To the majority he was just another of those awkward kids who hang around Gasoline Alley every May in the hope of securing a ride to fame. They thought differently of him when, as a novice, he won the richest race in America. Overnight he became the new hero.

Lockhart had gone to Indy intent on persuading the only person he knew there, mechanic Ernie Olson, to let him understudy for Bennett Hill. The ploy worked, and in a series of heady practice laps he took their Miller round faster than its more experienced driver. Olson had him stand by as Hill's relief, but on Memorial Day it was Peter Kreis whose ride he took over when the latter became too ill to compete in his Miller. Under grey skies Lockhart rattled many cages as he battled for the lead with established stars Dave Lewis and Harry Hartz. By the 72nd lap he was leading when the race was stopped because of rain, and then he staggered onlookers by pulling out a margin of five miles (virtually two laps) in the restart by the time the race was finally flagged-off at the 400-mile mark when it started raining again. He had amassed a lot of dirt track wins since he leaped to prominence in 1924, but this was totally unexpected.

The Brickyard win was the icing on Lockhart's racing cake, but he wanted more. Much more. For years he had dreamed of attacking the Land Speed Record. Now, through Indy, the dirt racer had a platform. People began to listen to him. He and Olson began working on a very special Miller, which they took to Muroc Dry Lake the following April. On the 11th, the 91cu in car achieved an average of 164.85mph, with a one-way best of 171.02mph, temptingly close to Henry Segrave's then very new outright record of 203.79mph. They learned a lot. With more power and superior aerodynamics, they knew they had a chance.

The man who did the most listening was Lockhart fan Fred E Moskovics, President of the Stutz company. He shared his ambition to break the big record, and pulled together a consortium of wealthy sportsmen who put up $20,000 to

Frank Lockhart's engineering talent bordered on genius, and in the cockpit his driving ability staggered the AAA fraternity as he won the 1926 Indianapolis 500 at his first attempt.

go with the $15,000 Moskovics himself put in and all of Lockhart's race earnings, which included leader fees from the 1927 Indy 500 which he seemed set to win before a conrod broke.

The *Black Hawk Stutz* would swallow all of his winnings, the consortium's money and more, but doggedly Frank and the brilliant Weisel brothers, John and Zenas, persisted, working with full use of Stutz's facilities at Indianapolis. At the time a typical record car shoehorned one, maybe two giant aero-engines into a massive iron girder chassis. Lockhart and the Weisels chose another theme: lightness and aerodynamic efficiency. The Stutz would be pencil slim, with spats fairing in the wheels. Like Malcolm Campbell's latest *Bluebird*, the shape was derived from wind-tunnel tests, and Lockhart and John Weisel pioneered ice cooling instead of using a conventional water radiator with its drag-inducing air intake. The V16 engine comprised two Miller straight-8s with their crankshafts geared together and the blocks linked at 30 degrees on a common crankcase. Two centrifugal superchargers, using the special intercooler that John and Frank had earlier invented to cool the compressed air/fuel mixture on the 91, boosted the 3-litre V16 at 30psi and it produced an estimated 560bhp at 8,300rpm, not bad for 1927.

Two independent engineering assessments – in the Curtiss Airplane Company wind-tunnel and in the Army facility at Wright Field – gauged its potential to be well over 280mph, at a time when the record had barely scraped past 200. And both calculations had assumed a maximum power output of only 525bhp...

The delicate-looking Stutz was finished in white and its wheel spats were left natural aluminium; the *Black Hawk* part of its title referred to the Stutz plant's location at Indy. When it appeared at Daytona Beach in February 1928 it was not alone. Stiff opposition came from Campbell's Napier-engined *Bluebird*, which had already held the record at 174.88mph in 1927 with a 450bhp Napier Lion engine, and now boasted vastly refined aerodynamics. And then there was Keech's *White Triplex*, also known as the *Spirit of Elkdom*. If *Bluebird* was a truck in comparison with the *Stutz*, the *Triplex* was a locomotive, as crude as Lockhart's racer was cunning.

Back in Philadelphia, wealthy wire magnate Jim White had been pondering the problems of high speed on land. Segrave's 1927 success with the £5,400 Sunbeam had paved the way for multi-engined cars, and White reasoned that if

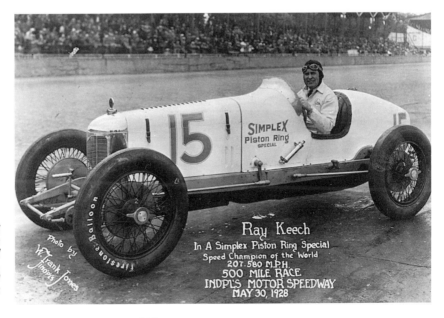

His Land Speed Record rival Ray Keech was a highly accomplished dirt and board track racer who feared no-one. By irony, his 1929 Indianapolis 500 victory was won in Lockhart's old Miller.

103

one wartime Liberty V12 could take Parry Thomas to 171mph, three of the 27-litre units should reach 220 with ease. It was a wild idea, on which he lavished all of £725, but the lack of fundamental engineering understanding was underlined by the crude machine's other 'attributes'. The three Liberties were crammed into a modified short-wheelbase truck chassis – popular rumour had it that the side members were from a railroad track –giving a total of 81 litres and a minimum of 1,200bhp, although White's imagination soon expanded that to 1,500. One Liberty was mounted ahead of the intrepid driver, beneath a sheet metal cowl, the remaining two side-by-side behind him, open to the breeze. There was no clutch or transmission, the only brakes were on the rear wheels, and White placed no importance on aerodynamics beyond adding a pointed nose and a tiny screen as a token to protect Keech from the elements. "Streamlining is bunk", he declared roundly. "The Land Speed Record is all about power, and we have more of that than anyone else." Despite its creator's name, the monster was painted a dull blue-black.

Science met brute force that month, but it was Campbell who snatched the record, despite bad conditions and more than one fright when *Bluebird* hit a serious bump midway down the course. On their home ground, the American contenders hit trouble.

In its early tests the Stutz disappointed, running into clutch slip and lack of power. Then poor airflow into the supercharger inlets was diagnosed and was corrected by the fitting of scoops. Three days after Campbell's successful run, Lockhart was fully aware that he shouldn't run as a squall was blowing up. He was frequently physically sick before a big event, and the proximity of the crashing Atlantic waves and the poor visibility unnerved him. But the 24-year-old had to make some sort of show. It was the classic situation many record-breakers have since encountered; pressure made them run when they shouldn't. For Lockhart, it came from his precarious financial situation and the AAA timing officials, who were ready to quit because of the bad weather.

Just after four in the afternoon, heading north from the Halifax River end of the course, he wound the significantly improved *Black Hawk* out to around 200mph when it hit a patch of rain, ran into soft sand and slewed out of control. He corrected, headed for the soft dunes, and then speared seawards as he over-corrected. Like a skimming stone the 2,750lb racer skipped across the waves

Lockhart's Black Hawk Stutz racer epitomized everything scientific, the prodigy working with John and Zenas Weisel to fashion an elegant cigar-shaped machine which bristled with innovation.

before coming to rest in shallow water. Lockhart was trapped in the cockpit as spectators rushed towards him to effect a dramatic rescue by human chain.

His manager, Bill Sturm: "So terrific had been the force of the impact that the body was bent and Frank was pinned in the car. A man came running into the surf with a rope. Another went under the water and tied the rope to the front axle. A hundred willing hands tugged. Slowly the car was pulled from the water. In the seat sat Lockhart – telling the workers how to get him out."

He was taken to the Halifax County Hospital with severed tendons in his right hand, bruised legs and shock, the latter made all the worse by terror of water, but he was not seriously hurt. Campbell was among his visitors. All Frank wanted to know when Sturm came by was how long it would take to effect repairs.

Conditions were scarcely better when the *Triplex* came to the line. At the wheel was 29-year-old Keech, a dirt track and board racer of some repute in Pennsylvania and neighbouring states. At the time his principal success had come with victory at the one-mile dirt track at Langhorne, on Independence Day 1926, in a Miller. He was, however, a hardened veteran of a life-taking sport who reasoned that if he could master a killer like Langhorne in a sprintcar, two-way runs at Daytona Beach ought to be an easier proposition, no matter what the machine. As it turned out, that would be a moot point. He was muscular, outstandingly courageous and just wanted to get on with the job. I've never forgotten writer Richard Hough's description of him which made such an impression on me when I was 15: 'a giant of a man with flame red hair and hands like a crane's grab'. He was the perfect candidate for the job. He was careful to ensure, however, that his fee reflected the danger of the undertaking. He would earn every cent.

Faced with the engineering excellence of *Bluebird* and the Stutz, the AAA officials weren't really sure what to make of the *Triplex*, and were initially relieved when they found a reason to prevent it running: it had no reverse gear. With the direct drive the only means of reversing the monster was to push it backwards, against the compression of its triple Liberties. It was a ridiculous regulation, but White's men were equal to it. With ingenuity they rigged up a starter motor that drove via friction against a rear wheel and moved the beast back inch by inch. The AAA men weren't impressed, but couldn't find any reason to stop the car when it appeared with a complete auxiliary rear axle, mounted just ahead of the standard unit, which the driver could lower by depressing a lever. This brought two worm gears into engagement and reversed the motion of the front engine. To overcome the compression of the rear engines the gearing was around 500:1, but the device worked. "We managed to reverse the car at 36 feet a minute", grinned Keech, "but it complied with what the AAA had said it would accept as a reverse gear." The system had to be taken off before the car could run.

Keech made several runs to get the feel of the brutal *Triplex*, but his attack was to end ingloriously and he, too, joined Lockhart in the Halifax County Hospital. In its crudity the *Triplex* dispensed with any kind of firewall protection between the front engine and the cockpit, and when a water hose burst near 200mph his legs were badly scalded. Despite intense pain he somehow managed to bring the monster to an even halt a mile further down the course.

Faced with one serious accident and a near-miss, the officials declared an end to the speed week, but by late April both contenders had left hospital and were ready to try again.

The *Triplex* had spent more time in White's workshop at 11th and Olive Streets in Philadelphia and now had a firewall and a proper reverse gear incorporated, among minor modifications. The latter now comprised a conventional propeller-shaft through which all three engines drove, rather than the previous hit-and-miss direct-drive system.

Despite its lack of engineering sophistication, it performed well. Keech hit 203.97mph on his first run into the appreciable wind on April 22, just below Campbell's record, and then vented his temper on the hapless AAA officials when they sheepishly informed him that their timing apparatus had failed to record his second, which, with the wind, had been significantly quicker. Conditions were less favourable when he tried again, as the wind had become stronger still. Despite that, Keech squeezed more power out of the Liberties than ever before as he wrestled to maintain control. *Triplex* took off for some yards when he hit the bump that had troubled Campbell back in February, and then a backfire from the front engine badly burned his exposed arm. A lesser man might have been deterred, but Keech kept standing on the gas and averaged 207.552mph for those two hair-raising rides – 201.56mph down and 213.9 up – on the treacherous beach. He might have eclipsed Campbell's mark by only a fraction over half a mile an hour – the exact figure was 0.596mph – but in those days the rules did not specify a minimum increment. Besides which, Campbell himself had edged out Ernest Eldridge by much less than that – 0.15mph – back in 1924. As a result, however, the FIA would in future stipulate a minimum speed increase of one per cent. Keech and White could care less, the Land Speed Record was back in American hands after an abnormally brave performance.

Since his February accident Lockhart had recovered fully, and the damage to the Stutz – a bent frame and body panels – had been rectified back at the factory in Indianapolis. The kid now had something new to aim at and was anxious to go. Three days after Keech's success, on April 25, he came out again and began to work up to the 200mph mark, but again the fickle beach was in poor condition. The answer would have been to await improvement, but he simply couldn't afford to. Everything he had was riding on a successful attempt, the financial pressure was immense, and there was no time to wait. The timekeepers had again been anxious to leave on April 22, but Keech's new record had persuaded them to stay over for Lockhart's attempt.

Shortly after dawn he blasted up and down the course, limbering up for his record attempt by bagging a 2 to 3-litre Class D record of a staggering 198.292mph that would stand unbroken until 1960. It began to look as if Keech had been right to stick around in readiness to defend his new honours.

Nineteen minutes later Lockhart was dead.

Like his Pennsylvanian rival, he reached 203.45mph by his third run, the first of the outright attempt, running into the wind. At the end of it he slowed a little sharply, locking his rear tyres momentarily for around 100 feet. The error was to have fatal results.

Since he had begun the project, Lockhart had received a generous offer of $20,000 sponsorship from the Mason Tire Company. Such were his financial straits that he had no alternative but to accept, thus switching from the Firestones on which he had planned to run and on which Keech had been successful. Campbell had advised him to change his tyres between runs (advice he did not always follow himself), but Lockhart simply had his helpers make a visual inspection because taking off the wheel spats took so long. They passed them as OK. Unbeknown to anyone, a clam shell had cut his right rear Mason and he was estimated to be travelling at 225mph at 7.59am on his return when it burst.

During tests of a Firestone tyre linked to a dynamometer driven by a straight-eight Stutz engine, he had satisfied his curiosity on the likely effects of a blowout by firing a shotgun into the tyre as it rotated at maximum speed. The damage had been so severe that the engine was ripped from its mountings. Reality reflected that scenario all too faithfully as the little white Stutz was thrown down the beach. Its tail flicked to the left, then, as Lockhart corrected, it slid to the right, and the car speared into the soft sand which flipped it into a series of complete sideways somersaults. A group of terrified spectators had a

By contrast, Keech's White Triplex was a crude locomotive of a car, packed with power and precious little else as two Liberty V12s nestled behind him to augment the other mounted just ahead of the cockpit. It needed an abnormally brave man to wrestle the fearsome creation to the record at Daytona Beach in April 1928.

miraculous escape as it flew inches over their heads before pounding into the sand. Lockhart was thrown out during its contortions and by a cruel stroke of fate his body landed at his horrified wife's feet. This time America's non-pareil did not survive.

OTHER VOICES

Louie Meyer – three-time Indianapolis 500 winner

"Lockhart was not an educated engineer, but he had a natural gift. He came up with the idea for the intercooler when he was testing a supercharger on a Miller straight-eight and when the inlet manifold cracked he got a blast of hot air from it as he walked past.

"When he was testing different size orifices on the Stutz engine you could hear that supercharger screaming half a mile away! He was an excellent driver, way ahead of his time.

"Cliff Woodbury and I were caught up in the accident that killed Keech at Altoona. A whole section of fence was torn down just ahead of me and he ran into it at full speed. Had nowhere to go. He was leading at the time, after passing me four laps before. There was no red flag until I came by. There were six guys claimed that win and to begin with they gave it to Keech. Six months later they gave it to me. I was running second at the time and that was what I figured I deserved.

"I didn't know Keech well and there was something about a feud with Leon Duray, I recall, but he was all right. He never took trouble from anyone.'

■ ■ ■

A year later Segrave came out again, this time with the beautiful *Golden Arrow*, which boasted even better aerodynamics than the Stutz and a solid 925bhp from its single Napier Lion engine. The 'Mad Major' had to await good conditions for a fortnight, but that was the only glitch in a campaign that underlined just how slick were the British when it came to record-breaking.

The *Arrow* probably ran less than 20 miles in its life, yet Segrave calmly smashed Keech's record with a staggering 231.44mph.

As soon as he had heard of the *Golden Arrow* project, White knew he had to throw in the towel or prepare for a counter-attack. Keech, hardly surprisingly, had declined to drive the monster again, and had since exploited his record fame by securing decent rides on the lucrative oval-track trail. Instead, a number of other drivers were considered. White's favourite was Indianapolis racer Wilbur Shaw, who would later win the prestigious 500 three times.

Shaw had been in sad shape in 1928. His competitive spirit had been crushed by the death of his wife as she gave birth to their premature child. Such was his mental anguish that he threw himself into racing anything, anywhere, and began touring the half-mile dirt tracks. The AAA responded to his situation, and that emotional decision to compete in outlaw events, by suspending him, but a romance with Cathleen 'Boots' Stearns, the girl who was to become his second wife, finally set him back on the right road by the end of the year. The AAA had to have its pound of flesh, however, and though White offered to buy him out of his suspension by paying a substantial fine, officialdom refused to be swayed. Indeed, it was vindictive enough not only to refuse him the *Triplex* chance of glory, but also to keep him out of racing until May 26, 1929, and even then refused to allow him to compete in that year's Indy 500, only four days later. Thus the popular gentleman from Shelbyville, Indiana, whose efforts would later save the Indy 500 as an event, lost his shot at the Land Speed Record through a spiteful political wrangle. They were sweethearts, those officials, but they probably did Shaw a favour keeping him out of the *Triplex*.

Renowned racers Leon Duray, Bob McDonogh and Deacon Litz were all mentioned as possibles, but without Shaw White began to lose heart. Ultimately, however, he was persuaded to run by Daytona garage proprietor Lee Bible. He was determined that Shaw's loss would be his benefit.

The part-time barber was a tragic figure in Land Speed Record history. At 42 he was much older than either of his immediate American record predecessors, or any of the other candidates, and perhaps it was the wrong time of life to begin a career of speed. He had behind him some outings in local dirt track races, and had worked on the *Triplex* in 1928 when it had been based at his premises, but he was not a shooting star like Lockhart, nor an experienced grafter like Keech. Instead, he was an extra who won himself a walk-on part that would ultimately take him from obscurity to infinity. He saw the ride as his passport to fame, and a better life for his wife, son and daughter, and White capitulated in the face of the loyalty he had always shown the team. What he did share with Keech, however, was bravery beyond the norm, perhaps the more so given his more limited experience of fast cars.

And the rookie did well. His first run on March 12 was made on wet sand and in poor visibility due to mist, and yielded nothing better than 127mph initially. He massaged those three Liberties into harmony, however, and the manner in which he then coaxed the *Triplex* to a shade under 190mph suggested that he might, after all, stand a chance of success. The AAA officials certainly thought so, since they were impressed enough to sanction him to make an official attempt the next day.

Friday the 13th was brighter, with the beach in better shape than it had been for Segrave and with little sign of the expected inclement weather. Segrave nevertheless had advised him to wait until conditions were perfect, but the Floridan was all too aware that the *Golden Arrow* had barely been stretched by the Old Etonian. He was anxious to set whatever new mark he could, in the hope that the weather might earn him a respite by closing things down for the Englishman. He warmed up with 183.11mph on his first, southward run, intending to make several more to build up his speed. Then, driving north from the Halifax River, he progressed to 202.703.

As he cleared the mile tragedy struck. Maybe he lifted off too sharply after the

Always in the background to the story of Beauty and the Beast, and so little in the spotlight, lurked mechanic Lee Bible, the extra whose walk-on role would take him to his death on March 13, 1929.

run and those Liberties acted like a violently applied brake on the overrun; maybe the *Triplex* suffered mechanical failure. Nobody was sure. "Bible either stepped on his brake or cut his throttle too quickly at the speed he was travelling", said eyewitness J W Morgan, who had been responsible for establishing speed trials and record attempts on the beach in 1902.

OTHER VOICES

Barney Markham – timing crew electrician

"The *Triplex* was coming up the beach at high speed and running true, on course, when, about 300 yards away from the timing trap, it made a fish-like waver from its track. When that happened the car seemed to lessen its speed and then straightened out on the course again and hit the timing trap squarely in the middle.

"Then, right after crossing the trap, Bible cut the motors sharply; I could tell that by the way the exhaust suddenly slowed down. The car turned slightly toward the dunes for about 150 feet, when it made an abrupt swerve.

"Still in the same direction, it went into the soft sand high up on the beach and headed straight toward the high bank of dunes, front end first.

"As it hit the soft sand the car went into a corkscrew turning motion, front end first, and hit the steep bank of the dunes at an angle of about 45 degrees. When it hit the solid bank it disappeared in a thick cloud of white sand, and out of that cloud I saw pieces of the car and other objects fly into the air as if dynamite had exploded in the car."

■ ■ ■

One tyre and spokeless wheel rim rolled north up the beach for fully a quarter of a mile before ending its crazed flight in the Atlantic Ocean.

Veteran Pathé News cameraman Charles Traub had set up his equipment at the end of the mile, to record the run. No stranger to peril, he had been stationed in Miami for several years, and among his achievements numbered gathering news pictures from the underwater resting place of the *S4* when it was sunk off Florida to test a new submarine lung. He had also worked in a diving bell to collect underwater photographs of the ocean floor.

"If you want to see real action, you'll get it right here when that fellow takes his foot off the gas crossing the finishing wire. At that speed, something is going to happen!", Traub had told observers only minutes before the accident. He was still cranking away when he saw the errant machine heading straight for him. Traub ran for his life, but by a cruel stroke of fate the *Triplex* veered from its trajectory at the last moment and cut his fleeing body in two before its violence was expended. Ironically, his camera and tripod remained untouched.

Like Traub, the garage proprietor didn't have a chance once the *Triplex* had begun its maverick lunge. He was pitched out as it rolled to destruction and was thrown dead on to the beach just as Lockhart had been the previous year. His neck, legs and arms were all broken. The Americans had paid a heavy price in their quest for glory.

Said Segrave, who had been present to launch a counter-attack if necessary: "Deeply as I regret the sad occurrence, I wish to say that Lee Bible, like others who have lost their lives in automobile racing, has not died in vain. High-speed racing has been the chief source of development of safe and efficient automobiles for general use.

"I am in absolute accord with the decision of the American Automobile Association to end the meeting immediately, as a mark of respect for the two men who lost their lives today and for their families." He had nothing new to aim at, and had been beseeched to return to England by his father. Segrave was in any case too sensitive to the dictates of good taste even to consider rubbing more salt into America's gaping wound.

So the saga of Beauty and the Beast reached its brutal conclusion, but even then there was to be a tragic postscript.

After his beach success, Keech had been able to negotiate better rides. In June 1928 he won on Detroit's one-mile dirt track, and followed that with successes at Rockingham, near Salem, New Hampshire, in July and Atlantic City, near Amatol, New Jersey, in September. They were important victories, but of even greater significance had been the invitation to drive in the Indianapolis 500 at the end of May, in which he placed a good fourth behind Louie Meyer's Miller. Just over two months after Segrave had ended his reign as the Fastest Man on Earth, in March 1929, Keech scaled another motorsport pinnacle when he triumphed at Indianapolis, again driving his Simplex Piston Ring Special and beating Meyer by six minutes. He thus shared with 1914 winner René Thomas the distinction of being the only man in history to win Indy and set the official Land Speed Record. Two weeks later, on June 15, he lost his life in the Miller, racing on Pennsylvania's one-and-a-quarter-mile board track at Altoona, Tipton. By another of the ironies that surrounded the story, he was leading the 200-mile race when he crashed at the three-quarter distance mark, and was initially declared the posthumous winner.

In 1930 White made news again by announcing his plan for a four-wheel-drive car which would aim for 500mph (the record then still stood to Segrave at the 231mph Bible had died trying to better). Given the bloody events of 1928 and 1929, there was perhaps at large, somewhere, at least one American driver who had reason to be thankful that the grandiose plans never progressed beyond the wire maker's colourful imagination.

10
NIGEL MANSELL
Opportunity knocked

"Give Nigel Mansell an opportunity, and he'll wring its neck." – Peter Collins

The Englishman, so they say, fights best with his back against the wall. Nigel Mansell was no exception in his early years, but then he discovered the trick: you just knocked the wall down. It took him five Formula One years to learn the art of that destruction, but once he had it mastered there was no stopping him.

He is like Senna in so many ways, wreathed in the occasional controversy, hounded by the media. Everybody has an opinion on him, and invariably it is a strong one. He is right when he tells the nationals that he is their story: when Allan McNish's Lola crashed into the crowd at Donington's Gold Cup in 1990 and killed a spectator, for example, one paper published a story relating solely to Mansell's agony in straining a wrist the previous week testing at Imola. If he doesn't win, and usually his victories are dramatic, pure *Boys' Own* stuff, he's being attacked by his team-mate, or hits his head on a low stanchion en route the the winner's press conference. Or is announcing his retirement.

Ah, retirement. Will we ever forget that long drawn out saga of 1990?

Nigel Mansell is a theatrical performer with a taste for melodrama. And what could have been more melodramatic after his bold charge after Prost at Silverstone that year than to walk home, throwing gauntlet and gloves to the adoring crowd? He didn't quite throw the Ferrari as well, as an *Auto Hebdo* cartoon suggested, but perhaps he'd only had two Shredded Wheat for breakfast that morning.

The man is incredibly strong. Once when I interviewed him at Hall Green, in 1981, I tried lifting the weights he'd so nonchalantly raised into the air, and couldn't move them off their rests. Determined exercising has given him hefty forearms and shoulders, and a bull neck that can withstand high G loadings. I once saw him totally out of control after the startline shunt at Paul Ricard in 1989, and it was not pleasant. He is not the sort of man one would be advised to tangle with without the aid of at least one automatic weapon.

The strength runs right through him, and is not merely physical. Watching a video of his life story, being taken round Ballamain House on the Isle of Man, seeing the trappings of his undoubted success, it is all too easy to overlook the early days of struggle, or to gloss over them. Yet, as my old headmaster would say, they were very real. In the long term the days of poverty and struggle may have been a relatively short part of his career, but they were packed with uncertainty.

I find Ayrton Senna's commitment to his career enthralling, when you sit down and consider just what else he gave up to achieve it. Forget the wealth for a moment, and concentrate on the everyday things. His is certainly not a normal life.

Mansell, too, has that incredible application, and so does Rosanne, the quiet figure in the background, who has backed him every inch of the way. At times that must have been pretty damned hard to do. Yes, the Mansells were lucky to have a flat to dispose of in Nigel's quest for success. Yes, he wasn't exactly a bozo who knew racing and nothing else. It's easy to forget that he is a qualified engineer who worked for Lucas Girling, and thus had that to fall back on. But to give all that up, on what at the time was little more than a whim fuelled by relentless determination, took a special kind of courage. From both of them.

The story of how Mansell turned the offer of a Lotus test drive into the reality of a testing contract, and thence into a regular Formula One drive, has been told many times, but is still worth the retelling. In 1979 he was driving in Formula Three for the Unipart-backed team run by Dave Price, but the Triumph Dolomite-powered March 793s were little match for their Toyota-engined rivals. What should have been a rewarding retreat from the financial edge became a nightmare struggle. For Mansell it ended at Oulton Park, courtesy of Andrea de Cesaris. Eddie Jordan, now a Formula One entrant but then an aspiring driver, was just ahead of them. "I could see them battling in my mirrors, and it was getting heated. Then one lap de Cesaris just went for a gap that wasn't there, and I could see this Unipart March rolling over and over down the road."

OTHER VOICES

Dave Price – Formula Three entrant

"We were one of the only teams at that time to employ drivers, rather than take their sponsorship money to run them, and in all honesty he was the best of the bunch. If you looked at what he'd done in 1978, he'd actually done quite well with what he had available.

"I held these interviews, like I was employing mechanics, almost. I had all these guys down from my shortlist, and he just destroyed all the others, really. He came in and he had so much will to do it. He'd sold up everything, sold up the house, the car. I think they were living in the back of a car, him and Ros, then! He didn't have a pot to piss in. So I suppose I felt sorry for him, too. So we took him and Brett Riley.

"In all honesty, he never lived up to my expectations. His character hasn't changed at all in 10 or more years, and he still tends to whinge at times. He was always convinced that Brett had a better engine than him. Well, there was no such thing as a good Dolomite engine! They were all shit! That was a fact of life. He used to overdrive, I think, to make up, and he always wanted the rear wing dropped so he'd go faster down the straight. And then he'd scrabble round the corners and end up being slower. Nine times out of 10 he was slower than Riley. I always got the feeling he felt he wasn't getting the best deal, but I don't think either of them were, in all honesty.

"We had a good deal with March, and people used to reckon the Dolomite had 170bhp, but I reckoned they used to lose 20 while they were being delivered!

"That year we gave him a road car – a TR7! – and I think it was 40 quid a week and expenses. He was the sort then, and still is, that if you gave him the right equipment, then he could do the job. If we'd had the Toyota I think the two of them would have cleaned up.

"The day after the Oulton shunt he was typical Nigel. 'I'll be alright to race next week, don't worry.' He told me he didn't take any painkillers so he could feel when he was getting better. He told me before he drove our car that he'd been the same when he broke his back..."

■ ■ ■

Mansell aggravated that old Formula Ford injury in his back, this time breaking a couple of vertebrae. In the first accident, he'd returned to racing in a collar, and won. Now, two days after Oulton, the phone rang. "It was Colin Chapman, asking me down to a Formula One test at Paul Ricard! I knew there was a test contract on offer, and I was determined I was going to get it. I knew that some of the other guys who would be there were already higher up the ladder, and that the second regular seat was going. I didn't think I had a chance of that, so I thought it would be more appetizing to them and I'd get the test contract."

It was shrewd thinking that would pay off. Surreptitiously taking painkillers – an indication of how seriously he took things – he went to the South of France for the most important drive of his life. Peter Collins was there as team manager.

"I guess he was very aware of the enormity of the job he was being asked to do, particularly in view of the opposition", he recalled. Formula One drivers Eddie Cheever, Elio de Angelis and Jan Lammers were also there, as well as promising Formula Two racer Stephen South. All of them were vastly more experienced.

"He was in a lot of pain", Collins said. "He didn't make it apparent, but I knew about Oulton Park and I knew he wasn't right. But I didn't let on to the Old Man. Nigel applied himself well, he knew what he had to do. He was patient – he was the last of the five to get a run, and he had to wait until the last day – and although he wasn't cocky, he was confident. I remember clearly that there was a lot of pessimism from the Lotus people who were there because he was straight out of Formula Three. He'd never been to Ricard before, but he sorted out his lines in a road car, and when he got into the race car he did 10 laps, I think it was, and his times were something like 1m 32s, 22, 18, 15, 13, 12, 11, 10s. He was very quickly down to a time. He was confident with the power, and precise. It was a typically Nigel performance. He was strongly in control of the situation, and he got down to a time in less time than either Cheever or

Lammers, who'd been in Formula One for a year.

"Elio was the most impressive and he got the second seat alongside Andretti for 1980, but Nigel was the next best. He ran a standard 79, and I felt he had the most potential given his lack of experience."

Mansell got the test contract, and a valuable £2,500 per test session, but still that wasn't going to be enough to live on. Collins, who like former journalist and now Williams team manager Peter Windsor could see potential others at that time couldn't, created a factory job for him as a technical progress chaser, and found him a Ford Escort road car to go with it. He also sourced Team Lotus' external engineering contract work, using his technical background when visiting potential contractees. Opportunity had knocked, and he had grabbed it instantly. Others in the past, such as Jim Crawford and Rene Arnoux in 1975, had not been so adept. That opportunist streak never disappeared, as those who saw his moves in Mexico in 1990 appreciated.

It went further than that. In his first full test, at Silverstone, he went faster than Prost's McLaren, and created no amount of consternation in the Colnbrook team, which promptly suggested that Lotus had better engines.

"Every time we'd tested up until then it had been for half a day, but this was a pukka two-day test. I was determined to do well. Everything just clicked and I was really able to get into a rhythm." That rhythm took him to the fastest-ever Lotus lap. On his next outing, on the Brands Hatch Club circuit, he knocked three-tenths off de Angelis' best time. After that he produced a four-page technical report which proved instrumental in sorting out the troubled Lotus 81.

"Everybody says that Alain Prost is brilliant at chassis setting", said Collins, "but Mansell is better. Look at Imola in 1990, when the Ferrari 641/2 came out. Prost was jumping from car to car, and it was Nigel who sorted out the new one. Prost was wanting to race the 641/1. Nigel got his sorted a lot sooner. It's all a

The legend of Mansell's refusal to accept defeat has its roots in incidents such as this one at Dallas in 1984. After vying for the lead with eventual victor Keke Rosberg, he collapsed with exhaustion while trying to push his crippled Lotus home in the broiling heat.

myth that he can't set a car up as well as Prost." Frank Dernie, former aerodynamicist at Williams and now chief designer at Ligier, concurred. "He is a very, very quick, strong, determined driver, forceful rather than aggressive. He knows what he wants, and is very clever at setting up a car."

Collins would be a direct beneficiary of Mansell's impressive physical strength at Rio, in 1981.

OTHER VOICES

Peter Collins – Lotus team manager

"I was swimming off the beach by the Intercontinental Hotel, where we were staying. I'd been used to body surfing back in Australia, but I didn't realize the vicious rips and whirlpools there were at that section. I found out later that six or 10 people drowned that day I got into trouble.

"I could feel I was getting into difficulties and yelled to the beach, where Nigel and Elio were sunbathing with Rosanne. They both came in to help me. Elio lasted two or four minutes, and then started to get into trouble himself and had to head back. Nigel stayed with me. I'd be dead if he hadn't.

"I was breathless and my arms and legs had gone, they were just like lead. The rip changes every 30 minutes or so, and we were still struggling when it changed, having been in the water for around 35 minutes. The undercurrent subsequently hit us and pushed us in, but I took a mouthful of water and I really thought that was it. All the while Nigel was swimming with me, pushing me, swearing at me to keep me going.

"With the second wave I felt sand beneath my toes. I dug them into it. I was absolutely knackered, but that gave me the final will to go on. Nigel was still swimming.

"We finally made the beach and I was totally exhausted. Then we realized that Elio was still out there, in trouble. Nigel took three deep breaths and started straight back in to get him, but Elio finally made it himself with a bit of a struggle.

"I'm not exaggerating when I say I would be dead if it wasn't for Nigel. I'd taken a lot of criticism because I'd put myself out to help him when he came to Lotus, and he repaid that. We were close even before that, and now it's something we both remember."

■ ■ ■

The previous year his Grand Prix debut had been surrounded by all the drama we would later come to expect of Mansell. Through the summer of 1980 he had combined Formula Two with the Ralt-Honda with his Lotus testing, and Chapman finally rewarded his persistence in Austria. Mario Andretti had become increasingly disenchanted with Chapman's refusal to sort the Lotus to his liking, and it was obvious he would not be staying for 1981. This time, Mansell knew full well that a pukka ride was there for the taking. He got the oldest 81 and just scraped in on the back row.

"I was on a high, just sitting there on the grid. The old adrenalin was pumping round. I was concentrating on the job I had to do when I began to feel uncomfortable. Fuel was leaking into the cockpit, and I began to feel like I was sitting in a bath of it. It was incredibly painful.

"There I was, about to start my first Grand Prix, and I was getting the most incredible stinging pains in my backside. Everyone kept asking me if I wanted to get out, but how could I? There was no way. You just don't do that when you're about to make your Grand Prix debut!"

They poured water in to alleviate the pain, but within laps of the start it had evaporated. For a time he enjoyed his run, before the pain came back. He soldiered on, getting as high as 13th, ahead of Keke Rosberg's Fittipaldi, before the engine blew up on the 41st lap and put an end to the immediate agony. It might not have been a shattering debut in terms of sheer performance, but it was to establish the legend of Mansell's physical endurance.

"Carrying on was the right decision; it showed I didn't give up. I got a good press because of it. But the problems started when I got out of the car and discovered that my hamstrings had shrunk where they'd been immersed in petrol for so long. I had to have them stretched for months afterwards."

OTHER VOICES

Peter Windsor – friend and former journalist

"I first met Nigel at a Silverstone Formula Three race in 1978. I watched him qualifying at Stowe and Club in the white March he'd sold his house to rent. His ability through those two corners was mind blowing! It was perfect judgment allied to car control. Before the race I went and introduced myself to him in the pits, and was very impressed. I was a firm believer the moment we shook hands and when I looked into his eyes I could tell he was very special. It was unusual to see a Briton so keen he'd run 10 miles a day and fire off 30 sponsorship letters a day. Who sacrificed his house.

"In that wet race he was a fantastic second with a misted visor. We saw one another every two weeks or so and I wrote sponsorship proposals for him. That winter I won a Guild of Motoring Writers award of £500 and put it into his career, which gave him a bit more publicity.

"Peter Collins and I were old friends from Warwick Farm, and when he eventually got the assistant team manager's job at Team Lotus I introduced Nigel to him and then on the Saturday at Silverstone we introduced Nigel to Colin Chapman. Peter took Colin to watch Nigel down at Woodcote. You could tell Nigel, he always ran his Dave Price March's wing three holes lower than anyone else. There were no good Dolomite engines, but Riley always got the best there was, so that was the only way Nigel could hope to compete.

"We took Nigel to Colin again afterwards and Peter kept trying to persuade Colin to have a driver test programme at Ricard. Nigel phoned me after his first run and said he was really shaken. He'd spun at the corner leading on to the straight. He said he wasn't sure if he could drive a Formula One car after all. But later he did a fantastic job.

"Later, when nothing appeared to be happening at Lotus, through David Phipps, who had connections with the team, I suggested him as the driver for the Ralt-Honda. Peter then agreed to tell Colin that March was pressuring Mansell to sign and that we could lose him, so Colin finally agreed to put him on a three-year deal. The chances he'd drive a Lotus were still small, though.

"In the meantime I'd done a million proposals and Victor Gauntlett liked the one we'd sent to Pace Petroleum. He wrote a cheque direct to March Engineering for Formula Three, and I managed to persuade Gerard Larrousse to let him have works Renault engines as the rest of his budget. It looked good until the anti-Mansell thing started at March and everyone lost interest. Nigel whinged and complained like hell even then!

"He was working as a buyer at Lotus and phoned me one day, shattered. He'd been to a company at Milton Keynes and they'd told him the March guys had said he was going to lose his drive. He and Rosanne had taken a camper to the French/Italian border at Monaco, while the team flew out and stayed in the Holiday Inn, so we were less than impressed. The whole thing was a disaster and it all collapsed.

"The Ralt-Honda was the only thing left, and eventually, after he'd blown off

Tom Gloy, I think he proved to Ron Tauranac that he was better than Ron thought.

"When Mario had gone home on one occasion Peter finally persuaded Colin to let Nigel have a test run at Silverstone. He called me that night and said, 'It was a disaster... I'm only pulling your leg! I did a 12.8s!'. He'd done the same times as Elio first time out. Colin and Nigel Stroud couldn't believe it! Then at Brands, Patrick Head and Carlos Reutemann were impressed, too.

"Mario tested the 81B after the German GP and it was awful, but he suggested that Colin might let Nigel race it. It was a dreadful car and that's the one he debuted there. He did a good job.

"I think he was better still at Zandvoort, which was the big point in the year. Elio had qualified with 20 minutes to go and Nigel had the 81B again and wasn't in. Colin let him out in Elio's car. It was one of those times when all that hard work and drama could have gone one way or the other. A moment of truth. He qualified it just three-tenths off Elio's time. It was just stunning. One of the most impressive things I've seen. When you looked at Moreno and Palmer in similar situations in later years, not doing that really set their careers back. Nigel just maximized that opportunity and did the job."

■ ■ ■

At Brands Hatch in October 1985 he finally made the breakthrough when he won the Grand Prix of Europe for Williams. The success opened a floodgate and would sweep him beyond the victory score of Stirling Moss as the most successful English driver in history.

There were other dramas. In Montreal in 1982 he sprained his left wrist in an incident with Giacomelli. In Dallas in 1984 he collapsed with heat exhaustion while pushing his car to the line. He concussed himself hitting the wall at Detroit the following year, then was hospitalized with more after a 201mph tyre failure on the Mistral Straight at Ricard in the next race. There was dehydration at Brands Hatch in 1986, where he swayed precariously on the rostrum, the toothache and subsequent headache from hitting an overhead gantry in Austria in 1987, the Suzuka shunt that ended his championship chances that year. Chickenpox at the Hungaroring in 1988. Cut fingers after winning at Rio in 1989...

It was the theatricality that started to grate. Like Eddie Sachs, Mansell is a character who loves to be loved, and by the same token he needs sympathy. He surrounds himself with acolytes. Every time he gives his all, but he needs to know that the effort has been recognized and appreciated. To understand the man, you have to understand that. It's quite an endearing trait, in a way, but after a while it gets a bit like having to assure a friend continually that you still like them. The constant struggle to prove himself left an indelible scar on a very sensitive, emotional man, and it became a habit he simply couldn't break.

At Monza in 1990 he limped towards us. What was the trouble this time? "I was getting some socks from the drawer in my hotel, and I pulled it right out. It landed on my big toe. I've never known such pain!", he said, and he limped away, a man in agony. The previous month my wife had dropped an iron on her big toe whilst getting the kids out of the car. In shepherding them across the road and into the house she had no time to dwell on her pain, and refused to thereafter. I'd rather have liked to see the two of them meet up at Monza...

Against the amateur theatricals, though, there was always the bravery, and Nigel Mansell is Brave. Against all advice, he raced at the British GP in 1982, his Canadian-damaged wrist in a special cast. The Kentish circuit is a bad, bad place for a man with a stiff-sprung Formula One car and such an injury, but he hung on as long as he could before finally calling it a day. I watched spellbound there in 1983 as he literally fought the appalling Lotus 93T around in an automotive equivalent of alligator wrestling. It was an awful car, but there was absolutely no questioning the commitment with which he willed it over Brands' notorious bumps and dips.

His pole-winning lap at Silverstone in 1990 was also something to behold as he balanced the Ferrari right on the very edge. But it was a competition for John Player, which pitted one of its racing cars against one of its racing catamarans, that really brought home the Mansell commitment. The deal was that he and Bob Spalding would drag race each other at Holme Pierrepont in 1982. That was fine for Bob, since it is a pukka watersports park, but Mansell only had a narrow path to run down, and grass at either end of it to act as run-off area. Despite that he didn't bat an eyelid, nonchalantly spinning the Lotus 91 to a halt at the end of each pass. He won, too, 3 litres of Cosworth V8 propelling him to 116mph in 5.4s compared to 3½ litres of Johnson V8 pushing Spalding's Velden to 100 in 5.7s.

Brave, too, was his drive from the pit lane to fifth at Estoril in 1985 when he overtook car after car by listening for the change in its engine note as the driver lifted off, then counting one before doing likewise as he dived inside. Brave he also was during first qualifying at Monaco in 1985, where his Williams was troubled by a throttle closure problem that overtaxed the brakes.

Grey-faced, he said: "It's one of the few times I'll ever admit to being scared in a car. It's the one thing you don't need round here." He refused to drive it the following day if the problem persisted, but it didn't. After a stunning lap on Saturday afternoon, he started that race from the front row, alongside Senna...

The days with Lotus promised much as he tried to forge a similar kind of relationship with Chapman to that Andretti had enjoyed in the good times. Against that, however, had to be measured continuing animosity between Nigel and team manager Peter Warr, who had returned to the fold in 1982. "Mansell won't win a Grand Prix as long as he has a hole in his arse", Warr once said. As Chapman's 'protege', Nigel was on reasonably firm ground, although Windsor remained convinced that even Chapman never really appreciated just how good Nigel was. Warr could only bite hard as he saw the Briton's pay increasing. Chapman had already boosted it at Monte Carlo in 1981, and again at Zolder where he scored his first championship points with a good third place drive. Warr and Mansell clashed frequently.

"I was a bit cheeky to Colin at times", admitted Nigel. "But I think he quite liked that. He didn't like people to be too obsequious. At the same time, he didn't like to be told what to do, or rushed into anything. I had to be careful to be patient. When he told me to do things, though, I never thought twice about doing them." Nevertheless, the boss had seriously considered replacing him with Jean-Pierre Jarier for 1981.

When Chapman died at the end of 1982 Nigel's position became much more vulnerable. Mansell believed Warr resented his relationship with Chapman, with whom Warr went back a long way. Warr in turn felt Mansell was acting like a superstar after his Zolder success the previous year. Mansell stayed aboard for 1983, but only just. Warr once told him that Warwick was his number one choice, and that Nigel was behind "three or four others" in the list. It was de Angelis who got the first Renault turbo-powered 93T. John Player's demand for a British driver kept him on the payroll for 1984, too, but by mid-season Warr had snatched Ayrton Senna away from Toleman, and it was obvious he would partner de Angelis for 1985.

Those seasons ultimately brought little in terms of tangible results: that third at Zolder in 1981, fourth at Vegas, third in Rio the following year, fourth at Monaco. Fourth again at Silverstone in 1983, and a brace of thirds and a fourth in 1984. When he had qualified seventh at Long Beach in 1981, Windsor said to Ron Dennis: "What do you think about that?", whereupon Ron said, "I don't think about Nigel Mansell", and walked away... What had Collins originally seen in him?

"Nigel was a committed driver from the first time he drove a Lotus. When he was on the throttle, he was on it. He had good car control, if a little brutal, and when he was on the limit he wasn't super-ragged. That lap he did for us at Ricard in 1979 was driven in exactly the same way as his pole position lap at Silverstone in 1990: with controlled aggression.

"I saw back then what I see now. A bloke who was dedicated and absolutely convinced of his own ability. I thought he had it and that he would make it."

Monaco 1984 had given the best indication. Burdened by grief for his mother, who had just died, he finished third in the early French GP, and then in pouring rain at the Principality he had overtaken Prost and led for five glorious laps, pulling away from the Frenchman. In the pits Gerard Ducarouge was having a fit, screaming at him to slow down, to accept that he had the race in the bag, but Mansell was on a high. He lost control on a white line going up the hill to Massenet on the 16th lap and walloped the wall, and the moment of glory was over. He sat on the Armco with his head in his hands, but his time would come. What was telling, what many tended to overlook, was that he was running Goodyears where all the others who were going quickly in the wet (bar Stefan Bellof) were on Michelins...

It seems ironic now that Williams signed him as a good number two, expecting little more of him than to act as Keke Rosberg's back-up. The winter of 1984 would be the first in which he could truly be certain his seat was safe for the following year. Like many a racing driver before him, the Finn was less than enthralled at Frank Williams' choice of partner for him and said so, but later he would come to modify his tone. Businessman John Thornburn had run them both at McKechnie Racing. "In my 19 years of motor racing, I reckon this lad has the best potential since Jimmy Clark", he declared, and his sheer belief was instrumental in launching Mansell's career. He thought Nigel was better than Keke...

OTHER VOICES

Keke Rosberg

"It's absolutely true that I didn't want Nigel in the team with me. I told Frank that, and still he went ahead! I based my judgment on stories I'd heard about him, and we spent part of the season learning about each other. But after a bit it became clear that a lot of the stories I'd heard weren't true. He was a very good team-mate, one of the best I've had. We became good friends. Now my son

Niko thinks it's great that Dad knows Nigel Mansell!

"I suggested to Jean Todt that he tried to get Nigel for Peugeot when he had 'retired' from Formula One. I would have been very happy to have him there as a team-mate again."

■ ■ ■

Mansell's relationships with other team-mates would not be so fruitful. When Rosberg left for McLaren for 1986, Nelson Piquet moved in. He and Mansell would fight for the World Championship in the following two seasons, Prost beating both in 1986, Piquet's superior finishing record taking him to the 1987 title, even though Mansell won six races to his three. The following year in Rio, with Piquet now esconced at Lotus, a row blew up when copies of Brazilian *Playboy* hit the streets containing an interview in which Nelson made contentious and offensive comments about Mansell and Rosanne.

In 1990 Nigel's relationship with Prost also reached rock-bottom. At Estoril it even looked suspiciously as if Mansell deliberately drove at his team-mate as they left the startline, the two front row Ferraris veering so close together that Senna and Berger in their McLarens burst into the lead from row two. At best, Mansell made an appalling start; at worst, he deliberately tried to intimidate Prost. The cynics amongst us concluded that his negotiations with Williams and Camel were at such a point that Nigel desperately needed to win a Grand Prix, in whatever manner was required.

When he went to Ferrari, of course, everything was sweetness and light, and that dramatic win in Rio first time out cemented the relationship. The church bells rang all night in Maranello, and the tifosi took him to their hearts. A year later it was Prost's turn, and as the season gathered momentum the little Frenchman stamped his considerable personality on the team. Mansell, like many a second-year Ferrari driver before him, found himself getting shallow treatment. It wasn't always easy to identify, but that only made him feel worse. The feeling of persecution grew in direct relation to Prost's tally of victories (five in all) and his own list of retirements. Complaints against the fairness of his treatment were, in such circumstances, perhaps inevitable.

It also hurt that Prost got so much credit for setting up the car. "Prost did the engine work after his falling out with Enrique Scalabroni at Imola; Nigel did all the chassis work", said his close supporters, but that didn't quite explain why Prost had markedly better set-ups for Mexico, Ricard and Silverstone, all of which he won. The euphoria of Rio and the opportunism of Hungary the preceding year seemed a long, long way away as Nigel became mired in the politics. His dismal 1990 season raised the inevitable question: would he ever win the World Championship?

How close he had come in those halcyon days of 1986 and '87 as he matured! He took five victories in the first year, all of them in the same thrusting mould, redolent with that controlled aggression. The Williams-Honda was a combination of the best handling car with the most powerful engine, and it was damn near invincible, except that inter-team rivalry with Piquet let Prost keep himself in play all year until that dramatic puncture in Adelaide literally snatched the title from Mansell's hands.

"I *can't* believe it", he repeated over and again after that cruel fate, and few drivers have ever had to face such crushing disappointment. He had driven beautifully, done everything he needed to to secure the crown, and then in a moment it had gone. "It took me a long time, a very long time, to get over it", he confessed.

The detractors believed it would break his spirit, yet he came back as hard as ever in 1987. This time the tally was six wins, and again they came the hard way. And again there was disappointment as he crashed during qualifying for Suzuka. He went out of the championship struggle on a stretcher.

If 1988 was a lost year as Williams, deprived of Honda power, trod water with Judd V8s in the last year of the turbos, it was also cathartic. He clashed many times with designer Patrick Head as they argued about reactive ride suspension, and he endured a number of frights when it went wrong. But he came to terms with losing the championship, came to accept that perhaps it didn't matter quite so much. The consolation was that at least everybody could now see what the Chapmans, Collins and Windsors of racing had seen earlier than most, and he built on that. "The championship is fine", he said. "If I win enough races I will win it. Now I am looking at it totally differently. I go out to win each race now, and I'm going to let the championship take care of itself." Rather than worry about the whole, he would let the parts and the results therefrom speak for themselves. "If it comes my way, fine", he said. "If it doesn't, it's not the end of the world."

Despite the disappointments of 1990, when it seemed that Prost had tucked him up nicely and effectively reduced the upper strata of Formula One to a two-horse race between himself and Senna, his believers stood firm. "With a little more fortune he would have won both the 1986 and '87 titles", said Collins. "Yes, he made mistakes, but so did the team, and it made the sort of mistakes that didn't affect his team-mate. Give him a reliable car and he has the ability. I still firmly believe that only two drivers have the ability to run races right on the very edge, and they are Senna and Mansell."

The retirement saga dragged on through the latter part of 1990. Was it simply sour grapes, was he genuinely disaffected, or was it a means of taking himself out of the Ferrari equation for 1991 so that he could then change his mind once the Prancing Horse had signed somebody else? The questions raged, and never received full answers.

In 1989 Mansell had invited a group of journalists down to his Ferrari dealership near Bournemouth, 'to set out his store'. "I've had up to 14 personal sponsors", he began, "all of whom have required something from me at races. I've begun to realize just what pressure I've been putting on myself and I came close to overloading." He was speaking in terms of time, not income. The sponsors had been very helpful for the latter. "Now I don't have any deals apart from Ferrari and Marlboro. It's a great weight off my shoulders and I'm not afraid to admit it."

He promised more open channels of communication, and they stayed pretty much unclogged right through until that July 1990 announcement. Even then they were clear, until the rumours of a reversal of that decision began to circulate. It took them all of a couple of hours to start rumbling round the paddock.

I don't for a moment question that he was in a state of real emotional turmoil, and it surprised him, I believe, just how many offers he got from a variety of unexpected sources. There was talk of a third Marlboro Penske in CART, of being a glorified tester for Footwork, of sharing a Peugeot with Rosberg. Even, had Senna have gone to Williams, of taking his seat at McLaren.

One of the things that had triggered his decision to quit was the way in which talks with Williams for 1991 had gone awry at Silverstone, just before That Announcement. Jean Alesi had become upset to hear that Mansell was in the 1991 equation, having himself signed a deal with Frank Williams on February 2, 1990. Now it was Mansell's turn, as Frank informed him that signatures on contracts had to wait as he was now courting Senna instead. The inference was clear, and it hurt a man as proud as Mansell. Senna was first choice.

Eventually, at the Belgian GP at the end of August, Honda stepped in to break the deadlock between Ron Dennis and Senna and ensure that the star driver stayed at McLaren, and gradually Williams and Mansell reopened their dialogue and feathers were smoothed again. Money was the stumbling point for some time, and publicly Mansell still maintained that nothing had happened that would make him change his mind about retiring. He still spoke of his plans to indulge his love of golf, of spending more time with his family. What he said was true enough, he was staying retired, but we all knew what was being discussed in camera. Yet Rosanne, astute lady that she is, counselled him not to quit if his heart was not in it.

Two things happened which indicated how Mansell underestimated the media. At Monza, in early September, he specifically called everyone together. "Categorically", he reiterated, "the situation has not changed. I am retiring, I am not talking to anyone and I'm not racing next year." Again, it was true enough, but it seemed the media was becoming a useful bargaining tool in his negotiations. He continued the denials right through the Spanish GP weekend, even though it was believed that only Martin Donnelly's accident had prevented the announcement of his signing on the Friday. By Monday it was finally official. The Great U Turn had been accomplished. "It was an incredible commitment to come back", he said. "To unretire was the most historic thing I could have done in my life."

The other thing was the bitterness he expressed at the way Derek Warwick's actions at that time, in the aftermath of his team-mate Donnelly's accident, had taken the lion's share of the publicity and overshadowed his non-retirement story. After all his own success, and the plight in which Derek found himself at that time, it seemed particularly churlish. Perhaps he had never heard about the boy who cried wolf.

He sought the counsel of senior media members, incorrectly assuming that they would pass on a tacit invitation to others to attend a 'summit' in Adelaide to discuss the situation. He had an audience of one, and another Cold War began. "I intend to drive a human bulldozer through anyone who is not positive about me in 1991", he declared. It made interesting reading. The Born Again racer of 1989 appeared to have changed again under the pressures of all the polemics, only to be all smiles again by February 1991.

It remained to be seen whether the return to his Williams roots would work the oracle. When he left in 1988 the mechanics threw a party. Frank Williams' views were not entirely complimentary. "The trouble was, he'd become the complete superstar", he said. "We'll miss him, no question. The guy is immensely quick. But I'll miss him as a driver, not as a bloke. With Alan and Carlos and Keke I remember the good ups, even though we had plenty of downs.

The hero at home: at Silverstone for the 1991 British GP he was simply in a class of his own as he thrashed Senna's McLaren during the height of Williams-Renault's Indian summer.

But I never felt that way with Nigel." Another senior Williams employee said: "The pity is that you can't just helicopter him in from his hotel, plug him in the car, and then just helicopter him out again."

Water passes very swiftly under the Formula One bridge. After two years without a charger at the wheel, Williams was only too pleased to persuade Mansell back. "He has developed a sense of humour", he said. This time around morale soared, as it only can when a team recognizes the presence of a winner in its midst. And Mansell, for all that we criticize aspects of his personality, *is* a winner. On his first serious run at Paul Ricard in January 1991 he was fastest of all in an interim car. "This time round he has matured so much", added Williams. Further proof of that came throughout the season as he battled with Senna for the World Championship.

I have seen him victorious, aggressive, injured, theatrical and melodramatic, but up until the German and Belgian GPs in 1990 the one thing I had never seen him do was give up. I still don't quite believe the evidence of my eyes there, and they were indeed sad days when emotion and Ferrari polemics appeared to get the better of him. "Nigel is incredibly sensitive as a driver", said Windsor. "He's a front-end driver, he can turn in on the brakes the way Prost does, he can find the grip, use less road than Senna or Piquet." With oversteer, his style was stymied.

At the end of the day, what really matters is how a driver performs on the track. Give Mansell the right equipment, and he will challenge for the lead. His fans adore him, not only the normally phlegmatic British who invade home tracks when he wins, but also the fickle tifosi. Perhaps the media is just too close. Nevertheless, he is a driver one can admire without necessarily liking. One day, when he really has retired, maybe we shall look back and say, "He really was bloody good, Mansell, wasn't he? And he was *British*". "He's got where he is by sheer hard work and determination", said Dernie, "but there is a natural gift in there too."

If self-belief, determination, towering commitment, uncanny car control and sheer balls were their own reward he would have won at least one title before 1991. The tifosi certainly thinks so. In the winter after he'd left Ferrari he received a vast trophy on which was inscribed the legend: 'To our World Champion, 1990'.

11
RICK MEARS
Wichita lineman

"There are no supermen in the world. Everybody puts his pants on one leg at a time."

There are two little guys that I worry about in Milwaukee. Nine or 10, they'd be. I'm worried that they're walking around with the wrong impression of one of the most rounded sportsmen I've ever met. Rick Mears was at a particularly tricky point in his explanation of oval racing technique when they intervened, seeking an autograph. They were polite, and normally Mears would have obliged instantly. But he was warming to his point, anxious that it should come across accurately.

"Give me a second please, guys", he said in the soft Californian drawl that always makes the expression 'Clint Eastwood in a race car' spring into my mind. A little crestfallen, they walked outside with their notebooks. Mears completed his point, then excused himself and went out to look for them a minute later. They'd gone. I just hope they didn't go thinking he's aloof.

That was 1990. Mears was by then a triple Indy winner, five-time pole-sitter, the first man to lap the Indianapolis Motor Speedway in excess of 220mph, second only to Mario Andretti in the all-time dollar earning stakes, and as approachable as he had been back at the Watkins Glen Six Hours in 1981, just over a month after the nasty methanol fire at Indy that had given him facial burns. In 1991 he again increased his Indy pole and victory tally. He took the pole with a super-cool run – just after a heavy shunt caused by car failure…

Rick Ravon Mears is the sublime speedway driver, and a lot more besides, one of nature's gentlemen without the typical racer's need to feed his ego at someone else's expense.

In his career he's done just about everything he could have done on the USAC and then CART trails. After a career off-road he switched to motorcycles and then did a year and a half of SuperVee before graduating to USAC Champcars, as they were then known, in 1977 with an ageing McLaren. He joined Penske for the 1978 season and has stayed there ever since, in what could well be the longest driver/team relationship in history. He is unfailingly polite, and as reserved as he was in that first year with the Philadelphian's team. You could look a long time at Mears, without ever spotting a trace of braggadocio.

He was, and is, a modest man, who was genuinely surprised how quick he was in his early days. "You always wonder, you know, go searching in the back of your own mind whether you can do it or not, until you've done it. Up until the last couple of races, when I started qualifying up there with everybody", he

The smile is genuine, and not something turned on and off depending on how his racing is going. The supreme artist of oval racing, Rick Ravon Mears stands out as the gentleman of current motorsport.

said at Pocono in 1978, "I was always searching. Am I doing it right, or am I doing it wrong?" He is a thinking driver, full of self-analysis. "After a while it kinda lets you know they aren't completely supermen – but some of them are!"

A dogfight with Al Unser Snr at Milwaukee that year taught the idealist some valuable lessons as he earned his USAC spurs. "It didn't matter where I was at, he was there. Oh, I was impressed, but I should have expected it, really. I haven't always done things that way myself.

"Up to then I'd always felt that I'd take my line and if the guy could get by me that meant he was quicker. That meant I was doing something wrong and I needed to go quicker. I wouldn't distort my line to keep him from passing me, but I'd never had to run for those stakes before, either. That tended to change things a little bit. Once I saw that those guys were doing it, I started to do it, too." He won that race, his first Champcar success, but he still blocks a lot less than the majority of his rivals. Cleanliness has always been one of the hallmarks of his style.

"The two cleanest guys out there are Al Junior and Rick", said Bobby Rahal, "and of everyone, Rick is the cleanest. Absolutely no question. He's the kind of guy who, no matter what the situation, will never, never let you down. You always know what he's gonna do, that he's gonna be fair."

"When I started I was impressed by Foyt, Rutherford, Al and Bobby Unser, Mario, Sneva", said Mears, "because you could run close to them, you could run with them and not have to worry about them doing something to surprise you. The top guys today are the same. And again, you get back in the packaways and there are some who do surprise you, and you wonder what they're doing out there. When you get up there into that first 10 group they're all pretty consistent. Some get a little wilder than others at times, but nothing serious."

Despite the success that's come his way, he hasn't lost sight of the basics, and will always give full credit to his equipment and the people who make and prepare it. "You know, back in 1977 I frightened myself more trying to qualify at Indy with the McLaren than with the Penske in 1978. Running 182 in that car was twice as hard as running 200 in the Penske. The car just makes a world of difference."

His historic deal with Penske had its roots at the Colorado 500 motorcycle meeting, organized in the fall of 1977 by Wally Dallenbach. "There were about 30 of us there, Bobby and Al, Parnelli Jones, Dan Gurney, Penske and myself, my brother Roger. Roger (Penske) and I got to talking and I said, 'I hear you're thinking of hiring Pancho (Carter) for next year'. He says, 'No, not as far as I know. I heard you were going with Fletcher'. And I said, 'Not as far as I know'. I did have a deal possibly working with Shadow at that time, they were thinking about getting into Champcars, and he said, 'Before you make a deal with them give me a call, I got something in mind'. That's all that was said.

"Next time I talked to him was at the Michigan race, which was the next race, and the following Sunday after the race I went to his house and that's where we laid everything out, what was going to happen."

That day they laid the foundation of the relationship that went into its 14th straight season as this book was written. Along the way, they captured those four Indy wins, the 1979, '81 and '82 National Championships, more than 40 runs over 200mph at Indy, those six Indy poles and a staggering closed course record of 233.934mph set at Michigan International Speedway in November 1986. In that session he ran 24 laps, 14 of them over 200mph, 12 of those over 215 and nine of *them* over 220. They ran 227, 221, 223, 228, 225, 231, 221, 233 and 223...

For a man with that sort of scintillating ability, it is strange that Mears had no real aims when he came into Indycar racing, nor does he profess to have any now.

"When I was in off-road and SuperVee I never thought about USAC Champcar racing, other than when I went to watch them run, or something like

that. I never set it as a goal. I never set any goals. I figured if I worked hard enough at anything I was doing it would make the opportunities arise, which is how it's worked out so far. So I never really set any goals."

And Formula One? "That's not a goal, either", he said back in 1978, "but if it comes around, I'll try it! I feel like I need a lot more experience before I can really get into that. I just enjoy racing, enjoy running whatever I can get in. I like to try anything once. A split programme like Andretti's would be a handful, definitely, but I feel like I've got a lot to do in this area that I'm in right now before I could think about doing something in something else. I've got a lot to prove here, a lot to prove to myself. I don't like to disappoint myself, that's why I don't set goals.

"I suppose the nearest I get to a goal is as far ahead as winning the next race. It's not really a goal, either, and it hasn't always been winning. It's always been to do better than I did the time before. Whatever I've done I go out and say, 'I want to do the best job I can do', and see what happens."

The Formula One opportunity did arise, however, in March 1980. The plan was to run him in a third Brabham at Long Beach that year, and in readiness he tested a BT49 alongside Nelson Piquet.

"We did two tests at Ricard, and the third test was the one at Riverside. Basically, that's just what the whole thing was, a test." The popular story at the time was that Rick withdrew when he learned that Ecclestone expected him to pay for the privilege of racing for him, but he refuted that firmly. "They wanted me to come out and try out, and basically Bernie and I sat down and talked about everything as far as dollars and cents were concerned, and we came to an agreement on all that and it was just a matter of me making up my mind, taking the final decision whether I wanted to.

"The way it all came about was that at that time CART was just coming about, when CART and USAC were having their clash, and we didn't know for sure what was going to be taking place. Whether CART and USAC were going to get together, whether it was going to survive or not, or whatever the case may be. Brabham had approached me already, and I kinda wanted to get my foot in

What might have been: in 1980 Mears tested a Brabham BT49 at both Paul Ricard and here at Riverside at a time when it was quite possible he might join Nelson Piquet on the F1 scene. Circumstances conspired against such a move, and he would remain in America, but he was very quick. He had satisfied his curiosity and proved to himself that he could have handled it, and to him that was sufficient. It was F1's loss.

the door in case something went awry with CART. So I said, 'OK, let's give it a try'. Plus I wanted to know for myself. I've always been the type that I could be running in one series, and if I was leading the points championship in the series and something else came by, I'd skip a race and go do it. I enjoy trying something new. I've always enjoyed doing that, so it was another opportunity. Plus there was everything you hear about Formula One.

"The first thing I learned when I got into Indycars is there are no supermen in this world. You know, everybody puts their pants on one leg at a time. Everybody seemed to hold a pretty high regard of Formula One drivers, like they were better than everybody else. So I kinda wanted to find out for myself."

He had never driven a ground-effect car before, nor sampled Formula One, nor even seen Paul Ricard, which at that time still had the flat-left kink past the pits. Despite all that, he was very quick.

"We went fine, we went fine", he said easily. "I think I got to within half a second of Nelson, which I knew I could make up with more time on the track. I wasn't gonna do something stupid. I wasn't surprised at being quick, it just proved the point to me that there are no supermen in this world. It's a combination of a lot of things that makes a guy quick."

OTHER VOICES

Herbie Blash – Brabham director

"He turned up at Ricard with this lawyer from Las Vegas – I think his name was Simon Simmonds – and when they first turned up it was, 'Hey, this is France!'. It was a whole new world to them. They were so American, they hadn't travelled at all.

"He wasn't that impressed with the car, really, when he first looked at it. He was very straightforward. He jumped in, did three or so laps and came in, and he said it was very positive. He couldn't believe the brakes or the cornering forces. And, of course, Ricard in those days had that long loop, where everybody's neck goes. He was so cool, calm and collected. He didn't show any emotion at all. Eventually his neck started to give out a little, but he was so

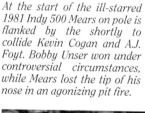

At the start of the ill-starred 1981 Indy 500 Mears on pole is flanked by the shortly to collide Kevin Cogan and A.J. Foyt. Bobby Unser won under controversial circumstances, while Mears lost the tip of his nose in an agonizing pit fire.

ultra-cool. And *very* quick. Nothing fazed him out at all.

"I think he really wanted to do Formula One. The only problem was that, like the rest of the Americans, he was happy back home. He was happily married then and he didn't fancy moving everything over to Europe.

"I went to watch him out on the circuit and he was *very* smooth. The guy would have made it. He was a World Champion, I think."

■ ■ ■

"I felt good about it, and I satisfied my own ego. I knew I could make up time and I was taking it easy, I didn't want to make any mistakes and look like an idiot. It took a little time to get used to it, it's just like anything you jump into.

"So we did the two tests there and then we went to Riverside, which was a track I knew, although it wasn't really the same because we had chicanes put up in about three different places so we could test the Weismann gearbox. We ended up about 3 seconds a lap quicker than Nelson. I know where the time was made up. After the run Gordon Murray said, 'I can see where you're working out most of the time, around Turn Nine'. It's my favourite corner on the whole race track. Nelson didn't like that one. It's slightly banked and right up against a wall. The chicanes really changed the track from what I knew, though, so when we ran quicker than him there, that really satisfied my ego that I could do it if I wanted to. That we could be competitive without a problem."

OTHER VOICES

Gordon Murray – former Brabham designer

"He was very sensible, that certainly came across. And very conscious that he shouldn't bend the car. He was very smooth and quite impressive. And a nice person, too, which always goes a long way to helping. Very, very bright, intelligent. I watched him out the back at Ricard and Riverside, and thought then just how smooth he was."

■ ■ ■

"I enjoyed it, it was fun. But I enjoyed the States, I enjoyed the Penske team, which I'd just been with for a couple of years. I didn't really want to give this operation up. There was a lot more here that I wanted to accomplish yet, and I liked the variety of having both, the speedways and the road courses. I'd only won at the Speedway (Indy) once then.

"I couldn't do both, I'd have had to give one or the other up. So weighing it all out in every respect – well, you gotta do what makes you happy. And I didn't feel I would be as happy in Europe, with all road races, no ovals. The travel would have been tough, too. It was one of those things that weighed in; we could have handled it, but... I don't really regret not doing it. I satisfied my ego, satisfied my curiosity that if we wanted to go there and run, we could. It's like everything else, you've got to run with the right team and the right equipment. I don't care who you are, if you don't have that you aren't gonna get there. Nelson won the World Championship the next year, so it might have been good for me. Maybe. You never know."

FISA firmly quashed an attempt by Long Beach organizer Chris Pook to field Rick in the third BT49, citing the regulation that a fresh driver can only be added to the entry list, *force majeure* aside, if a formal application is made within a specific time period. Pook's approach was made to Bernie Ecclestone and FOCA at a time when FISA and FOCA were at war. While Bernie took the view that Pook had effectively complied by informing himself as race organizer,

FISA disagreed. It was Formula One's loss more than Mears', whose raw speed and smooth style would certainly have made him a very strong candidate in the European series.

He was born in Wichita on December 3, 1951, and he inherited his love of machinery from his father Bill who, when not farming, indulged in a little racing himself in stock cars and modifieds. "The last race he ran he went out and won the dash, won the heat, won the 100-mile final. And he got about 60 bucks to split with his owner. He said, 'Hey, it's just not worth it. I get in a roll, break a finger or an arm and can't run the tractor, I can't make a living.' He just stepped out, but from everything I read and heard, he was a shoe. He stood on the gas!"

Today, Rick's mother and father go to some races, manning the Mears Gang fan club's racewear trailer.

"I can remember playing with models, building models, then I got into racing slot cars, then go karts a little bit, then motorcycles. It's always been something like that, something mechanical." His career resume reads like the Hall of Fame put together, but success has come at a price.

He was leading the 1981 Indianapolis 500 as he came in for his second fuel stop, having started an uncharacteristic 22nd after trouble in qualifying. As crew member Bill Murphy pulled the dry-break coupling from the Penske's fuel tank union, the one-way valve jammed open, spraying methanol in all directions. Within seconds the car car was alight, the fuel burning with invisible flame. Team manager Derrick Walker suffered burns, too, and in agony, Rick jumped from the car as his helmet caught alight. In a race distinguished by a very low standard of fire-fighting, he had to quell his own burns by grabbing an extinguisher from a marshal. Bill Mears also had to help.

The Indy fire took the tip off his nose, but what happened at Sanair, the 0.876-mile tri-oval just outside Montreal, in September 1984, was altogether more serious. It was the one major mistake of his driving career, and he was quick to shoulder the full blame for it.

"It was a combination of things. First off, me. It was my fault. I put myself in a position I shouldn't have, at a time I shouldn't have. It was just one of those things where you get over-anxious. At the beginning of the year we'd had a slow start and I figured we needed to start catching up. Then we'd won the Speedway and that put us up into the hunt in the points series.

"We'd done a test at Sanair and nobody else had run there, so we had a little bit of an advantage going into the weekend, and I wanted to keep it. Sanair's a bullring, it's hard to get a clear lap, and I wanted to get a good clean lap to see where we were at. I was behind Bobby Rahal and Scott Brayton, I believe it was, and as I came out of Turn Three I could see it was a clear track ahead of the others. So once I got by them I'd have a clear lap.

"It's a three-cornered track and as I came off of Three I had a run at Rahal and was committed. As I pulled out round him he pulled out to go around Brayton, so I had to watch him and I saw a guy, Corrado Fabi, warming up down on the apron. I stayed as close to Rahal as I could because I was already committed, going through there like that as this car was coming out of the pits. As we went through I'm watching Rahal's corner because I gotta stay right on him to make sure I miss Corrado. As you go by you watch him out of your peripheral vision, watch how fast you're going by, how long it takes before you're gonna clear him. So I was watching Fabi going by and watching Rahal, and I thought, OK, it's clear, we're gonna make it. But Fabi was warming up, and just as I went by him he stood on the throttle and picked up speed. So instead of me going by, he started staying with us. I thought we were clear, but we hit as I pulled on to my line, and I went under the guardrail. So it was a combination of me being over-anxious and putting myself in a bad position. In a race, obviously you don't have guys warming up, but in practice you do."

As the Penske March went under the guardrail it tore off the front bulkhead and smashed both of his feet.

"I drove a car for the first time five months later. I was in the hospital, basically, for three months, two months in Indianapolis, another month in California, then in a wheelchair another month or so after that. I'd still use the wheelchair or crutches to kinda hobble around at the end of five months, and we went to Phoenix to test and they basically had to pick me up and sit me in the car.

"At that time I had everything just padded up. My ankles were bad and I just couldn't use them very hard. They were tender. Fortunately, you don't have to brake much on an oval, and I left-foot brake everywhere. Matter of fact, I didn't use the clutch before the accident either, so that was a plus. It was one less thing I had to worry about."

At that point he broke off to sign an autograph, handing the book back and saying, "Thank you very much", unconscious of the fact that the hunter clearly felt the gratitude should have been the other way around.

"If you were in Formula One you probably wouldn't have done that", I ventured. "That's another reason I didn't do it", he shot back, good naturedly. "That attitude, I swore I'd never be like that. I wasn't raised that way, and I'm just not like that, anyway. That's not my make-up. I don't agree with it.

"Anyhow, we did the test and I ended up running quicker than Sullivan, so that was worth six months' therapy, to get back in the car and run that good. First time out I went out and warmed the car up, came in and stopped, then I went out and started leaning on it a little. When I came in the guys leaned over and said, 'How is it?', and I said, 'It's pushing a little bit in Three and Four, but it's neutral in One and Two', and they just cracked up and started rolling on the ground. I'd forgotten about my feet already and was thinking about the car, and they were wanting to know what my feet were like. It felt good to be back in it, to take my mind off everything else.

"I didn't have a problem getting back in the car after the accident, because I knew what caused it. If I had done something that I didn't know, something had happened where I'd made a mistake and didn't realize it or whatever, yeah, it would make me think about it. But if something happens and I know what caused it, OK. Every time I've ever spun a car, I've known exactly what caused it. Either I ran it in too deep, jerked it, or got on it too soon. You know, I screwed up. It'd drive me nuts if I didn't know what caused it. I couldn't get back in the car. But by knowing, either what I did or what broke, it's one hell of an incentive not to do the same again!

"But it took a long time. A long time. I've still got pain, every day. I broke every bone in my right foot, half of them more than once, and half the bones in the left foot. Obviously, in 1985 I didn't run the road races, and it wasn't the matter of shifting because I wasn't using the clutch anyway. It was just the matter of being able to brake harder. We did a lot of playing, changing brakes and master cylinders, looking at power assistance, all kinds of things like that to help out. And as we kept working and running with these master cylinders I kept building up strength, also. For a long time I had to run a different size master cylinder to the other guys, which gave me a lot more travel in the pedal, which I didn't like.

"I started road racing again the following year, and now I use the same master cylinder as everyone else. That year, 1986, we had a car, the PC15, that didn't work on either ovals or road courses, so I still couldn't drive on road courses! I'd run the March on the ovals and continue development work on the 15 on the road courses. So I'd be quick on the ovals and slow, qualify anywhere from third to 10th, on the road courses. That thing wouldn't handle on anything. Period.

"At the last race of the season the team had more Marches and kinda shelved the 15, but Al Unser decided he was gonna use it for the Marlboro Challenge. I didn't like it for Al's sake, but I liked it for mine. In fact, we sat on the pole with it at Sanair. It was the first pole for Chevrolet. That was good, satisfying."

What he omitted to mention, because he isn't the type to, was the sportsmanship he displayed to stand-in Unser Snr late in the 1985 season when he stepped down from the final oval race, the Jimmy Bryan 150 at Phoenix, so that Al could continue his quest for the National Championship. Al won that one, and went on to beat son Al Jnr by a point for the title, and in recognition of Rick's sportsmanship Al handed over the symbolic No 1 to him for 1986. In that troubled year he was instrumental in developing the Ilmor Chevrolet engine that now dominates CART, taking the pole at Indy and Pocono (at a record 223.401mph), leading more laps than anyone at Indy, and finishing only two seconds behind Rahal and Kevin Cogan. He stuck with Penske throughout its '86/'87 drought, and was rewarded with his third Indianapolis victory in 1988, winning immediately afterwards at Milwaukee and taking the poles at Pocono and Michigan, too. In 1989 he was second only to Emerson Fittipaldi in the National Championship, winning again at Phoenix and Milwaukee, and finishing the year tops at Laguna Seca. It was the year that took him right back to the front line, and the Californian success was his first road course victory for eight years. He backed it with another, the Marlboro Challenge, at Nazareth in 1990, which supplemented another Phoenix success, despite a tangle with clumsy backmarker Randy Lewis.

OTHER VOICES

Ken Anderson – damper specialist

"The two best drivers I've ever worked with are Rick and JJ Lehto. Even after the Sanair shunt, on a road course Rick would always be on the Friday pole. Then Danny would get the set-up for Saturday and would be able to brake that little bit harder and therefore go that little bit faster."

■　■　■

Mears has always adapted easily, and attributes his success partly to that. "One thing that's kinda helped me, and I'm not bragging at myself or whatever, is being able to adapt quick. I feel that's probably what helped me make the switch to Champcars. I've never had to really teach myself, do something over and over. It's just come fairly quick to a certain point, then you have to start and work at it. But I guess what helped me in Champcars is that once I made a few laps I felt I knew exactly what it needed. And then you just start doing it. That's part of the game.

"When you've got a good car, that works good and runs fast, it's hard getting to the limit, to make it do something, because it's working so well. You can get into two off-road cars and they're identical and they feel completely different. You can get into two Indycars and they're identical and they feel completely different. They don't work the same, and that takes adaptability to figure it out. I felt that was just what you were doing, adapting to another car. The way I figured it in my mind, I felt that was one quality that a driver had to have; the ability to adapt and change to what it needed at the time. You look at Parnelli, you look at Bobby, at Al, at Mario, you look at any of them... Foyt... that run quick, they can run quick in anything they get in. They figure it out."

He is the recognized master of sustained speed in the claustrophobic speedway environment of the groove and the wall. Indianapolis, he says, is a one-groove track when you're going quickly. The groove is where the car works best. One line is the centre of the groove, and the driver works his car a little either side of that. The art is in being able to move the groove, of finding a way of getting on the power earlier and carrying greater speed to the end of the

straights. On the speedways, Mears has few, if any, peers. "He's a diesel engine", said 1990 rookie and former Formula One driver Eddie Cheever. "Thump, thump, thump, just so utterly reliable."

One of his greatest drives came at Michigan, in 1984, when he finished third, only four seconds adrift of Mario Andretti and Tom Sneva despite a faulty pop-off valve. At Pocono that year he lost by 0.27 of a second to Danny Sullivan, but triumphed for the second time at Indy. Journalist Jeff Hutchinson missed that race, but arrived the following day when the traditional victory photographs are taken. "It was raining, so not much was happening, but even so, Rick must have told his story a thousand times since the previous day. But when I asked him if he'd mind telling me about his victory, he just sat down and ran right the way through it all over again." At the same event in 1991 he signed autographs hastily, explaining, "Sorry, guys, I have to meet the press in three minutes". Formula One, where were you?

"Rick is the best guy I've ever seen on an oval", averred Sullivan, and he echoed the thoughts of many. "He's so good I don't know where he seems to get that extra speed. In that respect, he's the yardstick for all of us."

I'd often felt that making the switch from road courses to ovals and back again all through the season must be particularly difficult, bearing in mind that you aren't supposed to try and catch slides on the speedways, but Rick soon punctured that myth.

"I caught one today", he said at Milwaukee in 1990, where he started from pole. He said it quietly, without affectation. "On my quick lap, on the steering graph you can see it. I do it from time to time, but I don't want to do it very much!"

According to the book, if you get into a slide at somewhere like Indianapolis, you don't apply opposite lock, you steer against the slide, to try and spin the car away from the outer wall. Many are the cases in the Methodist Hospital who have tried to catch a high-speed slide and found their rear tyres gripping again just as their car is pointing at the concrete...

"I've corrected them at Indy", Rick continued, "but I don't ever want it to get to that. I might get it to where I release pressure on the wheel. It kinda goes against all your instincts not to try and correct a slide. The reason I say I don't want to get to that is that normally if it's gone into a slide and you have to

Mears and Penske have become as synonymous as Clark and Lotus. His entire USAC/CART career has been conducted in Roger Penske's cars, and it has never crossed his mind to seek pastures new.

Mears and wife Chris (in black overalls) celebrate his fourth Indy 500 win in 1991. That year he had sent his public relations representative Susan Bradshaw a bunch of flowers on one occasion when (erroneously) he thought he had offended her. And the day the official photographs were taken at the Speedway his manners in excusing himself from signing autographs for journalists, so he could keep to his schedule, were at stark variance to the majority of his F1 counterparts.

correct it, it's already on its way. It's too late. There's times when you can catch it quick enough, but the big one is what you're talking about, and that whips back in the other direction. And that's what hurts you.

"I'll get it to the point where it's still sliding and it's one of those slides where you say I'm not going to go any more. When you take that second bite is usually when it gets too much. What you have to do is wait. And the instant you feel that tyre starting to come back, starting to catch, turn the wheel back in the other direction *before* it comes back. If you wait until it hooks and then starts back, and try to stay with it, it's too late, it's already gone in the other direction. You can't unwind it quick enough. It's why, as soon as you feel it slowing down and starting to catch the bite again, you'd better be back this way. That's the hard part, not to go too much. You can go a little."

And all this on a circuit where all you have to do is drive at 230mph and turn left four times a lap...

"Yep, that's it. It's easy! And there are so many stages of that. You can be wide open all the way round the track and you're dead slow, if you haven't got the car set right. There's neutral, push, loose, and all these stages in between. You go from where the tyres are actually scrubbing, and you can go from here to here", he said, indicating parameters. "You can go through all these stages and never slip a tyre, and they'll be a tremendous difference in speed. Just because of the way the car's loaded up, the angle, the wind-up in the wheel versus the tyre. Different things. Right about here, say, is fast; anything other than that it starts binding up a bit, maybe. That's the hard part, learning to feel all of this.

"Most drivers drive off the basis that when the car slides, they catch it. At Indy, and on the speedways, you have to learn to feel what the car's telling you before it does it. You need to be super-sensitive. You gotta learn to work off all those *readings*, not those *feelings*, learn to *read* all of that without the car doing anything. So you can go from here to here in your parameters and go 10 to 20mph difference within these ranges without ever slipping a tyre. It's all just in load and feel, and it's very fine, fine, fine adjustments, be it ride height, attitude, wheel rates...

"You can learn it. I've been fortunate in that I was, you know, born with it, basically. I thought sure, everybody does this, but then over the years, talking to guys, I found out that not everybody does feel it. So I've been fortunate. I'm better at that than stab and steer. I get nervous when I run in stab and steer situations, I don't like driving like that. I like driving smooth. And that's like in the Brabham, the one thing I did learn, you had to pitch and toss a ground-effect car like that far more than we had to. I'd trained myself all along to drive very precisely, very smooth. That's why in the Brabham I got to the point where I wasn't gaining any more, so I had to give her a pitch, jump on it, use a few kerbs. I thought everybody stayed off the kerbs..."

Mears' ability to read cars has made him the yardstick, taken him to 28 career victories up to 1991 in a National Championship that has habitually been much more competitive, in terms of the number of potential winners each season, than Formula One. Along the way his personality has remained utterly unchanged, unaffected by success or status. In Bakersfield, where he lives, the South High School has a Rick Mears Scholarship Award, and Mears himself was on the receiving end at the end of 1989 when the Associated Press sportswriters in America voted him the Driver of the Decade after considering drivers from all motorsport disciplines. They might just as easily have changed Driver for Sportsman. He is proud when he says, "To this day I've never had to put a dime in a car. I don't feel it's right. I feel like anything I do ought to be on my ability, as to what I'm doing."

Finding a man totally at peace with both himself and his profession is about as rare as finding a five-lap qualifying tyre, yet Rick Mears radiates an inner calm, and is in the same control of his ego as he is of his Penske as the Indy wall flashes by, inches away, at 230mph. Despite his protestations to the contrary, there are still times, particularly when it comes to qualifying on the super-speedways, when you suspect that Chris Mears must hold out her husband's trousers in the morning and watch him vault into them. Both legs at once.

12

RON MUSSON, BILL MUNCEY and DEAN CHENOWETH

Racers unlimited

"Anything other than death is a minor injury." – Bill Muncey

The Coast Guard's vessel was big, cruising and minding its own business. Ready to swoop into action on Seattle's Lake Washington if the call came. You never knew with the thunderboats, those 5,000lb Rolls-Royce Merlin-powered missiles that those crazy guys raced bow-to-bow for a living. Most of the crew had seen the big hydroplanes before, and knew what they were capable of when the forces of nature got out of kilter with the wishes of the man at the wheel.

It took the Coast Guard boat 11 seconds to sink, all 15 tons of it. Bill Muncey had scored a direct hit, amidships, and the crew never knew what hit them as the entwined boats disappeared. Even the captain was taken totally by surprise when *Miss Thriftway* slammed into his vessel at 150mph. He left the engine running as he ordered everyone to abandon ship. By the time every man had disembarked, the medics had already radioed ahead the bad news. Muncey made the hospital, but was listed DOA. They were wrong, though. Somehow the 30-year-old racer had given death the slip despite being taken unconscious from the water. His kidneys had been torn loose in the impact (not for the first time) and he had other serious internal damage, but none of it worried him too much. "Anything other than death", he had always maintained, "is a minor injury."

That was Muncey for you, wisecracking all the time, but with the hard edge to his comments of a man who has appreciated first-hand life's little ironies.

That accident occurred at the start of the 1958 Gold Cup in Seattle. If the big hydroplanes are the aquatic equivalent of Indycars, the Gold Cup is the Indianapolis 500. It was typical of his glittering career, of his coolness under pressure. The big unlimiteds don't have brakes. Instead, the driver throttles back and, as more of the hull comes into contact with the water, hydrodynamic drag slows it down. When you're doing 160 and something goes wrong, though, you don't back off in a hurry. Do that, and the stern will drop as the propeller slows down and slips beneath the surface, and more likely than not the tunnel between the two sponsons at the front floods with air as the bows rise. It's the classic recipe for a violent backward somersault – the blowover – as Muncey well knew.

"I didn't have time to be frightened", he said later. "My hands were full trying any which way to miss that frigate!" With a broken rudder he had no chance. As the other boats made the left turn, he washed out of the lead and across the bows of his rivals. Roy Duby just kept *Gale V* off *Miss Thriftway*'s stern as

Muncey speared straight on into the Coast Guard craft and earned his latest spell in hospital. He was well used to the feel of starched sheets.

Even by that stage of his career Muncey was assuming the proportions of the legend he would become. Like Mario Andretti, he was always ready with the instant quip. Reporters loved him, waiting with poised pens as he delivered yet another Munceyism. He had an outward gruffness that cloaked a rare sense of humour and honour, and a relentless streak of competitiveness. "I really can't stand to lose", he would say, "and losing is something I have never been able to come to terms with. OK, I admit it. I'm a poor loser, but I don't see anything wrong with that as long as you stay a good sport." In his career it was thus fortunate that he did a lot less losing than any of his rivals. From 191 races, he took 62 victories.

Hospitals couldn't keep Muncey for long, however regularly he might visit them. Two months after the Gold Cup incident he was back on his feet. Within six he was reunited with the rebuilt *Thriftway*.

When grocery store magnate Willard Rhodes told him the one final prize he sought from racing was the World Speed Record for propeller boats, Bill accepted the challenge despite grave misgivings.

"Anything other than death is a minor injury." The press loved Bill Muncey and his instant quotes, and they loved his sheer pleasure in winning. In the history of Unlimited hydroplane racing, only Commodore Gar Wood in the Twenties and Thirties came anywhere near his charisma.

At the time Donald Campbell was the fastest man on water at 260mph, but the *Bluebird* used the pure thrust of a jet turbine. With no drivetrain his boat literally blew itself across the water. The propeller record had been going nowhere for some years since Jack Regas had come the right way out of his attempt in Hawaii Kai at 195mph, and increments were becoming increasingly smaller as the challenge became harder still. The outright record was no cakewalk, but the propeller record was just as dangerous. If its potential increases were diminishing, the risks were multiplying by a frightening factor. As Dean Chenoweth, one of Muncey's strongest rivals, would later put it, "Running around 200 is like running through the twilight zone."

Thriftway had been designed and built by Ted Jones, 'The Dean' of hydroplane racing, whose *Slo-Mo-Shun* boats had redefined the standards in the early Fifties. Yet over the past two seasons in Jones' boats Muncey had been dogged by the sort of misfortune that makes some men seek less esoteric pastimes. In early 1958 he was piloting the first *Thriftway* in a race on the Ohio River when it literally disintegrated around him. He was rushed to hospital with ruptured kidneys, surface cuts and severe bruising. His stomach had been torn loose, and he had almost bitten right through his tongue. In the rebuilt boat he'd then speared the Coast Guard craft during the 1958 Gold Cup. He could be forgiven for feeling less than enthusiastic about his chances third time out, attacking an increasingly dangerous record.

As the days of the attempt neared, his sense of foreboding grew. His first experience of 190mph in test runs did nothing to allay his fears; 170 in a race was one thing, but 190 was a whole new deal, pushing to the very outer edge of skill and luck. It was Russian Roulette with only one blank in a six-cartridge chamber.

Without fail the *Thriftway* ran into terrifying rudder flutter every time he edged it over 180. It got so bad it was all he could do to keep his grip on the wheel, and Muncey was no wallflower. Keeping his foot down, trying to tough it out, did nothing for his sang-froid. After his recent bad experience with rudder failure, his misgivings were understandable.

A less committed man might simply have walked away, but that wasn't Bill's style. He felt he owed something to Rhodes. It wasn't just that Rhodes had already laid out a lot having the course surveyed and hiring officials; their relationship went back a long way. Bill was an intensely loyal man, prepared to have that loyalty measured up front if necessary. Rhodes had done a lot for him, and provided him with competitive equipment after years of struggle. Muncey had already repaid him by winning, but with him things like that went deep. He would go ahead with the attempt, even if it meant paying the ultimate price.

In 1960 Ron Musson really had no right to race deck-to-deck against Bob Hayward's markedly more powerful Miss Supertest III during the Harmsworth Trophy, but his skill with Nitrogen Too marked him as one of the sport's great competitors. In Muncey's opinion, nobody could handle one of the Unlimiteds the way Musson could.

February 16 dawned cold, a bad sort of day to die. Muncey strode up to Rhodes, kitted out in the life-jacket that he'd designed himself and which had already saved him twice. "Willard", he said, "I'm gonna do this once for you. We either make it, or we don't make it. But I'm *never* going to do this again."

Then he climbed aboard the white-and-red hydroplane, fired up the supercharged V12 Merlin and headed out on to the course. The *Thriftway* crew knew that Lake Washington was marginal, as if they needed any further complications. There wasn't really sufficient room for acceleration, and that meant Bill had to make a left and a right under a bridge before he could get up to real speed. With grim determination he took the *Thriftway* under that bridge at 145, and was edging 185, with full rudder flutter, as he entered the measured mile. He saw 200 as he came out of the traps.

Without a pause he turned and gunned back into the return run required by the international rules. Again, the rudder fluttered like a trapped bird's wings, and again he kept his foot planted to the bulkhead. It was a typical Muncey performance. He could have walked away, but instead he chose to fight – and conquer – the demon that lived out there on the lake.

He averaged 192.001mph through the mile, slower than Regas' 195.329 over the kilo, but a new record nevertheless over the Imperial distance. Rhodes knew when to be satisfied. In 1962 Roy Duby upped the kilometre record to 198 and the mile to a hair over 200, but nobody else has driven a propeller boat faster across such distances to the present day. Duby, a typical product of the unlimited genre, was still riding motorcycles in Florida 30 years later and, aged 81, reportedly drag racing the local kids.

OTHER VOICES

Bruce McCaw – hydroplane aficionado

"My sort of impression knowing Bill, not well, but for a long time, was that the guy had a huge ego and he was sometimes awfully difficult to get along with. And he had one hell of a temper. But he was a phenomenal boat driver. It's very difficult to criticize his abilities because he was as good as they came. And he was uncanny, bursting with personality. Somebody you respect, but don't necessarily want to throw your arms around.

"We had a name for Muncey that applies to a lot of people: A legend in his own mind. And there's a certain amount of that in it. But he was also very similar in some nicer ways to Mario Andretti. They were very similar personalities in some respects in that both virtually epitomized their respective sports.

"The thing that stood out most about Bill was that he just did *not* like not winning."

■　■　■

With his background Muncey was an ardent safety campaigner, a man who'd seen many friends die. In the space of two years in the Sixties alone he saw aces such as Ron Musson, Don Wilson, Rex Manchester, Chuck Thompson and Bill Brow perish, and he didn't care to see something as precious as life wasted.

In Bill's mind Musson was the greatest of his time, a peerless driver capable of extracting the maximum from his equipment without ever overtaxing it. Bill, a hard man on his own machinery, appreciated and admired that.

"I thought Ron was the best there ever was", said Bob Burd, historian of the Unlimited Hydroplane Hall of Fame and Museum in Seattle. "The way he could start races was so impressive. He judged the starting gun to perfection every time, and could cross that line smack on the nose. Nobody could get near him on that. He and Dean Chenoweth, they were the best.

"Ron was just a prince of a guy. He used to be the newspaper boy for one of my uncles. He was only a little guy, so small in fact that my wife Winifred can get into his race suit that we have in the museum. But one hell of a driver."

Musson moved into the tricky unlimiteds in 1959 in the famous *Hawai Kai III*. It was a good ride. There was about him the skill of Jim Clark, that inner confidence that created such a calm exterior when he was driving, and it quickly became appreciated by the hydroplane fraternity.

Before each heat there is a five-minute period in which the drivers mill about, jockeying for position for the flying start, which is signalled when a large clock indicates that the warm-up period has expired. The art is in hitting the start/finish line in the right lane for the first turn, at maximum speed and bang on the dot that signals the start of the sixth minute. Any driver who crosses the line too soon receives a one-lap penalty. Musson was a master at starting, and could calculate exactly the dwindling time while also manoeuvring himself into the most advantageous position. His skill allowed him to pick any of the first turn lanes that he wanted, but usually it was the number one lane, the most prized and therefore the most difficult.

The unlimiteds are more than 30ft long, weigh up to 7,000lb and in those days their Rolls-Royce or Allison aero-engines propelled them up to 170mph – 250 feet per second. Behind them, the propeller threshed up a mountain of water, 100ft long and 60 high... the famous roostertail. It's a glorious sight, unless you happen to get wetted down in the first turn. Drivers have been injured by the cascade of hundreds of gallons of water.

At 170, only the tips of the two sponsons up front and the rudder and half the propeller at the stern support the boats as they ride on a cushion of air, and the first the driver knows of a blowover is when he sees the waterline disappearing from his horizon. It's a balancing act between the forces of nature and the brute power of a machine with sufficient torque to rotate round its own propeller. Donnie Wilson once said, "With an unlimited you have tremendous power at your disposal. The challenge is how much of it to use, and when to use it."

They would bob through the turns as the driver tried to read the changing water conditions. Musson, the little public relations man from Akron who loved racing, could read them like his favourite book. At the Harmsworth Trophy one year he enthralled the spectators with his dramatic battle against Bob Hayward's *Miss Supertest III*, even though his Allison-powered *Nitrogen Too* gave away the better part of 600 horsepower to the Canadian challenger.

He won the Indiana Governor's Cup race at Madison that year, and added the Mapes Trophy at Reno the following season, when he also took the Silver Cup on the Detroit River. He joined lubricant magnate Ole Bardahl's team for the 1961 season, and they never looked back. Muncey narrowly beat him to the 1961 High Point Championship, and in 1962 he was third in a new Ron Jones boat that was set up to slide and opposite-lock around the turns like an Indy roadster, instead of bucking through them like an untamed mustang. In 1963 he added his first Gold Cup. For the following two years he was unbeatable, both on the Detroit River and in the High Point table.

Musson was an easygoing character, enormously popular with his rivals and the fans alike. Nobody had a bad word for him. "He was a good driver, a hellraiser, a wonderful guy", recalled McCaw. "He just loved to have fun. He had a devil-may-care attitude. He and Manchester, of course, that was a very close situation because Ronnie drove for Ole and Rex was married to Ole's daughter Evelyn. He was an incredible guy, always a gentleman. Sure, he took his racing very seriously and he liked to win, but he was philosophical when he didn't."

When Musson and Manchester were both killed on the same weekend, Bardahl was very nearly finished. On the day that became known as Black Sunday, June 19, 1966, as Ford was winning for the first time at Le Mans, Musson died when the revolutionary *Miss Bardahl (4)* disintegrated on the Potomac River during the President's Cup race in Washington DC. The Ron Jones-designed craft placed the driver ahead of the engine, Formula One race car-style, but Muncey for one was dubious of the new concept. They had a lot of trouble with the propeller shaft bearings on the new boat, and crew chief Leo Vanden Berg wasn't sure they should race it, but Musson's old faithful *Miss Bardahl (3)* was out of commission. It was race or spectate. Musson was a racer who didn't give the second option another thought. He would drive the boat. Typically, he wasn't prepared to run for second or third place while they sorted it.

The 38-year-old champion was pushing it hard, vying for the lead on the second lap of the second heat, when she broke up. The crew suspected that

The long drought in Muncey's career ended with the Atlas Van Lines, designed for him by Jim Lucero and nicknamed the 'Blue Blaster'. The combination was unbeatable in the late Seventies, but in Acapulco in 1981 the boat flipped as it raced into the reddening sun, and on the still waters the legend died.

another bearing problem had ripped out the transom, causing the green-and-yellow 32-footer to rear into the air at 170mph before crashing down nose first. Musson died instantly of a broken neck. The nonpareil, with 16 victories and two World Championships from only 47 races, was gone.

Less than three hours later, Manchester, in *Notre Dame*, collided with Donnie Wilson's *Miss Budweiser* in the final heat and both men succumbed. By tragic irony, Manchester was awarded the win posthumously on the basis of points scored in previous heats. "Those weren't recruits we lost today", said Muncey. "They were the best we had."

The grief-stricken Jones went into self-imposed exile for four years. Muncey remained sceptical of cabover boats, as the rear-engined craft were called, but after reviving his career in the early Seventies he was persuaded to make the switch in 1977 with the *Atlas Van Lines* designed by Jim Lucero. If Muncey himself was like Andretti, Lucero was the unlimited's version of race car designer John Barnard, an articulate, farsighted, innovative man. They gelled perfectly, and Muncey and his *Blue Blaster* ran riot. They were second in the High Point series, correcting that in the following two seasons until the opposition began to catch up in 1980. By then Muncey had accrued those 62 career wins, four world titles, seven Nationals, a record eight Gold Cups and the status of a legend. He was indestructible, the perfect ambassador for the unlimited circus. The Munceyisms still flowed thick and fast, and the bad days of the late Sixties and early Seventies were a thing of the past. Even then, though, in that 10-year doldrum period between his last High Points success

Ron Musson was an Unlimited racing Jim Clark, a quiet, small man who could become a tiger in the cockpit yet always remained charming outside it during his reign in Miss Bardahl (3). When Miss Bardahl (4) flipped during the 1966 President's Cup on the Potomac River, he stood unmatched in his dangerous profession.

with *Miss Century 21* in 1962 and his return to the top in 1972 with *Atlas Van Lines (5)*, he had driven a lot of second-rate machinery with his inimitable first-rate talent.

Yet behind the wisecracks, Muncey was troubled by his advancing age, and the sure knowledge that he couldn't go on forever. He won the Evansville Cup race in July, but that was to be his final victory. At the UIM World Championship meeting in Acapulco on October 18 the legend died.

Just before the meeting he'd been interviewed in San Diego, and his interviewer made the error of referring to him as 'The Old Man'. Bill got bitter and the conversation terminated prematurely. "He was an old man still trying to live like the kids," said Burd. "I took him on a tour in Seattle that year to visit handicapped kids – he was always good with that sort of thing – and he was a guest speaker. Well, he came right out and said he would do anything he had to to win. He was a one for psyching out the younger guys, too. He wasn't the cleanest player in the world. He'd get those guys freaked out before they even got on the water, pull tricks on them, get them shellshocked. That time he got killed, why, he knew the boat well enough to know where the redline was..."

At 52, however, he had reached a crisis, unable to see any value in himself other than as Bill Muncey, hydroplane driver. The fans adored him on a Villeneuvesque scale. He *was* unlimited racing and everything it stood for, but still he couldn't see a role for himself outside of that big blue boat. Some say he committed suicide that day in Mexico, that he could see no future for himself. Nobody really buys that sort of emotional stuff, but maybe he had got to the point where he threw too much caution to the wind. He loved the sport with a passion that killed him.

"I can fly this sled", he told Lucero as he went out that afternoon, the rear wing set to fly the *Atlas* lighter than ever before. He was where he always wanted to be – out front, ahead of the pack – when too much wind got underneath her and blew her skywards. "I can make the moves I need to keep out of trouble", he had said, but this time they were not enough. He broke his neck as the boat crashed back on to the once glass-smooth water, and under the reddening sun which some say had blinded him temporarily, a man of immense magnetism succumbed.

When Musson had been killed there had been the inevitable outcry, yet little had been done to change a sport with a dark reputation as a widow maker. When Muncey died, however, it shook the unlimited fraternity to its core, every bit as much as had Clark's death exploded in the world of Formula One motor racing. Muncey was the living legend, the epitome of the sport, and yet he had perished.

It took some years, but the thunderboaters took a long, hard look at themselves, and radical changes were effected by the end of the decade. Traditional methods of construction – wood, screws and aluminium – were discarded in favour first of honeycomb aluminium, epoxy glue and glassfibre and then aerospace carbonfibre composite techniques. Safety capsules with enclosed, reinforced cockpits became *de rigeur*. Just as the car racers had discovered by the end of the Sixties, so the boaters came to appreciate that it was far safer for the man to stay with the machine, rather than to be pitched into the medium. Control was significantly enhanced by safety straps, and the death toll began, at last, to dwindle. It was all way too late to benefit Muncey, but it was the best epitaph to a giant who had loved the sport without reserve, and embraced it until it had *become* his very life before taking it.

His protege Chip Hanauer would take over his mantle and race for the team run by his widow Fran. And he in turn would quit, champion for the fifth time, at the end of 1990, the active driver with the most wins to his credit. Yet ask aspiring unlimited drivers today who their greatest inspiration was, and the chances are that their reply will still be Bill Muncey.

Alas, the changes come too late for Dean Chenoweth, too. He had so nearly escaped when he announced his retirement in late 1974, but *Miss Budweiser*

owner Bernie Little persuaded him back. 'Dynamo Dean' had been tempted by Little's new toy, a Ron Jones-designed monster powered not by the venerable Merlin, but by the more powerful Rolls-Royce Griffon. They had a tough year in 1979 as they sorted the concept, and that autumn it got worse. Anxious to salvage something, Little took a shot at Duby's mile record on Lake Washington.

Chenoweth, relieved to have blown away the 'roostertail anxiety' of his retirement years, had wound the red-white-and-gold craft out to an estimated 220mph when disaster struck. Maybe a weld on the rudder bracket sheared, maybe he hit something in the water. The distinctive roostertail broke into a ragged pattern as *Miss Budweiser* cartwheeled across the calm surface. The 42-year-old Chenoweth was tossed overboard like a rag doll. Just before the run, crew chief Dave Culley had forced him to wear a new flak vest. It saved his life.

Doctors at the Harborview Medical Center were astonished at his physical condition. A pelvic fracture stabilized overnight, about six months faster than normal. He had cardiac bruising and eight broken ribs, but he would be back. Two months after the accident he was back to his usual 10-mile daily run in the rolling hills of Tallahassee. A month later he finally outran Florida State Seminoles training coach George Henshaw, the terror of his football charges. "When I beat George", said Chenoweth, "I knew I was back!"

In 1980 and 1981 he and Little cleaned up in the High Points Championship, adding two more titles to the brace Dean had won back in 1970 and '71. He and Muncey were the cream of the crop, and with the latter's demise Chenoweth stood alone, the yardstick by which all others were judged. He won the World Championship in which Muncey died and was pushing Hanauer for the 1982 honours when the circus pulled up at Pasco, Washington. During qualifying for the first heat *Miss Budweiser* barrel-rolled at more than 180mph. This time

Throughout the opening two years of the Eighties Dean Chenoweth and Miss Budweiser brought worthy competition for Muncey, and upon Bill's death Dean became the yardstick by which other Unlimited racers measured themselves.

Most men would have headed back into retirement after experiencing the sort of 220mph accident that befell Chenoweth in 1979, but the dynamo fought back to fitness in a recovery that stunned doctors. Like Muncey he couldn't keep away from the big boats, and paid the price in 1982 when the Bud flipped backwards at 180mph.

Chenoweth stayed in the cockpit, even when the boat smashed back on to the water, but the first unlimited racer to have survived an accident at over 200 never regained consciousness.

"They were the two best, Musson and Chenoweth", said Burd. "Dean was a carbon copy of Ron in every respect, only the years separated them. They were great guys, gentle, fun, honourable. I'll never figure how Bernie tempted Dean back.

"He should have quit after that accident in Seattle in '79, but he just couldn't keep away. When he was killed he was like Muncey, redlining it. The boat was set up for 180 and he was doing 190."

They were *racers*, all of them, Musson, Muncey and Chenoweth, who competed in one of the most dangerous sports. They were poised on the knife-edge every time they took their sleek racers out on to the water, prepared not to tiptoe, but to run full pelt across their aquatic tightrope. They appreciated the risks only too well, yet still each of them knew only the one way to drive: standing on the gas.

13

ALAIN PROST

Little big man

"I am an open man. And, one thing: I never lie. I ne-ver lie."

They were very sad questions, those posed so often at the end of 1989. Was Alain Prost really all washed-up, even if he had just snatched away his third world title? Was Formula One's one-time yardstick now a psychologically defeated man coming to terms with his fresh status as second-best?

Never before had we really seen such a titanic clash of greats as we did with Prost and Ayrton Senna. In Alberto Ascari's 1952–53 heyday, Juan Manuel Fangio had had an inferior car. When Fangio had better equipment in 1954 and '55, Ascari was the one similarly handicapped. Stirling Moss was either Fangio's team-mate, or had Ascari's problem when he wasn't, and he reached his maturity after the Argentinian's retirement early in 1958. Stirling's accident four years later then prevented full comparison with a flowering Jimmy Clark, who himself would be dead before Jackie Stewart and Jochen Rindt had got themselves into fully competitive cars.

Thus in 1988 we saw for the first time two true superstars, each close to their peak, sharing the McLaren team. It had to be an explosive situation. And it was.

An interesting insight into Prost, often overlooked: in 1987 McLaren was *his* team. Keke Rosberg had discovered that unpalatable fact the previous year when it refused to alter the MP4/2 to accommodate his driving style, which was better suited to oversteer than to the car's inherent strong understeer. Prost, it was inferred, had pulled political strings to ensure the handling trait remained what it was. Ron Dennis gave him the power of veto on the choice of team-mate for '88. Dennis wanted Senna – every team boss wanted the gifted Brazilian – but was prepared not to take him if Prost said "No". And how easy it would have been to do just that! Instead, he was sportsman enough to stand up and be counted, sufficiently at peace with himself to put himself in a position where the comparisons would finally become direct. Above anything else, the little Frenchman with the curly hair and battered nose *is* a sportsman. Where would be the ultimate satisfaction in remaining the best, if one had denied one's leading opponent a chance to compete on equal terms? He knew he was inviting the wolf into the parlour, but he was bold enough to answer the knock on the door and to open that door wide. What he didn't know was just how debilitating the resultant relationship and feud would become for both of them.

How they must privately curse one another! Without the other, each would now have a fantastic record for GP victories, not that Alain's 45 by the end of

144

1990 is exactly shabby as it is...

Prost knew all about Senna's reputation, even played a little joke on him when they first tested the new McLaren MP4/4 in Rio. Not for nothing do his friends in the French press call him by a nickname other than 'The Professor': they call him 'The Terrorist'. Prost was due to run, come in, and hand over to Senna. He pulled into the pits, but remained in the car as a new set of tyres was fitted, just long enough for Senna's patience to break and for him to begin to mutter, "It's not fair..." before slipping the belts and jumping out. It was a subtle bit of one-upmanship that built on the advice he had already given his new partner on getting quick times out of the older, tricky MP4/3.

Prost took the opening race in Rio, just as he had on four previous occasions, including his glorious revenge on his previous employers in 1984 on his first new outing with McLaren after Renault had sacked him at the end of 1983. As the season progressed, however, he became acutely aware of Senna's qualifying speed and the depth of his commitment. At 33, he himself was no longer quite prepared to take such risks, and he wasn't scared to admit it. He'd done all that himself, back in 1984 when Niki Lauda was on the receiving end of a faster team-mate's performances. Memory spans are short in Formula One, though. Some of the French press in particular began to suggest that his best days were behind him. The two factions had never enjoyed a happy relationship, ever since he had left McLaren at the end of his fraught debut year in Formula One, gone to Renault as number two to Rene Arnoux, and comfortably eclipsed his fellow countryman. Prost was the upstart who knew how to win, Arnoux the martyred country boy made good.

"Once, in 1982, I was refuelling my car just after Arnoux had won the French

GP by refusing to obey team orders", said Prost. "The attendant said to me, 'I'm really glad you screwed that bastard Prost, Mr Arnoux'. Typically, Prost saved the man's dignity by refusing to enlighten him, even to the point of substituting cash for the credit card he had been about to proffer. There is compassion in his nature and it can extend even to those who dislike him.

That caring side of his character is illustrated by the trip he made from Cannes to Paris in a Ferrari F40 to pick up the young boy who was suffering from muscular dystrophy. They spent much time together as Alain gently showed him what Ferrari life could be like. "It was one of those moments", he said, "when you suddenly realize that nothing that happens in motor racing is very important."

As he tested early in 1991, rebuilding his battered motivation, he continued in similar vein as the Gulf war moved closer. "I still have the love of driving when I'm in the cockpit with the wheel in my hands", he confirmed. "I have never lost interest in working with the Ferrari team from the technical point of view." But his growing distaste for the way in which sportsmanship in Formula One was declining had its expression as he added, "I lost the taste for this milieu a long time ago, long before Suzuka.

"What is happening in car racing now is meaningless compared to what is happening in other parts of the world. It's a little bit disappointing, however, especially when one does the job as I do, when you see people who take completely ridiculous top-level decisions. A little bit alarming."

He was alluding to some comments made in the recent past by FISA's president, Jean-Marie Balestre, who had mentioned 'people with big mouths', although he himself had been very, very quiet since the bitter disappointments of Suzuka and Adelaide. "I've decided not to say too much, but to concentrate on my job which, however, will not prevent me from opening my big mouth", he declared with some of his old humour. "If I don't say anything, it's not at all to give *him* pleasure, but to give *me* peace. When I have something to say, I'll say it."

That trait was ever the case, and had surfaced already in that dreadful season with McLaren in 1980. It was his rookie year and one in which the team's performance was the catalyst for John Hogan of Marlboro bringing in new management in the shape of Ron Dennis and John Barnard and laying the foundation for the team's subsequent greatness. Prost was consistently faster than his experienced team-mate John Watson, for a variety of reasons, and was acutely aware of how Wattie must have been feeling. He liked John, and when he once came across a little paddock humour at the quiet Ulsterman's expense, he was outraged. To this day he despises the nature of the perpetrator.

In those 1988 races there was little to choose between Prost and Senna as they eked out their 150-litre fuel ration in the final year of the turbocharger. Prost was the more frugal and could run more power as a result, but though he won seven races and scored more points altogether, Senna won eight times and took his first title. That season was the first in a long while, certainly the first since 1985, the year of his first World Championship, when he no longer had direct control or influence over his situation. Like Senna and Mansell, he is an emotional man, and he had trouble dealing with the on and off track pressure exerted by his team-mate.

As in 1984, when he won seven races but ultimately lost the title to team-mate Lauda by the record low margin of a mere half a point, Prost remained gracious in defeat. Ironically, had Monaco not been stopped before half-distance and thus counted for full instead of only half points, and even had he finished behind the fast-closing Senna, the six points he could have taken for second place would have been sufficient to win him that year's title. In 1983 he had seemed set on course for his first, only to see it slip away into Nelson Piquet's eager clutches as Renault failed to respond to BMW's late performance improvements. By then some of the internal acrimony at the Regie had evaporated with Arnoux's switch to Ferrari, but when Renault lost the title for the third year in succession somebody had to carry the can, and that somebody was Prost. He ran all the way with it to McLaren, and never looked back.

In 1985 he made sure of his first Championship in devastating style, dominating even though the competition was stronger than it was to be during Senna's first Championship year, 1988. And, against expectations, he became the first driver since Sir Jack Brabham in 1959 and '60 to win back-to-back titles when, despite the superiority of the Williams-Hondas, he stole the final race in Adelaide after a brilliant recovery from a puncture.

Losing in 1988 was thus something he accepted. Indeed, such is the character of the man that his greatest concern was the disappointment that his son Nicolas would feel upon learning the news.

There was, though, something else, a shred of suspicion. Senna had won the Japanese GP at Suzuka after a brilliant recovery from stalling on the grid, yet Prost couldn't understand then, any more than he can now, how the Brazilian, his economy inferior all year, could have used five *litres* less fuel than him in that race, after such a dramatic charge...

It set the shape of his 1989 season, which began with a brilliant, yet little appreciated drive to second place in Rio, where clutch failure obliged him to soldier through on two sets of tyres to everyone else's three. And then came Imola, and the real break with Senna.

They had exchanged words after Portugal in 1988, when Senna's car had swerved towards him as he tried to overtake down the pit straight, but they appeared to have re-established cordiality when the pre-race agreement not to overtake before the first corner was broken at the Italian race. It was an unworkable agreement, which Senna denied ever existed, but he himself had proposed it in the first place, in front of witnesses. Afterwards Prost was as angry as his friend Gilles Villeneuve had been back in 1982 with his Ferrari partner Didier Pironi, following a similar breakage of a pre-race arrangement. The parallels between the two ran even deeper than they appeared to on the surface.

"I thought it better not to talk, you know. I had to think. What do you do in that kind of situation? You can hit him..." He broke off to laugh. "But no! That might be the right solution. I'm not joking. I mean, that could be best because

In his Renault years it was fashionable to dislike Prost, who was too often seen as the underling of the faceless Regie leviathan. Only later did the basic humour in his personality find a better chance to express itself, and did it become apparent just how talented he had to be to have won nine GPs in the yellow turbocars.

then we could come back friends, maybe, later. Sometimes it's a question between men..."

Back in his karting days he had dealt thus with Francois Goldstein, even though he had had to jump up to hit the six-footer! But it had worked, and to this day they remain firm friends.

"After Imola I called Ron the next day. I said I needed to think about retiring for the year, maybe. Only because I remember the story of Gilles and Didier, because I remember too much. I was close friends with Didier and even more with Gilles just before the end. And I remember very well. Gilles called me the week before he died because he wanted some help about his brother coming into Formula Three with a Martini chassis, and I tried to help him a little bit. He was calling me maybe once or twice a day, and every time he was calling me about Didier, and he was very, very angry. I couldn't believe it. When he had his accident, I was absolutely sure what had happened. It was unbelievable.

"I said to Ron, 'I know this situation and I'm not going to react the same', but then I felt so bad, so demotivated, that I said, 'What do you want me to do? I'll stop to the end of the year and start again next year. It's up to you.'"

His relationship with Ron Dennis, at one time so warm, would become a casualty of the feud, one senses to the lasting regret of both men.

Perhaps it was melodramatic, and perhaps he was now having more off days than before, when consistency had always been his hallmark, but he was well and truly off his game psychologically. The smouldering fire at McLaren was then stoked again when he accused Honda of providing Senna with a better engine in Mexico, of manipulating the management chips to give his team-mate greater power.

He was quite open and straightforward about it. "It is difficult to compare engines, because Honda provides different specifications for different circuits. But I asked them, and looking at the chart I could see there was a difference there. I don't mean it was done on purpose, but I just want to understand. For sure the way I drive is very different to the way Ayrton drives, but in a race like Mexico I don't understand. Honda tried to tell me the difference we could all see in the chart was in my driving style. But I can't accept that, that's why I was upset.

"I had softer tyres and for sure I was a bit faster than him everywhere in the first part. When you are behind a car like that you can *feel* you're quicker on the chassis side, so you know exactly what any difference can be down to...

"On the third lap I was quicker than him in the fast corner – and also because of the tyres, let's be honest – and I was right behind him. I was absolutely sure on the long straight that I would be able to overtake. And there was absolutely no gain for me on the straight!

"Then when I stopped for tyres and was on a fresh set, he came up behind me and just overtook me – poof! I was at least as quick as him in the fast corner, but he just overtook!

"The trouble is, they admit the problem to me and to the team, but not to the press. McLaren understands this, too. I understand that it is difficult for Honda to say your engine is bad; or we gave a better engine to Ayrton. That isn't the case, I never say they do it on purpose, but for sure there is a problem."

The situation reached fever pitch in the middle of the season as he pondered his future. At the time I interviewed him in *Motoring News*, quoting such comments. Nigel Roebuck did the same for *Autosport*. Honda's Osamu Goto then took the trouble at Hockenheim to 'educate' us both. It was, he told us, a simple matter, one that we had not understood. Prost did not know how or when to change gear properly! Mr Goto did not at that time elect to enlighten us as to how Prost had to that point managed to win 38 Grands Prix, nor did he ever do so, since he maintained his silence by the simple expedient of thereafter steadfastly ignoring either of us whenever he encountered us in the paddocks. In private, Honda had hauled Alain over the coals, going through each article

Perhaps the greatest drive of his career came at Suzuka in 1987, when he fought his way back to seventh place in the McLaren MP4/3 after sustaining a puncture on the opening lap. But for that, he would have walked the race.

word by word, line by line. "Did you really say that?" he was asked time and again. It would have been easy to deny it to avoid embarrassment, to lay it off against the press, but that is not Prost's way. "I have been quoted exactly, with complete accuracy", he replied.

By the French GP at Paul Ricard, early in July, he had finally made up his mind to leave McLaren at the end of the year, but even then there was talk of a year's sabbatical prior to a return in 1991 when Senna had retired or left.

By the German GP, as it became clear he was moving ever closer to Ferrari, his relationship with Dennis and McLaren had soured further. It finally broke when Ron watched, in outraged astonishment, as Alain gave the passionate tifosi his trophy after winning the Italian GP at Monza. To Prost, who'd spoken out again in qualifying when Senna proved nearly two seconds faster, it had been nothing more than a spontaneous, if inconsiderate, gesture. To Dennis it was tantamount to treason.

Senna was busy agitating Honda behind the scenes, and in Estoril demanded that Prost should be sacked. As it was, he was obliged to make an official public apology, but remained unconvinced that Honda hadn't been playing power games. To his detractors – a surprising number in view of his character – he was whining because he could no longer hold a candle to Senna, in either qualifying or the races. To those who admired his personality and performances, it was out of character, so much so that it was indeed an indication he felt something beyond his immediate understanding and control was taking place. The truth will probably never be known, but Prost has never been the type to indulge in self-deception. If he thought he was genuinely no longer a match for Senna, he is the type to concede the fact rather than come up with all manner of excuses to disguise it.

The World Championship was finally settled in his favour when Senna collided with Brundle's Brabham in the rain at Adelaide. It brought him much less satisfaction than the previous two, his greatest professed delight being that Senna hadn't won it. It had been his toughest season ever, in which his stock had fallen again in some quarters to the level it held in his unhappy Renault days. He admitted he drew little enjoyment from racing within the acrid McLaren atmosphere, that probably he had stayed a year too long. Certainly, he wore his emotions on his sleeve more than in any other season, but his charged state did not fully explain how so consistent a performer could have had such an up-and-down season, robbed of victory at Hockenheim, and so comprehensively blown-off by Senna at Monza.

Suzuka proved he could still rise to the occasion, and lead even Senna when his motivation was sufficient. And it proved that even he, when pushed hard enough, could dig deep into his reserves to find the ruthlessness that comes so much more easily to his arch-rival. Until the shunt it had been a brilliant performance.

In the late Eighties and early Nineties it became almost *de rigeur* to establish oneself in one camp or the other, in Prost's corner or in Senna's. It was a foolish situation which quite overlooked the brilliance they shared. In fact, the two have many, many similarities besides an ability to extract the absolute maximum from a race car. Both are top athletes, both are committed to success to a degree unfamiliar to 99% of people outside of the crucible of Formula One. And both, when the mood takes them, can be incredibly devious, manipulative and ruthless in pursuing their own ends. Only their methods differ.

So, too, do their driving styles. Prost is super-smooth, in the Moss, Clark, Gurney mould, clipping apexes with uncanny precision, lap after lap. He is deceptively fast. Watch his car flowing around a circuit and it looks slow. If the race driver's art is to slow everything happening to him at 180mph to the rate others would understand at 40, then the Frenchman, 'The Professor', has the ability to slow everything that the car does outwardly, too. He rarely spins, always drives with an economy of movement that is a joy to watch. He turns in under the brakes, and finds grip that others don't. And he is fast. Just as Clark was. The latter point is so easy to overlook. His drives at Spa in 1986 after initial contact with Berger, and Suzuka in '87 after a puncture, were glowing examples of his ability to drive very, very quickly and to fight back. And Mexico in 1990 showed to perfection the inner calm and iron self-control that make him such a deadly rival. It would have been so easy to charge too hard early on after his poor qualifying runs, but he bided his time, avoided overtaxing his equipment, and was there when it mattered at the finish. The superfast 1984 qualifying laps may be few and far between now, but that was another superb performance.

Senna, by contrast, though smooth, always looks like a man in a hurry. He often sounds it, too, using that unique throttle-blipping cornering style.

So many times Suzuka has been a dramatic venue for the Frenchman. In 1989 the controversial incident with McLaren-Honda team-mate Ayrton Senna all but settled for him his third World Championship, and also set the scene for the Brazilian's extraordinary retaliation a year later...

Aggression oozes from every pore, and his ruthless precision and commitment going for gaps is breathtaking. To watch him in action at close quarters, such as at Monaco, is truly awesome. The only other driver I have ever watched who comes close in that respect (and very close at that) is Michael Andretti. Traffic has always been Senna's *metier* and Prost's Achilles' Heel, the Brazilian ripping through it on the principle that it is better to be ahead of the accident than to get caught up in it. Prost is more circumspect, and there perhaps he betrays the length of time he has been in Formula One.

Damp or greasy tracks are also Senna's meat and drink, and few will ever forget his sheer mastery of the conditions at Suzuka in 1988, when he stalled at the start and then slashed through the field to catch and pass the more cautious Prost. There, while the Frenchman could post the odd really quick lap during the chase, Senna could do them regularly.

Prost, however, rarely makes mistakes. Certainly not mistakes of the magnitude of those that have befallen Senna over the years: hitting the barrier at Monaco in 1988, tripping over Schlesser at Monza later that year, clashing with Mansell at Estoril in 1989. The biggest mistakes Prost has made over the past years of his rivalry with Senna have been to underestimate his rival continually, and to leave him even the tiniest gaps. It happened at Montreal in 1988, again at Silverstone in 1989. Each time, he said, he was obliged to give way to prevent an accident.

On two other occasions, of course, he also gave Senna tiny gaps, and each time the consequences were far-reaching. Each time the incidents happened at Suzuka...

Perhaps if he had tried to keep going after their 1989 shunt at the chicane everything might have been different. For 46 laps of that race Prost was pure magic, blasting away from a surprised Senna after altering his rear wing setting on the grid to give himself greater straightline speed. Senna's only chance was at the chicane, and I still believe the only way his move on Prost would have worked would have been to lean on the Frenchman's McLaren going into the absurdly tight right-left flick. At the speed he approached, there would have been no way to get round the corner cleanly, without contact. Such tactics have always been anathema to Prost. The last contact mistake he had made had been with Nelson Piquet at Zandvoort back in 1983, where he had been quick both to admit guilt (with some mitigating circumstances) and to apologize to the Brazilian.

He has never been one to harbour grudges in the way that Senna does. Four times after the heat of Suzuka had subsided in '89, he tried to shake hands, to bury the hatchet. Each time he was rebuffed. "Words can be very nice and if put together can be very beautiful", Senna would say. "But actions say more. Action is real. Words can be all play." He would make much of the manner in which Prost spoke his mind at McLaren, and again at Ferrari in 1990.

"Look", said Ayrton. "In the past three years he has criticized me, he has criticized the management at McLaren, he has criticized Honda, he has criticized me again. Then he goes to Ferrari, and he criticizes Ferrari, he criticizes its management, his team-mate again, Goodyear... I tell you, it makes me laugh." Put that way, it looked like a long list of complaints, until you looked at how many times Senna and Mansell had also complained over the years. Then it looked normal fare from a Formula One driver. And like their complaints, much of his had justification.

They finally shook hands at Monza in 1990, in what looked like a genuine, spontaneous decision. Both spoke of sportsmanship, of how their renewed rivalry in different marques was good for the sport. Both men appeared to mean what they said.

Then Suzuka blew it all apart again, left Senna with a tainted World Championship, much as he believed Prost's 1989 title had been tainted. Again, Prost had left the tiniest of gaps, certainly not enough to contain another

Formula One car at the moment when it mattered. Senna, despite his own protestations, hit the Ferrari's rear wing hard enough in the 150mph corner to snap it clean off. Afterwards he still maintained he had struck the side of the red car. Tellingly, mere fractions of a second after the impact, Prost already had the Ferrari on opposite-lock to counteract the resulting slide.

The incident finished any vestige of relationship. "What he did today was disgusting", said Alain. "He did it deliberately. I am sick of him trying to represent himself to the world as something he is not. He is a man without value.

"It is important that all rules are accepted. Any weakness, and it is finished." He gave a little boy smile as he spoke the words, as if he was almost apologizing that there had been controversy yet again. In the circumstances, it is difficult to see what else he could have done at Suzuka to avoid an incident that appeared to be a pure product of his rival's pique at having to start from the side of the grid he did not prefer.

Prost had spoken of retirement for the first time after Imola in 1989, but it would not be the last. He finally elected to go to Ferrari for 1990, and did so with a fearsome commitment. "You have not seen the real Alain Prost this year", he said at the end of 1989. "This is like 1982. A shit year. If I'm driving like this at the end of 1990, then you can call me wanker."

He mentioned quitting again after the 1990 Portuguese GP, in which he was convinced that Mansell had deliberately steered at him – his own team-mate – at the start to discourage him from trying to lead. Prost desperately needed to win that race to keep his Championship hopes alive. Mansell, too, had needed a win to keep his own currency high during negotiations with Williams and Camel for 1991. Afterwards, third-placed Prost was sickened by the effusiveness Senna and Mansell showed to one another, as if they were deliberately trying to rub his nose in it.

He mentioned it a third time after Suzuka, went through much of December that year in a state of flux. Frankly, it became tedious. And sad in a way, to see one of the world's two best Formula One drivers agonizing so publicly. There was, however, little new in the situation. He had been through it before with McLaren and Renault in the early Eighties, and the cynics saw in it a subtle – oh, so subtle – method of putting pressure on Ferrari to do things his way. Oh yes, 'The Terrorist' can be a very apt sobriquet...

OTHER VOICES

Steve Nichols – Ferrari engineer

"It's interesting that when Alain was at McLaren I never worked directly with him at races, just in testing, as engineers used to alternate duties. That interchangeability of engineers was a pretty good system.

"It was a little bit odd at Ferrari because they all assumed that I was Alain's man. I'm sure Nigel never trusted me because of that. Of course, I'd had opportunities at tests and races to see that Alain was very good. When he returned to the McLaren team in 1984 he was still a little inexperienced, but he was very quick and dedicated and would just push, push, push, like Senna does now. Niki Lauda had to put himself up to another level, to elevate his game.

"Niki used his experience and wits, where Alain was very quick and less experienced. He was not only quick, but he learned pretty quick, too. He was taking it all in from the Old Master. He learned a lot about race and test strategy, finding out what's important and what isn't. He gained quite a lot in those years.

"Now it's come full-circle, he's the Old Master, and there are other things in his life now. Inevitably he's not so hungry. But it impresses me to what degree

152

In his first year with Ferrari Prost staggered his critics with five splendid victories for the Prancing Horse, including a hat-trick in the middle of the season which launched his challenge to Senna for a fourth crown.

he can motivate. He's pretty damn strong, pushing, working hard. It's not so much on the circuits, but in qualifying at Monaco, qualifying and the race in Spain, and qualifying in Suzuka he was impressive. But it's the way he pushes off the circuit, too, days and days and hours and hours of testing, pushing all the development. That's 90% of winning races, and 99% of winning the Championship. Just being quick may be only 1% because out there they're all quick.

"His most impressive feature is how sensitive he is to all that a car does. He can tell us, too. Some of them can't tell you, they just say it's good. You tend to think, 'OK, so we'll all go home then!'. Give the same damn car to Alain and he'll come up with a list. Then he'll say, 'Don't get me wrong, it's very good', and you think, 'Thank God'. Then he'll say, 'It's just that it can be improved'. All this much more information comes from him than from others.

"We were both amazed at Ferrari how bad some basic things were, which reflected the position it was in with an all-new car. There were loads of initial problems on reliability. That's not a criticism of Ferrari, the drivers or John Barnard, just a statement of how development had progressed. We developed the package, really fine-tuned the chassis, ordered up finer springs and bars. That sort of thing.

"Some drivers don't fine-tune, they just carry the car on their backs and change their style. Alain isn't very good at that, only because normally he doesn't see the point. He much prefers to really work with the car so it does as much of the work as possible."

■ ■ ■

From the very first day at Fiorano he impressed the team, and his use of the electro-hydraulic transmission sent engineer Pierguido Castelli into raptures. Of course, there was much of the honeymoon period about those early days, and like Mansell the previous year, Prost consummated his new marriage with an

153

early win in Brazil. It would be the first of five, a score beyond any expectation, but the successes brought their own pressures.

Prost's arrival within the team was like Niki Lauda's had been at the end of 1973. He had very clear ideas concerning what he wanted and what standards he expected, and he knew all too well, as did Nichols, just what was required to beat McLaren and Honda. He retaught the team the mentality of winning. He embarked on a stringent programme of testing and, just like Lauda, who had clashed with team manager Daniele Audetto, so he clashed with Cesare Fiorio. There was also friction with Mansell, who became jealous of the manner in which he had integrated, of his ability to speak Italian, of the strength of the relationship he had forged with the engineers. None of that was Prost's fault, but rather a product of his brand of total commitment. It seemed, however, that Prost and controversy were now inextricably linked. But compared to most of his rivals, his overall style was more that of a ballet dancer compared to a punk rocker.

He is an essentially straightforward individual, willing to commit himself to the attainment of goals, but also possessed of a strong perspective on life. "It is a game, to be played to the full, but also to be enjoyed", he said, "and to be enjoyed with honour." The competitive instinct is as deeply rooted in the shaggy-haired Frenchman with the Mr Punch nose as it is in any race driver worth his salt, but above anything, Prost likes to win cleanly, fairly, to see sportsmanship uppermost in any contest.

By the start of 1988, long before McLaren's orgy of winning began, he had already done enough, with 28 GP victories to his credit, to win a permanent place in the list of all-time greats. He had won two World Championships, missed out narrowly on two more, and was recognized as Top Dog. At that time, in McLaren's family atmosphere, he enjoyed his racing, excelled at it, was ever at the centre of the action in any event in which he participated. The feud with Senna upset his equilibrium, made him even consider retirement to set up his own team for 1990 with Renault engines and John Barnard as design chief.

Was he then, by 1990, the past master gamely hanging on too long, who should perhaps have hung up his helmet after his 1988 title defeat, and gone to rest on the laurels of a glittering career? The results firmly refuted such questions. In 1990 Alain Prost drove with all his old fire and motivation. Never more was his mastery of car set-up so starkly underlined, either. Ferrari had the best handling chassis of the year, and Prost's almost always had a better set-up than Mansell's. Interestingly, when he had to take over the Frenchman's spare car after the startline shunts at Spa, Mansell eventually retired it, complaining that it was dangerously plagued by terminal oversteer. Rosberg had been unable to come to terms with the McLaren's understeer, Mansell with the Ferrari's oversteer. Prost had set up both, could adapt his smooth style to any exigency.

OTHER VOICES

Keke Rosberg

"Alain was a completely different kind of driver to, say, Gilles. More the Niki Lauda type. But I think Alain is quicker than Niki. In those years when I knew Niki I don't think he was, if you take the whole driver, that brilliantly quick. He was brilliant using his strong assets and trying to make his weaknesses strong.

"If you look at his physical condition he could never be a fighter, anyway, whatever he was doing with his guru. At the end of the day the strength was missing, but with his driving style and mentality it was never a problem for him. Don't misunderstand me. Lauda never suffered from his physical condition, but he could never do what Mansell is doing, or what I was doing.

"Nelson, Nigel, Alain, they're all in the same mould, but Alain is also brilliantly quick and his level of motivation is very high over all the years.

"He's very clever. Like Niki, clever enough to engineer himself into the right situation to win. His head rules his heart. Gilles and I were maybe too much the other way."

■　■　■

The turn of the decade of Formula One did not lack for controversy or acrimony, and more often than not, Prost was at its epicentre. He hated every moment of it. Yet though a victim of his own emotions, in his love life as well as in racing, he remained his own man. Refusing to race in the rain at either Silverstone in 1988 or Adelaide the following year were crushingly disappointing acts from a man so revered, yet one had to appreciate his feelings and the honest would also admire his belief in his own principles. Neither decision can have been easy to take, and it took a special kind of courage to stand by them. "What is the point to drive when you cannot see?", he asked. "When it is slippery, OK. But when you cannot see? It is just a waste of talent." He had not forgotten Didier Pironi's accident at Hockenheim in 1982, when the Ferrari driver had crashed over the back of his Renault in pouring rain, simply because Didier had not been able to see it in the gloom...

No matter what his personal and professional problems are off the track, I have never seen them reflected in his driving. In so many ways he is a more worldly, naughtier version of Jim Clark, and he reflects the Scot's nature as he stands today one of the few Formula One topliners who still holds to the old credo of giving his rivals racing room. They still do it in CART, but in Europe such courtesy and respect between rivals is becoming increasingly rare.

Clark, however, had Colin Chapman to produce him race-winning cars, to make sure the team was competitive. In an increasingly technical world, Prost has that other dimension, his ability to force the pace of development in a team. He is like an iceberg; it's what you don't see that matters, that ability to do so much more, behind the scenes, than just winning more races than anyone else.

Too often for some, he is a man who is unable to remain silent when troubled, and it is sad that his career has latterly come to wear that taint of controversy. He cares deeply for sport and for *the* sport. History will remember him as the most complete driver of his era, perhaps of any era, a true contender for ultimate honours in the list of all-time greats.

14

TOM PRYCE

Racing is also this

"I personally believe that those three – Roger Williamson, Tony Brise and Tom Pryce – were far more committed racers than James Hunt." – Trevor Foster

There was much of Jim Clark about Thomas Maldwyn Pryce's character, and perhaps that was why I identified so instantly with him. He was quiet, humble, utterly devoid of any side or pretention. I remember watching him at the International Trophy race meeting at Silverstone in 1972, standing by his Royale, deep in thought. Just as I was about to walk over his attention was called elsewhere. It would probably have been a toss-up which of us would then have been more shy on first meeting.

The record books reveal only one victory for him in a Formula One race – the 1975 Race of Champions at his beloved Brands Hatch – but oh, could Tom Pryce ever drive! In the Formula Three race supporting the 1972 Race of Champions he had simply pulverized the Hunts and Williamsons to take a tremendous victory. He won by 15 seconds, and his rivals were so incensed they protested that his Royale RP11 must be under weight. It wasn't.

That day at Brands Hatch in 1975, the same raw ability had simply been geared up another notch as he took pole position for the Race of Champions and then savagely cut the lead he had allowed Jody Scheckter to establish after making a poor start. He had that sinister black UOP Shadow slithering beautifully round the greasy circuit as he ate up the Tyrrell's lead. Just as he was preparing to pounce, the South African's engine scattered, and Tom romped home to victory and a standing ovation. He set fastest lap, too, and matched it again in a race in which he had trounced luminaries such as Ronnie Peterson, Emerson Fittipaldi and John Watson.

Brands Hatch was *his* circuit. He lodged just down the road at West Kingsdown when his childhood love of cars and motor racing had taken him to England to compete in the racing driver's school Motor Racing Stables' Formula Ford races that counted towards the *Daily Express* Crusader series. The prize was a new Lola T200, the deciding race the support to the 1970 International Trophy race at Silverstone. Tom walked it. With the Lola went fuel, oil and tyres, and he moved permanently to the south to work as a mechanic on the MRS cars.

The short-wheelbase T200 wasn't the easiest car to drive, as Tom found when he shunted it heavily coming out of Clearways in his first race with it. "There was this pile of junk sitting on top of the bank, and I just didn't have a clue what to do with it. I didn't know a thing about the business, where to get it fixed, or

who to approach." It sat in a Brands lock-up for days as he wondered what to do, but a trip to Arch Motors and £50 later he was back in the right direction. The incident was typical of the man who didn't open a bank account for years after moving from an agricultural engineering background in Ruthin, and who usually spoke only Welsh to his highly supportive parents.

The Lola taught him the car control he later displayed for Bob King's Royale company in SuperVee and the short-lived F100 sportscar series in 1971. It was a poor formula, but a good way of getting experience at someone else's expense. In the Royale RP11 in 1972 he was also running away with the Oulton Park Good Friday Formula Three race until he had an unaccountable spin, and at Monaco he broke a leg when, having stopped at Casino Square with engine trouble, he was run into by Peter Lamplough. "I just couldn't believe it. I just froze on the spot", he admitted. Nevertheless, five weeks later he was back on pole at Brands Hatch and the momentum continued. By 1973 a menu of Formula Three, Formula Atlantic and Formula Two won him the top Grovewood Award for aspiring drivers, and Formula Two drives with Bob Harper for 1974.

In 1973 he had been invited to test one of Ron Dennis' Formula Two Motuls and had got a drive in one courtesy of property developer Chris Meek. Characteristically, Pryce was modest about his selection. "He had drawn up a list of names and I seemed to be the first one who was home when he rang!" At Norisring he had led until brake failure dropped him behind Tim Schenken. By chance, he then became involved in the unusual Token Formula One project when Meek put up the money for a Cosworth DFV for a car which had been created by Rondel's Motul designer, Ray Jessop, and Rondel backer Tony Vlassopulo made up the rest of the budget.

They raced the car in Silverstone's International Trophy race, four years after he had won his Crusader Lola, and then he made his Grand Prix debut at Nivelles in the Belgian GP, where he qualified an excellent 20th, but retired after Jody Scheckter struck the car as he limped it to the pits with engine trouble. Then came Monaco and the turning point. The organizers refused to allow the Token to start, and instead Vlassopoulo offered him one of his Ippokampos Marches in the Formula Three race. "I wondered if it was the right thing", Tom admitted, but he thought of the potential Token sponsors who would be present and went ahead. He won the race going away, dominating in a style rarely seen in the highly competitive formula. "When I'd won, all I thought was that we had some money to go towards the Token. I never dreamt there would be so much fuss."

Suddenly, everyone wanted Tom Pryce's signature on a Formula One contract. His press-on style had been evident for a long time, and frequently drew comparisons with that of Rindt and Peterson, so perhaps it was fitting that it was Shadow team manager Alan Rees, who knew both stars well, who won the day on behalf of the team's owner, Don Nichols.

"Tom was my choice when Brian Redman quit after Monaco. I was very keen on him. I thought what he did at Monaco at that race was almost unique because he wasn't in Formula Three any more. It is a terribly difficult race to win, for a number of reasons, and he came back on a one-off deal and won it in a very impressive way. That was one of the most impressive things I remember about any driver. It's very difficult just to win it, let alone do what he did and come out of a different formula. We needed a driver then, and he was the obvious guy."

First time out in a Shadow DN3 at Zandvoort he qualified 11th, but collided with Hunt at Tarzan just after the start. Next time out at Dijon he was sensational.

"Suddenly Tom went out on the normal Goodyears we were getting at Shadow in those days", recalled former Shadow mechanic, now Jordan Grand Prix team manager, Trevor Foster, "and he was *very* quick. He qualified third, right behind Lauda and Peterson and ahead of Regazzoni, and people just couldn't believe it. The garages at Dijon are literally the same now as they were then, and he just came in and sat quietly in the corner. He had this plain white

As the media waxed lyrical about the Hunts and Williamsons of F3, Pryce burst into the limelight with a dramatic victory for Royale in the 1972 Race of Champions supporting event.

racing suit, the one he'd always had, with just 'Tom Pryce' written on it and his blood group, and that was it. He just couldn't understand what all the fuss was about, that's the thing. It didn't overawe him at all. Everyone wanted to interview him, wanting this and wanting that, and he said, 'All I'm doing is just driving a Formula One car'."

He scored his first World Championship point at the Nurburging, and blended unobtrusively into the milieu of Formula One. Alan Henry, journalist and close friend: "He and Nella were very quiet. You've got to remember she was a child almost. She married him at 19 and was a widow at 22. Talk about growing up in one compressed space of three years. They were very private people. They were both good company with a good sense of humour, but they kept themselves away from the main company at the races. Very much the way that Martin Donnelly and his fiancee did in 1990... I remember them sitting there at Monza, dining alone. That would have been Tom and Nella. Nella didn't like motor racing, she was scared of it." Like Clark, Tom was utterly unassuming out of the cockpit, but a tiger within it. Funnily enough, he ate his finger ends as well.

OTHER VOICES

Trevor Foster – former Shadow mechanic

"When he won the Race of Champions at Brands he drove just brilliantly in the slippery conditions, just got totally in control. He used to slide the car around a lot, but you never felt he was out of control. Some guys you watch and you think, 'He's throwing it around, which corner is he going off on, how long can he hang on to it?'. But with Tom you always felt that he *could* hold on to it.

"He was very, very good, totally natural. He wasn't particularly smooth, but he always looked in control. Very aggressive with the car. Not super-technical, but he would drive whatever. He wouldn't drive until he'd blown the engine or destroyed the car, but if he had a small problem he'd still carry on. He did a Formula Two race at Rouen for Team Harper, where he was running second, and round the hairpin at Nouveau Monde it kept jumping out of first. He said, 'It was great fun because I had to give it full boot to get the back out to get round, putting it on full opposite-lock while holding it in gear with the other hand'. He was very much like that, like Roger Williamson in many ways. They just wanted to drive. Tom would gladly have driven both Formula Two and Formula One. When he had the opportunity to drive a Team Harper Chevron he said, 'Yeah, course I will, if I can physically be there. I'll drive it'. He wasn't particularly worried that he didn't have a BMW engine, or he didn't have this and he didn't have that, you know? For him the pleasure was driving or racing. It was great. He used to come up to the workshop, just call in, walk round, talk to all the fabricators, everybody. They thought the world of him. That's the way he was.

"He could never quite believe how good he was. The thing with him was he was a superb natural talent, but in a much quieter way than Roger, less cocky. Tom was almost sort of afraid to ask for things.

"I remember Reesie going berserk with him one day when he'd done three or four Grands Prix and said, 'Ray Jessop has asked me can I test his Formula Three car tomorrow at Goodwood?', and Reesie was hanging off the wall! That was typical Tom. 'No problem, I'll just check it out with Alan...'

"On one occasion he came into the transporter and said to Reesie, 'Look what I've got for myself', and he'd got a Heuer watch. He'd got one for Nella, too. And Reesie said, 'Well, what did you get for that, then?', and Tom said, 'Just the two watches'. Reesie went mad at him. Tom thought he'd got a blinding deal because just for a small patch on his overalls he'd got these two watches. Reesie said, 'You should have had at least this much money', and really revved into him.

"He did a deal to drive a GM Opel Commodore once, and as part of the deal he got the loan of it for a year, and he thought that was mega because he got the car as well!

"A lot of guys you get to meet, and they do change as they go up the ladder, but I'll tell you what, Tom was definitely one that you could have said would never, ever have changed. Normally the thing about racing drivers is this firm belief that a lot of them seem to have that to get on you have to be selfish, because that's some of the reason why the good guys are quick. But Tom was never, ever, selfish, and if he walked into the hotel bar and you were there, he'd still always buy you a drink. Always. He'd just walk straight up, even if he'd come back late from a meal and was going to the lift. He'd divert, just have five minutes, and say, 'Right, who's having a drink?'. Then he'd buy a round and then he'd say, 'Right lads, I'm off, I'll see you tomorrow morning'. Always, without fail.

"He'd never slag anybody off. I remember at Kyalami, when we were running reasonably well there in 1975. He was running well in the points and he picked up a puncture. He came into the pits and we put a new rear on and off he went. He said, 'Well, I think I just ran up a kerb once too often'. He never got uptight, he wasn't ranting or raving.

"I think in '75 he was still on a very sharp learning curve and things were still catching him out. When he fell off at Silverstone after taking the pole, he just came back disappointed, but not depressed. Disappointed was the only way you could say it; he never used to get into massive depressions. He'd just say, 'Sorry, that's down to me, I just turned in too early, or got too sideways, or whatever'."

■ ■ ■

At the beginning of that year he'd been pushed around rather when Shadow tried to swap him for Ronnie Peterson, who was at that time struggling desperately with the uncompetitive Lotus 72. There was actually a Shadow DN5 in Interlagos with Ronnie's name on the side, and there was poor Tom somewhat bemused in the middle of it all. Later he would become the team's darling, but then he was the new boy, Peterson had the experience that the team sorely needed, and there was little question of Jean-Pierre Jarier going since he'd taken pole position with the new DN5 in the opening race in Argentina and then went on to dominate in Brazil. To get Ronnie, Pryce had to go, no matter how promising he was.

Tom himself certainly didn't want to leave. Everyone within the team was convinced he'd have a better long-term future at Lotus, and Colin Chapman was quite keen, but Tom just said, "I don't really want to go. I like everybody here".

"He was always happy to stay", admitted Rees. "He had a strong sense of loyalty. Too strong. Tom was going to get a good deal, anyway, because Chapman was pretty interested in him. It seemed to suit both sides. It would have suited Tom, too, although perhaps he wouldn't have appreciated it at the time. He would have gone to a better team, not at the time, maybe, but overall he'd have done well out of it.

"The deal was done, but John Logan, President of UOP, Shadow's sponsors, didn't want to do it right at the last minute. He didn't like the whole aspect of it, and obviously, when you do these deals, you negotiate it all out and then you tell the people what you're doing, and that's why it all happened – or didn't happen! – at the last minute. He didn't like what had been done."

Henry believes it would have been worse for Tom to have gone to Lotus at that time. "If he'd turned up at Lotus when there was a 78 or a 79 he'd have been Chapman's darling. But if he'd gone there when they had their backs to the wall, he'd have been broken by Chapman and would have ended up like Bob

Typically Tom. At Zandvoort during 1975 he had the Shadow DN5 well cranked up, although he was later to smooth out his style after repeated admonishing from team manager Alan Rees!

Evans. If Evans had come along a year later it might have been all so different for him."

The matter blew over and Tom settled back down. At Monaco he qualified on the front row alongside Lauda and ran third behind Niki and Ronnie until crashing, at Zolder he was sixth, and at Ricard he tried a new, smoother style forced upon him by Rees. It hurt, but it worked. "I can see the sense in it, but it all seems so slow in comparison!", he complained. "Besides, I *like* throwing the car around. I *like* oversteer."

His best performance came at Silverstone, where he took the pole and led the British GP on laps 19 and 20 before he got caught out by a rain shower at Becketts. "The previous lap I'd made a mental note that it was getting damp", he confessed. "It was my own fault." He had been under intense pressure from Pace, Scheckter, Lauda, Fittipaldi, Hunt and Regazzoni at the time.

At the Nurburgring he was set for second place to Reutemann when a loose fuel filler cap resulted in him sitting in a bath of petrol, and as the pain obliged him to ease his pace, Laffite and Lauda passed him. In Austria he drove beautifully in the rain to work through the field into third place by the finish.

OTHER VOICES

Alan Henry – journalist and friend

"At Anderstorp, in Sweden, there's a fast banked corner leading into a tight left before the pits, and he'd been belting round in practice in the DN5. The entrance to the pit lane came off just beyond the apex of this right-hander and he got himself out on a wide line because he was either pushed out by someone or going round the outside of someone. He suddenly realized the only realistic

161

place to go was the pit lane. He was so embarrassed that he came in and said, 'Two notches off the rear wing', and went steaming straight out again. They subsequently wondered what the hell it was all about. He told me later he was too shy just to come in and drive straight through and say that he'd screwed up!

"He was immensely serious about motor racing. It's very difficult when a bloke is a good friend actually to get a measure of just how committed he is to it. He was a very quiet person, and that was a by-product of his shyness and the fact that he really did come from a country boy background. He talked to his father in Welsh, they used to converse in it. I remember going to his house and being absolutely astonished that they were on the phone just jabbering away in Welsh.

"I think that he had a gentleness about him that reflected in the way he drove a racing car. I always thought that he had the star quality, to a lesser extent, that radiated off a driver like Andretti. I'm not saying he was an Andretti, but there was an element of him being a somebody when you met him. You thought, 'This bloke's a bit special'. Perhaps if he'd been around 10 years later he wouldn't have been pushy enough to get as far as he got in the Seventies. I think his only disadvantage was that he wasn't assertive enough.

"Reesie understood Pryce. I always felt Reesie understood Tom in a way that Jack Oliver didn't, in a way that Don Nichols didn't. I think Reesie was always clever with racing drivers in that respect.

"Brise and Williamson were more abrasive because they were more worldly. If anything, there was a tameness to Tom's personal character which might have affected him in the end. But he was a very, very nice person. When you got to know him you could talk about anything for a long time, just sort of meander off on conversations about everything and anything."

■ ■ ■

UOP pulled out at the end of 1975, leaving Shadow with no real money and thus precious little development. The cars suffered and a change of Goodyear tyre construction and wing regulations mid-way through the year also hurt the team as it was unable to adjust the cars to compensate. Jarier's interest and application waned, but not Tom's. The team was struggling, but more often than not he outqualified his team-mate and outraced him. He was running second in the opener at Interlagos before fading brakes and worn tyres dropped him a place to Patrick Depailler, and his fourth place was the highlight of the British GP after a brilliant battle with Gunnar Nilsson's Lotus 77. The new DN8 arrived at last for Zandvoort. A year before it would have gone to Jarier, but now Tom was recognized as the team leader. He qualified it third and finished fourth. His brilliance was obscured by the murk in the season's finale at Fuji, where Niki Lauda's withdrawal and James Hunt's success in the World Championship overshadowed everything else. There he was closing on leader Hunt in the rain when rubber from his front tyres clogged the side radiator ducts and overheated the engine. It was another lost opportunity after a terrific drive through the field that again revealed his true flair.

OTHER VOICES

Alan Rees – former Shadow team manager

"Jochen Rindt was a very intelligent driver, and so was Jackie Stewart, but I don't think Tom was as intelligent. He had the same sort of car control as Jochen, but he wasn't as worldly.

"Tom would have got to the top, though, somewhere around where Nigel Mansell is, I would think. You need to be able to work it all out, and I don't think either Tom or Ronnie could have done that. Nigel's never won the World Championship, but he's a hell of a quick driver... Tom would have been the quickest driver of his day.

"Yes, he was unworldly in some of his deals. Pretty naive. It would have changed to a certain extent, probably to a large extent. That wouldn't have been a problem that would have held him back, I wouldn't have thought.

"The wet was an extension of his car control. In those days the guys with really good car control were that much better in the wet. He was a calm guy, and it took a lot to irritate him. In fact, I can't ever remember him being upset. Certainly he could get excited, but I don't remember him losing his temper, ever.

"He was tremendously popular with the mechanics. He was one of them, with his farming background, working on tractors and all that. Perhaps he was more popular than anyone I've known. It wasn't just through his background, but also because of the way he'd be with them, and would handle them. His relationship with the mechanics and with people in the team was absolutely excellent. Jean-Pierre (Jarier) was a bit arrogant, but a fantastic driver. The pair of them were well matched, but he just didn't have Tom's determination. He was nowhere near as close to the team as Tom was, and Tom was easier on his car.

"I remember him best for his tremendous car control and because he was such a really nice guy. Too nice, really. There were hints that he didn't really know why he was good. but we never actually had a discussion about it. I think he was probably a bit surprised that he could do as well as he did. Perhaps that's the best way of putting it."

■ ■ ■

When it rained at Kyalami for the first practice session for the 1977 South African GP, Pryce and the Shadow were in a class of their own, just as he so often was when the weather intervened to redress the imbalance in machinery.

The new season started with similar promise in 1977. At Interlagos he was again on schedule for second place, this time to Lauda, when the DN8 lost its oil pressure a few laps from the end. John Surtees got on very well with Tom, and there had been a chance he might have driven for the former World Champion's team that year. Shadow had owed him money from his 1976 contract, but when it secured further support from the Villiger tobacco products company and Italian financier Ambrosio, that was all settled. In 1974 he'd earned £6,500 for the balance of the season. That had risen to £10,000 for 1975 and £30,000 for 1976. Fresh terms had been agreed for 1977 as he led the team. Perhaps, at last, things were looking up. Certainly, when the teams moved to South Africa for testing prior to the Grand Prix, he was able to carry out some much needed

running to sort the DN8. It was the first serious mileage since its introduction, and now there were several modifications to try.

It rained during practice on Wednesday morning and was wetter still in the afternoon session. Tom went out in the Shadow and just blitzed everybody, his 1m 31.57s being an average of a shade under 100mph. Lauda was nearly a second slower. It dried up the following day, and this prevented him from repeating the virtuoso performance; I remember reading with anger a national newspaper's suggestion that the 'rabbits' had been put in their proper place. Tom qualified only 15th and made an awful start, for reasons we will never know. At the end of the first lap he came round in 22nd place. Bit by bit he scythed through the backmarkers until he had his sights on a group comprising Laffite, Stuck and Nilsson dicing for 11th. He was tucked right in Stuck's slipstream going down the main straight when the tragedy occurred on their 22nd lap.

At the end of his 21st lap, Tom's team-mate Renzo Zorzi had rolled to a halt opposite the pits. The fuel metering unit was malfunctioning, and as it pumped petrol into the engine's vee a small fire erupted. He pulled the onboard extinguisher to douse it after he had climbed out. On the pit wall two eager marshals saw the smoke and, against all reason, decided to run across the track to fight it. At that point the track was on a slight curve with a shallow dip before the point at which Zorzi had stopped. As they sprinted across, that dip temporarily hid Laffite, Stuck, and Pryce and Nilsson, side-by-side.

The first marshal just made it. The second, 19-year-old Jansen van Vuuren, during the week a ticket clerk at Jan Smuts Airport, was lugging a 40lb fire extinguisher and was thus marginally slower. Stuck just jinked round him, but Tom had no chance, nowhere to go. He was trapped on the left-hand side of the track with Nilsson to his right. The Shadow struck and killed van Vuuren and threw his body across the cockpit and the rollover hoop, then high into the air like a rag doll's. His extinguisher hit Tom full in the face. He was doing at least 170mph and he had no chance. Its driver already dead in the cockpit, but his right foot still flat on the throttle, the Shadow continued to speed down to Crowthorne, where it veered, out of control, to the right before colliding with Laffite's Ligier as the Frenchman turned in to the right-hander. The DN8 continued into and through the catchfencing and into the outer wall at almost unabated speed.

OTHER VOICES

Trevor Foster

"Kyalami was horrific, because the race was going on. The guy with the extinguisher was hit virtually straight in front of where we were; as it was then you went over the brow in front of where we were at Tyrrell. Obviously we were concentrating on the marshal and all we saw was him run over. You think that there's plenty of time to lift off, but there isn't. The guy just went up in the air like a rag doll and came down just at the side of the track. And because Tom's car carried on, I never thought anything else had happened. I couldn't see down to Crowthorne, and when he didn't come round again, and because they didn't stop the race, I thought that he'd probably pulled off with a bit of damage to the car down the bottom. Nobody knew any different. I went down to *parc ferme* and remember talking to Jimmy Chisman, with whom I'd worked at Shadow and who'd gone to Brabham when I went to Tyrrell, and I said, 'Are you alright, then?', never knowing any different. And he said, 'No, I think Tom's dead. He's had a big shunt at the end of the straight.' And then, of course, it all came out what had happened.

"I remember Alan Rees telling me that Laffite couldn't believe it because he

The seeds of disaster are being sown at Kyalami in 1977. After his dreadful start Tom races back through the field, having already passed Brett Lunger's March and his own team-mate Renzo Zorzi. Soon after Zorzi's car would grind to a halt opposite the pits and Jan Smuts Airport booking clerk Jansen van Vuuren, acting as a marshal for the weekend, would take that fatal decision to render assistance by running across the track directly in the path of Tom's speeding car.

didn't know quite what had happened, and when they both shunted and he got out and walked over to Tom's car, he thought Tom had died in the actual accident.

"Tom really was a super guy. It's hard to evaluate the two characters of Roger (Williamson) and Tom. Roger was far more of a lad. On the grid you could talk to him, but he used to get this sort of glazed look of concentration, where Tom'd be sitting there even at the Grands Prix, and you could talk even with two minutes to go. They approached it in slightly different ways. They were different characters, but in the way they approached it overall, they were the same. Never overawed by anybody. Tom was very open in his praise of people, but I don't think he ever thought he was as good as Ronnie Peterson. He never wanted to be a high-profiler, he really just wanted to turn up and drive the car, do a good job and go."

■ ■ ■

Alan Rees

"As he was coming through the field there was only one more in that pack that he had to overtake, and that was Stuck. Stuck was the one who avoided the guy who ran across the road, and he did it so quickly that Tom was left out there. He wouldn't even have known about it. He wouldn't have known anything about it, I'm sure of that. Stuck obviously saw the guy at the last moment and just swerved, and Tom was right in his slipstream. He would have taken Stuck that lap down the straight."

■ ■ ■

Alan Henry

"I was down at Crowthorne and saw it all, although it didn't register with me what was happening at the time. I just saw a car out of control. I walked up the left-hand side of the track after it was over in a fairly zonked frame of mind

165

because there was no doubt about Tom. And Surtees popped out of one of those little caravans the teams had, took me in, sat me down and gave me a whisky, which I always thought was a nice gesture. I appreciated that a lot. I remember Jenks' face as well, going into the press room which was at the start/finish line. He had been up at Leeukop, at the other end of the circuit, and hadn't the faintest idea this had happened. He sort of breezed up to pick up an information sheet. I haven't seen the wind so taken out of his sails as it was then by sheer disbelief.

"Tom's buried at Otford, and I remember the memorial service at Ruthin was more of a tearjerker than the actual funeral. His father was very supportive and helped him a lot when he won that *Daily Express* Crusader Championship and with it the Lola. It was his father who suggested he had those vertical black stripes on his helmet because he lap-charted the Motor Racing Stables races and could never tell him from anyone else when he was coming round.

"Tom was certainly quick enough to go all the way. It would just have been a matter of calming himself down and getting the right equipment."

■ ■ ■

I'd just left college and was working for Dexion in Maidenhead that Saturday, building a warehouse storage system and running in and out to a college friend's car to listen to the radio every so often. After Williamson and Brise I couldn't believe the news.

Immediately after the accident Tom's wedding ring went missing from his body, but after an ultimatum had been issued by the organizers, it was returned with the same callous anonymity with which it had been stolen.

The very stupidity of the accident – a moment's rashness from a young boy whose only aim was to fulfill his role to the best of his ability – simply heightened the feeling of loss and futility. In the tragedy it was easy to forget just how loyal Tom had been as he remained at Shadow despite offers from several other teams, notably Lotus, Tyrrell and Surtees. And other things, such as his stunning drive in a Lancia Stratos on the Tour of Eppynt before he crashed. Or his doting parents, his father, the police sergeant in Ruthin, his mother, who shared Nella's mistrust of the sport.

To the very end he was a racer. During his charge back through the field only four other drivers – Watson, Lauda, Scheckter, all of whom went the distance, and Pace, who completed 76 of the 78 laps – set faster laps. That was how hard Tom was trying in his 22 laps.

He was gentle, a man who remained unspoiled despite his new environment, and who admitted there were times when he'd far rather have been away from the commercialism of the sport, back with Nella in the converted oast house they had bought in Kent. It boasted only two silver trophies. One, the size of a silver egg cup, was his from that Race of Champions victory. The other was won at a gymkhana by Nella when she was 13. He had gone motor racing not for the glitter and the glamour, but for the fun and the pleasure it gave him to hold a car in a wild oversteering slide with the throttle wide open. His only fear of death was typically caring; he worried how it would affect those he left behind.

Tom Pryce was one of the people after whom I named my elder son. I hope one day he might grow up proud to share the name of someone who set such an example in his behaviour and his attitude to life and people.

15

DAVID PURLEY

Prodding the tiger

"No. I like having my own team. It's like being back in the Army. I'll stay as I am."

David Purley died as he had always lived, riding on the edge of a risk. He was 40 years old when his Pitts Special failed to come out of a dive over the sea near Bognor Regis, and thus perished an extraordinary man.

Motor racing will forever link his name with Roger Williamson's after his heroic attempt to rescue his fellow Briton from his upturned March during the Dutch GP at Zandvoort in 1973, but 'Purls' himself was no mean driver. Throughout his career he would, however, remain underrated.

Quite probably that was because he never took it with that ultra-hard edge of professionalism so many of his colleagues did. Life, to Purley, was for living, for having fun. He loved his racing, but he also had a strong sense of perspective.

He was born into a wealthy background after his father Charlie had graduated from fishmongering to create Lec, one of Britain's largest manufacturers of refrigerators. "We'd got one lorry and one shop on the sea front, but just to keep the right image Dad painted number 17 on the front of the truck and repainted it every other week to give the impression that we'd got a fleet of them!" David arrived a few weeks after the Second World War had ceased and grew up to pursue an erratic academic career at a progressive co-educational school in Devon. He was expelled, "when an alarm clock rather embarrassingly failed to go off when it should have done...". Perhaps it hadn't been that progressive after all.

For a while he worked in the vehicle maintenance depot at Lec, but developed the passion for flying that would eventually lead to disaster one summer evening at the beginning of July 1985. At 17, he was at one stage the youngest private pilot in the country, and he became Lec's first company pilot after two brushes with the local CID, which took a dim view of the pleasure he derived in beating up the seafront. "I chose that for two reasons. I might mature a bit quicker and I might avoid killing myself!"

When he took up motor racing in 1968 it was through neighbour Derek Bell, and before long his roadgoing AC Cobra had been modified and pressed into service. I remember watching him thrashing it round Brands Hatch on a Saturday afternoon *Grandstand* TV programme, and he was a spectator's delight. He had a spectacular approach to life, and it had its expression in the way he drove the car.

By that stage he had seen more than most men do in a lifetime. After flying

Happy-go-lucky and possessed of a particular disdain for fear, former paratrooper David Purley would have made the perfect Fifties Grand Prix racer.

all over Europe and Africa for Lec, he and Charlie Purley fell out. Purley jumped on his motorbike and roared off to London, finding work on a demolition site for six months for £48 a week. "Then winter came and I reckoned that perhaps demolition work wasn't such a good idea after all. So there I was driving along the Chiswick High Road when I saw this Army Information Office. I went straight in and joined up in the Coldstream Guards."

Within a year he was at Sandhurst, selected as officer material. It led to two adventure-packed years of service, six months of them active in Aden at the time of unrest there. On one occasion the armoured car he was travelling in ran over a mine. Six of his fellow occupants were killed, but he walked away. Just before he embarked on his motor racing his parachute had failed to open and he had had a miraculous escape riding down atop his senior NCO's inflated 'chute.

"I was the first jump on the port side and my platoon sergeant was first on the starboard. Unfortunately, we hadn't mastered the technique of jumping from a Hercules and we collided under the belly of the aircraft. My parachute got tangled up and I floated down from 10,000ft on the top of his 'chute, looking through the hole in the centre at his tin hat. If I'd chosen to scramble off the edge and my tangled 'chute hadn't opened I'd have been a goner." His sergeant was knocked unconscious as they landed, but Purley escaped with nothing worse than a broken ankle.

Earlier still, he had escaped from a near crash in crocodile-infested waters in Port Harcourt, in Nigeria. "We were in a single-engined Commanche 250 and I took it down low over the mangrove swamps between the Sahara Desert and Sierra Leone to see the crocodiles feeding. We nearly provided them with their menu because the plane started misfiring and wouldn't gain any height. When we finally staggered into Bathurst I had sweated off nearly a stone in weight!"

In later years, as is often the case with men who are not inhibited by the fear of death, he would be accused of having a death wish, but nothing was further from the truth. Purley loved life and everything about it. In motor racing, with its team spirit, he found the ideal outlet after he'd left the Army and bought himself a Datsun dealership in Middleton-on-Sea.

After a Chevron B8 he graduated to Formula Three with a Brabham BT28 and later with an Ensign. The Grand Prix des Frontieres at Chimay was a flat-out blind in dangerous conditions. It was tailormade for Purls, and in 1969 he

Determined that a little drop of rain shouldn't prevent the race going ahead, Purley clinched the 1976 Group 8 Championship with his Chevron B30 at the Tribute to James Hunt meeting at Brands Hatch.

168

beat James Hunt's Lotus 59 by a whisker. He won the race again for the next two years, and later revealed how he would scream into his helmet at the most difficult sections. "It was a trick we used for getting the adrenalin going in Aden", he would say with his lazy smile.

In his first Formula Two race, at Oulton Park in 1972, he started from pole position in his Lec-backed March 722, but it was an otherwise troubled year. In 1973 he moved up to Formula One with a Lec March 731G, and in Holland came that dramatic rescue bid. He and Williamson had been racing together when Roger's March crashed and overturned. Purley stopped immediately and single-handedly attempted to right the car as craven marshals stood and watched. The harrowing television footage revealed the sheer frustration, exhaustion and, ultimately, the desolation he suffered.

Through his tears he said, "I just couldn't turn it over. I could see he was alive and I could hear him shouting, but I couldn't get the car over. I was trying to get people to help me, and if I could have turned the car over he would have been alright, we could have got him out."

Later, when the immediate grief had receded, he admitted, "I didn't even think about the heroism or any of that rubbish. I just did what comes naturally to a trained soldier who sees a fellow in trouble."

It was that sort of modesty and humanity that made David so immensely popular, and he was awarded the George Medal for gallantry for that selfless act of heroism. Tom Wheatcroft said of him, "I liked him as a fella. You couldn't have got a nicer fella than David."

It took him a while to get his enthusiasm back, but by 1976 he had won the Shellsport Group 8 series for big single-seaters in the UK, driving a Lec-supported Chevron B30 with the Cosworth GA V6 engine. His performance in the final race, at the Tribute to James Hunt meeting at Brands Hatch, typified his character and ability. Because he was on pole they asked him to inspect the circuit when it began pouring with rain just before the start. A lot of drivers didn't want to go out. Entrant Mike Earle told his boys to get the Chevron warmed up, since it was Purley who was doing the inspection.

When he came back he said nonchalantly, "Yeah, it's perfect". "What about the flood at the bottom of Paddock?", somebody asked. "Well, you don't *have* to drive through it", he replied. He led all the way, set fastest lap, and his victory set the seal on his championship-winning season.

In 1977 he moved back up to Formula One with his own Lec CRP1, designed by Mike Pilbeam and again run by Earle. Usually he would just turn up in a pair of jeans and a tee shirt, but Earle took him up to London and got him neatly kitted out ready for a sponsorship meeting with Conoco, the fuel company. At first Purley intended going with Earle as pillion passenger on his new Kawasaki, but was finally dissuaded. Nevertheless, he turned up for the meeting a sartorial disaster, dressed in brown trousers, red shirt and green jacket...

"He was born 20 years too late", suggests Earle. "He would have been the ideal Fifties driver. He would sit in the bar all night, literally, drinking and drinking, and tip up the next morning, all bright. 'OK chaps? Right, let's go!' He used to love it. Absolutely *love* it.

"What was good about him was that he was frightened of no person. He just had that about him. It didn't matter who it was. If someone told him it couldn't be done, he'd just go and do it.

"He knew nothing about racing. *Nothing.* You've got to understand that. He just raced cars. He would literally come up to you after a race – I know it sounds like exaggeration, but it's true – and say, 'Yeah, I was down there and I was following a bloke in a red car with a red helmet', and you'd say, 'Lauda?', and he'd say, 'Yeah, that's the one'. It was like that all the time. The only blokes he knew were Wattie and Andretti." In the Belgian GP at Zolder that year he qualified 20th, but he actually held the lead briefly during the tyre stops as the track dried. Later, he would know Lauda rather better, and Lauda would certainly not forget who David Purley was.

Earle: "The good thing about Zolder was not so much that he led it or was second, depending on whose lap chart you look at, the interesting thing for me was that before anybody stopped in the wet he was up to seventh, and that just allowed for Andretti and Wattie taking themselves off on the first lap. So he'd overtaken a lot of people. The car was good in the wet, it was obviously too soft and a bit spongey, but I mean it was OK. And he was leading the race and Niki was charging up to go up the inside of him, and Dave held him up. He finally came in for tyres, and as he came down the pit road I thought, 'There's something wrong', and I realized he'd switched the engine off. He didn't want it to overheat...! We lost about half a lap. Like I said, he knew nothing about motor racing! He finished 13th.

"Afterwards, we were packing up and Niki came up to have a quiet chat with him, you know, with about 48 journalists, a whole army of people around him. He actually walked up to Purley and was wagging his finger and saying, 'You must have known who I was', and Purley just said, 'I was leading then. If you wanted it, you had to get it.' And Niki started with his finger again, and Purley said, 'If you wag that at me one more time I'm going to break it off and stick it right up your arse.'

"Niki described Purley as one of the rabbits, so we raced with a white rabbit after that. Then Purley called Niki a rat, and Niki got a rat on his car. At the end of it they were good friends."

At the French GP at Dijon two meetings later, Surtees was running Patrick Tambay. When he failed to qualify, Big John offered Purley the drive. He was desperately short of cash and Earle advised him to take up the offer, but he said, "No, I like having my own team. It's like being back in the Army. I'll stay where I am." It was a decision that was to cost him dear.

During the second pre-qualifying session for the British GP at Silverstone, less than a fortnight later, the throttle stuck open as he approached Becketts. The Lec hit the barriers at more than 100mph and stopped within 5ft. It was a massive impact. He made the Guinness Book of Records for the most destructive accident anyone had survived.

OTHER VOICES

Mike Earle – friend and entrant

"People do not realize just how serious it was. He very nearly died, and even after that he nearly lost a leg.

"Brian Henton came in and pulled up and called me over. I thought he'd say Purls had run out of fuel out on the circuit, but he said he'd had a really big one round the back and they were stopping the session. When we got there they'd parked all the escape vehicles round the car. We took tools with us to take the rollhoop and the dashhoop off so we could get him out, and all that. Martin Dixon" – Earle's second in command – "ran round the corner, and when he saw it he just dropped. Just the shock of it.

"It was absolutely unbelievable. His knees were up here, by his shoulders, his head was sideways, back through the rollhoop. He was conscious and he was starting to suffer. He kept asking the doctor, 'Is Mike Earle there?' I went up and I said, 'Yeah, what do *you* want?'. He kept saying, 'It's the brakes, it's the brakes'. I said, 'No it wasn't, I can see the marks on the road.' Then he went quiet and the doctor pulled me to one side and said, 'Get him into an argument, will you?'. He wanted me to keep him going. So I said, 'I don't know about you'. He said, 'How bad am I?'. So I said, 'You're alright, but you've messed the car up. Useless.' He said, 'Oh no, will it be ready for tomorrow morning?'. And I said, 'Well, if you are, it will be'.

Rabbit leads Rat. Purley holds a momentary lead in the 1977 Belgian GP as Niki Lauda rushes up behind the Lec in his Ferrari. Their celebrated altercation afterwards resulted in Purls calling Lauda a rat, and Lauda calling him a rabbit. Thereafter each raced with such animal symbols painted on their cars, and a friendship developed.

"It took us 45 minutes to cut him out and get him away, and another 40 to get him to hospital. At that point I didn't think there was any way. We stayed there all night. He had 17 breaks in each leg and three breaks in his pelvis. The following morning a lot of the shock had come out. His head was like a water melon. It was a really tough time for him, but he always kept saying, 'Oh yeah, I'll be back. I'll get back'."

■ ■ ■

When he first came out of hospital his left leg was two inches shorter than the right and he had to wear a built-up shoe. He told Earle, "I can't go on like this, it's bloody hopeless. I feel such a wally. I can't do anything. I can't run". Running had been one of his favourite pursuits.

"Gail, his girlfriend then and later his wife, was a lovely girl, very tall. I told him to get two inches taken out of the right leg and he said, 'Piss off. Have you seen the size of Gail? I'm already shorter than her!'."

Instead, Purley went to Belgium to see a specialist. He pinned the left leg top and bottom, then broke the bone in the middle and parted it by half an inch. He then let it calcify before breaking it again, and he kept doing that until he got the full two inches back. It was a long, agonizing process that took the whole of 1978, but eventually he was ready to start full rehabilitation. Out on the Lec airstrip he started riding a bicycle, but the snag was he couldn't put his leg down whenever he stopped, so unless somebody was there he'd just fall off. He developed a system where he'd ride off down the runway, and then scream as he came back down so somebody would go out and hold the bike so that he could get off. When he'd mastered that he moved on to take part in motorcycle enduro events. For David Purley, nothing had to be easy.

After that, it was time to come back to motor racing. He made his comeback at Thruxton in the Lec and finished reasonably well up, but ground effect had rendered the car obsolete. "Now I've had a look at it I know I can still do it", he told Earle, and he bought a Shadow DN9.

I watched him drive it to fourth place at Snetterton, where he ran in the leading group until dropping back in the final stages, and I saw just how haggard he looked as he sat drinking a bottle of water in the car immediately afterwards. What I didn't know then was why he didn't get out of the car in the pit lane.

Earle had said to him, "Bloody well done, *I'm* impressed. And if I'm impressed with you, that's bloody well done". Purley had smiled at him as we stood around clapping, then he said, "Do me a favour. I don't want to look a wally, but I can't move. Take the car round to the transporter and I'll get out there". So Mike had pushed it round and four of them lifted him out.

OTHER VOICES

Mike Earle

"In my opinion, for what it's worth, he was a much better driver than people gave him credit for. Because of the Roger Williamson thing he became known as 'Brave Dave', and all this sort of stuff, and I think he got sidetracked a bit by it all. I think he came to enjoy the fame of that. But he was a very good driver. The stories about Purls seem totally over the top, but he was that rare thing, a man who really was larger than life.

"He was a crafty old fella when he decided he wanted to have another go. He called me and said he'd like me to run it, but Greg Field and I had formed Onyx then so I said, 'No, I don't want to know'. I didn't really relish the thought of him doing it all over again, to be honest. He was a friend. And then he said, 'I've got so and so to run it', and he knew he was a total waste of space and that really I wouldn't let him do it, so I said 'OK. But first of all we'll take the 002 Lec car to Goodwood, very quietly, no-one there. Jump in the car and you drive it. No-one will see you.' All the time he raced he hated testing. When he won that Group 8 championship, all through the winter Derek Bell tested the Chevron while David was in Australia. He came back a day earlier, went quicker and said, 'Fine, thanks very much'. So I said, 'We'll go up to Goodwood, do a bit of testing, make sure you're fit'. He said, 'Oh bloody hell, do I have to?'.

"We'd done an 8.8s with the old 001 car, and this one was a bit better, so if we couldn't do that with it, forget it. He kept saying, 'Bloody hell, do you mean it?'. He went out and he was immediately on to it after three or four laps, and his ninth lap was an 8.4s. We showed him that going past the pits and, of course, he was out there on his own on the track. So he braked, reversed up the pit road and said, 'That'll do then, won't it?'. And he meant it! He got out of the car and went home. He didn't want to drive it any more because it wasn't racing.

"He was an amazing character. In some ways he was like his old boy, Charlie Purley. The sense of humour was there, but it was off at a tangent. He reminded me of this bloke I knew once who picked up a bird one year when I'd just started racing, and although she wasn't a hooker, it was clear she wouldn't mind being paid. Well, that particular day he'd had a little bike go missing from his pit, and this bird started telling this bloke she'd had a bad day and had had her purse stolen, and all this, pushing for a little money. This guy took it all at absolute face value because he didn't think that way, and said, 'Yeah, it's funny, isn't it? I've had a really lousy day, too. Somebody stole my monkey bike as well!' He just didn't realize what she was after! Purley was like that with *his* sense of humour."

■ ■ ■

Such was his irrepressible lust for adventure that he was very closely involved in engineer David Gossling's plans to create a British Land Speed Record contender in 1976, using fuel pumps from the stillborn Blue Streak rocket programme in a car called *Project Blue Star*. The whole thing appealed immensely to Purls, and as ever, Earle was involved. It was he who suggested they get some order into it and aim for the Sound Barrier, and Gossling had

172

progressed things to the point where the Cranfield Institute was heavily involved, and the Duke of Edinburgh had agreed to become a patron.

They built a full-scale mock-up of *Project Blue Star* and I went all the way to Rufforth, from Darlington, to see it in the summer of 1976. *The Northern Echo* had got its wires crossed; Purley was showing it off that day at Brands Hatch...

Driving home from another late night's work in the summer of 1977, Gossling's MGB left the road in a gentle accident, went into a ditch and turned over. He was killed. The project died with him, but Purley would have been the perfect driver for it, just as Innes Ireland would have made a fine replacement for Donald Campbell when he expressed interest in carrying on after the 1967 *Bluebird* tragedy. Purley and Ireland had much in common, not the least of which was their paratrooping background and their ability to imbibe. Earle described as fascinating just sitting back and listening to their conversation. He also remembered laughing at Purley's grasp of the egg-shaped 'Cranfield Capsule' survival cell for *Blue Star*.

"Purley, being a totally non-technical person, said, 'Yeah, well, great, what does it do?'. They told him, 'In the event you crash it's like an egg and squeezes out the hole and it's so strong'. And he said, 'Well, won't I get dizzy?'; 700mph down the road in an egg. 'Will I get dizzy?' The bloke said, 'Yes, but you'll be alive'. He really did want to do that project."

Swayed by subtle pressure from his family, David finally retired from motor racing and took more of an interest in the management side at Lec, but the craving for excitement led to the purchase of the Pitts Special. Life was tamer, and he still needed his kicks. He just couldn't keep away from risk.

OTHER VOICES

Mike Earle

"His death was another piece of David. Although he and the family were wealthy, he always wanted to save money. I always used to say to him that his Silverstone accident was caused because I wanted two more guys – there were only seven of us and we built the car and we built the engines. We had our own engine shop. I said I want two more guys and we can have a T-car – and he said no. That day of the accident we had a fire in the morning, and it was the extinguishant that turned like cement in the rollers and made the throttle stick open. I always said to him, 'If we'd had those two more blokes, you'd have just jumped into the T-car'.

"When he decided he was going to take up aerobatics he and another friend went and bought a pair of Pitts Specials in bits in the States, shipped them over, and he got this old boy to build them in the hangar. He was always coming in and asking if we had a bit of lockwire, and all that. And he finished them and there was a guy who lived down our way and flew for either the Rothmans or Marlboro aerobatic team. David rang him and asked him if he'd test it out for him. The guy said, 'Yes, no problem'. He came down and asked who built it, and when David told him the guy said, 'Thanks very much, but no thanks!'.

"Purley had never flown a Pitts before, and they don't have any flaps, so he just jumped in, fired it up, got to the end of the runway and started doing bits with it. When he came back in to land he suddenly realized he's sitting a long way back and the thing's got quite a long nose and the propeller was huge. They hang them on these huge propellers. The danger was that the prop was going to hit the ground if he didn't get it right, and he couldn't see the runway. And he suddenly realized he had no flaps. He must have gone over 25 times, because he didn't know how to land the bloody thing! Then he suddenly clocked it that if he kicked it sideways he could see and just get it within 10 feet of the ground and drop it down. That's just the way he was.

"Two weeks before he died, this friend of his had got a new Pitts and he fetched it down and said, 'Try this'. And the engine actually stopped totally and he crashed it in a field and just destroyed it, rolled it into a ball. Christ, I don't know how he got out of that. One of the people involved in that made him an offer for his, and he thought, 'OK, yeah, I'll sell it. I've had enough fun out of it. I'll pack it all in'.

"On the Monday night he went out for his last flight in it, and he knew there were Derek, Wattie, myself and Graham Burrows down below because we all used to play tennis at Graham's house right on the seafront, so he dive-bombed the house a couple of times. We were all sort of saying, 'Bugger off, Purley, you're distracting us', and then we could hear him out in the distance, out over the sea. Then we heard noises and one of us said, 'Oh, it sounds like Purley's engine's playing up', and we were right in the middle of a rally and almost at once we all threw our racquets down and ran out on to the beach. We met this little old man coming up and he said, 'A little red plane's just crashed into the sea'. Derek wasn't there at that moment, he hadn't arrived to play, but Wattie and Graham and myself all piled into Graham's boat and we zapped out there, and we were the first ones out there by about 15 minutes.

"On the way out they were saying, 'Cor, he's done it this time', and I'm saying, 'Nah, nah, nah, don't you believe it. He'll be out there, he'll be floating around, probably broken a leg and an arm and saying, 'Bloody hell, it's taken you a long time to get out here'. And I honestly, honestly believed that. I really did. I expected to see wreckage, but when we got there there was nothing, a few pieces of red paint and one of his Dr Scholl's sandals that had floated to the top. We couldn't see anything. Three or four hours later they found him, still in the plane, and they got him out the following morning.

"What happened was that a piece of rubber had come away inside a fuel hose and blocked one of the inlet ports in the injection pump as he came off the top

Wearing one of John Watson's helmets, Purley had his most impressive comeback race after the Silverstone shunt at Snetterton in 1978 after replacing the spare Lec with a Shadow DN9. He finished fourth after a gritty drive, and had to be lifted from the car afterwards.

of a roll, and as he flattened it out and aimed at the sea, the engine lost probably 10 to 15% of its power. People who saw it go in said the throttle was wide open until it went in, so he was obviously trying to get it back. It went in at a 45-degree angle, and the cockpit and the fuselage sort of jacknifed together. The thing that hurt him was that the seat belts didn't have doublers behind the panel, and the straps pulled out the back of the seat and he went on to the dashboard. He had severe chest injuries, but he was still alive when he went in because he'd ingested water. His injuries were enough to kill him, but he was alive for a while...

"And that was it. We all came back, and I could not believe it. All the things he'd been through. Bloody Aden, the parachute accident, the armoured car. All the accidents he'd had. He was a real adventurer. He loved life so much the last thing he wanted to do was to die. He just loved life. He really loved it."

■ ■ ■

The motor racing world mourned David Purley. He had shaken off his rich boy image, and eventually left the sport on his own terms, walking unaided. He was a man of unique character and immense popularity, a free spirit who never lacked the courage to prod the tiger within himself yet one more time, even when he knew that, one day, it would finally bite back.

Today the spare Lec is proudly displayed at Tom Wheatcroft's Donington Collection. In the background is the remains of the original, which stopped from more than 100mph in a matter of feet. At the time his was the fastest recorded deceleration a human had survived.

16
JOCHEN RINDT

Champion lost

"What gifts hath Fate for all his chivalry? Even such as hearts heroic oftenest win; honour, a friend, untimely death..." Anon.

Jochen Rindt! The name somehow demands an exclamation mark behind it. Everything he did was done with speed and a style that captivated the hearts of thousands of enthusiasts the world over. Jochen Rindt! Even now, more than 20 years after that day when tragedy snatched him from the world title that was to follow, it sets the mind tingling, instantly conjures up mental images of a racing car being driven to its absolute maximum. Of a long-faced man with a flat nose and tousled hair, who would inevitably seek the sustenance of a cigarette whenever he stepped from the cockpit.

They said he was arrogant, aloof. Perhaps he was. Rindt was not a man used to being told what to do. Even as a schoolboy he had rebelled against authority. Orphaned at one in 1943, when his German father and Austrian mother perished in a bombing raid on Hamburg, he was brought up by his maternal grandparents in Austria. His father had owned a spice mill, his mother had studied law. Their child had talent and intelligence and grew up used to a comfortable standard of living. From an early age he knew what he wanted and had the acumen to make sure he got it. Self-sufficiency came early, too. Such resourcefulness took him quickly from a tuned Simca Montlhéry to the Alfa Romeo he needed to beat similarly equipped rivals. His grandmother was persuaded to fund it...

It was when he burst on to the British motorsport scene on Whit Monday 1964, with a quite stunning victory over Graham Hill's new Cooper-BRM in the Formula Two race at Crystal Palace, that the fraternity began to sit up and take notice.

Who the hell is this Jochen Rindt?, they demanded to know. Jochen was only too pleased to enlighten them. That day in south-east London he snatched the crown of the Formula Two category, and he never relinquished it. It simply became *his* formula.

The previous day he had given warning of his awesome skill by starting the Mallory Park race from pole position, although not being in gear when the flag dropped had set him way back. He then fought through the field, triggered a multiple shunt, but still brought his car home third behind Jim Clark and Peter Arundell. After that and the Crystal Palace drive it was clear that Rindt's was no ordinary talent. Oddly enough, it had been Hill's first Formula Two race, and his Cooper was handling abysmally, with faulty dampers, a broken rear anti-roll bar

Rindt and Colin Chapman had a stormy relationship during their two years together, yet each knew he needed the other. Moments after this photograph was taken at Monza Jochen was killed when his Lotus 72 veered into the barriers at Parabolica.

and horrendous understeer as a result. Rindt, nevertheless, drove brilliantly that day to take a clear victory. At one stage, by his own admission, Hill had taken all the available road to get by him. "Afterwards I thought it was a daft thing to do because if I'd done anything wrong he'd have had absolutely nowhere to go. I put him in an unfair position." Like Clark, a believer in giving his rivals racing room, Hill apologized afterwards to the newcomer. Jochen merely shrugged. To the wild youth who had terrorized his hometown of Graz during roadgoing duels with Helmut Marko, it had been nothing. Any sign of weakness, then, had been thoroughly discouraged. Consideration was a weakness.

Certainly, Rindt could be difficult. If he took against somebody, no amount of persuasion could make him change his mind. The celebrated journalist Denis Jenkinson, of *Motor Sport*, was never convinced of Rindt's talent, and said so on numerous occasions. He described him as a leadfoot with tremendous reactions, but little natural skill. He was determined not to recognize him even as a serious racer until he won a Grand Prix.

Rindt had yet again looked like doing just that at Montjuich Park during the 1969 Spanish GP until his monumental accident when the rear wing on his Lotus 49B collapsed. He missed Monaco while recuperating, and therefore was not party to a conversation that was, temporarily at least, to cost Jenks his most recognizable appendage.

After Saturday practice he had declared, "Rindt won't win a World Championship race this year", to the general astonishment of the assembled company. In fact, he was very nearly right.

In the past he had bet his beard against the Allard dragster getting below a certain elapsed time for the standing quarter-mile. It had succeeded in doing so, but Jenks had saved his beard by driving the machine himself and recording a competitive time. *Motoring News* reporter Andrew Marriott recalled the incident and immediately challenged him to bet his beard on his latest controversial declaration. Commentator Robin Richards drafted a pledge on a table napkin and handed it for safe keeping to Brands Hatch supremo John Webb, once Jenks had signed it in front of witnesses Pat Mennem, of the *Daily Mirror*, Anne Hope, of the *Sun*, and John Langley, of the *Daily Telegraph*. In due course, Jenks was to be smooth-shaven.

177

Jochen might have been amused had he been there, but it is unlikely. He disliked Jenkinson to the point where he would pointedly ignore him if he were a third party to a conversation he was holding with someone he did like. Even if the second party included Jenks, Rindt, even more pointedly, would not. To him, people he disliked simply did not exist.

Yet behind his sometimes forbidding mien lurked a sparkling sense of humour that became evident to newcomers only if Jochen decided to allow them to enter his inner circle. The trick was in getting into it.

"He was one of the most laidback guys you could meet", said Mike 'Herbie' Blash, a mechanic at Lotus during the Rindt days and now director of the Brabham team. "I would say he was like a Fifties driver in the late Sixties. He wasn't hard on his people, even when the car went wrong. And as far as being arrogant, well, that was more his looks than anything else. He wasn't that good looking, but he was a really nice guy to work with. He was a mate. But yes, if he didn't like you, then he didn't like you."

OTHER VOICES

Pat Mennem

"He and I were stuck at Geneva Airport on one occasion and we talked a lot. I went to see him in Switzerland, and when he was in London I took him to lunch, introduced him to the *Mirror*'s editor. I liked him. He was not arrogant, but he was more intelligent than most of them, and much better read. He had a very rounded knowledge, of the environment, astronomy, government affairs. Quite astonishingly for someone whose parents were killed by the RAF, he had no hang-ups about the British at all. It didn't trouble him.

"He was very competitive, intensely so. Whatever you were doing he had to beat you, even if it was noughts and crosses, skiing; anything he had to do he had to win.

"His most outstanding quality was that he never complained. When he was persevering with the Cooper-Maserati I used to say, 'What's the trouble?', and he'd just say, 'I've got cockpit trouble. I can't make it go fast enough'. He never went on about brakes, tyres or whatever.

"And I've never seen anyone go round Montjuich Park, in Barcelona, like he did. He used to *fly*. It was an unbelievable sight. He was really wound up..."

■ ■ ■

Rindt came into motor racing his own man, and stayed that way as he climbed right to the top. He did not suffer fools gladly along the way. He was, however, a simple character, totally apolitical. All Jochen Rindt wanted to do was drive the world's fastest racing cars, and to *win*. It was not so much arrogance as independence, very much as it would later be with Ayrton Senna. And, as it transpired, Jochen reversed the usual trend; the more he won, the nicer person he became.

As he struggled in Formula One with uncompetitive equipment in 1964 and '65, it was Le Mans, of all races, that provided him with the means to shine. If ever a man and an event were ill-suited to one another, it was the Austrian and the French classic, yet when he was victorious there in 1965, the circumstances were typical of the man. He was paired with the American Masten Gregory, a driver who placed greater reliance on his own powers of retardation than he did a car's by regularly abandoning ship post haste when a crash seemed imminent. Even when the machinery was travelling at considerable speed... They were well suited, given their respective senses of humour, but Jochen had about as much intention of pussyfooting through 24 hours in Luigi Chinetti's outclassed

Ferrari 250LM as he did of leaving his next cigarette unlit.

Everything about that race seemed wrong. Jochen got a late release from BP to drive the Shell-backed car and missed all but the final practice session. After he'd worked up to fifth place after the first hour – no mean feat amongst all the works Ferraris and Fords – the starter motor broke. An hour and a half later the distributor failed. Jochen did a lap on six of the 12 cylinders and prepared, like the team, to pack up. Gregory insisted they check the distributor, mainly to disprove the popular theory that he had simply overrevved and damaged the valvegear, and by the time it was changed and a faulty condenser was located, they had lost nearly half an hour. When Masten finally found Jochen, he was in his street clothes, about to leave in his hire car. The only reason he hadn't actually gone was that it was boxed in. Gregory was a persuasive individual, and lured Jochen back into the event. Rindt had one condition: they would drive flat-out. Win or bust. They won.

For 21 hours they flogged that 250LM, and in all that time they treated Le Mans like a Grand Prix sprint. Jackie Stewart was driving the tardy Rover-BRM and would regularly be lapped by the sideways Ferrari. As he was, two fingers would be visible in its cockpit...

They took the lead just after dawn, fought a successful battle with the similar but markedly more healthy car of Taf Gosselin and Pierre Dumay. As an indication of the true Rindt, he conceded when Gregory implored him to let him drive the final stint, appreciating what that would mean to the likeable American. Masten nursed it to the flag as the differential lock began groaning more and more, and later, as the car was driven back to the paddock, the differential failed altogether. Jochen was also astute enough to admit that it would have broken a lot earlier than that had he been at the wheel...

When Masten Gregory found Rindt in the paddock, about to leave for home, he persuaded him that their Ferrari 250LM could be repaired during the 1965 Le Mans. There and then they made a pact to continue, but only at maximum speed. Twenty one hours later the wilting car took them to victory, breaking its differential as it was driven to the paddock...

OTHER VOICES

Alan Rees – former Formula Two team-mate

"Yes, he was arrogant, but not in the way people talk about him. You could say anything to him. He had a great sense of humour. This is why, to call him arrogant, in relation to joking with him and saying what the hell you liked to him, is not right; he wasn't arrogant. To people who didn't know him, though,

I'm sure he came across that way. Once you were accepted by him it was alright. If he accepted you and got on with you and liked you, he wasn't at all arrogant. He was a funny person, really.

"In those days we just got in and drove, and all the set-up was really in the design of the car. We didn't even change dampers and roll bars! You didn't have this fantastic downforce that they do now, and if the thing understeered, really, you just changed the way you drove into a corner. Jochen would just drive round everything, absolutely everything, no matter what. He could do anything.

"I only really knew him from a Formula Two point of view, and there's no doubt we had the best cars, which suited me fine! Those Brabhams were definitely the best cars. They were better than the Lotus and the Matras.

"We worked together from 1965 to '68. He had his own car in 1964 and I also had my own car that year, and we got quite close during the season because we were the only private owners who were anywhere near competitive. It was after that that we got together in the same team.

"In Formula Two he invariably won races, even against Jimmy and Jackie, but he had a better car. Don't misunderstand me, I think Jochen was just as quick a driver as Jimmy, which is saying a lot. It's very difficult to draw a difference between them. The only difference I would say is in the way they looked on the track. Jochen would perhaps be a little more flamboyant than Jimmy, but they had exactly the same sort of skill. It just came out a little bit different on the track. Jimmy looked a little bit more organized and under control, but the skill was almost identical, I would say, between the two of them. The Brabham made the difference, I think."

■ ■ ■

If Formula Two gave Rindt a showcase for his extraordinary talent, it was to be many years before he finally succeeded in unlocking the trophy room in Formula One.

Cooper's Climax-powered cars were little threat during the final years of the 1½-litre formula, but initially the Maserati-powered contenders looked promising in 1966. At Spa, Rindt looked fabulous. This was the race which began on a dry track, but was radically altered by a sudden rainstorm at Malmedy. Eight cars, including Stewart's BRM, spun on the opening lap when a river flooding across the road at Burnenville took drivers by surprise. As the downpour continued, Jochen recovered from a massive spin, flat-out on the Masta Straight, and moved ahead to lead from Surtees' Ferrari. The Austrian made maximum use of his full wet Dunlops, but as the track began to dry slightly, the Ferrari's Firestone intermediates swayed the result in the Englishman's favour. Rindt then ran into trouble with the differential, but nevertheless finished an excellent second. In an otherwise fruitless year, he repeated that at Watkins Glen when, as Chris Amon would four years later at Spa, he waited endlessly for a BRM engine to break. This was the H16 installed in Clark's Lotus, which held together to give the Scot his 20th World Championship victory. Jochen himself had another three years to wait for his first, at the same circuit.

After something of a cold war with Pedro Rodriguez at Cooper in 1967, Jochen was only too happy to move to Brabham in 1968 after his own plans to have Robin Herd build him a Formula One car failed to materialize. That design subsequently became Bruce McLaren's successful M7A. The year began well with third place at Kyalami in the Championship-winning BT24, but the quad-cam Repco V8 in the new BT26 was a dismal failure, plagued by unreliability. The only other race Jochen finished all season was the German GP, when he finished third in appalling conditions.

For all that, he enjoyed the year, revelling in the relaxed atmosphere. He and

On his full wet Dunlops Rindt was brilliant during the opening stages of the wet Belgian GP in 1966. Where the likes of Stewart and Hill spun and retired, he survived a wild gyration on the Masta Kink and seemed on the verge of his maiden victory until the rain eased and Surtees came through to win in his Ferrari, which was running on Firestone's more suitable intermediate rubber.

Jack were perfect partners, and despite the car's power deficit, Rindt established himself once and for all as one of the fastest men in Formula One. He wanted to stay for 1969, and Jack promised him the Cosworth engine to match the Brabham's recognized handling excellence, but now Colin Chapman was convinced of Jochen's ability. The previous year he had been the only entrant not interested in his services; then he had had Jim Clark. Now Jimmy was gone, and Chapman had become the pushiest. His financial inducements finally became too much for Jochen to resist. "He was one of the best we ever had", said Sir Jack. "Absolutely fantastic. He was very good in the team, he never complained, and we almost had him back for 1970; the deal was done, until Chapman offered an awful lot more money..."

On paper it was a blessed marriage, not merely one of convenience. Despite Ron Dennis' efforts as Jochen's mechanic at Cooper and Brabham, Jochen's grasp of technicalities remained lamentable. "He was", remembered Blash, "the type of guy that would turn up, jump in the racing car, get the job done, and then disappear. Technically, *useless.*" Jochen felt he needed Chapman's car – "The Lotus is the fastest car in Formula One; I need to be driving it." – while Rindt was the fastest driver and Chapman desperately needed somebody to take over Clark's mantle, even though he still had the services of reigning World Champion Graham Hill.

Rindt, however, was not Clark, not when it came to accepting Chapman's ways. Where Jimmy left much of his direction to the Lotus chief, Rindt was his own man and did things his way. In time-honoured fashion the 49Bs were quick, but they were also fragile. Jochen was second to Stewart in South Africa and then achieved the first of that year's five pole positions at Barcelona. He was leading comfortably when team-mate Hill crashed as a result of rear wing failure, and before Graham could flag him down, his own car suffered a similar fate. It was a massive shunt from which he was desperately lucky to emerge with nothing worse than concussion and a broken nose. It was his first serious accident and it made a major impression on him. During his recuperation he wrote an open letter to every European motoring magazine urging that wings should be banned. Chapman was not amused, having been a pioneer of them in Formula One...

"I remember Chapman sending Beaky Sims and myself up with a hacksaw to

181

cut the rear wing off Graham's car because we could see it had broken", said Blash. "We got up there just as Jochen went off. He was lucky to get out of that."

Jochen also had very firm ideas on what direction Lotus should be taking. 1969 was the year of four-wheel-drive experimentation, and as usual Lotus was in the vanguard. Rindt had a hearty detestation of the Lotus 63 from the very outset.

"Jochen started to get nervous about the cars after driving the four-wheel-drive car and after that big shunt at Montjuich Park", recalled Blash. "He didn't like the 63, not one little bit.

"There was a time I remember at Zandvoort, in 1969, when it was introduced, and we had two 49s and two 63s. He walked into the garage and saw the cars, and he told us he'd already told Chapman he wasn't going to drive the 63. So he said to Chapman, 'Why have you got those here?', and Colin said, 'Well, they're here for you to race'. Then Jochen said, 'I'm not racing one of them'. So Chapman said, 'Come over here', and he took him round the corner, and as Jochen walked away I remember him turning round and waving his finger, 'No way'. And then he came back, and he'd got his own way!"

Heinz Pruller, the indefatigable Austrian reporter and broadcaster and Rindt's biographer, tells the story of how Jochen purloined a placard from a Dutch Volkswagen dealer on his way to the circuit one day. It read *Bargain, for sale*; he placed it on the 63's nose...

The fragility of the Lotus worried Rindt all through 1969. It had been the one real reservation he had had about joining the team, and here were his worst fears being realized. It prompted countless arguments with Chapman. White-faced paddock encounters were common between the two for much of the year.

But Jochen Rindt was not a man who let his anxieties affect him in the car. He was one of the coolest drivers to set foot in a race car, as his debut at Indianapolis in 1967 proved. He was immediately in trouble with the entrenched authorities at the Brickyard because of his cocky attitude to the mandatory rookie test. "And you know what?", said former Formula One driver Eddie Cheever, himself a rookie in 1990, "They remembered him all those years later. Some of them still felt sore about it! I had my run-ins with FISA, and the guys at Indy warned me that they didn't want anyone behaving like Rindt did!"

The old school at Indy had been impressed by Jochen's apparent

As he waited for the right F1 car, Jochen Rindt assumed the F2 crown from the moment he burst on to the European scene at Crystal Palace in 1964. At Rouen in 1967 he heads arch-rival and friend Jackie Stewart round the Nouveau Monde hairpin.

unflappability, however. When he crashed his Eagle in Turn One he calmly steered the fiery machine into the wall, standing in the cockpit, and then stepped off at the last moment. When measured, it was found that his pulse rate had risen a mere two beats, his blood pressure by only 6%... "Jesus, when they took him for a check-up at the hospital, he went in the front of the ambulance with the driver and offered him a cigarette!", said Cheever.

Two years later, the frailty of the Lotuses didn't slow him down at all, but it really made him think, fuelled by his friendship with his close neighbour, the safety-conscious Jackie Stewart.

The rows continued. By Silverstone, Chapman was so determined to persevere with four-wheel drive that he had actually sold off all but one of the 49Bs and there weren't any Lotuses during the first practice session, such had been the rush to prepare them. Graham Hill actually bedded-in a Brabham BT26 as a favour to Ron Tauranac. Jochen, watching the other drivers at work with a stony face, was blistering in his criticism. "This", he said, "is like a Barnum and Bailey circus, in two different rings." He and Chapman had another flaming row. Chapman ended up 'buying' the other 49Bs back from John Love and Jo Bonnier. The scene was set for one of Jochen's greatest drives.

It marked the first true occasion on which he and Stewart looked destined to race to the flag. "Jochen and I were virtually identical in ability, and the Lotus and the Matra were so evenly matched, too", recalled Jackie. Their off-track friendship was enriched by a deep respect they had for one another on the track. The crowd that day was treated to an awe-inspiring duel. Earlier in the season Jochen had driven a brilliant race at the sodden International Trophy, scything dramatically through the field to a sensational second place behind Jack Brabham once a misfire had cleared. Now, from the pole, he leaped into a narrow lead from Stewart. By the end of that first lap they were already three seconds clear of Denny Hulme's McLaren. For once, it was one of those days when the action for the lead held all attention. The Lotus was a shade faster on the straight, the Matra more secure in Silverstone's fast corners. After five laps Stewart slid into the lead, but Jochen was there again 10 laps later. This time he stayed there, with Stewart never more than three seconds adrift, often much closer than that, until the gap was suddenly less than one at the end of lap 61. "Jochen, technically, was driving superbly", said Stewart. "No opposite-locking, just driving by the book." "I would say he had quite a bit in hand then, maybe half a second a lap", said Alan Rees. "He wouldn't drive it sideways if he was comfortable."

The next lap Stewart led by five seconds, and the lap after that Jochen sped into the pits. The left endplate on the rear wing was peeling back. Fearful it would cut the rear tyre, Stewart had drawn alongside to signal Jochen, such was the etiquette of that bygone era. The mechanics tore the plate off with their bare hands and Rindt resumed just before Jacky Ickx could deprive him of his place. Later still, he lost even that hard-won second position when the Lotus, agonizingly, ran short of fuel. His pit stop dropped him to fifth, then a late lunge took him back to fourth ahead of his friend Piers Courage. Said Stewart, "Either of us would have been content had we finished second that day".

"He was pissed off. Oh, he was *really* pissed off!", said Herbie. "It was exactly the same problem Clark had had at Monza in 1967. The car carried as much fuel as it could. We even had a special tank just behind the radiator for the longer races, and of course the hot air exiting the radiator used to heat up the fuel. That really was his race..."

Rindt and Chapman had a long, cathartic conversation at the Nurburgring and cleared the air a little. Colin even managed to persuade Jochen to drive the hated 63 in the non-championship Gold Cup race at Oulton Park a fortnight later. He finished second to Ickx. At Monza he finished in a similar position in the 49B, this time to Stewart, who led him across the line by a mere eight-hundredths of a second. Inches past the line the Lotus had gone ahead. Jochen cursed poor pit signals, realizing too late that it was the last lap.

Jenkinson's beard was finally doomed at Watkins Glen, where Rindt's first victory was as clear-cut as any of Stewart's that year. From pole, Jochen led until lap 11, yielded for nine laps to Jackie, and then moved ahead for good. To round off a perfect day, Courage was second.

Again, his future seemed unsettled. He had proved himself to be the fastest man in racing, and was now emerging as one of the most rounded performers, too. His reputation for being hard on his machinery was receding. For a long time he considered returning to Brabham, and Jack was prepared to retire there and then if he signed. But once more Chapman topped everyone else's offers, and promised him the car to end all cars – the Lotus 72.

He had come to accept Colin, but he didn't like him. He was also fully aware that Chapman's real preference was Andretti, whose Firestone commitments still prevented him undertaking a full programme. "Jochen wasn't awed by Colin, but then nobody impressed him", said Blash. "He feared nobody. He was his own person and did what he wanted to do. He didn't really like Chapman. Their relationship didn't really get better once the 72 was sorted, either."

The Lotus 72. If anything revolutionized Formula One in the Seventies, it was Chapman's beautiful chisel-shaped car. It would eventually prove everything he said it would be, but its birth was very painful. In early testing, team driver John Miles had an unpleasant experience when one of the shafts that connected the inboard front brakes to the wheels broke. At Jarama, for the Spanish GP, the same thing happened to Rindt when the retaining bolts sheared. It seemed like 1969 all over again, and all the old worries came flooding back.

Monaco in 1970 was, perhaps, his greatest triumph, a victory snatched despite all odds, just as Le Mans had been five years earlier. The two successes came after he had already written off his chances of winning. I can't think of any other driver who could get away with that sort of couldn't care less attitude and still retain his reputation, but what Jochen could do when he was fired up more than excused him those small lapses of commitment.

He went to Monaco in ill humour, having again refused to drive the 72. Lotus took along one as a spare, but the design was undergoing serious modification back at Hethel. Jochen lined up in the 49C, a lacklustre eighth on the grid, and began the race in a pessimistic frame of mind. He could be mercurial, and his mood was low that day. By that stage of his career, he had also begun to develop a distaste for fighting lost races. He was a sleeper for the first 35 laps, finally passing Henri Pescarolo's Matra for fourth place on the 36th. He disposed of Denny Hulme's McLaren five laps later, but even then it wasn't until Amon's March halted on lap 61 that he finally sensed the chance of victory. Bit by bit he began to pull back the 13s deficit to Brabham, but Jack seemed equal to the task until he was badly baulked by Jo Siffert as the Swiss struggled with fuel feed problems. From nine seconds on lap 76 the gap had halved next time round. Stewart had taken pole position with a lap in 1m 24s, but on the penultimate lap Jochen took seven-tenths off that, and a further tenth off that on his last. Truly, it was a remarkable recovery.

As history recorded, Brabham made a minor error lapping Courage's De Tomaso going into the old hairpin on that last lap, and slithered into the barriers. Rindt was concentrating so much that he didn't realize it was the BT33 as he ducked round the obstruction and charged for the line. "The thing that'll always stick out in my mind is that he didn't even realize that he'd won", said Herbie. "When he came back to the pits, I remember the smile on his face. He just couldn't *believe* it..."

Though he refused again to drive the 72 at Spa, Chapman's weapon had been honed for action by Zandvoort, where Jochen won with ease. That victory came without joy, though, for even before he accepted the laurels he had seen Courage's helmet lying beside his burnt out De Tomaso and knew his friend had

At the 1969 British GP the two fought their sternest duel, and Rindt appeared to have the Scot's measure until a rear wing endplate on his Lotus tore backwards. Later fuel starvation lost him second place, too, and led to another blazing row with Chapman.

perished. As Nina Rindt, the Finnish model he had married in 1967, consoled Sally Courage, none of them knew that Jochen himself was living on borrowed time.

Coming so soon after Bruce McLaren's death, Courage's had shattered the tight-knit Formula One fraternity and made Jochen yet more aware of his feelings of vulnerability. He hated the 72's inboard front brakes, and said so often, but Chapman, as Andretti would discover, was not one who took kindly to having his drivers suggest design modifications. And despite misgivings, Jochen knew that the 72 was the car that could win him the crown. The French GP at Clermont-Ferrand had brought him one of the luckier wins of his career, and then he triumphed at Brands Hatch when Brabham ran short of fuel in the closing stages. That, however, was not quite so clear-cut as the stewards decided to measure the Lotus' rear wing height.

"It was too high. We got the car in the transporter and we knew the wing was too high", remembered Blash. "They had two stays supporting it at the back and we had to lean on these stays and push the wing down. Chapman was there urging us to do it. The only problem was we leaned too hard and the stays buckled and dropped the wing something like six inches! While that was going on, waiting to see if we'd won or not, I remember Jochen was sitting with Twiggy – she and Justin de Villeneuve were mates of Bernie's – and when it was announced that he'd won he was just delighted."

The World Championship was coming into focus, especially after he had triumphed at Hockenheim, narrowly beating arch-rival Ickx. The two had never got on, and Jochen particularly savoured that success. Arrogant and aloof though some may still have felt him to be, with his dislike for signing autographs or conversing much on race mornings, he declared, "A monkey could have won in my car. Thank you, Colin". It was his last victory.

As was his custom, he gave his mechanics his victory laurel. Beaky Sims took it and placed it at the spot where Jimmy had died.

As Jochen prepared for the Italian GP at Monza, the rumours were rife. Rindt was setting up his own team, taking Jochen Rindt Racing, his Formula Two outfit, into Formula One. There were even, some said fanciful, suggestions that Jackie Stewart might be part of the deal. Others suggested he would retire to concentrate on business interests such as the Jochen Rindt Racing Car Show, in which he took immense pride. Certainly, those close to him had detected a reduction in his sheer enthusiasm for the sport since Piers had died. At other times, he had indicated that if he secured it he would exploit his World Championship before calling it a day.

OTHER VOICES

Alan Rees

"In 1970 we stayed friends, but our paths crossed a lot less because he was doing the Lotus and I was doing something completely new with March. If we saw each other, fine. But it wasn't the same once we stopped working with each other.

"He wouldn't have retired for two or three years, I wouldn't have thought. He enjoyed it too much, and he didn't really have anything else to do at that time, although he was always looking for things. He wanted to get involved in business, and he was always looking, and he started this show, and all that sort of thing, but I think he'd have gone on and he would have found other things as he went along.

"I certainly remember him tremendously for his sense of humour. That's the first thing that springs to mind. It wasn't a kind sense of humour, but it wasn't unkind, either. I think it was somewhere in the middle. He wasn't totally unkind to everybody, but he enjoyed making jokes at people's expense. That's the first thing I would think of, more than anything else. And then I would think of his driving, about his really high level of natural ability, and his car control. All of those top guys have it, but Senna and Prost today, they don't drive like that. Whereas in those days Jochen would just drive round every corner and the car would be sideways..."

■ ■ ■

In Austria, Jochen had driven a superb race, dropping three places after lifting off for oil flags, and then fighting every inch to regain them and close on the leading Ferraris of Ickx (now coming into the picture more and more) and Regazzoni before his engine broke. However, Miles had had another worrying front brake failure.

On Friday afternoon at Monza, Jochen had experimented without the wings on the Lotus, and found he could pull far more revs on the straight, even if the gearing wasn't right. It was rectified for Saturday afternoon, when the 72 was geared for a maximum speed of 205mph. Nowadays it seems crazy to have removed the aerodynamic appendages, but in those pre-chicane days Monza was a slipstreaming race and Austria had already revealed the Ferrari to be very quick. Herbie Blash put that decision into better perspective: "Some people hadn't run wings the previous two years. And the 72 was a very aerodynamic car which produced plenty of downforce because of its wedge shape. When I look back on it now, it doesn't seem a stupid thing to have done, in the circumstances of the time. You had more straight than you did corners at Monza then, and the big thing was to get down those straights as fast as you could." Miles, however, had found his 72 horribly unstable without its wings.

Jochen was pushing hard on his third flying lap on the afternoon of Saturday, September 5, and had just overtaken Denny Hulme as he entered the Parabolica. He was braking at the fastest part of the circuit when the Lotus suddenly darted to the left and slammed into the guardrail. The nose went beneath it and was ripped off. The 72 had a fabricated frame which carried the inboard brakes and was bolted to the front of the monocoque. It was torn off. Jochen preferred not to wear the crutch straps on his six-point harness, fearing

1970 finally brought him the car he had so desperately sought: the Lotus 72. Initially he hated it and refused to drive it, but when he finally did he won four races on the trot to pull out the lead that would make him the sport's only posthumous World Champion.

he might not be able to escape quickly enough should the need arise. He slid down in his seat and was partly thrown out of the gaping hole at the front of the chassis. His jugular vein was severed by the main buckle, but though he must have died instantly, the vagaries of Italian law obliged official comments to suggest he had died in the ambulance en route to hospital. Once again, the inboard front brake shafts were blamed.

OTHER VOICES

Herbie Blash – former Lotus mechanic

"At Zandvoort one year he came in and, still in the car, took the helmet off, and one thing that he always wanted was a cigarette. He was sitting in the car just puffing away on a cigarette, and as he drove down to *parc ferme*, there he was with the cigarette hanging out of his mouth. Quick? The quickest. The first lap

187

he was right on it, just like Ronnie would be. Absolutely balls to the wall.

"A guy who loved racing, but wasn't in love with it? I'd agree with that. He had a sense of perspective on it. Right at the end, it was just the start of big money for the drivers, and I think he suddenly realized there was a lot of money to be made, and he became very money orientated.

"At the end of 1970 there was talk of Jackie and Jochen actually driving together. Either with Roy Winkelmann or maybe Bernie, because Bernie was running his Formula Two team, Jochen Rindt Racing. Jochen would have liked Jochen Rindt Racing to have gone into Formula One. But at that particular time Chapman was also talking to Stewart, trying to lure him to Lotus. But Jackie didn't want to go, he was always very nervous of the cars then.

"I'm sure Jochen would have carried on for another year or so. But I think he'd have left Colin. I think eventually there would have been a Superteam, with Jochen and Jackie. Who they were going to drive for I don't know, but the two of them were so close, and they wanted to drive together.

"The only person that Jochen used to look up to was Bernie. He thought Bernie was the greatest thing since sliced bread, because Bernie was serious, and because Bernie was also very funny. Jochen used to like to gamble, used to like to play, and Bernie was that type of person. Bernie was really his best mate.

"We socialized. Numerous times we went out to dinner. But again, Jochen wouldn't hang around the circuit. With Graham in the team, Graham would sit down and write from one to 20 and then he'd come up with 20 jobs. Chapman would list one to 40. So we'd just sit there and keep working, working. And Jochen would say, maybe, 'Change the gear ratios', and that was all! He would drive round problems. I can't think of one time when he was really technical at all.

"There haven't been many since like Jochen. You'd have to say Villeneuve was in the same sort of class, obviously Peterson, too, and by the looks of it, Alesi might be that sort of driver as well.

"At Monza, Chapman shot off immediately. Just went. Nina was at home in Switzerland, so we had to get his belongings from the hotel. Bernie arranged *everything*. I had to take Jochen's car back up to Nina at Begnins. When I arrived at Geneva there were all banner headlines in German, *Jochen Rindt killed*. As I drove up to the house Nina was at the bedroom window and waved like mad. I can imagine now that it was as if it was Jochen coming home, although of course it couldn't have been. There was nobody in the house, just Sally Courage and Nina. There I was, what, 21 years old?, sitting there on the settee between these two women. What can you say in a situation like that?

"All of a sudden, Natascha, who was six and upstairs, cried out, 'Papa, Papa'. Both girls burst into tears, and there I am, 21 years old and not knowing what life's about, with one arm round Sally Courage and the other round Nina."

■　■　■

Judged by any standard, against any yardstick, Jochen Rindt was a great driver. In Formula Two he could take on anybody, even Clark. In Formula One he was reaching full maturity. As Hockenheim proved, pressure didn't worry him in the slightest, nor did the need to tiger through in adversity.

After all the years in uncompetitive or unreliable machinery he was within reach of the summit when fate reached out for him that bright afternoon at Monza. As cruel as the act of taking him had been denying him the satisfaction of knowing that when he died he had already achieved his dream of becoming the World Champion.

17

PEDRO RODRIGUEZ

No wasted weekends

"He didn't agree with all the safety campaigns that people like Jackie Stewart did – he believed that when it's your turn to go, you gotta go, regardless." – Jo Ramirez

How well I remember July 11, 1971. It was a warm Sunday in Harrow, mere days after the French GP. With memories of a sideways BRM P160 being hurled round Paul Ricard by a little man in a silver crash helmet, I was desperately looking forward to watching the following week's British GP at Silverstone.

I was walking down the stairs at home when I met my father coming up. "Have you heard about Pedro?", he asked. It was always that way in our family, even to my mother. Pedro. In England, he might not have been known outside racing, but in our household he needed only that one name, like he was a friend we all saw regularly. I didn't need to take in the almost awed tone in my father's voice, nor to see the look of parental concern in his eyes, to *know*.

The little Mexican had been due for a weekend off from his schedule of racing for BRM and John Wyer's Gulf Porsche team. He was busier as a racing driver than at any time in his career, but a weekend without a race was two wasted days to a man who lived his life on the edge with supreme fatalism. And certainly by that stage of his burgeoning career Pedro was never a man to waste anything.

BRM was aghast at his final negotiations to drive Herbert Muller's Ferrari 512M at the Norisring, an awful concoction of a track set in the old stadium where the Nazis had held their wartime rallies. He was to have driven the CanAm BRM there, but its Chevrolet engine blew up on the test bench. The organizers had made much play of him during pre-event publicity, and were desperate that he still be there. They offered significant blandishments, even tried to persuade JW Automotive to enter a Porsche 917, but there was insufficient time to prepare one. Everyone at BRM would have preferred him not to race there, but were sufficiently acute to realize how much racing meant to him. Only later were they to realize the awful price of leniency.

Poor Tim Parnell. He was then team manager for the Bourne equipe, and even today there is bitterness in his voice when he recalls Pedro's decision to race that weekend. "We'd gone to Silverstone, we were all ready for the British GP, we'd tested, the cars were looking good and fit, and then some stupid idiot rang up from the blinking Norisring and they kept pestering him, pestering him to drive this bloody car there. It was an old clapped-out car that'd been doing some film work. And they offered him so much money, they kept offering and he kept turning them down, and I said to him, 'You're crazy to go there, Pedro, to drive a bloody clapped-out car', but the money they offered was too

189

In his early days Pedro (right) played second fiddle to younger brother Ricardo (left). The latter's death at the circuit later named in their honour affected Pedro deeply, and it was some years before his own career assumed its initial momentum.

much, and in the end he just went. And it was absolutely ironic. The *ironic* thing was that he got into the lead with the thing; he should never have been in the lead with this clapped-out car, but there it was. And of course, in Germany they thought it was fantastic. Tragic. Your life's thrown away in a clapped-out car in a clapped-out bloody race."

Yes, the money had finally proved irresistible. But Pedro's real motivation, as ever, had simply been racing.

He put the Ferrari on the front row for the first heat, mere tenths behind Chris Craft's winning 7.6-litre McLaren, and was leading, as one knew he would have been in such circumstances, when he came up to pass a backmarker on lap 12 under braking for the Esses. Some say that a tyre failed, others that he collided with Kurt Hild's modified and slow Porsche 910 spyder. Something made the Ferrari veer to the left and hit the barriers before plunging back over to the right, where it smashed into a bridge abutment. It was a massive impact, which instantly ruptured one of the Ferrari's fuel tanks. It burst into flames immediately, and it was three minutes before the prompt marshals had him out. They were helped by his former JW team-mate Leo Kinnunen. *Paris Match*, as it so often did, captured the ghastly consequences, and as Pedro was finally released and carried away on a stretcher, he was already beyond hope.

"To me, Pedro was the greatest driver of his time... I mean *the* greatest", said devastated JW boss John Wyer. "He is irreplaceable."

"He would race anything", said Jo Ramirez, the Mexican who came over with Pedro and his brother Ricardo, worked with Pedro at JW, and is now part of the McLaren management. "If someone offered him a wheelbarrow he would go and race it. That weekend I had just bought a house in Maidenhead, the first house I ever bought, and he used to live in Bray, which was very close. He and his girlfriend Glenda were coming to dinner that evening, and he called me on the Friday and said he was going to race for Muller. I said, 'Oh well, no problem,

190

there's always a next time.' I never even saw the news of the race and completely forgot about it, and on Monday morning I learned that he was killed. I couldn't believe it."

"All that, for a funfair race", said his JW mechanic Ermanno Cuoghi.

He died that evening, and a light went out in my life. Donald Campbell had been my retrospective hero at that time, but Pedro had been the first active driver with whom I had identified in my adolescent years of racing passion. Now he was gone.

Whenever I think of him I am taken back to the days when my enthusiasm for motorsport hadn't become tempered by the cynicism bred from dealing first-hand with so many of its current personalities. To the eager walk to the newsagents on a Wednesday morning for *Motor* and *Autocar*, and the frantic sprint there on Thursdays for *Motoring News* and *Autosport*. Oh, was it ever a bad day when any or all of them were delayed! To days when I would peek quickly at the race reports, and then torment myself by refusing to look again until I'd reached school, whereupon I would hide somewhere to devour the words of Mike Twite, Mike Cotton, Pete Lyons or Jeff Hutchinson, hanging on to phrases so that whenever I came to recall certain races, I could trot them out verbatim.

The first motor race I ever saw was the 1968 Race of Champions at Brands Hatch, when we sat at the back row of what is now the Lanfranchi grandstand, me the pubescent 15-year-old able to tell the older guys with whom I had gone who was driving what, and bristling with pride because Mike Spence had put his V12 BRM – my team! – alongside Bruce McLaren's pole-winning McLaren M7A, with Pedro back on the third row. The Mexican's car needed a late plug change on the dummy grid and he got away after everyone else, yet he was so fired up that sunny March afternoon that he devoured the field, all but McLaren. My heart sang as the green P126's orange snout flicked one way then another behind Stewart's awkward Matra, while all the time, from the depths of the cockpit, a little fist waved angrily.

Stewart was warm about Jim Clark, Dan Gurney and Mike Spence when we talked for this book, but his voice was emotionless when he spoke of Pedro, clipped and impersonal.

"He was very Mexican, excitable and fiery, Latin. He was very lethargic out of a car in many ways, but if he got upset at airports or with rental car companies or with traffic, he became very Mexican. As he did in a racing car.

"I mean, Pedro at the beginning of a race was one to be avoided. First lap, second lap type of thing. His eyes were all over the place all of the time, like Rene Arnoux's. You look at people's eyes, it tells you a lot in a racing driver. You can see some are absolutely hyper, some are more subdued, some of them are forcing themselves to be that way. Then you look at the other ones who have got that calmness..."

Jackie was at odds with both Pedro and Jacky Ickx for refusing to give up Spa in support of his campaigns. He could never understand their fatalism. Pedro, for his part, would have nothing to do with the Grand Prix Drivers' Association's 'militants'. "If the organizers want to put on a race at Spa", he said, "then I will be there."

That afternoon drive at Brands was as close to a display of Latin temperament as Pedro ever got in a racing car. He was unusual in that he never mixed very freely with the other drivers. He tended to stand back, and Parnell sometimes used to ask him why he was like that. And Pedro would smile and say, "Well, it's just how I like to be. I don't really like to know the other drivers. Or for them to know me too well and perhaps know how I think and react to all these things."

"And there's no doubt about it", said Tim, "when you're out on the track and you're competing with someone you're not really sure of, and you know that they're the sort of lad who doesn't spend too much time looking in the mirrors, and he's got his line and gets on with it, and if these guys want to get by him, well, it's up to them to get by, it's a good policy." Chris Amon found that out to his cost trying to pass Pedro during qualifying at Monaco in 1970.

OTHER VOICES

Jack Oliver – BRM and JW Gulf Porsche team-mate

"His English wasn't very good. He had that very Mexican way of speaking, like the guy who approaches and asks if you want to buy 'pictures of my sister'. I didn't see the Anglophile side of him.

"He was a fiercely competitive bloke, especially with his own team-mate. That's probably why he drove so strongly in all locations and conditions, regardless of whether the car was competitive. He always gave 100%. He was not the sort of bloke you get particularly close to, maybe because of nationality. Very fiery, very possessive. There was strong inter-team-mate competition and not a full exchange of information between us on the cars, perpetrated mostly by Pedro, as I remember.

"We had a distant relationship, he was just another competitor. Quite often people in the same car are very competitive. It's the same car, you see, so you can't use that as an excuse..."

■ ■ ■

Nevertheless, socially he could be good company, even-tempered. It took a lot to get him really upset, and the storm soon passed. He was simply not the type to harbour anything. "The car would get him mad, of course", said Parnell. "He was so competitive he wanted a car he could compete with. If stupid things went wrong with it, and if things went wrong with it that he'd already identified as problems, then of course he did get steamed-up, and quite naturally so. But he was a wonderful guy to work with, certainly. When BRM lost Rodriguez and Siffert we hit rock bottom again."

BRM was hardly at the top in 1968, although in the early races Len Terry's P126 and its Bourne-built P133 derivative were actually quite good until the numerous Cosworth-powered teams and Ferrari and Honda honed their development. All through the season his fighting spirit blazed through regardless.

At Jarama he led and was a possible victor until he slid off on oil. At Monaco he did the job properly to remove two wheels at Mirabeau after brake failure, whereupon he walked away with breathtaking insouciance. At Spa he was hounding McLaren until he began to run short of fuel on the last lap. McLaren won. At Zandvoort he was third in the wet after a dramatic climb through the field. And at Rouen he actually squeezed past eventual victor Ickx to lead for a lap in the appalling conditions before dropping back to fight tooth-and-nail with Surtees' Honda until his gearbox failed. He set fastest lap at that one.

After that the results were thin, confined to a survivor's third in Canada and fourth in Mexico on the circuit now named after him and Ricardo. The point was that Pedro always tried in the car, and Formula One in those days never had the certainty of car performance that often renders today's races so dull. Back in mid-1968 you never quite knew whether the BRM would pop up near the front of a race, and that was a delicious uncertainty to an avid schoolboy.

That was what I so loved about Pedro. His ability, like Moss, to make the impossible possible. To pluck a result from nowhere while his team-mates floundered near the back of the grid, victims of their own psyches.

As he would prove later with the Porsches, his stamina was outstanding, and time and again he would step from his victorious car with nary a bead of sweat

Magic moment: at the author's first motor race – the 1968 Race of Champions – Pedro harried Stewart mercilessly in the Matra as he recovered from the late plug change which had obliged him to start from the back of the grid. He passed the Scot, to finish second only to Bruce McLaren.

dampening his brow. Yet, incredibly, he never concerned himself with physical fitness. "The joke about him was that lying flat on his back reading a book was the only exercise he was ever seen to take", recalled Cotton, to whom he was as legendary a figure as he was to me. "But anyone who could control a car like the 917 in the wet had to be an outstanding driver. His car control was amazing."

In the rain, of course, he was simply sensational. Rouen and Zandvoort in 1968 had been landmarks, but nothing matched his awesome mastery of Brands Hatch in 1970 where, in the BOAC 1000kms, he finally had the machinery to match his talent. "It was as if he has sleight of hand in the wet," said Chris Amon at the time.

That afternoon Pedro wove a magic spell with that blue-and-orange 917, walking away from a class field in torrential rain. Even when Clerk of the Course Nick Syrett had him black-flagged after 20 minutes for passing under a yellow flag that he simply hadn't been able to see in the murk, Pedro simply sat calmly during his lecture, staring straight ahead, before blasting back into the fray. His rhythm altered not a bit after the hiatus...

"When it rained he was the most remarkable man I've ever seen race", said Parnell. "The other drivers used to joke about it and say, 'Well why doesn't someone tell Pedro it's bloody raining!'. Ridiculous, absolutely ridiculous! The way he could balance the car."

On an oily track he was in his element, and I still believe he would have won that Race of Champions in 1968 had he started with the rest of the grid. That BOAC race in 1970 he *did* win. He lost a lap during his telling-off, yet by lap 20 had made it up to deprive Amon of the lead. His overtaking manoeuvres against wet-weather talents such as team-mate Jo Siffert and Vic Elford defied belief as he snaked into Paddock, and he made the rest look like club racers as the fearsome Porsche 917 squirmed its way round the Kentish track. New bodywork had done much to tame the original beast, but it was still a driver's car. And what a driver he was that day, lapping the entire field by half-distance. *Elford* was *five* laps behind at the flag. Pedro's stunning success lives on as a treasure in the minds of all who witnessed it.

No less impressive was his display at Zandvoort in 1971, where he battled all afternoon with Jacky Ickx's more powerful Ferrari. Ickx was heralded as the Rainmaster, but Pedro was at least his equal and the two of them fought such a gripping duel that they lapped the entire field! Pedro should have won that Dutch GP, but the fuel metering unit went off with 10 laps to go and he suffered a chronic misfire that killed his chances. Ickx, quicker when the track was drier, eventually won by eight seconds.

Looking back, so many glittering drives stand out. He *made* sportscar racing in 1970 and '71, and in a great car he, too, was great. Races surrendered to him. Despite victory at Reims in 1965, Pedro's true ability in a sportscar wasn't fully recognized for years, although JW team manager David Yorke appreciated it in 1967 when he put Pedro in the Mirage at the BOAC 500. He was flying until his driving partner, Dr Dick Thompson, spread the car over Clearways. Under Wyer and Yorke his true ability would finally blossom.

"At Daytona in 1971", recalled Ramirez, "we were leading the race, and three hours before the end the gearbox packed up when Oliver was driving. You cannot change the box, but you can change all the parts, everything inside. Not the actual case. We had to use levers and hammers and we got Pedro out after an hour and a half's work. We had just to throw everything in and hope it was alright. By then we'd lost first place, but then it started raining. Rain at Daytona? Round the banking there in the 917 in the rain, he was incredible... We all sat waiting, hoping the car was going to be alright, and he just went by and put his finger up, and then he went out carving seconds and seconds..." He and a car-sick Oliver won, just as he had the previous year with the quiet Finn Kinnunen. That year, Ferrari's 512M was little match, although Roger Penske and Mark Donohue got theirs working very well in the two North American races to give JW a hard time. Pedro retaliated in a mighty scrap at Sebring, and the Ferrari needed more tank tape than the Porsche, although there wasn't much in it! Penske was *very* upset with that one!

And then came the Austrian 1000kms at the Osterreichring, the race many rate as his best ever. Predictably, he led the opening laps before losing almost six minutes having a faulty battery changed. JW blamed him for using the headlights too often! Outwardly calm, Pedro just zipped back into the event, never once questioning that he might not have a chance of making up his two and a half lap deficit. Apart from a 12-lap stint for co-driver Dickie Attwood, he drove the entire 170-lap distance single-handed. Clay Regazzoni led in the Ferrari 312P, and though he eventually made the mistake that handed the victory to Pedro, the little Mexican had already clawed his way back on to the same lap, and was gaining, gaining, gaining... Cotton was at that race: "It was an amazing drive, four and a half hours. And when he got out of the car he was so cool. He wasn't even sweating."

For me, though, Spa in 1970 was his greatest race. The event where he slapped BRM's critics so firmly in the eye. He loved the place, loved its challenge and its danger. This was no artificial track, but a driver's circuit. Yes, Armco was sprouting, but there were still trees and houses close to the tarmac, traps into which the unwary might fall. It was Formula One without a safety net, and Pedro was in his element.

At the time he was still dangerously underrated by his rivals, yet his victory there rates among the finest Formula One drives. He never put a wheel wrong, as Chris Amon was quick to admit. The perennially unlucky New Zealander had spent the entire race just waiting for the BRM to break, or for the volatile Mexican to make a mistake. Instead, both were perfect. "He never put a wheel wrong, just drove beautifully", admitted Chris with reluctant admiration. "He was just so precise, everywhere. If it hadn't been for finishing only second, it would have been beautiful to watch."

"When we went there everybody had been rubbishing us and we'd been struggling to get back", remembered Parnell, "and he was *magic*. Through the back curves of the old Spa circuit, they all said to see him drifting the BRM through them was just fantastic."

In the end, Pedro finished a mere 1.1s ahead of Amon. As he climbed from the car he was literally as fresh as when he'd started the race, despite the intense pressure the March driver had sustained on him throughout. As he pulled off his crash helmet, not one thick, black hair was out of place.

The United States GP at Watkins Glen should have been his that year, too, once Stewart's new Tyrrell had retired. Instead, he wound up second, having left the pits after a late fuel stop as if hole-shotting with Don Garlits.

"Oh well, that was my fault, with a petrol job", Parnell recalled. "We couldn't carry enough fuel. Very funny thing about Watkins Glen. It was the end of the year, always held in October time, the BRMs always went well there, but they always used a hell of a lot of fuel there. We crammed as much on board as we could, but we just hadn't got enough. We topped him up on the line again, and we just hadn't got enough. Oh, he was bloody upset about that. Bloody upset, he was. Quite naturally so. Well out in the lead and he ran out on the second lap from the end. Oh, we finished second, but $50,000 went down the drain. Money was important to him. Compared to the money they get today it was all peanuts, but winning meant more to him."

Whatever he drove, Pedro would never give up, even when the machinery was below par. He went to Indianapolis with a Huffaker MG Liquid Suspension Special in 1964, and though he ended up in the wall when the left rear wheel fell off after a lap, he had been standing on the gas from the start of qualifying right up until that moment. American observers had been impressed.

His finest hours came in the appalling conditions of the 1970 BOAC 1000kms at Brands Hatch, when grown men gasped at the sleight of hand he displayed on the treacherous track surface. The race surrendered to him, and he and the Gulf Porsche 917 finished five laps ahead of their nearest rival.

That was one of his few serious shunts, and three years later he broke an ankle and smashed a heel in a shunt at the Enna Formula Two race with the wooden Protos. He was dicing for second with Jean-Pierre Beltoise, and after being thrown from the car he maintained that position as he slid personally across the start/finish line. He had to have his injuries set without anaesthetic, but he endured the pain with typical stoicism. Another nasty moment came at Zandvoort while testing the BRM in 1970 when a tyre failed. "He is one of the most intelligent drivers round today", Yorke said of him. "He can analyze a situation almost before it develops."

If he could charge with the best of them, he was also capable of nursing his equipment. Nothing exemplified that better than the South African GP in 1967. His Cooper-Maserati was cumbersome and uncompetitive, but by taking care of it he brought it home first for his maiden GP win, and temporarily topped the World Championship points table.

That year he teamed with Jochen Rindt, who took great pains to discomfort him at every turn. But it worried Pedro, a man who preferred not to get too close to his team-mates in any case, not at all. It even amused him highly when Rindt, having failed to take him to the cleaners at backgammon, jumped planes rather than continue together! Interestingly, even at that stage of his revived Formula One career he gave little away to Jochen, and when their cars were comparable, their times were, too. Pedro, however, was much easier on his equipment. He scored more points, and the win that Rindt didn't manage. Team manager Roy Salvadori reckoned they had equal potential.

At the end of the year, against medical advice, he made his comeback from the Enna shunt for his home GP. By then the Cooper was even less competitive, but in a race of attrition he brought it home an exhausted sixth. That, too, was typical of his refusal ever to give up.

By the end of that year his future was mapped out. 1967 had been his first serious year as a professional, even though he had been in Europe since he and his younger brother Ricardo had driven an OSCA together at Le Mans in 1959. Between those two extremes lay sorrow and uncertainty. Both of Don Pedro Rodriguez's sons had matured in a childhood indulged by vast wealth. Years later, when Jim Clark and Sally Stokes travelled to the Mexican GP, Pedro met them at the foot of the aeroplane steps. "I asked him", said Sally, "how on earth he had managed that, but he just smiled at me..." Don Pedro had some interesting connections...

When Pedro was 11 he raced motorcycles. Three years later he was racing cars. At 15 he had a Porsche 1500. He was 18 when he first went to Le Mans. Ricardo, in fact, had had *his* Le Mans entry turned down in 1957 because the AC de l'Ouest felt that 16 was too young an age to race there!

The younger Rodriguez was the faster, and certainly the more spectacular, but his extra speed came at the expense of his equipment and, at times, his personal control. As Pedro languished out of the limelight, uncertain if he wanted to devote his life to racing, Don Pedro's wealth helped Ricardo to sign with Ferrari for the 1962 season. He had attracted Enzo Ferrari's attention not only by his father's folding stuff, but also through his activities in Europe with the Italian sportscars and an astonishing qualifying performance in one of his cars at the 1961 Italian GP at Monza.

Ramirez came over with them, age and nationality creating a close tie with Ricardo in particular. "He was more my character, whereas Pedro even then was much more reserved. I got on well with them both, but I went to Italy in 1961 with Ricardo when he had his first Formula One race, when Von Trips was killed. I was the team gopher in 1962, when I used to travel to all the races with Ricardo, Bandini and Baghetti."

Ricardo lost his life exiting the Peraltada, still one of racing's most exacting and exciting corners, while practising for the 1962 Mexican GP. Ferrari hadn't gone, but it was unthinkable that the hometown hero should not race. He was trying to win the pole in Rob Walker's Lotus 24 during the final session when he lost control and was killed instantly. He was only 20. The accident was put down to a blend of youthful exuberance and nationalistic pressure, but Pedro always believed it had been due to tyre failure.

The incident had a profound effect on him. As Ramirez moved on to Maserati (and thence to Lamborghini and then Eagle), Pedro pondered his future in racing, whether he really wanted to carry on. After a while he did so, helped by victory in the Daytona 1000kms sharing a Ferrari 250 GTO with Phil Hill, but his involvement was more as a gentleman amateur. He liked to race, but he

He should have won the 1971 Dutch GP, too, as he fought tooth and nail in his Yardley BRM against Jacky Ickx's Ferrari in the rain. He eventually finished eight seconds adrift after a fuel metering problem, but even so they lapped the entire field.

liked also to live in Mexico where he ran his successful European car dealership. The days were yet to come when he would become the comfortable Anglophile, living in Bray with his white Bentley S1 and his beloved deerstalker or flat cap. He would race occasionally for Team Lotus in Formula One, standing in for Clark at the French GP at Reims in 1966, when Jimmy was hit in the face by a bird in practice, but though he ran well there, he was not highly rated.

"Pedro was very introverted", Ramirez recalled. "Ricardo was very extrovert. They were good friends, but I never had quite the same friendship with Pedro as with Ricardo. Ricardo and I were like two brothers, and we used to do a lot of things together. Pedro was a bit serious at times, I think he took life too seriously... I think he thought about giving up after Ricardo was killed, but it didn't last long. I think that Ricardo was perhaps a little bit more mad about racing at first, but then Pedro began to take his very seriously."

Once BRM had won the battle with Cooper for his services in 1968, he settled down. Even in 1969, when BRM boss Louis Stanley took that unfathomable decision to 'rest' him in Parnell's then private BRM team, he kept his spirits up, although he eventually had to abandon ship for an old but marginally more competitive semi-works Ferrari. He soldiered it to sixth at Monza.

As he returned to BRM for 1970 life held so much; he had a competitive if fragile Formula One car, and the Porsche 917 to master in a sportscar championship that, in those days, was as exciting as the single-seaters. He adapted more easily to European life than had Ricardo, and he led a peaceful existence in Bray, even if the presence of his estranged wife Angelina did create problems from time to time as he was then living with his girlfriend Glenda. "It was a bit sticky", Ramirez admitted. "It was for me, too, because I liked them both. I was never too sure about Angelina, but Glenda was alright." "When he died it was tricky writing the obituary", said Cotton. "We weren't sure which of the women should receive our condolences."

With better machinery, Pedro's talents were honed. His technical feedback became more assured, as did his ability to set up a car. "One of the things I most admired, and it's something you don't see very often in modern drivers, although perhaps Senna is a little bit like this", said Ramirez, "was that he would get to a stage in qualifying where he'd realize the time, and that he'd changed the car about as much as he could and still have the chance left to set a time. Then he'd decide to go out and stay out and get himself used to how the car was, sort of adapt himself to it. I think modern drivers, they wouldn't do that. They'd probably refuse to drive it."

"He knew what he wanted from a car", said Cuoghi. "He knew about the little details, about understeer and oversteer. He could help you to make the car better."

His mechanics loved him, not just for the small presents he bought them from time to time, nor even just for his big heart. He could be intensely considerate. When Ignazio Giunti was killed in the 1971 Argentine 1000kms, Pedro took all of his mechanics out that evening to get them drunk and help them forget.

He was also tremendously popular with the fans, and he always had time for the people who paid to get in. He appreciated, through his own love of racing, that other people's love for it could have expression other than actually driving fast cars.

OTHER VOICES

Tim Parnell – BRM team manager

"He was a hard man to overtake. He was quite hard on his cars at times, but he could nurse a car along, especially when we did the CanAm with BRM, and in the other sportscars. It was amazing how he could get a car home. When he knew there was something wrong with a car, and knew basically what the problem was with it, he would get it home.

"1969 was a difficult time. We were all depressed at that time. BRM was going through a bad patch then. The H16 was a brilliantly engineered piece of machinery, but as a racing car it was very, very difficult. It had brought the factory to its knees, really. It was so difficult to maintain the cars and to keep them going, and everybody was down. When you get situations like that everybody gets low, even after the 1968 season. Then, at the end of that, he came with us and we had the two-valve engines that were built for commercial purposes. They were built mainly for Matra, which had the V8 engines for their sportscars and were going to have a V12 for the sportcar programme. Eventually it just became a commercial engine, and when the H16 was struggling it was decided to develop it into a four-valve. We were down then, and so was he. Then, of course, he rejoined the team for 1970.

"Without a doubt he was a great part of the history of motorsport. A fantastic sportscar driver, without a doubt. I suppose as a sportscar driver he was one of the greats. And he was getting with it in Formula One; I wouldn't be doing him an injustice, I don't suppose, if I said that. Everything was coming right for him."

"He had terrific spirit, terrific comradeship. He always mixed well with the team. He'd come and eat with the mechanics. If I said, 'Where shall we meet?', he'd say, 'Oh, we'll go and eat with the mechanics'. We all used to sit down and eat together, things like that.

"Oh, that Tabasco sauce of his! That's it, he'd carry it with him. He'd play some amazing tricks on some of the drivers when they weren't looking, and sprinkle some of it on their food. George Eaton, he did that to; he caught Mike Spence, too, and he caught Piers once, as well.

"He was a man of mystery... well, there was a mystique about Pedro. His style

Pedro Rodriguez as his legion of fans remember him, in brown Yardley BRM anorak and wearing his beloved deerstalker. Of all the BRM drivers team manager Tim Parnell can recall, he enjoyed the greatest amount of fan mail.

and the way he was such a fearless little driver. He was an amazing person; he had a fantastic fan club. Of all the drivers who drove for us at BRM – Mrs Walker was my secretary and Tony Rudd's before that – she said they'd never had such a fan mail as they had for Pedro Rodriguez."

■ ■ ■

The success that meant the most to him came at Le Mans in September 1968. Then he was still vastly underrated, even as a sportscar driver, but perhaps it evoked happy memories of Ricardo as he and Lucien Bianchi finally steered their JW Gulf Ford GT40 to the American marque's third successive triumph. "When they first came over here they started at Le Mans", Ramirez said. "That was the big thing then, and I think it always stayed that way for Pedro."

Somehow Pedro *knew* he was going to win that race, and went into it with supreme confidence. His stamina was staggering, and he drove far longer than Bianchi. And he was very upset when Yorke refused to let him finish as well as start the race! As they drove the victorious GT40 to the paddock afterwards, Pedro wanted all of his crew to sit on the roof with him...

In 1971 the BRM was fundamentally more reliable, the P160 evolution from the Spa-winning P153 competitive on all types of circuit. Pedro beat a good field to win the Rothmans Spring Cup at Oulton Park in April, and was quick everywhere else. The weekend before he died, only Stewart's Tyrrell was ahead of him at Paul Ricard. His years of effort, it seemed, were just about to be rewarded. At last his Formula One star was truly ascendant.

A week later, his love of racing finally took him to the wrong place at the wrong time. Had anyone tried to warn him that morning in Germany that his time had come, he would not have railed against the cruelty of life. He would have accepted his fate calmly, with a philosophical shrug of his shoulders, a flash of those warm brown eyes and that quiet smile playing at the corners of his mouth that simply said, 'You cannot argue with God's will'.

18

EDDIE SACHS

Death has a thousand doors

"In the long run, death is the odds-on favourite."

Nobody, not even Pierre Levegh at Le Mans, was as obsessed with a race as Eddie Sachs. He lived for Indianapolis, for the chance to race in the 500. They threw him out of the Speedway, the first time he went, when they found he didn't have the right pass, but he would return, despite the humiliation.

"I'll be back", he roared at the security guards who escorted him to the gate. "Remember the name – Eddie Sachs!" A J Foyt suffered a similar indignity, and the two would share a mutual respect as their fortunes improved.

Edward Julius Sachs, born on May 28, 1927 in Bethlehem, Pennsylvania, was not normally an aggressive man. Oh, he could be when it mattered, when he was driving a sprintcar high up by the wall at Langhorne, or a Champcar on the ovals, but his overriding characteristics were optimism and determination. He had them in spades. It was just that he was totally consumed by his burning ambition to win at the Brickyard, that day in 1953. "My Indy", he used to call it, and there were stars and stripes in his eyes.

Most of the time he was an affable, intensely garrulous man whose sense of humour became a legend. Just before the start of the 1963 500, for example, he marched cheerfully behind the Gordon Pipers on the main straight, waving happily to his fans. They called him the Clown Prince, but the clowning was often a useful cloak for the depth of his obsession. He failed his rookie test in 1954, the first time he got to Indy legally, and again in 1955, and for a long time he had to endure the jeers of his rivals. One race programme listed him as Eddie Saxe. The clowning helped cover his wounded pride, too.

Everything about his early days seemed to embrace failure. He aspired to be a baseball star, then a professional footballer, but he proved miserable at both sports. When he went to a motor race at Greensboro in 1947, however, he knew he had found his metier. But though race driving became his passion, he proved equally inept. He hung around Dorney Park Raceway, in neighbouring Allentown, for night after night, but whenever he took to the track his performances in stockcars were woeful. Whatever it took to be a driver, it seemed, had been left out of Eddie Sachs' personal makeup. But he persevered. He would joke about his lack of ability, and admitted that when he did take part in his first sprintcar race he scared himself to death. "I spent each corner howling with fear, and when I got back to the pits I shouted 'I'm safe!'", he clowned.

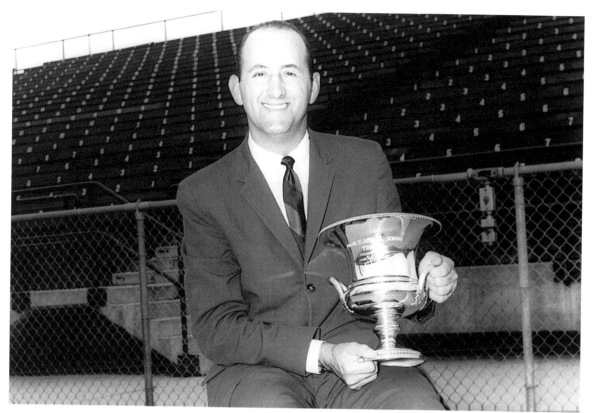

Few men ever worked as hard on their driving style as Edward Julius Sachs. He knew nothing about the way in which cars worked, was the despair of his mechanics, and never even really understood why he was quick, but A.J. Foyt believed him to be one of the hungriest drivers he ever

Eventually, Dorney Park's Lou Heller took pity on him and began to teach him the rudiments of his profession, and little by little he began to improve. "The trouble was, Eddie knew absolutely nothing about what a car was doing", veteran chief mechanic Clint Brawner would later lament. "If the car was wrong at a certain corner, he would instinctively correct for that before he got to the bad point. It was uncanny, because he never knew he was doing it!"

There was nothing he wouldn't do to be near Indy. For a while he washed cars in the vicinity, or collected pop bottles so he could claim the deposit when he returned them to the local grocers. He had unsuccessful spells as a bellhop, even ran a bar. Anything to be near the Brickyard's month of May action.

In 1956 he finally got to watch it from the right side of the wire with a badge that said he was a driver. He drove the Glessner Special to 34th fastest time in a field of 33, which left him as the first reserve. By then, however, his prowess had been evident on the gruelling midget and sprintcar circuit, and he would record his first victory that July in the USAC 100-miler on the one-mile dirt track at Lakewood Park, Atlanta, in the Glessner Special. At the end of 1956 he ended up second in the Midwest sprintcar series, and third in the USAC Midget National Championship.

A year later he made the breakthrough at the Brickyard. He qualified the Schmidt Special second only to Pat O'Connor, but his race ended after 105 laps. Undeterred, he went to Monza in that watershed event in June when Indianapolis came to Europe. He acclimatized faster than any of his rivals in the Jim Robbins Special and led the first of three heats for a while, running fearlessly wheel-to-wheel with O'Connor, Tony Bettenhausen and eventual winner Jimmy Bryan. He finished fourth in that heat after the big car kept bottoming on the bumpy banking, and he and O'Connor were again wheel-to-wheel at 170mph in the second heat. When O'Connor split a fuel tank, victory for Sachs seemed certain, until two camshaft securing bolts sheared and prevented him either finishing that heat, or starting the third. He was classified eighth overall.

Soon afterwards he suffered facial injuries and a crushed hand bone in a midget race at the 16th Street Speedway, opposite the Indianapolis Motor Speedway, but he returned as determined as ever. If Eddie Sachs had started out a bum, he'd come a long way in a very short time. He underlined that in 1958, which brought him USAC 100-miler victories at Langhorne and the Indiana Fairgrounds. Only the fearless and the talented ever won at the former venue, which even the bravest drivers treated with respect. There was another retirement at Indy after only 68 laps, again after starting from the front row, while at Monza's second Race of Two Worlds he again led the first heat and was fighting Luigi Musso for second place behind victor Jim Rathmann when the Jim Robbins car threw a rod. By the end of the year he had won the Midwest Sprintcar Championship.

He maintained his record for front row starts at Indy over the next two seasons, but finished neither race, but his reputation was further enhanced by more USAC 100-miler wins at Syracuse and Trenton. He won at the New Jersey track in 1959 and '60, and would win again twice in '61.

That year's 500 boiled down to a classic shootout between Foyt and Sachs. Qualifying had claimed the life of legendary hero Tony Bettenhausen while he was trying to sort out Paul Russo's roadster as a favour to the gnarled veteran, and his death cast a pall of gloom over the other drivers, especially as other veterans Bryan and Johnny Thompson had recently lost their lives in accidents. Sachs was more sensitive than many to such things, but became only the third man in the Speedway's history to take the pole two years in a row, joining luminaries Ralph de Palma and Rex Mays.

At the start Jim Hurtubise jumped into the lead from Sachs and Don Branson, but the latter strained his engine almost immediately. After a five-car incident Hurtubise's engine went sour and rookie Parnelli Jones came dramatically to the fore and stayed there, despite a facial injury. When his engine in turn lost its edge, it became Sachs v Foyt. Troy Ruttman and Rodger Ward, past winners both, intervened briefly, but it was the two hard-chargers down to the wire over the last 200 miles. Eddie had the slightly faster car, but Foyt just wouldn't give up. They traded the lead lap after lap, and would swap it

The tears of a clown. At Indianapolis in 1961 Sachs tours into the pits after losing to Foyt, as ever waving to the crowd. Only minutes earlier he had been waving a victory salute until fears about his right rear tyre prompted him to make a precautionary stop. A year of anguish later, he reconstructed the same situation and proved to himself that the tyre would easily have lasted the few miles that separated him from the success he so desperately wanted.

10 times over the last fifth of the race. They both made their final scheduled pit stops, and this time Foyt caught and passed Sachs for the lead, the Bowes Seal Fast Special suddenly quicker than the Dean Van Lines Special. Between laps 170 and 183 of the 200, he opened out a 20-second lead. Foyt couldn't figure it, unless Sachs' engine had lost power. It hadn't. There was a much more simple reason.

A jammed fuel line had prevented Foyt's crew fully filling his tank during his stop, so his car was lighter and therefore fractionally quicker. Fifteen laps from the end he was called in for an agonizing eight-second stop. Foyt boiled back out, charging as if nothing else in the world mattered, which to him it didn't. Sachs, meanwhile, looked an easy winner.

But it would all go wrong for him. He had a huge lead, and was waving to the fans as he reeled off the last 10 laps. In his pit, chief mechanic Brawner and car owner Al Dean couldn't believe that they were about to win the 500. Sachs' tearful wife Nancy clutched nervously in the stands, refusing to be escorted to Victory Lane until she knew, for sure, that her husband really had won. So much had gone wrong for him in the past.

In the car, Sachs began to detect the unmistakable signs. The handling was going off, and he felt the warning vibration. He watched a thin strip of white rubber begin to show through on his right rear Firestone. It couldn't be happening, but it was. He was going to lose the 500, so cruelly close to home. He thought the rubber would peel right off. Sachs and Foyt had been taking their equipment to the limit, but ironically Foyt's fuel problem saved him. With its heavier load, Eddie's car had used up all its rubber, it was that simple.

Sachs had only seconds in which to make the most crucial decision of his life. He had the 500 in the palm of his hand. Did he stay out and risk an accident, or did he come in for a fresh tyre? He agonized all the way round the lap, and then came diving in. Al Dean cursed him. Brawner cursed him even more, desperately close to tears. One of his mechanics was so upset he fell to his knees and his hammer, trapped in a rear wheel, was thrown skyward as Sachs and the Dean Van Lines Special rejoined the race.

Just as he left the pit road Foyt went by, and Sachs lost his race by 8.3s after a shade over three and a half hours of racing at 139mph. He never came as close again. A year later the Dean crew re-enacted the incident out of curiosity. Eddie's tyre went the full distance. Safely…

The disappointment might have crushed a lesser man, but once he had cried like a kid he accepted defeat with grace. But why had he stopped? Why not risk those final laps? Foyt certainly would have, come hell or high water. Perhaps that was the vital difference between two fearsomely determined men.

Both had watched in horror as Bettenhausen had cartwheeled to his death in front of them on the pit straight in qualifying. Afterwards Eddie had sat on the pit wall with his head in his hands, crying his eyes out. Foyt never cried. His reaction was to slam his helmet as hard into his garage wall as possible. That, too, was one of their differences. Eddie was fearless, but maybe he just lacked that final haze of red mist.

He was the first to admit that he had fumbled the most important catch of his career, potted the cue ball along with the black. There had seemed good reason for stopping, although Brawner was adamant the tyre had had enough tread for three more laps. When Foyt went to Victory Lane Eddie had stood quietly on the edge of the milling crowd, kicking the dust, a wistful expression on his face. There was no bitterness, and that was typical of the man.

"I'll get it yet", he said. "I used just to want it for myself. Now I want it for my family. Someday, my son will stand in a school playground somewhere and he'll be able to say to the other kids, 'My daddy won the 500'."

He added, with candour that was also an inherent trait, "I have only myself to blame. With a safe 26-second lead after A J's stop and only 10 laps to go, I became over-confident and slowed down too much through the turns. I failed to drift properly, turned too sharply and put all the wear on the right rear tyre. I first saw the canvas on lap 195, and figured I'd rather be second than dead."

OTHER VOICES

Chris Economaki – publisher of *National Speedsport News*

"You gotta speak loud to me. Eddie Sachs' engines have ruined my hearing...

"He was a character. Of all the race drivers I've ever met, Eddie was the one who was the least gifted to begin with. Everything he had at the end of his career he had had to learn fact by fact, lap by lap, the hard way. God gave him nothing. He was not a natural born race driver. He was a natural born *showman*. He was a very personable guy. Extremely homely. Not a good-looking person; he had a big nose and was sort of an odd-looking guy. But he was very determined, and a nice guy.

"I got him his very first pit badge at Indianapolis, and a month or two later we got a package at home and it was an electric coffee maker as a gift in appreciation of me getting him in at the Indianapolis Speedway. He had a great way with words. He was criticized when he had his first qualifying effort at Indianapolis. It was on the last Sunday. In those days it stopped at six o'clock, and if you were in the race you were in it, and if you were waiting to go you had to wait until next year. So he went around and he qualified, and when the chequered flag waved it took him like five minutes to make the cool-off lap. And everybody said, well, that was poor sportsmanship. You know, he should have come in and let the other guy have a chance, because the gun went off and qualifying was over. At the victory dinner after the race he got up to get his cheque and he said he had been criticized because of the length of time that it took him to take his cool-off lap. And he said he learned that from watching the Indiana University basketball team play basketball, because when it had a one-point lead it held the ball for the last three minutes. And of course basketball is big in Indiana, and they had to agree with him, you know.

"So he was that kind of guy. He had a way with the press and so forth. He was a very, very talented guy and he wasn't afraid to talk.

"Clint Brawner, for example, his crew chief at Indianapolis, was a superb mechanic, but he wasn't good on pit stops. After the drivers' meeting at one of his 500s, he went to Brawner and he said, 'Clint, I want to buy two tickets, the best seats for you in the house, and you can watch the race from the grandstand'. And the mechanic just blew his *stack* about the *audacity* of a driver wanting to chase him out of the pits on race day! He was that kind of a guy.

"Indy 1961? Well, there are some people who believed, knowing Eddie, that he really didn't want to win because he liked being the underdog. I find that hard to believe. The canvas was showing on the right rear tyre. He was a sensible guy, and he didn't take crazy chances. He knew that if he stayed out there the chances of that right tyre blowing were high, so he stopped and, of course, that gave Foyt the win. Why did he do it? It's a question that'll never really be answered accurately because he's gone.

"He was a great sprintcar driver. When I was starting out announcing, he was driving an old bucket of bolts, and he was colourful then. He used to stand up in the seat. Eddie Sachs did one thing no other driver ever did, then or now. When he won a race he would slow the car way down and take his helmet off and he'd finish the cool-off lap with his helmet in his lap and wave to the people so they could see what he looked like. I've never seen a driver do that, before then or since then. As I say he was a natural showman.

"He, er... he, er... im*preg*nated this young lady from Dayton, Ohio, not his wife Nancy, and when she delivered the child he entered into some contract

204

with her, I forget the specifics of it, to pay her a sum of money every year until the child was, I don't know, 15 or 18 years old, because he felt responsible. Of course he was killed shortly thereafter, and I don't know what became of that."

"When Eddie was around you always knew it. He was the centre of attraction. Sort of a showoff, but in a nice way, a positive way. He had a lot of friends and he was a superb driver at the end of his career, he really was. And, of course, the way he went was terrible."

■ ■ ■

At the 1961 victory banquet the Clown Prince revealed yet another side to his nature when he paid tribute to the efforts of Jack Brabham, who had raced to ninth place in the rear-engined Cooper that would lead to the greatest revolution the Brickyard had known. When he thanked the Australian and Englishman John Cooper for making Indy a truly international event, he meant every word.

He was back in 1962, driving the Dean Autolite Special. He hit the wall on the first weekend of qualifying, and thus started way down in 27th slot, where he qualified on the second weekend. In the race he was the fastest of them all, and came through the field to third, only 20s behind winner Ward and nine behind Len Sutton. "He drove a brilliant race", admitted Brawner. "But if only he'd gotten on it in qualifying, and started from the front, he would have won it hands down."

The crowds loved him, took him to their hearts with genuine affection. It wasn't just his clowning, or his habit of taking over an interview. Once, after he'd won a sprintcar race, he kept talking into the microphone until the crowds were leaving in the gathering twilight. It was the way he drove, too. Like Foyt, he handled a car as if every race was his last, determination oozing from every pore. As A J said of him when they duelled for the 1961 Indy 500, "I glanced over and I could see his teeth clenched. I've never seen a look of determination like the one that was on his face".

Langhorne, in Pennsylvania, had a fierce reputation. It was the kind of one-mile dirt oval on which heroes won and the less wary died horribly. It was not the kind of track on which to take unnecessary chances. When Sachs won the USAC 100-miler there in June 1958 he had the crowds screaming for him, lap after lap flirting with the wall mere inches from the outer guardrail. He lived life out on the edge, and they loved him for it. He gave them something back, too, and they loved him even more for that.

Not everyone appreciated his outspokenness. When he won the USAC Midwest Sprintcar Championship in 1958 he made an impassioned plea at the victory banquet for better-paying races. It went down like a lead balloon. "Worst thing I ever heard", growled Duane Carter, USAC's competition director. His fellows concurred, but Carter secretly agreed; the speech had been written for Sachs on the kitchen table at the Carter family's home...

When the boot was on the other foot, Sachs bore criticism nobly. If a journalist took a shot at him, no matter how cheap, he would simply buy more copies of the paper and write a letter thanking the writer for the publicity and enclosing an autographed picture. It took a lot to upset him.

At Indy in 1963 he was running fourth, behind Parnelli Jones, Jimmy Clark and Foyt, when he spun twice. The first time, in the southwest turn, he just kept his Bryant Heating & Cooling Special off the wall. The second time was as a result of the left rear wheel falling off. That time he smacked the northwest turn wall hard. Moments later, calm and collected, he walked into his pit, bowling the wheel ahead of him like a kid with a hoop, and waving to his adoring fans. At the noon luncheon to celebrate Jones' controversial victory the following day, the subject of the manner of the Californian's success was again aired. For a long time his Watson roadster had been leaking oil, but entrant J C

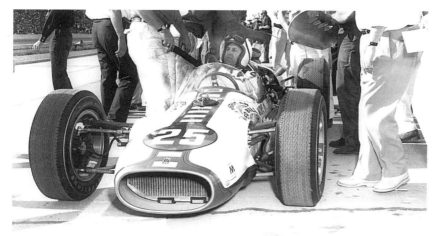

Agajanian had persuaded official Harlan Fengler not to black flag his man as Jim Hurtubise earlier had been. It came to a confrontation between the Establishment and the Newcomers, and Indy being what it was in the Sixties, the Establishment won. Clark simply shrugged his shoulders and vowed to play the game by the Americans' rules the following year, but Sachs, irrepressible as ever, was unable to hold his tongue and told Jones flat out that he had spun as a result of the oil his car had spilled, and that Parnelli hadn't deserved to win. Jones, like Foyt never one to accept that kind of criticism with grace, decked him with a punch.

Hours later, hearing of the fracas, writer Jep Cadou tracked the bruised Sachs down to his motel room and persuaded him to pose for a mocked-up picture of the knockdown. Eddie laid on the floor obligingly, with a small chequered flag in his mouth. It made the front page of the *Indianapolis Star*...

The 1964 event was to have been his last 500 appearance, his last attempt to scale his personal Mount Everest. He'd told Nancy that the previous year, too, and had cut down on his other racing activity, but this time she sensed he meant it. Away from racing he handled public relations for Al Dean's haulage firm, and the entrant had offered him an executive position in Detroit. Eddie was expected to take it.

Ford had offered him its new V8 that year, and he collaborated with Ted Halibrand and his chief mechanic Wally Meskowski and their new rear-engined Shrike. Halibrand was already renowned for his cast magnesium wheels, but this was a fresh departure that embraced the new technology brought to the Speedway in 1961 by Brabham and Cooper. Sachs went out to meet it, unlike diehards such as Foyt and Jones, who had serious misgivings about the 'funny cars'. Back in 1961 he'd been shocked to find that Brabham was quicker than him through the first turn, where he'd always prided himself he was as fast as anyone. His best was 138mph to the Cooper's 140, and right then he knew the writing was on the wall.

Named after the bird of prey, the Shrike was designed by Norman Timbs, the man behind Mauri Rose and Bill Holland's famous Blue Crown Specials which won the 500 in '47, '48 and '49. It had four cast magnesium bulkheads wrapped in a thin magnesium skin, and was among the lightest of the new cars that appeared that May. With magnesium's flammable properties, it was also among the potentially most dangerous.

Sachs caught the Turn Two wall with it as he acclimatized to the techniques required with a rear-engined car, and thus had to qualify on the second weekend. He was the fastest that day, but lined up in only 17th slot, right behind rookie Dave MacDonald in one of Mickey Thompson's ill-handling Sears Allstate Specials. The Californian road racer was having trouble adapting to Indy's concrete walls and non-existent run-off areas, and Foyt hadn't been able to resist needling Sachs about it before the start. "That's the guy you're followin' out there today, Eddie."

At the start Sachs actually edged ahead of the red car going into Turn One, but MacDonald had a better line and repassed the American Red Ball Special going into Turn Two. The Thompson car had never been run on full tanks until that point, and the extra weight affected the tyre contact patches. Despite grip thus reduced since qualifying, MacDonald was driving flat, his car twitching violently as he slid it through the turns. He had moved up from 14th to 10th and was challenging Walt Hangsen for ninth as the leaders passed the pits for the second time. Coming out of Turn Four, MacDonald hit a notorious bump and the unstable Thompson car was immediately pitched into a violent spin towards the infield wall. As it struck it the car erupted into a ball of flame, which it then spread across the entire width of the track as its momentum carried it back towards and into the outer wall. The incident immediately spread a mushroom of thick black smoke across the Speedway. Bobby Unser, in the Novi, caught the back of Ronnie Duman's Watson roadster and both spun as they cleared the smoke. Johnny Rutherford barely avoided the Red Ball car in his Watson and stood on the gas to put flames out, while Bob Veith, too, had a lucky escape, his rear-engined MG Liquid Suspension Huffaker tucked right in behind MacDonald as he spun. "I got through it all right", he told nervous reporters, "but I didn't see how Sachs was going to make it."

"MacDonald's car exploded like a bomb", said Rutherford. Sachs liked to wear a slice of lemon on a string round his neck as he raced. Rutherford later found it on the cockpit floor of his own car...

"The morning of the 1964 Indy 500 there was a double-spread advertisement in the Indianapolis morning papers from Marathon gasoline", recalled Economaki, "and it said, 'Watch Eddie Sachs. He's riding on five tanks of Marathon gas'. And that new car, the Shrike, was made of magnesium bulkheads, and there were five fuel tanks around him. And, of course, when he ran into that mess there, not only did the gasoline explode in the car, but the car itself burned because magnesium is a flammable metal. And that accident was the reason why gasoline is outlawed in Indycar racing today, because alcohol is much harder to start to burn. Rubber fuel tanks followed, too. So his legacy was a safer series, actually."

As rookie Dave MacDonald spun his ill-handling Thompson out of Turn Four on their first lap, it slid back up the banking after hitting the inner wall, right into Sachs' path. Eddie didn't stand a chance. In the holocaust that ensued, America's Clown Prince of racing perished.

Sachs didn't make it. With nowhere to go he tried to run high, but piled straight into MacDonald's broadside car and immediately the conflagration engulfed the Shrike, with its 60-gallon gasoline fuel load. Eddie never had a chance. MacDonald died an hour later in the Methodist Hospital, but Sachs was killed instantly, the victim of massive neck and chest injuries. The great dream was consumed along with the dreamer.

Just after he had been handed the crumpled note which said simply, 'Sachs,

fatal', Indianapolis 500 'voice' Sid Collins ad-libbed this moving eulogy:

"Some men try to conquer life in a number of ways. These days of our outer space attempts, some men try to conquer the universe. Race drivers are courageous men who try to conquer life and death. They calculate their risks, and in our talking with them over the years, I think we know their inner thoughts. In regard to racing – they take it as a part of living.

"The race driver – who leaves this earth mentally when he straps himself into the cockpit, to try for what is to him the biggest conquest he can make – is aware of the odds, and Eddie Sachs played the odds. He was serious and frivolous – he was fun. He was a wonderful gentleman. He took much needling and gave much needling. Just as the astronauts do, perhaps, these boys on the race track ask no quarter and they give none. If they succeed they're heroes, and if they fail, they have tried. It was Eddie Sachs' desire, I am sure, and his will, to try with everything he had, which he always did.

"So the only healthy way, perhaps, we can approach the tragedy of the loss of a friend like Eddie Sachs is to know that he would have wanted us to face it as he did – as it happened, not as we wish it would have happened. We're all speeding towards death at the rate of 60 minutes every hour. The only difference is that we don't know how to speed, and Eddie Sachs did. And so, since death has a thousand or more doors, Eddie Sachs exits this earth in a race car, and knowing Eddie, I assume that is the way he would have wanted it."

How good was the driver behind the jester's mask? Foyt once said of him, "I had always marvelled how he could handle a car. He could take the worst-handling pig that ever sat on a racetrack and go out and just manhandle that thing into looking like a winner. It's why he was so hard to get past. Most drivers have a bad day now and then, but more often their cars have a bad day. With Sachs, you had to fight like hell every day because he didn't have many bad days and it didn't make a damn if his car was having a bad day or not. He *made* it go." And yet he didn't know a con-rod from a con-man, had absolutely no clue why he was fast.

Eddie Sachs had been hospitalized 15 times from race car crashes, but he always came back. "I think of Indianapolis every day of the year, every hour of the day", he would say. "When I'm sleeping, I dream about winning it. I love it all, from the first to the last day of May." His friends wanted him to quit, fearful he would kill himself, but still he came back. "I'll quit the day I win Indy", he promised. "Then I'll hustle out to the largest exit gate and tell everyone, 'Hey, I'm the guy who just won the 500, me, Eddie Sachs'. And then I'll quit racing and die in bed someday, very happy. I know if I keep on driving I'll die in a car, but I want Indy too much to stop."

His enthusiasm also set him in the *Miss Such Crust IV* unlimited hydroplane for a race in 1963, but by then he had another love. He was becoming increasingly hooked by the stock market, at times even to the detriment of his racing.

Every year at Indy they helicopter in a copy of the *Indianapolis News* with the winner's name as a banner headline. They handed a copy to Foyt in 1964, just after he'd drunk the victory milk. "There was a big smile on my face when they handed it to me", said A J. "Then I read it: FOYT WINNER IN 500; SACHS, MACDONALD DIE. It took a lot away from my second victory."

Eddie Sachs was the emotional clown who had fought back defiantly from his initial rejection and embarrassment at the Brickyard, but whenever he got into his car, the clown vanished, to be replaced by a different person. In the cockpit he was great, and he knew it. Better still, his countless fans appreciated that, and let him know. That was what mattered. Few drivers ever needed the support of their fans the way he did. Eddie loved to be loved.

He had always cried when the Star Spangled Banner was played before each 500. Now, in their thousands, it was their turn to cry.

19

AYRTON SENNA

The philosopher king

"I am not designed to be second or third. I am designed to win."

There is a tendency in motorsport, irritating that it is, to pigeon-hole. So and so is like such and such. A is like X. It is, however, a convenient means of shuffling the ever-growing pack, of putting people into some sort of perspective, even if the sheer individuality of the subjects make that difficult. The trick is knowing who to compare with whom.

How on earth do you quantify a driver like Ayrton Senna?

History has never seen a World Champion so complicated. Prost is Prost. Time was up until 1988 that you didn't hear the bad words about him that had been so commonplace in his Renault days, but his feud with Senna reopened some old wounds. You never heard bad things about Jim Clark, because there was nothing bad to know. Stewart was much the same, bar the whinging of the anti-safety brigade to which nobody with any real sense paid much attention.

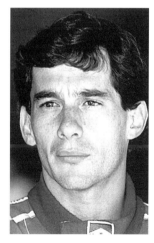

A portrait of the racing driver as philosopher king. Only the man himself really knows whether he is arrogant and aloof at times, or simply a deeply vulnerable personality cloaking himself in a protective shell.

But Senna? There are times when he makes that original Ice Man, Achille Varzi, look like Mr Therm. Senna used to be so easy to understand in a racing car, a driver just totally committed to winning, period. But since 1988, 1986 almost, he has become difficult to understand even in the cockpit, and out of it he can be so many people. He is a driver with more different facets than a diamond. An enigma best understood by assessing a series of vignettes. He's a bit like Mansell insofar as that for every anti-Mansell story there is a pro-Mansell counterbalance.

After the furore of the Warwick Affair early in 1986, when he was so roundly condemned for refusing to have a driver of Derek's calibre as his team-mate, Senna withdrew from the British specialist press. Prior to that, while not always the most voluble character, he was a ready talker if you chose your moment. An obvious enthusiast, just like the rest of us. In rare moments, such as after his drive at Montreal in 1985, he was positively garrulous. He hadn't won that race; that day in June his Lotus 97T had been delayed by a detached turbo pipe and lost five laps, but he had loved every moment of his blistering recovery. It earned him a new lap record, and afterwards he bubbled over at the thrill of his chase of Keke Rosberg's delayed Williams, and the narrowness of the gaps through which the Finn thrust it. Nigel Roebuck once played me a tape he recorded with Senna at the time, and it took me a while to place the speaker, so unexpectedly conversational and animated was the Brazilian.

At his post-race press conferences in 1988 and 1989 he frequently seemed bored, restless. In Hungary in '88, understandably angered by the inevitable background noise as a support race began just as he was answering journalists' questions, he stormed out. The Italian press doesn't care for *prima donnas*, even if their language coined the phrase, and a resultant heated debate with writer and technical artist Giorgio Piola ended with Senna throwing a punch. That was unwise and less understandable. Piola's artistic talent is no less than Senna's for driving. He stands 6ft 2in and is only marginally narrower and less solid than a Sherman tank. Senna was fortunate that the blow did not connect and that Giorgio did not react; I still cannot fathom out why. Indeed, Piola later apologized to McLaren's Ron Dennis for the incident, even though it was not of his making.

There are often days, it seems, when Senna has his enthusiasm for the media flipside of his job well under control. When a party of English journalists finally pinned him down for interview in Jerez that year, he sat and talked for 22 minutes. I know, because I watched him start his stopwatch as he seated himself... Yet when Swedish journalist Freddy Petersens interviewed him in Adelaide that November, a more relaxed Ayrton insisted on a second session to wrap everything up. McLaren MP4/4 designer and engineer Steve Nichols recognized an air of change in his driver after he had clinched his first World Championship in Suzuka that year, and it began to manifest itself at his first race as champion of the world.

In his Spanish interview session, he had spoken quietly of his feelings for his homeland, his belief that he is only in Europe for a short stay, his love of going home to his father, Milton da Silva, who built him his first kart when he was four and used to penalize him if he spent too much time with it and ignored his studies. To his mother, Neyde, whom he lionizes, his sister Viviane and her children, and his younger brother Leonardo, a frequent spectator at his races.

I was reminded of the immense wave of sympathy his comments had evoked in me when I'd interviewed him in the Silverstone paddock in 1983, at the height of his Formula Three feud with Martin Brundle. It was one of those glorious sunny days in July, a week before the British GP, yet Ayrton still felt it was cold. "He hated the country's climate in his earliest Formula Ford days", recalled entrant Dennis Rushen of Rushen Green Racing. "In fact, he used to refuse to run our Van Diemen in testing unless Robin or I had pre-heated his gloves..."

That day, as we sat on his silver Alfasud and talked, he came across as a lonely, slightly unworldy young man still yearning for Brazil, even though it was his third season of living abroad. As our background was the mounting pressure his very success created.

"Every time I won, to start with, I began the next race with people thinking, 'Is this the one he'll lose?'", he recalled with a sad shrug. "When the break did come, at Silverstone, it was almost a relief."

The greatest pressure comes from within, however, and he has always been his own hardest taskmaster. He approaches everything that interests him with an intensity that is awesome, having sacrificed all other pursuits to achieve his goal. He acknowledges that readily.

"Sure, I am intense about anything I do. It's something I get from my father, who is the same way. It's always been my attitude to go deep into a thing, to concentrate and do it properly."

Those less used to such single-mindedness, to whom play is as important as work, have trouble *understanding* his level of commitment, even if most can appreciate it. And perhaps it is small wonder that he clearly does not suffer fools gladly. His whole life is geared several notches above that of a normal person, and out of the car his mental processes frequently work as fast as they do at maximum speed within it. You don't make small talk with him very easily, but get down to specifics and you'd better know what you want to say, how to say it, and what you are talking about if you don't want to find yourself

Many believed Senna to be the moral victor round Monaco's sodden streets in 1984, as he was closing steadily on Prost when Clerk of the Course Jacky Ickx decided to stop the race prematurely. Within months, he had walked out of his Toleman contract and headed for Lotus.

addressing thin air.

A lot of his apparent brusqueness at races is due to his continuous cerebration about his car's set-up, track conditions, race tactics. His former colleagues at Lotus, tyre fitters Kenny Szymanski and Clive Hicks, still tell the story of how he used to sit at home in an armchair mentally driving laps of the next circuit on the calendar... In Senna's time, Formula One had progressed far beyond the happy-go-lucky cavalier, more into the age of the test pilot. He works with a test pilot's mentality, endlessly logging minutae.

The brusqueness has also, I have long suspected, been a hard shell he has deliberately developed over the years, since the carefree days. It really began to form in the Formula Three year as his inherent shyness was often mistaken for arrogance, and his forthright views on subjects germane to his challenge tended to endorse the views of those who felt him aloof.

At that time he was still desperately homesick, especially when he felt he was sometimes cast as the evil foreigner out to beat the homegrown goodie Martin Brundle, and the shell helped against that, too. When the Warwick Affair blew up in his face, certainly to some extent because of the official line run out by team manager Peter Warr at Lotus, who effectively played the two ends against the middle as Ayrton stayed out of reach in Sao Paulo, the shell came into its own and he has never seemed so open since.

The inevitable loneliness that is a corollary of his distant stance is something with which he has come to terms.

"When you are driving the car you are lonely", he said in Adelaide in 1990, the day after his public row with Jackie Stewart over the Suzuka Incident. "It is just you and the machine. All the effort and all the people who helped make it are behind you. It's just down to you. That's OK. But when you are travelling all round the world, week after week, different hotels all the time, that is not an easy situation.

"The public, other people, they are not where I am, they are not sitting where I am sitting, they are not standing where I am standing. Therefore they cannot experience what I experience. Therefore it would be very difficult for them to understand, for them to interpret me correctly. I cannot complain about my life because I have as a whole a fantastic life. Some things are very difficult to cope with. They hurt you a lot, they really hurt. But on the other hand there are lots of fantastic things. In my mind, my heart, my private life, which can also make my life a beautiful life. But no-one is perfect, and no life is perfect. The main thing is that you have peace, with your own personality, your own feelings, your own thoughts. If you have that you can do almost anything. You can face up to any kind of trouble, any kind of fight. You can get hurt, but you can fight it.

"Over the years it doesn't get any easier to come back to Europe. I don't like to come to Europe. If I could I would come late to the races and leave immediately on Sunday night, but that is not possible. That would be the optimum. It's difficult." His mood lightened. "Maybe the answer is 16 races in Sao Paulo. Well, maybe one in Rio!"

The whole question of his personal commitment to success is thrown into further perspective by his dealings with Toleman. Right from his Formula Ford days the Witney team had been interested in his ability, MD Alex Hawkridge genuinely being one of the first outside club racing to appreciate it. He and Ron Dennis offered him F1 contracts which, with remarkable foresight, he turned down. Both offered to pay his way through Formula Three, but Senna did it himself, sourcing money back home from Banerj and Pool Jeans to pay his own way. Even at that stage of his career he didn't want to be pinned down. The first Formula One car he tested was a Williams FW08 at Donington Park midway through 1983, and predictably he drove it as fast as it would go.

It was the day he tested for Toleman at Silverstone – when Brundle tried the Tyrrell for the first time – that was truly historic. Members of the Toleman team were initially sceptical about the ability of a Formula Three novice, champion or not, until they realized that his second flying lap was the fastest any of their cars had ever circulated the Northamptonshire track! From then on they were fully paid-up, card-carrying Senna converts.

Hawkridge has had time to mellow in his feelings about Senna's move from Toleman to Lotus at the end of 1984. In his heart of hearts he knew the relationship was unlikely to last, not so much because the team couldn't come up with fully competitive machinery – at the time it was fast making progress – but possibly because the canny Brazilian had foreseen future events regarding Toleman's 1985 tyre supply contract and opted to jump ship.

OTHER VOICES

Alex Hawkridge – MD, Toleman Group Motorsport

"Of course he was absolutely, totally right, and I can say that now that time has healed some of the rift. He was ruthless in identifying what he wanted and going about getting it, even if that meant going against a contract. That was no barrier to his progress.

"When he came to sign our contract, he read it over the phone to his Brazilian lawyer and started objecting to our best English legalese – and we all agreed with him! Then we went down the road for a drink and it was as if he switched off and became a different character. There was no outward sign, but he began telling jokes.

"He could be giggly and schoolboyish on occasion, but he was also a sterile individual at times, or certainly gave the impression of being able to control his emotions so that he seemed like it. He knew what he wanted and he made it happen.

"When we suspended him that time at Monza in 1984, when he walked out of our contract to join Lotus, I wanted to teach him a lesson. I knew stopping him from racing was what would hurt him most, but I wanted him to leave us knowing that there is a price to pay for everything you do in life. It shook him rigid.

"But... we never had a better driver in one of our cars...

■ ■ ■

Socially, in his early days, Senna was shy and retiring, the type who sipped his drink quietly at parties, the loner in the kitchen. Later, he became quite proficient at greeting new people with a particularly earthy Anglo-Saxon expression before Rushen pointed out that what he had taught him was actually luridly offensive!

After three years of getting his own way on virtually everything at Lotus, when the deal to join McLaren for 1988 finally became common knowledge a lot of his detractors rubbed their hands gleefully at the prospect of the one-man band becoming an island in the Woking team, to the detriment of its harmony. Even within McLaren International there was a measure of apprehension, as engineer Nichols readily admitted.

"But within a very short time he fitted in really well", said Steve early in 1988. "We were worried we might get another Mansell-Piquet situation." For a while, things remained fairly harmonious, but by the end of the following year the worst fears had been realized and the Senna/Prost feud came to make Mansell and Piquet look like a couple of squabbling toddlers in a kindergarten.

Senna knew full well how important it was to get on within a team environment when he first moved to McLaren, and initially he and Prost got on well enough and each indulged in a little gentle gamesmanship. There were, however, rumours that Prost had had to advise him how to get the best from the interim MP4/3 Honda in the very early days, when the testbed car had its characteristic strong understeer. Ayrton was, above all, smart enough to realize that if he couldn't crack it with McLaren, there was nowhere else to go at that time, particularly if he wanted to keep a Honda engine behind him. It was all new ground to him, but he had fitted in quietly with Elio de Angelis in his first year at Lotus, and set about doing the same at McLaren with minimal delay. The other thing that was crystal clear was that if he beat Prost, the recognized yardstick, there would be only one conclusion the world could draw about his own abilities. Tantalizingly, the issue would never become that clear-cut.

The gamesmanship continued through the year, with one or two hiccoughs. Prost, whose small error in leaving Senna a gap in Montreal became a major one when the Brazilian found just enough to snatch the lead, had then avoided possible contact by accepting the loss and conceding the corner. Later, on the rostrum, he received a spurt of sprayed champagne straight in the eye. That, he felt, was deliberately rubbing salt in the wound.

The greatest strain came in Portugal, though, where Senna lunged at Prost as Alain tried to slip into the lead. It was an amazing manoeuvre, more blatant even than his celebrated baulking in qualifying at Monaco in 1985, and reflected the desperation with which he sought the title. Words were exchanged afterwards. "Portugal is over, I say nothing about it here", he commented drily in Jerez a few days later, and it was clear that Prost's assessment of the situation, and the depth of his anger, had shaken Ayrton. "I said to him, I didn't realize that you wanted the Championship so badly you were prepared to die for it", said Alain.

Warmer relations were re-established, however, and both genuinely believed their partnership was better than either had originally expected, but then came Imola in 1989. There, said Prost, Senna reneged on a pre-race agreement not to overtake before the first corner. The row snowballed. Prost, beaten into second place, was so disgusted he threatened to retire there and then. Eventually, he took the decision to quit McLaren, once so much his own team, and to go to Ferrari for 1990. Senna watched events, apparently unmoved.

The incidents were not over. In Portugal, Senna clashed violently with Nigel Mansell, later accusing the Briton of a driving manoeuvre which could have killed him. Although Mansell was suspended from the next race, in Spain, this was a penalty for failing to respond to the black flag which had been waved at him at Estoril after he had reversed his car in the pit road. (A year later Mansell duplicated the driving manoeuvre which had so insensed Senna, and afterwards, the pair of them were all smiles over what was generally taken as a deliberate attempt by both men to discomfort Prost. Senna explained how dangerous it would have been on this occasion to cut over on Mansell and try to deny him. In fact, the circumstances were identical...)

A week after that Portuguese clash, Senna deliberately ignored black and red flags during qualifying at Jerez and was fined $20,000.

The worst came at Suzuka, where Prost staggered Senna by leading for 46 laps before they clashed violently in the chicane. In my own opinion, Prost was probably 35% at fault for, yet again, leaving his rival a gap. Give Ayrton any kind of gap, and he'll try to take a mile. The Brazilian was 65% guilty because he put himself totally at the mercy of a man who had already made it clear clemency need not be expected. He recovered in brilliant style, and had apparently won a dramatic race that kept his World Championship chances alive. Then FISA disqualified him, and when McLaren appealed, the governing body launched into a blistering witchhunt against him which sullied the sport.

Many felt that, while action against Senna's apparent hotheaded streak should have been taken long ago, this was a manufactured excuse. Senna himself stated openly that FISA President Jean-Marie Balestre was trying to manipulate the Championship in Prost's favour. It was an ugly, extraordinary situation, which saw Senna winter under the threat of licence exclusion for 1990 unless he apologized.

In his sprintcar days, Mario Andretti had the likes of Don Branson to straighten him out whenever he transgressed, and he transgressed a lot. Branson was a grumpy guy who didn't suffer wayward rookies gladly. Senna had no Branson, but neither did he seem to have the ultimate respect for others that Andretti did.

In Adelaide in 1989 Senna and Ron Dennis' co-director Creighton Brown had held a charged press conference in which the Brazilian bared his soul. They

Clive Hicks, Kenny Szymanksi and team manager Peter Warr dance with delight as Senna punches the Portuguese air following his first GP success at Estoril in 1985. The pretender had staked his first claim to Prost's throne.

wanted, they said, our help, to pressure FISA into observing justice.

"You leave a lot of things behind you when you follow a passion", Ayrton said then. "Anyone who prevents an athlete from going to the highest place strikes a major blow to his mind and motivation. In that situation everything goes against you in your heart. Why go on when you are unfairly treated?" His voice was thick with emotion as he admitted he felt like going back to Brazil for good. "But I am a professional and a human being, and my values are stronger than those who would try to stop me. I don't want those with the power to use you to put forward bad values. I have often paid a high price for staying quiet.

"For a good performance in the car you need to go right to the limits. Now I am in a position where I cannot make any mistake. Any failure in the car, or any other car around me, is down to me. Is this fair? Is it fair to put such a weight on anybody in such a dangerous profession?

"I refuse to walk away from the fight. It is my very nature to go right to the end."

The cynics, myself among them, had a field day. There was Ron Dennis, the man to whom only the electronic media seemed important, suddenly trying desperately hard to curry favour, to call up his good old written word troops in the defence of justice. Yet at the same time there was nothing remotely amusing about the genuine tears welling all the while in Ayrton's eyes. Nothing at all. I found it a deeply humbling experience to see somebody so intense about a subject that they were prepared to open up their innermost feelings to a bunch of people, many of whom would probably use that frankness subsequently as something to throw back in his face.

Of course, the whole affair was duly sorted in time for Phoenix in 1990, Senna having made an apology of sorts. Effectively it was made with a finger raised at FISA. He won that race, after exercising commendable self-control when Jean Alesi immediately repassed him for a lap after he had overtaken the Frenchman's Tyrrell. On the face of it, Senna had won all round, but beneath the successful exterior lay deep doubt.

"In Phoenix I just couldn't understand the car or the engine. I couldn't feel them. I just lost all sensitivity. I had no motivation. I had no feeling for the car, not even in the pit lane. Only when I was driving the car on the circuit. But even the win there wasn't enough to motivate me. It was only the people in Brazil at the next race, and the positive thoughts they had for me, that gave me the ingredients to restart."

The Suzuka Incident 2, less than 10 seconds into the start of the 1990 Japanese GP, again raised yet more fundamental questions over his driving, just as had his earlier incident when lapping Satoru Nakajima, which had cost him victory on home ground at Interlagos. In Japan he had lost the battle to have pole position switched from the slower, right-hand side of the track to the grippier left, which had been a perfectly reasonable request. (FISA did subsequently change it, early in 1991.) And he knew that, should Prost get his Ferrari in front at the start of a race vital to both of them in their Championship quest, he would be long gone. The McLaren was no longer the superior car, even if its Honda engine remained the best powerplant. But did he deliberately push Prost off, knowing that he himself needed no extra points, whereas the Frenchman desperately did?

The incident will be debated as long as there is racing. The likes of Dan Gurney and Chris Amon believed Prost should not have given Senna even the tiniest gap. Jackie Stewart was adamant that Senna was at fault. "There are a lot of invitations around, like the one Alain appeared to offer for a fraction of a second, but you don't accept them all", said the Scot. "Sure there are gaps in motor racing. The trick is to find one wide enough for your car", said Mario Andretti.

The harmony temporarily established between the two greatest drivers of their time, when they had publicly shaken hands at the post-race press conference in Monza a few weeks earlier, was forever shattered. "As a man he has no value", said a trenchant Prost.

Senna refused to accept the remotest blame, to voice a word of regret. Prost, he claimed, had deliberately closed the door on him. "One who could not afford to take a chance, did so", he said. What he said next was even more enigmatic. "As I walked back from that first corner, I left there all the pressure from last year."

Had he really born the grudge for so long? His final comment seemed to confirm that he had. "I dedicate this Championship", he said, "to all those who tried so hard to take it from me." He rarely drinks, but later that night at the circuit restaurant he made a one-word toast as he indulged in vodka: "Prost!".

It was a tragic end to a year in which he seemed to have made such progress in his dealings with others. On the track he had had that minor contretemps with Nakajima at Interlagos, and had then unceremoniously bundled Nannini out of his way in Hungary, but on the plus side was his blistering record of pole positions, and his newfound circumspection in nursing a McLaren that was less than 100% competitive. That was only for two races, at Ricard and Silverstone, but a brace of third places was an indication of fresh maturity. At last it seemed he was developing the sort of inner peace that Moss, Clark and Villeneuve had had all along.

And those pole position press conferences became nothing short of compelling. At Jerez, the day after Martin Donnelly's savage accident, his eyes had again been moist as he expressed his feelings, and launched into a tirade against the actions of Nelson Piquet and Olivier Grouillard, over whom he had so nearly stumbled during his qualifying effort.

"I saw the two cars fucking around", he said, and he is not normally given to swearing, "and it was totally unacceptable in modern Formula One qualifying. It is really sad; we have all seen yesterday what an accident can cause us. If I had hit either of those cars today I could have taken off. It is really crazy."

The previous day he had staged his most impressive performance. Donnelly's accident had cast a pall over the paddock, even when it became known he had survived. Ayrton went to him on the track, and again later in the medical centre. After that first visit, he sat quietly in the McLaren motorhome, alone, gathering his thoughts. When qualifying resumed, he drove round Jerez faster than anyone ever had. It was Neville Duke taking the Hawker Hunter through the Sound Barrier at Farnborough in 1952, only moments after witnessing his close friend John Derry succumb in the crash of the De Havilland DH110. It was Jimmy Carruthers at Indianapolis in early May, 1973. He had visited the scene of the accident in which team-mate and friend Art Pollard had died, had then walked back to the pits, climbed into his Eagle, and kept it wide open to cover his next 10 miles at 195mph, his fastest speed ever. It was a repeat of what Ayrton had done at Brands Hatch in 1984 after Toleman team-mate Johnny Cecotto's shunt. It was pure, cold courage, an icy suppression of emotion. I had never admired Ayrton Senna more.

That courage so impressed me that I tackled him about it, two months later, when perhaps the intensity of the pain had dulled. He was one of the few drivers to go to the accident scene. Did he, as I did, fear that Martin was dead? Death is the race driver's greatest fear. It was the first time he had had to face what looked like death at a meeting. Had he deliberately ventured to the edge of the pit and looked over to learn something, to prove something to himself? Is that why he had driven so fast afterwards, too, to prove to himself his nerve hadn't been shaken? To prove something to the track? For the other drivers?

There was a long, long pause before he answered, and his eyes became sheeny.

"For myself", he said at last, and his voice was a whisper you had to strain to hear. "I did it because anything like that can happen to any of us. I didn't see anything and I didn't know how bad it was. I knew it was something bad, but

Arguably his greatest drive came at Suzuka in 1988, when he was left at the start in his McLaren-Honda. In greasy conditions he clawed his way back to the head of the field (passing Michele Alboreto, here, on the way) until he deposed team-mate Prost. The brilliant victory, a record eighth in the season, clinched for him his first World Championship.

people just go crazy and say all kinds of stupid things. I wanted to go to see for myself. I felt the need to know – if it was bad, how bad it was. The best way is to see for yourself and not to listen to other people. There was nothing I could do at that moment, but if I was there, maybe there would be something I could do. You never know.

"Afterwards, I didn't know how fast I could go. Or how slow."

There was another long pause. "Did you have to be brave to do that?", I asked. Another long pause. His eyes were now swimming, their lashes wet.

"As a racing driver there are some things you have to go through, to cope with. Sometimes they are not human, yet you go through it and do them just because of the feelings that you get by driving, that you don't get in another profession. Some of the things are not pleasant, but in order to have some of the nice things, you have to face them."

Whatever personal test he put himself through that day, he came through it with honour.

Beneath his sometimes dour mien lies a sharp mind and a sense of humour, although rarely at a track does he have either the time or the inclination to exploit the second facet. Even members of his team find him hard going at times. When he entered a Japanese restaurant to celebrate his 1988 World Championship victory with his team, two interested individuals, concerned with other areas of Formula One, rose spontaneously to applaud, only to observe virtual stony silence from those with whom the Brazilian was about to sit. And yet an interview with him is always absorbing, always frustrating. He is so eloquent that there is never enough time.

While his aloofness with his contemporaries may bounce back on him, that isn't the case with the elderly or the young, to whom he probably gets closest to revealing his true nature. Once, awaiting a medical appointment, he was kept hanging around as an elderly woman's ran well over time. Far from becoming impatient, he solicitously insisted on helping her to the door before entering the surgery.

I have watched him talking with small children, and seen the way in which his face becomes animated. His sister's children adore him, and it is clear just how important youngsters are to him. Some years back he received an award from children, and was visibly moved. Tears welled in those almost mournful brown eyes, and for a moment all thoughts of self control vanished. The aloof expression might never have existed as he paid tribute to them and said, "This means more than any other award to me because children, they are the honest ones."

Immediately after his victory in Japan in 1988 he began fretting about the role Marlboro intended him to play over the winter, and instead rushed back to his beloved Brazil to relax after the sustained pressure of his toughest yet most successful year. There were suggestions that he would retire when he won the title, but they were as wide of the mark as those that suggested he would not come back in 1990 after the war with FISA. He had threatened to retire during his personal low back in 1981...

There was also talk of marriage again, after his first to childhood sweetheart Liliane became one of the first casualties of his racing obsession.

"Whenever I have free time the least thing I want to see or talk about is racing cars, whether you can believe it!", he said by way of explanation. "The moment I leave I don't want to know about any testing, nothing. I want to enjoy all the other things in my life, because I know when I come back each March it is such a big thing. I fight for the opportunity to work out all the other side of my life, so when I come back I am completely charged."

Even before his first title he pleased himself, and he created quite an upset at McLaren when he did the personal deal with Banco Nacional on his overalls, something the likes of Prost and Rosberg had been trying to do for years. The world was literally at his feet at the beginning of 1989, when Nichols felt he could detect the signs of mellowing that had begun to emerge since Adelaide. In 1990 he was totally ruthless in his negotiations with both Williams and McLaren, using each to lever the other. Once, in his early days with McLaren, he had decided a point with Ron Dennis on the flip of a coin and found himself markedly the poorer. This time round the two headed into eventual deadlock, and as his McLaren talks stalled he agreed terms with Williams and actually signed a contract with them which would become valid that midnight. Before it did, Honda chief Nobuhiko Kawamoto stepped in to guarantee him the financial demands to which Dennis had not been prepared to agree.

But just as it seemed he had made such headway in 1990, Suzuka set all the uncertainty and controversy suppurating again. It clouded the brilliance of drives such as Monaco in 1984, or Suzuka in 1988, and his keenness, like Clark, to try other vehicles such as the series of rally cars he tested for the enterprising journalist Russell Bulgin in the latter's *Cars & Car Conversions* days. He would frequently phone Russell from his car while negotiating the M25 motorway in his Toleman and Lotus days, an indication perhaps of how he would keep up relationships with those who were uncritical.

He is misunderstood, because his brand of commitment is well beyond the understanding of many, frightening in its intensity. Yet for the many who vilify him, there are an equal number who see him as the fastest thing ever to hit Formula One. Nobody lacks an opinion on the most controversial driver of all time.

There is no earthly reason why a man who has succeeded so brilliantly at his chosen profession, through his own efforts, should swap his self-constructed shell for a behavoural mould fashioned by others, a social strait-jacket laced round him by those who would like to see him conform to their own expectations of what a hero should be. But it would be nice to see him more mellow, enjoying his racing as much as he did in the carefree days of 1984 and '85. The true tragedy of his career is that he is in danger of being remembered as the sober-faced Brazilian respected by most for his driving, yet disliked by many for his apparent arrogance. Had he been as outgoing as Gilles Villeneuve, it might all have been so very different...

"The day the positive side of my profession becomes even with the other side, or even goes the other way, my natural reaction will be to stop", he vows. "I have come close to it, but I fight for it, and I fight to make sure that the good thing grows and grows against the negative side. I like what I do, it is my life since I was four years old." I suspect he will carry on until he betters Prost's record for victories the way he annihilated Clark's record for pole positions. He could be ideally placed to set new marks that may never be bettered. The appeal of that

Monaco has become Senna's own personal playground. Shrugging off his 1984 disappointment, he won there in 1987, crashed inexplicably while leading in 1988, and then took the next three events. In each of the latter he started from pole position after qualifying runs that made even seasoned observers fear for his safety.

to him is obvious.

As Formula One entered the Nineties, it seemed that observers had to be split either into the Senna or the Prost camp, surely a ridiculous state of affairs with two such outstanding talents, ironically so similar in many ways, yet so disparate in others. The rivalry tainted both. Yet there is no pigeon hole for Ayrton Senna, in his era a non-pareil for sheer visual excitement and stimulation. And for controversy.

He is devout in his religious beliefs, with no fear about voicing them. "Monaco for me was a turning point", he said after crashing out of the lead there in 1988, and at the time his comment was misconstrued. We thought he was talking merely of learning how not to let his concentration drop. Later he claimed to have seen God there at the Portier corner, and after that his beliefs became more widely aired. He claimed to have seen God again at Suzuka's Spoon Curve during his brilliant drive to the 1988 Championship, and that he had been 50ft tall, wearing street clothes. There can be no denying the depth of his beliefs, but worrying both to him and other drivers is his feeling that at times he drives almost supernaturally, outside of himself. "It is something I don't understand, this feeling", he says guardedly, in his articulate, deliberate manner of speaking that weighs out each word carefully. Certainly, his faith helped him to put his serious accidents in Mexico and Hockenheim behind him in 1991.

Even the keenest competitors tire of the minutae of their profession. All work and no play, after all, can make Jacques a dull boy. Prost and Mansell relax with their golf, savour – sometimes even desperately crave – that quiet spell with a club and a little white ball. But not Senna. Not at races. He doesn't play golf. The last time he indulged in some public sport, on Bali beach after the 1988 Japanese GP, he sprained his wrist. When he really wants to unwind, he does so with his family or his radio-controlled model aeroplanes. In the height of his season, that is infrequent.

He is the man all of his rivals most fear, the one they least want bobbing in their mirrors, the one they all know will stay there the shortest time. They all admire him, even if they don't all like him.

Is he the arrogant Ice Man? Or just a man so very vulnerable that he believes his only form of defence is to use the maelstrom of his own fearsome talent as a weapon for attack? Only time, that great quasher of causes celebre, may answer such questions with authority and, perhaps, determine precisely where this occasionally flawed genius, motor racing's philosopher king, deserves to be ranked among the all-time greats of the sport.

20

RAYMOND SOMMER

Heart of the lion

"He was not merely above average, he ranked absolutely and beyond question with the greatest names in racing." – Luigi Chinetti

He was the quintessential underdog, the versatile devil-may-care idealist who would race to win, regardless of the odds. His duels with the works Alfa Romeos, armed only with his bulky Talbot and unquenchable determination, were evidence of a brilliance that never realized its true potential. Raymond Sommer, the gentleman driver, placed difficulties of his own making in his path, for it was not sufficient merely to compete. Had it been, the record books might have been swollen with his successes. Instead, the *manner* in which one competed was crucial, just as it would be with Gilles Villeneuve. To race and not to win, where the inequality of machinery made defeat inevitable, regardless of personal courage and commitment, was acceptable if one lost with honour. If one knew one had driven at the very edge of one's performance. That, to Sommer, was the true meaning of motorsport. The public, those whose own money had earned them the right to watch, loved everything about him, from his good looks to the way he refused to give up, from the stony blue stare with which he raked the start of every race to his love of unproved or lost causes.

To those who sat watching in the grandstands he was the epitome of the postwar racing driver, the gay cavalier who went into battle with a smile on his lips, the man to whom no adversary was too great.

Sommer's was a privileged background. His father, Roger, had been a pioneer aviator, which perhaps explained why he understood, and was so prepared to indulge, his third son's penchant for speed. In his early days, Raymond, too, had been hooked on aviation, as well as amateur boxing. Sommer Snr owned a vast factory which manufactured felt and carpets at Pont-à-Mousson, in the Ardennes district of northern France, and practically everything revolved around it. The workers lived there, and it was like his own little city. He owned all the housing for them, and the family was accordingly of considerable means. Raymond received a generous allowance, yet was forever mortgaged to the gills to pay for his hobby.

For all that, he was a man well versed in the value of money, and he lost little time once his career was established in ensuring that there was equality with his rivals when the organizers made their payments. He was fiercely proud of his independence, and wore it like a badge of honour. It meant he could ignore blandishments from works teams if he felt that to drive a works car would load the dice too heavily in his own favour. Instead, he chose the most sporting challenges; the fight was always more important than the weapons.

The tragedy of his career was the manner in which it was limited by the Second World War. When he went into it in 1939 he had twice been the Champion of France; he was approaching his thirties, and in his very prime. Behind him lay Maserati and Alfa Romeo drives in the major Grands Prix, and a brace of Le Mans victories for Alfa. The first had come in 1932 when he was partnered by Luigi Chinetti, who would later establish the North American Racing Team. Yet the unwell Chinetti drove for only three of the 24 hours. The victory owed much of its sparkle to Sommer's incredible durability, even though Chinetti had had a hard time persuading his young friend to be gentle with the failing car. The second success came the following year, this time in partnership with Nuvolari, whom he had beaten first time out in the Alfa at Marseilles in 1932. They won by only 10 seconds – a mere quarter of a mile – after a gripping duel with Chinetti's similar car. In the 1938 race he and Clemente Biondetti retired their Alfa Romeo 8C 2900 from an easy 100-mile lead after 22 hours. He came out of the war approaching his forties, his best years lost.

The youthful Sommer idolized Nuvolari, the Flying Mantuan, and the elder man was effusive in his praise of the youngster. The legacy of Sommer's admiration had its expression in his entire racing philosophy, which was so similar to Nuvolari's – race hard, and to hell with whether the car lasts. It had expression, too, in his attitude to others. Not for Sommer the aloofness that wealth sometimes brings. A gentleman on the track, he often went out of his way to help other drivers find the right lines during practice, and when currency restrictions hampered the British racer abroad, it was more often than not Sommer who would step forward, unbidden, with a timely offer of assistance.

In a racing car his courage and enthusiasm knew no bounds. He would never give up. When the exhaust pipe broke on his 1100 Simca Gordini at Lausanne in 1947 he refused to break off a dramatic battle with Bira's similar car; instead he drove one-handed as he grasped and then tore off the offending pipe with the other. By the finish he was a mere length behind the Siamese prince. That same year he drove his 4CLT Maserati into the ground at Spa in his chase of the Alfa Romeos of Jean-Pierre Wimille and Achille Varzi, only conceding third place to Consalvo Sanesi's Alfa 158 when the Maserati's chassis broke under the strain.

Sometimes a man with a 'closed face', at others kind and warm, Raymond Sommer cared more for the way in which he played the game than the result he derived from it.

His attitude brought him a particularly apposite soubriquet as the press began to write of Raymond, Coeur de Lion. His greatest characteristics were his big heart and his tremendous courage. Wimille was the smoother and perhaps even the better driver, but when he was killed, in the winter of 1949, Sommer stood as the best in France, the champion of 1937, '39 and '46. Even Ferrari recognized it, and he was the first to drive a GP car for Il Commendatore. It was a wayward machine, but Sommer succeeded in taming it.

Nothing typified his spirit more than the 1950 Belgian GP at Spa-Francorchamps. There his heavy Talbot Lago was ranged against the works Alfa Romeo 158s of luminaries such as Fangio, Farina and Fagioli and the Ferraris of Ascari and Villoresi. The Talbot, long the tortoise to the Italian hares, had no chance whatsover, but they had forgotten to tell that to Sommer. Unlike those of Etancelin and Rosier, his lacked the twin-ignition and triple sidedraught carburettor modifications, and gave away some 40bhp even to them. Yet within moments of the start he had caught and passed Ascari and begun a merciless hounding of Villoresi, driving the Talbot to the very limit. Three laps before the thirsty Alfas were due to refuel he passed the Ferrari going down to Burnenville and, incredibly, closed on third-placed Fagioli. When the Italian made a pit stop Sommer took over his place, and a lap later he was second as Farina peeled in. On the 13th lap he led as Fangio, too, stopped for fuel.

When Fangio returned to the fray Sommer was nearly a minute in front of Farina. He stayed there for another five laps, averaging a punishing 110mph. He

was so quick that Alfa Romeo even thought it had made a mistake, that he must be a lap behind. All three of its drivers were running without margin. Inevitably, Fangio and Farina hunted him down and repassed the big blue car. Equally inevitably, it later succumbed to engine failure when a con-rod broke, unable to stand the pace. The Alfas triumphed, but Sommer was the hero of the day as he worked his mesmeric artistry.

If he was never daunted, he also never had much mechanical sympathy. The deftness of hand on wheel was not matched by deftness of mind on machinery. In those days racing cars had few settings; usually just the tyre pressures, the friction damper adjustments and a choice of final-drive ratio. The Talbot had three available ratios, and whenever faced with a choice, Sommer would always opt for the lowest to give himself the highest possible engine revs.

So much did he believe in his own philosophy of fighting the good fight that he kept a diary in which he made meticulous notes of every aspect of his performance. His expectations of himself were always the highest; that time at Spa he gave himself only nine out of 10...

There were other brilliant showings. Before the war he had been the Miracle Man of Miramas when, in 1932, he had become the first man to beat the Alfa Romeo P3s in a fair fight. That day he took full advantage of a lap charting mistake by the Italians, but at St Cloud, in 1946, when racing resumed, there was nothing fortuitous about his victory for Maserati over the Alfa 158s. As it would later at Spa, the Alfa management found itself seriously questioning whether Sommer really could have been on the same lap as its cars.

He was at it again at Zandvoort a month after that Belgian GP epic, thrusting his Talbot after Fangio and Gonzales in their 4CLT Maseratis and Villoresi in the Ferrari. Gigi soon succumbed to his onslaught, perhaps mindful of the zeal he had shown at Spa, and then watched him again as Sommer launched after the leaders. Against all expectations, he moved ahead of both and began to pull clear. In his wake, Fangio began to wilt under the strain of overtaxed damping, and Gonzalez and Villoresi lost time refuelling and changing tyres. Sommer had started with half-full tanks, cunningly planning to combine his need for extra fuel with his anticipated tyre stop. He duly stayed ahead until, with the race in his grasp, he was halted on lap 37 when a rocker broke and bent a valve.

OTHER VOICES

Gerard 'Jabby' Crombac – Editor, *Sport Auto*

"I am a Swiss. My family worked in Paris before the war, but during it we retreated back into Switzerland where the food was better! As soon as the war was over my father had an important job in the department store business, and he rushed back to Paris, because in Switzerland we were financially very tight. I followed him, finished my school there, but in those times France was a little run down. I was a great enthusiast for racing and thought there was nothing much I could do there for the time being, so I went back to Switzerland and got a job with a friend of my father's who was selling curtains and material for upholstery in bulk, in a very large shop.

"We were working Saturday mornings, but one Friday night I declared I had a very bad cold and wouldn't be able to work on the next morning. And on the Monday morning there was a very good picture in the paper of a hillclimb where Toulo de Graffenreid had been winning with his Maserati. Pushing the Maserati and wearing racing overalls was J. Crombac! In a way, the boss, who was a great friend of my father, was very good about it. He called him and said, 'Look, I think your son prefers motor racing to curtains, and he ought to try and make a career there'.

"My father took me back to France and said, 'Look, I'll give you one year, pay

Sommer prepares for the Bois de Boulogne in October 1946 in the Maserati 4CL. He won, emerging from the shadow of Jean-Pierre Wimille, to whom he had been second the previous year.

for your lodgings and everything, to try and make your way into motor racing'. In Switzerland, a French driver had been coming to race there and I had been helping him, lap scoring, things like that. I acted as his secretary in Paris on the understanding that I wouldn't be paid. He was called Raymond de Sojay, and he was a great, great friend of Raymond Sommer. He raced a Cisitalia.

"True enough, after working from October until February there he organized a lunch between myself, my father, himself and Sommer, and Sommer couldn't refuse anything to him because there were some faults in the cupboard. Sommer said, 'OK, he can join me as a trainee'. He even paid me, and I still have the pay cheques.

"So I did the '49 season. I wasn't allowed to do internal mechanicking and I only once went to a race. I was based with the team in a Paris suburb. They would do a race and it was usually very slow to get back, so they would arrive sometime during the night of Monday or Tuesday morning, and I would arrive on Tuesday morning and would dismantle the bodywork, with its rows of little bolts which were flat bolts with two little holes, so you had to use a pronged spanner. As the whole thing was seized with castor oil, it took me a whole day. Then I had to wash the car in alcohol, which was the only way to get rid of the castor oil. I was cleaning, watching, sweeping the floor. Every evening I had to pick up all the tools and wash them and put them back on the rack in order, that sort of thing. I was greatly enjoying myself, but then I realized that I wasn't going to become the World Champion racing driver doing that. Raymond Sommer would never let me drive his car, and in the end I joined my father's firm, which allowed me to buy my own racing car later on.

"He was a very lunatic character. Sometimes he would come and shake hands with everyone, and be very kind, and sometimes he would arrive, you know, with a closed face, and he wouldn't talk to any of us. But that would only last about a day.

"He was not terribly mechanically minded, but he was interested in all sorts of things. This workshop we had was a huge place, a former laundry factory with

223

a tremendous chimney, which of course was useless, but he got a kick from looking at this chimney, which was going up to the fifth floor. He had a team of masons just building things in this factory. He'd say, 'Put me a wall in here, that will be the washing bay'. And the next week he'd say, 'No, I don't like it like that. Knock it down'. He enjoyed having things done. That was his hobby.

"He would never touch a car, but there was one thing he would always do himself. When we had completed the car we would put it on top of the truck, and in those days to strap the car in the transporter meant nailing wooden blocks around the wheels with huge big nails. And he enjoyed knocking them in. That was his fun.

"He was very kind, because in those days all-nighters were very common. We never went to a race without an all-nighter on Saturday night, that was common practice, and often we had several all-nighters to prepare the car during the week. He would always turn up with his wife during the evening and bring drinks and cigarettes. He was very considerate and very liked by his people. Even so he was a bit lunatic.

"We also maintained his road cars. He was a great car enthusiast. He had a Lancia Aprilia, which he used as daily transport. Unfortunately, my first job when I joined him was to clean the engine of the Aprilia, and I left the rag on top of the exhaust pipe, and he did a couple of miles and the car caught fire. That was my introduction to Raymond Sommer, but he was kind enough to forgive me.

"He had a very large BMW saloon, a 335 I think it was, the ultimate BMW just before the war. Spare parts were very difficult to find, so he had another derelict 335 in the corner for spares. He used the good one and the Aprilia as his road cars, and really enjoyed them.

"To help pay a little for the facilities, we also carried out maintenance on other cars. We had on full maintenance contract a Veritas-BMW which belonged to Alexander Orley, who was an American living in Europe.

"Harry Schell was a great friend, and whenever his Cisitalia was in Paris it was also maintained at Sommer's premises, and I believe he never paid. He also had connections with Sommer! The first race I officially went to as a mechanic he lent me to Schell to do the Lausanne GP in 1949 with the Cisitalia, which was a great kick for me.

"As far as a diary was concerned, yes, for sure he kept one. I have the logs,

Spa in 1950, and Sommer has just surrendered the lead to Fangio's Alfa Romeo once more, after the Argentinian's fuel stop. So hard did he drive the Talbot that Alfa's management believed there had been a mistake in lap charting.

although unfortunately I don't have the period I was working there, so I don't know if he mentioned me setting fire to his car!

"He was very much a thinker, that was a strong part of his character. It was an incredible diary. He kept detailed notes on hotels and so forth, things such as, 'Hotel so and so, ask for room number so and so. Never go back to that hotel, too noisy.' Or 'fleapot'. He rated restaurants, too, not only on the circuit, but on the road. 'Stop at so and so. Marvellous food.' Then he'd code the menu. It was a surprise to me when I discovered this; I was not aware of it at the time.

"He was very hard on his cars. One race, at Albi, was run in two heats. Stupidly, the finish line was in the middle of a hairpin. Fangio was there, and Sommer passed him going too fast to make the hairpin, but he still won the first heat. But, of course, he then couldn't start the second heat because he'd damaged the car!"

■　■　■

Coeur de Lion's quixotic streak drew him to lost causes, and the disastrous SEFAC, CTA-Arsenal and BRM V16 projects stung him. On the two latter occasions the much-vaunted machines broke on him on the startline, but typically he made the best of that 1950 British GP afternoon at Silverstone to dog Stirling Moss in the 500cc race. A race was a race to Sommer, no matter what the car, and despite Moss' advantage of a twin-cam head on his Cooper-Norton, Sommer never gave up the fight, and he thrilled the crowd as he held Alf Bottoms' similar car at bay by a mere second.

Such was the character of this impulsive fighter, to whom discipline and team orders were anathema. Watching him at Bremgarten in 1948, a young would-be driver was spellbound by his style, and thereafter resolved to drive with similar flamboyance. His name was Joseph Siffert. "I shall drive like Sommer", said the 12-year-old Swiss. "I shall attack."

Many feared Raymond Sommer, and towards the end some of his rivals were openly resentful. This confused and saddened him, for he was incapable of entertaining such thoughts himself. He was not always a happy man, but he was kind, considerate and compassionate. He played a crucial role in securing the release from the French authorities of Dr Ferdinand Porsche when the war ended. He was also instrumental in shaping the future of the German mechanic, Otto, who worked on Orley's car. Prior to the war he had been a works BMW racing mechanic, but during the hostilities he had been captured and became a prisoner of war. Sommer had an opulent house in St Maxime, on the other side of the Gulf of St Tropez. At the time of the Liberation he happened to be at St Maxime and he saw a bunch of prisoners milling about and, incredibly, recognized Otto amongst them all. He asked what he was doing.

At that time, anyone who wanted staff could 'adopt' prisoners, as long as they took over feeding and accommodating them so that the French Government was relieved of the responsibility to do so. Thus Otto was taken on as a gardener for Sommer's estate in St Maxime. When things settled down fully and prisoners of war were freed, Otto didn't want to go back to Germany, where everything was still in ruins, so he transferred to Sommer's workshop in Paris and became the mechanic responsible for Orley's car because of his BMW background. The whole episode was typical of Sommer's attitude to people.

He would fight physically when he had to, though, as his boxing showed. Typically, during the hostilities he preferred the life of a pilot, and he once shot down a German fighter using only a pistol. It gave him the sort of odds he liked.

He went to the Haute Garonne GP on the difficult Cadours circuit in a mixed frame of mind on September 10, 1950. His efforts so far that season had earned him the title Champion of France for the fourth time, and he had recovered fully from the illness of 1947, when he had inadvertently swallowed methanol at Pau. His achievements had been recognized by the Legion d'Honneur, but

only the previous week at Monza the continuingly aggressive attitude of some of his rivals had upset him. He still could not understand why others might resent him.

On the last day of his life, 'Coeur de Lion' hustles his 1,100cc Cooper round Cadours during the Grand Prix du Haute Garonne. Today, a memorial stone still marks the scene of his accident.

He was driving his 1,100cc Cooper when it suddenly left the course, hit a tree and overturned. He was killed instantly. Like Keke Rosberg, he had always had more stamina than the cars he drove, but now he was gone. A seized wheel bearing was generally suspected, but those close to him spoke quietly of how the steering had broken after a bent track-rod arm had been straightened by injudicious use of a welding torch.

What might he have achieved in top-line cars, this lone wolf who was so very much more than a rich playboy, had he not chosen to embrace his strict code of racing ethics? He epitomized the belief that success is not the true measure of a man, and he stood as a unique blend of modesty, aggression and determination. Today, in the Pyrenees, on the corner where he succumbed, a small plaque pays silent tribute to an indomitable free spirit.

21

JACKIE STEWART

The legacy of safety

"Get that boy signed up, quick!" – John Cooper

It was difficult to avoid John Young Stewart, the mastermind behind the whole thing, at his 1990 Mechanics' Grand Prix Challenge at Gleneagles. Not that there was any reason why one should have sought to, for wee Jackie is a throwback to the days when sportsmen were sporting, and a conversation with him is always rewarding. What made his accessibility remarkable is the general tenor of his lifestyle. Keeping up with him in his heyday as a thrice World Championship-winning driver was never easy; now it can be well nigh impossible. He's the only person I know with two carphones...

He has business links with Ford which go way back to 1968, when he signed to go Formula One with Ken Tyrrell. They take him across the globe, and today his schedule is busier than ever it was, even with the hectic pace of racing and testing. He also earns a lot more, and Jackie always was one with an eye for top dollar. Having seen him at work, it must be said that whatever the American giant pays him, it isn't enough. Time spent with him isn't found easily, but is invariably worthwhile.

At Gleneagles I came fully to appreciate just what a rounded character Stewart is. There he was, moving swiftly in his inimitable Spring-Heeled Jack fashion, addressing a problem here, organizing a detail there. As ever, expending incredible energy to make sure everything was a total success.

Before I met him for the first time, some years before, I walked in that twilight zone one does before meeting someone well-known with whom one already identifies quite strongly. You know so much more about them than they do about you, and the small talk can be tricky in that period in which they can either get bored and walk away, or get interested and stay. This was, after all, the man whose performance at Silverstone in 1967 had been a great influence on me.

Back then, my father had a Rover 90 on which we changed the clutch. Being one of those P4 Rovers on which weight was no object, an ordinary hydraulic actuation system simply wasn't good enough. This one had a finely engineered mechanical linkage which actuated a splined shaft mounted in the bellhousing, and thence the clutch itself. Inquisitively, I had dismantled it, cleaned it and reassembled it. It was only when we put the entire gearbox back in the car and had everything bolted up that we discovered the clutch linkage would no longer connect up. In moving the splined shaft I had reinstalled it so that the hole for the clevis pin was 90 degrees out; we had to pull the gearbox out again to rectify it. It's fair to say that I was not desperately popular.

I consoled myself that night with *Autocar*. It was the May 4 issue in which there was a report of the International Trophy race at Silverstone. And there, in one of those glorious 'heading towards the camera' shots taken at Copse Corner was the BRM H16. 'Jackie Stewart's fierce-looking BRM...', said the caption. I can remember it now with utter clarity. I was hooked. After that, Aston Martin P215s and Maserati 151s were never quite the same. I had discovered Formula One...

A man of his time. During his racing heyday in the early Seventies Stewart embraced modern styles with shoulder length hair, having developed rapidly into a worldly champion.

Any apprehension that first meeting held was swept away within minutes. Stewart is incredibly adept at putting you at your ease. I would notice that again, and be grateful for it, when we drove together one year at Oulton Park during one of his regular Ford advanced driving instruction days. Such was his manner that it was impossible not to feel relaxed, even when you had a triple World Champion sitting alongside critically assessing your driving. It was expert, effortless tuition, with a serious message. He was a marvel that day.

And there he was at Gleneagles, the victor of 27 Grands Prix and three World Championship titles, welcoming his guests with an easy charm. It was, perhaps, to be expected with those of us who already knew him well, but it was extended to our wives, too. Trish was made instantly to feel a welcome part of the scene, as if it was all laid on just for her. Other wives felt the same.

It was impossible to watch the man without being fascinated, just as his driving used to weave a spell on spectators. Here was someone very well known, who has always been dyslexic, yet for whom the problem was never diagnosed until he was 42. Consider that; throughout a brilliant career he was burdened, as he admitted, by the belief that he was simply a scholastic dunce. It was only eight years after he retired that his problem was correctly identified.

He is passionate that dyslexia should be recognized early in children, and when he appeared to talk about the subject on BBC's *Wogan* programme he proved impressively articulate. As he explained how the reading impairment had hampered him, the good Terry, for once prepared to let an interviewee speak at length, chimed in, "It hasn't affected your ability to count money though, has it?". Quick as a flash, Stewart responded, "Not when it's coming in!".

Son Paul may not quite have inherited his father's skills with a shotgun, but he does have the same reading problems. I remember his first press conference when he announced his Formula Ford 1600 race programme with Geremy Thomas' Carphone Group. Behind him on the dais was a wall on which Carphone Group was spelled out in large polystyrene letters. During the course of his speech they began to detach themselves, until only the letters r ho e rou remained. Aware that his audience of cynical hacks was sniggering more and more, the teenager turned round to ascertain the source of mirth. Upon seeing the calamity he said with commendable aplomb, "Now you know what I really see when I read Carphone Group". It quelled the laughter and prompted a round of applause.

At a similar age, Jackie was establishing a name for himself by winning the British, Scottish, Irish, Welsh and English trap shooting championships. When he narrowly failed to be selected for the British Olympic team in 1960 he began to look elsewhere and followed in elder brother Jimmy's tracks by starting to compete in club motor racing events in Scotland, driving friend Barry Filer's Marcos. By 1963 his exploits were drawing the attention of the influential, among them Robin McKay, who at that time managed Goodwood circuit. He made a call to Formula Three team owner Ken Tyrrell.

"He said to me, 'You're always looking for new drivers, well there's been a bloke going very quickly round here in an old Cooper Monaco. I thought perhaps you'd like to know'. So I called his brother, Jimmy Stewart, whom I don't think I knew, but he had been a racing driver. I asked him if he thought

228

his younger brother was interested in going motor racing seriously, and he said he did.

"It must have been March, and we had a test down at Goodwood and Bruce (McLaren) was doing all the testing with this Formula Three car. The idea was that Bruce would set a certain time and then Jackie would have a go. Well, he got in, and I told him to take it easy because he'd never driven a single-seater before. In three or four laps he was quicker than Bruce, so I pulled him in straight away and said, 'Look, this is silly, you're supposed to be taking it easy', and he said, 'But I was'. Hah!... Life's so unfair, isn't it? Bruce said, 'Let me get back in that bloody thing', so he got back in the car and went quicker, and then Jackie went out and went quicker still. Bruce was a terribly nice bloke, and he looked at it and said, 'Christ, he's a bit quick, this fella!'.

"John Cooper had been on the first corner, watching, and he came running up to me and said, 'Get that boy signed up, quick!'."

Stewart had an arrangement with Reg Tanner, of Esso, to drive Jaguars. Ken, ever the opportunist, tried to get Tanner to back his team as well when he sought his permission for Jackie to drive for him. Tanner wasn't interested in spreading his support, but he didn't mind Ken using Jackie. "'Please your bloody self', is what he said to me, and he's regretted it ever since!", grinned Tyrrell.

Bruce McLaren's secretary, close friend, and now purveyor of rare motoring books and ephemera, Eoin Young, was another who had cause to regret turning Stewart down. In 1964 Jackie had offered him a share of his income if he would manage his career. "I thought, what do I need to do that for?", said the New Zealander. The two celebrated their 'forty-eleventh' birthdays while we were in Montreal in June 1990, and it was Alan Henry's 43rd, too, and Stewart accepted an invitation to dine with us. The Tram Way burger joint was perhaps not entirely in keeping with what he was used to, and he did walk in looking very dubious, but he made the effort, and it was one of those spontaneous evenings you come to treasure. As ever, he was charm personified when his identity was twigged by our fellow diners and the requests for autographs began to flow. It was a great evening.

1964 was a wildly successful season that brought Jackie nine Formula Three victories. Much more than that, it catapulted him through Formula Two to Formula One by the end of the year. Having spotted his incredible rise, Colin Chapman persuaded him into one of his Lotus 33s in the Rand GP at Kyalami. He took pole position for his first Formula One race, but though he retired in the first heat when a driveshaft broke on the line, he made sure of polishing his reputation by winning the second.

Even then he was canny. Jim Clark was the dominant figure at Lotus, and ever would be during his lifetime. Jackie had been asked to compete in South Africa because Jimmy had slipped a disc during an impromptu snowball fight during a Ford Cortina press launch, and though they eventually became firm friends, Jackie was shrewd enough to realize where his future lay. BRM offered him a seat for 1965, and he jumped at the chance. At Monza in the September he outfumbled team-mate Graham Hill to win his first of those 27 Grands Prix.

If Stewart is remembered for anything besides his sheer success, it is for the dramatic safety crusade on which he embarked after crashing during the 1966 Belgian GP at Spa-Francorchamps. In those days the circuit was more than eight miles long, and though the start had taken place on a dry track, the field ran into a rainstorm during the first lap as they crested the rise at Burnenville. Jo Bonnier, Mike Spence, Jo Siffert and Denny Hulme all spun. Further on, at the Masta kink, Rindt looped into a series of wild spins, and then Stewart (who had just won at Monaco), Bob Bondurant and Graham Hill all lost it in their BRMs. Bondurant landed upside-down in a ditch, but escaped with cuts and bruises. Hill, seeing that Stewart was trapped in his car, rushed over to assist. The BRM was leaking fuel wildly, but after undoing the steering wheel they finally succeeded in getting him out. The entire incident left a lasting impression on the Scot.

"I was trapped for 25 minutes in a car leaking petrol. Can you imagine that? Bob and Graham only got me out after finding tools in a spectator's car. There weren't any doctors and they put me in the back of a van until an ambulance finally took me to the first aid spot near the control tower. There they left me on the stretcher, on a floor littered with cigarette butts. They thought I had a spinal injury, but though they gave me a police escort, the ambulance crew didn't even know the way to Liège."

In the light of what happened to poor Philippe Streiff at Rio in 1989, when he was left paralysed through lack of proper and speedy medical attention following a testing accident with his Williams, Stewart's words are even more chilling.

Jackie recovered his equilibrium quickly, but he soon launched himself into his campaign to have guardrails erected, trees cut down and the foolish risks minimized. Some drivers disagreed, including such fatalists as Rodriguez and Ickx, but most understood and appreciated what he was trying to do. Other observers, such as *Motor Sport*'s Denis Jenkinson, deplored his crusade, and wrote him off as a 'milk-and-water' nancy-boy. Stewart didn't care, and he pressed on regardless. Many of the things we take for granted today, such as a wall protecting those in the pits from those on the track, are a direct result of his campaign. As an indication of how ridiculous the situation sometimes got, in 1968 the RAC MSA declined to order protection from trees at Brands Hatch, 'because they are only small trees'. And this in the very year in which Jim Clark had died after running into the trees at Hockenheim...

He earned his right to voice his strong criticisms. At Spa in 1967, though he hated the place, he suppressed all emotion in the style he always adopted when racing and tigered to second place in the troublesome BRM H16. He actually led for a while before having to give best to Dan Gurney's Eagle, and thereafter drove much of the way hauling that big green monster around with one hand while holding the gearlever in engagement with the other. Through Eau Rouge...?

He nearly won there in 1968, too, driving his Tyrrell Matra with his right wrist in a special plastic brace after fracturing the scaphoid earlier in the year during a Formula Two accident in Spain. That time he ran out of fuel.

But for that wrist injury he might well have won that season's World Championship, taking three wins and finishing second to Graham Hill, only 12 points adrift. He had missed both the Spanish and Monaco GPs while his injury healed, and Hill had won them both. In Germany he was simply sensational as he won in fog and rain by over four minutes from Graham. It is true that he had the best wet-weather tyres, but that was nonetheless his greatest victory.

It was also one of the few times Tyrrell has ever made a driver go out when he didn't want to. "I remember it extremely well", said Ken. "On the morning of the first practice it was foggy, but the track was dry, and we used to go round the top loop and bed brakes and everything before going out on the long 14-mile track. We spent a long time going round the top loop and we lost the first 20 minutes of practice. By the time we went on the long circuit it had started to rain. And it rained through the whole of the rest of practice, so he qualified sixth. Anyone who went out and qualified on the long circuit when it was dry had a tremendous advantage. There was no warm-up in those days, but because of the conditions, which were awful – pissing down, and water everywhere – they laid on a special practice session on race morning. And Jackie didn't want to go out. I told him he had to go out and find where all the puddles were, and he accepted the logic of that.

"He had the best rain tyre, no question of that. He'd probably tell you it wasn't a difficult race for him because everyone else was so slow, and all he had to do was keep it on the island, but the mere fact that he finished so far ahead shows how good that was."

The following year, with the evolutionary Matra MS80, he blitzed the World Championship, clinching it with a split-second victory over Rindt, Beltoise and McLaren at Monza as the four of them spurted for the line. In fact the Lotus driver just edged ahead, but by then they had crossed the finishing strip. Stewart, as cunning as ever, had used a specially high fourth gear to avoid the need for a change to fifth before the line. The one gearchange that he saved won him the race and the Championship, and Tyrrell a lot of money.

"It was Jackie's idea to avoid that shift out of the Parabolica. It was a set-up that was peculiar to Monza with the slipstreaming we always had then. That was done not just to win the race at the end, but to win the leader money up for 25, 50 and 75% distance. The system is the same today, but it had only just started then, and the need for a special gear only really applied at Monza, where the slipstream battle meant that at any time you could be first or sixth. After all, sixth place was perfectly alright so long as you didn't lose the tow, but first was good at those special points. We used to give Jackie a countdown, lap 3, lap 2, lap 1. We earned a lot...! On second thoughts, I'm sure it was my idea, not his!"

Despite that success, they were forced to break with Matra when the French company entered into a deal with Chrysler and Simca, which precluded using the Ford Cosworth V8. Tyrrell and Stewart were happy to continue with Matra, but after testing the new Matra V12 engine in the back of the prototype MS9 at Albi that autumn, Jackie told Ken, "It's got no guts". "Which meant we had to look elsewhere. I went to McLaren, Brabham and Lotus to try and buy cars, but nobody would sell us any, so we were in the shit. And then this M-A-R-C-H outfit (named by linking the initials of its founders) started up and we got

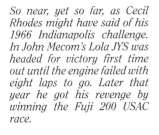

So near, yet so far, as Cecil Rhodes might have said of his 1966 Indianapolis challenge. In John Mecom's Lola JYS was headed for victory first time out until the engine failed with eight laps to go. Later that year he got his revenge by winning the Fuji 200 USAC race.

ourselves out of trouble. But the writing was on the wall; we either had to make our own car or get out of Formula One. That's when I approached Derek Gardner to design one for us. When we parted company, Matra's boss, Jean-Luc Lagardere, said to me, 'One of these days, Ken, you will come to me on your knees'. Ha, ha... I haven't seen him since then!"

1970 yielded only one win, and the trauma of the deaths of Piers Courage, Bruce McLaren and Jochen Rindt had brought unwanted further proof that the safety campaign had to continue. Never more was Jackie's courage called into play than at Monza, when he had to pull himself together in the immediate

aftermath of Jochen's accident to carry on with qualifying.

He had always raced with as little emotion as possible, supressing all feelings while in the car, deflating himself, "like a rubber balloon". At Monza he did not manage that until he was actually sitting in his Tyrrell March 701's cockpit. He felt devastated, unsure what to do, for once in his life, directionless. The first time he put his helmet on he had started crying, and he had to go to the back of his pit to regain control of himself. As the mechanics strapped him in he cried again, and was glad that his helmet and face mask hid his emotions. But out on the track he was an automaton again, fast, clean, precise, totally in control. He qualified the March fourth fastest, and the tears only returned when he climbed out at the pits. What made that lap all the more special was that he was not, like Clark, Rindt or Senna, the type of driver who found it easy to work up to a pole-winning lap. That day he dug very deep into his personal reserves.

He drove a heroic race there, too, running in the leading bunch and finally finishing second to Regazzoni. It was his last race in the March, and from then on Ken Tyrrell never raced anything that didn't bear his own name.

Stewart's 1971 and '73 titles were equally dominant, and he only lost out in 1972 because of a stomach ulcer, which took a little while to diagnose correctly. His style, as ever, was so fluid, so smooth, that it was all too easy to overlook one vital thing: he was also so quick.

His final year was perhaps his best as he battled with both Ronnie Peterson and Emerson Fittipaldi in the Lotus 72s. The way that he fooled the Swede on the first lap of the British GP, prior to it being aborted by the multiple accident provoked by Jody Scheckter when he lost control of his McLaren, was a demonstration of the Grand Prix driver's mind at its very optimum. He sold Ronnie the perfect dummy, and was long gone when the race was stopped. However, things worked out less well for him when the race was restarted and he went combine harvesting when the Tyrrell selected two gears at once going into Stowe and slid off through the crops, just as he was drawing up with the black-and-gold car. At the time there was a degree of scepticism about the cause of that much-publicized spin, but as Ken Tyrrell said, "Jackie was so easy on his equipment that if he said he had a problem with the gearbox, then he had a problem with the gearbox."

His drive at Monza was sublime. "We were at official practice there and after his first flying lap he came in and said, 'The car's awful, Ken. There's something wrong with it', so I said, 'Jackie, you've only done one flying lap and you've just beaten last year's lap record'. And his problem was, and I tell it to a number of drivers now, that when you haven't been driving for a couple of weeks it's so easy to go out and over-drive because you're not used to lurping along at 180 miles an hour. You frighten yourself, you know?

"The Nurburgring was Jackie's greatest win, but one of his best was the fourth place he took there at Monza that weekend which clinched him the title. The car had been a load of crap; he was moaning and groaning about it all through. 'It won't do this, it won't do that'."

He started sixth, was fourth on the first lap and stayed there until he sustained a puncture on lap 8 and dropped to 20th place; it was a long stop. Lap after lap thereafter he just went quicker and quicker. It was a fantastic drive, one of those days when a superstar drives in an absolutely spellbinding manner, like Clark there in 1967, Prost at Suzuka in 1987, or Senna at Suzuka the year after.

By lap 33 he was menacing Mike Hailwood for sixth, snatched it from him on the 37th, and then dealt with Carlos Reutemann and his own team-mate Francois Cevert to grab back his original fourth place by the 49th of 55 laps. At the finish, after an inspired performance in which he broke the lap record on the 51st lap, he was less than five seconds away from Revson's third-placed McLaren. His best lap of 1m 35.3s would have placed him third on the grid. Truly it was the stuff of legends as his three points proved sufficient to clinch

him the Championship. He had been troubled by influenza all weekend, but it had been a true champion's performance.

Tyrrell: "I said to him afterwards, 'What about the problem with the car, Jackie?', and he said, 'It seemed alright'. Hah!"

He and Cevert were very good friends, and though Francois showed every sign towards the middle and end of the season of being as fast as his team leader, Jackie never held anything back from him. He knew he was going to retire and had told Ken as much earlier, but Francois didn't know until much later, although he did before he died practising for the final race at Watkins Glen. "It is a matter of certainty, in my opinion", said Ken, "that Francois was as good as he was because of Jackie. Not necessarily because of the way the car was, or how it was set up, but because he had the advantage of driving with someone who was good, and therefore had the target to aim for." Cevert knew they both had the same equipment with which to hit the target, and Stewart defined the target for him.

On Sunday, October 14, 1973, that new record of 27 wins behind him, a week since Cevert was killed, he made an announcement. "From today I am no longer a racing driver. I'm retired and I'm very happy. I made the decision on April 5 as I had mixed emotions about racing for some time. I only told Walter Hayes of Ford Europe and Ken Tyrrell. If I had told anyone else it would have been unfair on Helen, who has never asked me to give up motor racing. How would she have felt, especially with the press around, watching me take part in my fifth-to-last Grand Prix, then the fourth-to-last, and so on?"

More recently he said, "Grand Prix motor racing has given me everything I have in life". He did not point out what he has given it back. He has been tempted back into the cockpit only for the purposes of track tests for the Elf fuel company. In 1977 he proved he was as quick as anyone in a wide variety of cars. Indeed, in the P34 six-wheeled Tyrrell he was faster than Ken's regular pilots. The 1988 series was less happy, but there has never been any doubt about Jackie Stewart's contribution to the sport. While he remains the epitome of the maxim that there is life after motor racing, he is also living proof that the famous needn't be surly, arrogant and unapproachable.

He has the knack, and that surely is what it is, of making everyone he comes into contact with feel as if they are the only one that matters. I've seen him do it at race tracks, Ford presentations and public dinners, and at Gleneagles the same smoothness was apparent again. To see it is to watch a consummate public relations genius at work, but also to see a retired sportsman putting as much back as he can with a grace that is disarming. It makes you wonder how many of today's current crop of racers might achieve a similar status. I found myself wondering what his compatriot Jim Clark would have become had he enjoyed a kinder fate, and hence came about this book.

Clark and Stewart were totally dissimilar in many ways. Jimmy was naturally reticent, something of an innocent abroad, while Jackie shook off his innocence quite quickly and matured into a man of the world. Clark hated making decisions, Stewart was as sharp as a crocodile's teeth with his. Yet both are tied together in motor racing folklore, not just by their mutual skill and birthplace, but by the manner in which they conducted themselves. Jimmy the farmer, Jackie the garage owner's son from Dumbarton who became a millionaire champion yet still returns to Scotland once a month and loves every minute of it.

In Jackie's early days with Tyrrell in F3 and then BRM, Clark was a source of great help. Stewart admired him and drew on him as his own career developed. And in turn, as Clark watched the maturation of Stewart, and the manner in which the younger Scot capitalized on his potential, it taught him a lot about the business side of the profession.

Like Clark, Stewart took immediately to Indianapolis. Indeed, he came very close to winning first time there with the Mecom Lola in 1966, only to stop with engine failure eight laps from home. He waved to the crowd as he walked in. Later that year he made up a little for that disappointment by winning the USAC race staged at Fuji.

OTHER VOICES

Ken Tyrrell

"As a driver, the thing that most impressed me, really, was his ability to do the thing that he made most obvious, which was not just that he was able to lap fast, but that he could do it every lap. However, he didn't find it easy to go out and do a pole position lap, so it would have been interesting to see how he would have coped with qualifying tyres, for example. But say he was racing against Rindt; he would wear Rindt down just by lapping within one-tenth of the lap before, always. The number of times in testing where he did five laps of the same time in a row was most extraordinary. But I don't think he was the sort of driver to pull out a really hot lap.

"He started races and got into his rhythm quickly. From a standing start he used to go like hell, very quick. His second lap round would be much more cautious, because he didn't know what had happened on the first lap. If he was out in front he could go out and know that the track was clean, see everything around him. Second time round he didn't know what oil had been dropped, who'd spun off.

"He was a very good reader of the car. He knew what the car was telling him. He would be a dream, today, for Harvey Postlethwaite. He doesn't want a driver who tells him what to do to make the car handle, he wants a driver to tell him *how* the car handles. It's then up to him to put it right. And that's what Jackie was very good at.

"The thing I remember is that in 1967, it must have been, he went and bought this very expensive house in Switzerland, and he really couldn't have afforded it, because I know what he was getting paid, and it was nothing, *nothing*. And I think he *knew*. He *knew* he was going to make it. He knew he was going to make the big time...

After missing out narrowly on the 1968 title, he made no mistake in 1969. Matra's MS80, allied to Ford's Cosworth DFV, proved almost unbeatable all season. Here at Clermont he ran away and hid as team-mate Beltoise fended off Ickx for a Tyrrell Matra one-two.

"Then he made this other decision to come with us in Formula One. The Formula Three thing was one thing, and Formula two was a natural progression, but to make the jump, to come with us when he could almost certainly have gone with a team that was better, and not someone doing it for the first time, he saw something. He saw something, didn't he? And he saw it right, didn't he!

"That's another thing. When we were doing Formula Two together we were using a Cooper chassis with a BRM engine, which was a waste of time. And we met Jabby Crombac, and he introduced me to Jean-Luc Lagardere, the boss of Matra. He said, 'We think we have a car, would you like to try it?'.

"It ended up that I sent them a BRM engine and they put it in their Formula Three car, and they flew it over to Gatwick and we picked it up. And now, this was autumn time, I had to call Jackie to ask him to come down and try the car. And he said, 'Och, Ken. What are you getting up to?'. Anyway, he came down, we were lucky to have such a good day at Goodwood, and off he went to try it. Then, when he came in, he just said to me, 'Ken, this is the best racing car I've ever driven!'. We did a deal for Formula Two.

"In June 1967 I had flown over to Zandvoort for the day to see the debut of the Ford Cosworth DFV in the Dutch GP, which of course it won in Jimmy's Lotus 49. I didn't really have any ambition to go into Formula One, but when I came back I sent a telegram to Cosworth and ordered three engines. They came back and said that as far as they knew they weren't selling any engines as they had an exclusive deal with Lotus. So I told them to keep my telegram anyway. JYS had been receiving overtures from Ferrari, so I went to Lagardere and told him that if he built us a chassis, we had the Ford engine to put into it. He agreed, so then I went to see Walter Hayes at Ford and said, 'You know, if we don't do something, this man's going to go off to Ferrari. The deal was that I had to buy the engines, for £7,500 each, and supply the gearboxes, which were standard Hewlands, and Matra supplied the chassis free of charge and replaced any bits, and provided us with an engineer, Bruno Morin. I asked Jackie how much money he wanted to come Formula One with us, and he said, '£20,000'. So I said I'd find it. So then I went back to Walter and told him I had to go out and find some money, but would he guarantee Jackie's 20 grand? And he said, 'Yes'.

"Dunlop wanted to stay in Formula One despite the hard time it was getting from Firestone and Goodyear, and stumped up a further £80,000. I went back to Ford and said that I didn't need its £20,000 after all, and I only found out quite recently that they had agreed to pay Jackie's 20 themselves, and the 20 that I didn't get they paid to him as well!

"Jackie and I never had a contract after 1964. Nothing was ever written down after that. It was all done on a gentleman's agreement. But he was always sharp commercially, and as he became successful his confidence grew and he knew he could push the point a bit further. But he never, ever gave me any financial problems.

"As a driver he had his ups and downs. We had a bad time at Oulton Park once. He complained bitterly about the car, and we had a few words, but I don't remember us having serious words apart from that. We were at the Nurburgring once at a time when the England cricket team were playing a test match, and he was complaining about the car, so I said, 'Look, you think you've got trouble; and England are 70 for four!'. He didn't like that very much! As a bloke, though, he was about same as he is now, actually. Easy company."

■ ■ ■

Today Stewart forges on. Behind him he leaves not just those 27 GP wins and three World Championships, but his legacy of enhanced safety on the circuits of the world. The diehards to whom racing had to be a blood sport pilloried him as he campaigned for sensible safety precautions, but history relates that the Armco rash for which he was directly responsible has been instrumental in preserving life. Lack of popularity was a small price to pay. Had there been suitable barriers at Hockenheim in 1968 Clark might very well not have perished.

"If there is anything I'm proud of in my career as a racing driver, it's what I campaigned for in safety, and got done", says the man who also introduced seat belts, fireproof overalls and full-face helmets to Formula One. "It shifted the whole emphasis of motor racing towards safety and what we enjoy today. It was very tough. There was bitter obstinacy. *Bitter* obstinacy. It came from governing bodies, track owners, national bodies, the media, but we achieved it."

Chris Amon reckoned that Stewart loved a scrap during a race, but was happier leading it, like Clark or Ascari. He could win in all conditions, in the rain at Zandvoort in 1968, in the fog at the Nurburgring that same year, in the heat at Ricard in '71, and in slipstreamers such as those at Monza in '65 and '69. In the latter year he was cunning enough to spot what little tricks Rindt was trying to play with his rear wing in practice, too. He was clean, as well, always giving rivals the room to race. While the deflated rubber ball approach worked, he was honest enough to admit that there were times on the victory rostrum when he found himself more absorbed in valuing the trophy than he was in savouring the actual success.

The example of Jackie Stewart as the successful business personality creates fresh hope for dyslexics the world over, and his crusading continues as he pushes forward the financial frontier of the Grand Prix Mechanics' Charitable Trust. Top-quality sponsors such as Marlboro, Courtaulds, Avis, TAG, Heuer, Ford, Labatt's, Olivetti, JPS, Rapid Movements, Canon, Benetton, Mobil, Camel, Rolex, Elf, British Airways, USF&G, Allsport Management and Footwork contributed to that Gleneagles weekend, all badgered by the irrepressible Stewart as he worked tirelessly to put something back into the sport, just as Jimmy had hoped to. The £400,000 raised by the 1990 shoot since he formed the Trust in February 1987 is testimony to his powers of persuasion and organization.

More recently he has embarked on another crusade. His son Paul had begun racing himself, and together they formed Paul Stewart Racing. But his continued exposure to both the lower and the upper echelons of the sport has left Jackie Stewart perturbed about driving standards.

"I think they are very low at present. I'm an RAC steward now, and if we can get official observers tweaked up, if it is the immediate responsibility of the observer to comment if a driver, for example, has conducted a potentially dangerous manoeuvre, then the Clerk of the Course can be told immediately and can instantly police it by bringing the guy into the pits with the black flag for a stop-and-go penalty, like they have in Indycar racing.

"We need to stamp out the problem in the lower formulae, because that way we can ensure that the next generation will be clean. We can't do much about the present generation in Formula One, but what's been happening in Formula 3000 in the last three or so years is real rock ape-type behaviour. We simply can't allow that."

During his career he had two publicized clashes with other drivers. Jacky Ickx spun him out of their battle for the lead in Canada in 1969, and three years later Clay Regazzoni dispatched him into the guardrail at the Nurburgring; neither incident was his fault. I admired him immensely in Adelaide at the end of the acrimonious 1990 season. Immediately after the Senna/Prost clash at Suzuka, the majority had blamed Senna. Two weeks later, wooed by the persuasive Brazilian during a press conference in which he roundly criticized Prost, many were duped into disbelieving the evidence of their own eyes. Suddenly, Prost became the bogey man, the culprit.

This was too much for Stewart, who asked Senna why he thought he got involved in so many incidents with other drivers. Senna flew into a rage, and later, when they met by accident in the McLaren motorhome, he refused ever to be interviewed by the Scot again. Had Senna won the race, Stewart would have had nobody to interview for Channel Nine television, and he had done his homework to tell Australia why. He had drawn up a list of 21 incidents the Brazilian had had since coming into Formula One in 1984.

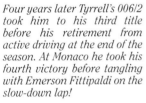

Four years later Tyrrell's 006/2 took him to his third title before his retirement from active driving at the end of the season. At Monaco he took his fourth victory before tangling with Emerson Fittipaldi on the slow-down lap!

From time to time, there have been suggestions that Stewart is worried about his identity in the sport, that he seeks reassurance. I put it to him one day, and he replied, "If that was the case, I think we wouldn't have called it Paul Stewart Racing, would we?". He enjoys being chairman of his son's team, of bringing on new drivers. He talks volubly of his Staircase of Talent concept. Gil

de Ferran, one of his Vauxhall Lotus drivers in 1990 and a Formula Three winner the following season, told me, "Whenever I have a long talk about racing with Jackie, I always come away having learned something more".

Some of the less palatable commercial facts of team life have not been lost on him, either. "I find it depressing that we are as amateur in so many different ways as we are in motor racing. It's a very unbusinesslike operation in so many ways, terribly transient as a society. By nature I've always thought of myself as very loyal to the people I form associations with. For example, I've been with Ford for nearly 25 years, Moet since '69, Rolex since '68. That creates relationships. In motor racing it is extremely difficult to get commitments and solidarity. A lot of that, unfortunately, is based on instability in the sport."

If it seems logical that Paul Stewart Racing will eventually graduate to Formula One, Jackie makes a good job of hiding the fact. "I haven't assumed that. Yes, it is logical in some respects, but we might run somebody's World Championship sportscar team, a touring car team, have a factory affiliation. We might go Formula One, or become a constructor, but it's too early to say. I had an opportunity to buy Team Lotus, one of two opportunities, but I realized I wasn't ready for it. I say that without fear of contradiction. I wouldn't have been capable of running it. We'll make mistakes where we are, but I'll be able to learn more, positively, from them than if I had naively jumped into a Formula One operation where mistakes are a lot more expensive. I'm not ready for it. I make no excuses for that, and I'm not shy to say it."

If you suggest his input, his return into the sport, is exceptional, he merely shrugs. "I like to think I'm putting something back, sure. Racing's been good to me, and I like to think I always have. I've always felt a strong commitment. I think there is a major obligation to do the appearances and sponsor-related programmes.

"All the companies I'm involved with are major multinationals. When they use somebody like me, they don't keep quiet about it. They project their image through somebody such as myself. If I go to address the Young Presidents' Club and do a 45-minute speech, the core of which is motorsport and the industry, I've probably got in that one room the best part of 400 of the biggest businesses in the world, and if one of those Young Presidents thinks that it might be worth looking into, that's 0.25%, and I've achieved something for motor racing.

"The way I see it, that's my role now. The aficionados are going to come to races, whether it's rain, hail or snow, so that's not my responsibility as I see it. It's more important for me to be doing the other group."

It isn't difficult to find people with respectful anecdotes about John Young Stewart, apart perhaps from the 1990 World Champion and the odd reactionary who never forgave him for helping to prevent racing drivers getting killed.

OTHER VOICES

Tom Wheatcroft – owner, Donington Park

"At Kyalami, in 1972, when we were over testing a Formula Two car for March, Jackie was there tipping Roger Williamson off during Formula One testing for the Grand Prix. 'They all think I change down here, but I don't. I take it in fourth, and that saves two gallons of fuel.' That sort of thing. We spent a lot of time with him, and that's one reason why I'm very close with Jackie.

"Nobody knew I were having the Grand Prix at Donington in 1990, but Jackie rang the minute he heard. He said, 'Tom, if you want me on the radio, want me to demonstrate anything, it doesn't matter what you want, I'll be there'. That's nice. That's better than two other British drivers I could name.

"We've got Jackie's Tyrrell in the Collection now. 003 were mine; I bought it off Ken. Ken wanted to give it to Jackie when he retired and asked if I'd swap it

for 006/2, so I sent it back. It went to Scotland, but a single-seater, well, nothing deteriorates quicker if it's left alone. He had it rebuilt, and then he tested it here. He said, 'Tom, if you want it back, here it is'. So it's back on display with us. At the Gold Cup he drove 006/2 and Paul drove 003 in a demonstration for us. That were very nice indeed."

■　■　■

It's the little things you appreciate about Stewart. Like the way he'll wait for you to turn your tape over before continuing a conversation, then go back to the point he was making if necessary. Little courtesies. When he won the 1969 World Championship he bought Rolex watches for all the members of the Tyrrell team. He had a deal with Rolex, and he bought them in Switzerland, then brought them to England, phoned the Customs and Excise and told them he was coming, paid the import duty, then took them down to Ockham and gave them all out. "He handed out the import duty slips, too", recalled Ken. "That was nice, wasn't it? Thoughtful."

Jackie isn't always quite so generous. When he was working on his book *Jackie Stewart's Principles of Performance Driving* with Alan Henry, AH thought it was a good idea to order a greasy breakfast to photograph as a contrast to the healthy custom-built muesli diet Jackie preferred. Stewart agreed, but refused point blank to pay for it!

He is a superb ambassador for motor racing, a World Champion who went out at his very peak. Go to any Formula One paddock now and the chances are you will still hear one journalist or another mimicking him at some stage. Always, it is done in an affectionate manner, such is the esteem in which he is still held.

22

LEE TAYLOR

In search of the ultimate

"I could barely speak the word California. When I had said that, it had taken so much I just couldn't remember what the second question was."

It took them 10 days to find Lee Taylor. Ten days in which his body lay strapped in the shattered hull of a rocket boat 200ft below the troubled surface of Lake Tahoe, across which the fatal rolling swells continued to wash over the now invisible traces of his broken dream. That dream that had dominated his life had finally ended up taking it. Some, even his friends, had always felt such a dramatic end was inevitable.

Sergeant Doug Struthers and the men from Douglas County sheriff's office spared no effort until they found the 46-year-old Californian. His desperate wish had been to set a new Water Speed Record in his attempt on Thursday, November 13, 1980, 'or to check out with dignity' if anything went wrong.

Well, things did go wrong. Taylor's beautiful *US Discovery II* danced a fatal two-step from sponson to sponson before rolling over and breaking up at 330mph, to the horror of spectators dotted like ants along the breathtaking snow-capped mountain skyline of the California/Nevada border. He did go with the dignity that was so important to him, but somebody still couldn't resist photographing the recovery of his body and sending the macabre snap to Australian rival Ken Warby 'with regards'. Taylor had made some enemies in his time.

For many years he was a complete mystery to me, nothing more than a name so often seen at the bottom of Water Speed Record tables, the man who'd taken away Donald Campbell's last record six months after his death. It stayed that way until a Saturday in 1976, when I saw my first photograph of his jetboat, *Hustler*, and fell hopelessly in love with it. And the more I came to learn of him, the more his story fascinated me. He was an ordinary football jock who went far enough to play semi-pro in the late Fifties and early Sixties, 6ft and 200lb of standard athletic college hunk. Yet he was also an extraordinary man who was hewn from the same vein as Campbell.

He was an idealist, even as his speedboat obsession developed and took its toll, but his life changed when he came close to dying in 1964 in *Hustler*.

He played football for the South Gate Saxons and the Fullerton Ringos as he planned a career in dentistry, and would play short-term pro-ball for the Challengers until his thirties. A scandal involving bribes and college ball players on the Pacific Coast Conference cost him the higher education athletic scholarship he'd won to the Washington State University, but it was that big

Lee Allen Taylor as he was in 1967, the year he finally realized his dream to become the fastest man in the world on water.

shunt with *Hustler* that really affected him.

One day he had turned up at the Firestone Boulevard garage of boat builder Rich Hallett, hauling a Westinghouse J46 turbojet on the back of a trailer. To the laughter of Rich's friends he instructed him, "Build me a boat around this one, Rich". The older man laughed, too, but not much. He knew Taylor was serious. After all, it was he who had introduced him to water skiing, and who had seen him set a new water ski speed record of 92mph at Long Beach's Marine Stadium in 1962, only weeks after he'd taken up the sport. No matter that the record had fallen within hours to speed skiing star Butch Peterson, Taylor had been bitten. Pretty soon, he and Hallett went racing hydroplane dragboats, with a lot of success. They were an odd couple, the jock and the master builder, who worked from his own innate feel for a boat and without any sort of detailed plans.

Just over two years after Taylor's death I met Hallett in his modest home in Downey, a rundown suburb of California not far from the Watts ghetto where the Vietnam riots broke out in 1965. "I didn't like Lee, but I didn't dislike him, either", he summarized, but his eyes twinkled as he said it. "He was good at things like water skiing, and he'd go really well for the first lap and then fall off! He was never in good enough shape to last five laps." Though he wasn't the type to crave personal glory, I got the impression that it had hurt Hallett when Taylor went off on his post-record round of interviews and chat shows in 1967. "I guess he kind of forgot all about his crew in all the excitement", said Hallett, who had nevertheless stayed friendly enough with him to be invited to the launch of his rocket boat 13 years later. "He was the kind of guy who could promote anything from people, but when it came to paying debts he just kind of forgot about things. He could have made a million dollars after he set the record, but he never wanted to be told how or when to do things. When he went on his record tour he kept all the money and none of the crew was invited." That, it transpired, was beyond Lee's control.

Back in 1964 their bond was close. They both lived on Quoit Street, and they lived, ate and breathed *Hustler*, 30ft of the most gorgeous boat any man ever fashioned from marine plywood and aluminium. She was painted white, with patriotic red and blue stripes, and an American eagle on her nose. She was the bee's knees, and a lot more of the bee besides. That bee had been the Marilyn Monroe of its hive.

They took her to Lake Havasu that April, and Lee had worked up to 260mph or more when the throttle stuck at the end of the fastest run. Until he died he couldn't remember what happened next, only that he'd gone water skiing two days earlier. Maybe it was just as well his memory bank had been wiped.

Due to a combination of things he landed in big trouble. He misjudged the fantastic acceleration, the engine only partially shut down at the end of the run because of a bent throttle return spring, and an underwater fin kept the boat running straight and true. Unable to deviate from a course that had *Hustler* headed straight for the bushy shore, he somehow scrambled out of his prone position in the cockpit and baled out while the boat was still doing well over 150mph.

I've sat in the same cockpit since, and I'm damned if I can figure out even now just how he managed to get out. It took me minutes, and I weigh a lot less than Lee did and I didn't have to fumble with any screen catches. Fear can lend unexpected speed to one's actions. Ironically, it would have been better for him if he'd stayed with Hustler, which suffered only minor damage that was repaired for $3,000. It would cost Taylor more than 10 times that to get himself back into shape.

He skimmed across the water like a pebble, and crashed over a small peninsula. When the US Coastguard found him he was partially submerged in 4ft of water. Nick Galish dived in and dragged him on to a large rock, and then strapped his unconscious form on to a stretcher. His helicopter partner landed on the rough ground and they struggled to load the stretcher on to the machine, but the pilot began to take off while one of the coastguards was still trying to climb aboard. As he jumped off the craft overbalanced. It sank with Taylor and the stretcher still aboard. Galish performed another heroic rescue and Taylor was rushed to a local Air Force base in a replacement chopper and then to the Sunrise Hospital in Vegas. He had multiple skull fractures and serious facial injuries from the first accident. The muscles in his left eye had been severed and its orbit crushed. The helicopter accident had smashed his left ankle. He was comatose and stayed that way for 18 days.

Surgeons wanted to amputate his left foot, but his father refused to let them. After numerous operations he would wear special glasses to correct a squint in his injured eye. The UCLA had rebuilt the orbit, the first time such an operation had ever been done.

When he came out of the coma they asked him two questions over and over. "Where are you from? What is your name?"

"I could barely speak the word California", Taylor said. "When I had said that, it had taken so much I just couldn't remember what the second question was."

His wife and daughters visited regularly, and so did friends from the boat world. He barely recognized them, and had trouble forming words. In the next 18 months he would have to learn all over how to walk and talk.

"I was like a grinning idiot. People came by, but I didn't know them. My daughters came to see me, and I knew they were my daughters, but I couldn't remember their names.

"I couldn't correlate things with an idea. For instance, I could read words, but I didn't know what they meant."

The first great triumph came when he read a sentence containing the word spectator. "It came to me what a spectator was. It was a major step. A victory. I knew what a word meant. I can't tell you how happy I was."

The prognosis remained gloomy, and many of his friends feared he would remain a partially crippled vegetable for the rest of his life. He attributed his survival to his superb constitution, and had other ideas. A nurse once left him strapped to the bed for his own safety, but had made the mistake of leaving an empty lemonade bottle on the bedside cabinet. He reached it, smashed it against the wall, and cut through his straps with its shards. "When she came back I was sitting in her chair."

The survival instinct, the innate stubbornness of a champion, was too strong. Less than two years after the accident the 'vegetable' was back aboard *Hustler*, ready to take aim at Campbell's record. "No one came right out and told me I was crazy for devoting so much of my time, energy and money to what must have seemed like a wild dream, but I guess a lot of people thought it", he said before the ill-fated run. The same people now voiced their fears for his sanity.

He was not the same man who had so idealistically breathed life into his ambition. Sometimes early on he raged or had crippling fits of terror. His left eye looked to the left, and his speech was slow and deliberate, like he was a child singing a song he'd just learned. Before long his sponsors began to get a little edgy. Harvey Aluminum, his largest, asked if another racer, Bob Stipp, could take a run in *Hustler* when Taylor seemed unable to get up to the speed necessary to qualify for APBA sanction to run for the record. When Stipp ran into a patch of bad water Taylor had advised him to avoid, and damaged a sponson, Lee got mad. Harvey pulled out when he withdrew from its sponsorship, Mobil too, and all over again he began the painstaking search for backers.

"He never was the kind to handle sponsors", Hallett remembered. "He told Harvey Aluminum to get lost, as well as several others."

"Putting Lee together with some people was like mixing fire and gasoline", recalled Jim Deist, the rotund cigar-chewing 'daddy of the drogue' who had designed the parachutes used to slow the boat down, and who now owns

On June 30, 1967 he sped across the surface of Lake Guntersville in Alabama to average 285.213mph in his gorgeous jetboat Hustler, finally breaking the record held by Donald Campbell which he had nearly been killed preparing to attack in 1964.

Hustler. "I really liked him, but with some, wrong guys, you just knew there was gonna be some kind of explosion!"

There were several as Taylor edged towards his date with destiny on Alabama's Lake Guntersville on June 30, 1967, less than six months after Campbell had died so spectacularly on Coniston. The Englishman's accident had had a profound effect on Taylor, who failed to get up to speed time and time again. One story had it that, because he failed so often, his faithful crew – Hallett, chief Paul Pribble, Tom Pavloski and Arnold DeBoze – resorted to subterfuge days before the record run. Pribble, it was said, set the throttle quadrant so that when Taylor thought he had 70% power he really had 100, and they moved the course markers further apart so he would get on the power earlier and stay on it longer. Sponsor John Beaudoin, a hard-hitting tyre dealer in Downey's neighbouring suburb Compton, was running low on patience and threatened to pull out if the speeds didn't start rising. Beaudoin, it seemed, had spread that story.

"I didn't know him before he got in the boat", said close friend Bruce McCaw. "Sure it was not easy, but just knowing Lee and the tremendous determination that he had; if there was something he wanted to do he'd just fly out there and do it. I suppose anyone might have had some reluctance to jump back in a boat that nearly killed them. I guess one of the things was he never blamed the boat for that accident, per se. My sense is he always trusted that boat. He really had a lot of faith in it. Every time we would talk about it, I could tell he really had a passion for it. He knew everything about it. Of course, had he stayed with it he would have walked away from the accident.

"He had a lot of confidence in it. There were some things he wanted to change, and I think he was running a little bit out of power without the afterburner. But I never heard anything about them changing the throttle settings on the run.

"Once we did a little film shooting at a show, and I guess it was the first time in a while he'd crawled back aboard, and while we were doing our stuff Lee was in another world. He was back driving that boat. You could see it in his eyes. He was totally at home."

On Friday the 30th Taylor drove *Hustler* faster than any man had ever driven a boat – an average through the kilometre of 299.181mph and a peak of 315.

243

But he only managed it one way, and two runs were mandatory to qualify for the record. On his return he ran into the wash of a pleasure craft, which cut his average to an agonizing 274, just two miles an hour under Campbell's record. Understandably, Lee exploded, but he calmed sufficiently for another effort. Beaudoin told him it would be the last. He averaged 285 and broke the record, despite the problems, despite the fear. This time they had to restrain him from going out again to try for the 300. It had been the last day before his APBA sanction expired.

After the whirlwind tour of shows that followed his success he went back to his business sharpening cutlery, surgical instruments and precision cutting tools. As Hallett had said, he could have made big money from the record, but he never really tried.

Maybe he should have quit then, to rest on the laurels of an emotional victory, but Lee was a man of vision, the slave of his obsession. He began to talk of the sound barrier on water, of building bigger and better boats until 750mph came into sight. He lost *Hustler* to Beaudoin in a protracted legal battle, so he and Hallett fashioned the full-scale mock-up of *US Discovery I*, which was similar, but with a much more powerful General Electric J79 engine. But the interest wasn't there from the money men, and the project faltered. Why did he still want to go faster?

"Travelling at speed on the water is my life", he explained in his new apartment in Bellflower, surrounded by the bills that had mounted during the *Hustler* project. "I don't need to wear goggles, but I stuff my ears with cotton. It's deathly silent, even running all-out. There is no sound because the jet is behind you. Everything is behind you. Up there in the nose you feel like a man atop a rocket. It's just you and nobody else. I am moving rapidly away from the sound, anyway. There is no cooling breeze giving me a sense of speed. It's eerie – hot and eerie. Running, the temperature in my fireproof suit gets up to 140 degrees. It's all very swift – and dangerous.

"You have a feeling of wanting to go faster. You have a strong desire to go faster. You are euphoric. It's a feeling you want to go on and on. I had that euphoric feeling when I set the record, and I want it again."

OTHER VOICES

Bruce McCaw – business manager during *US Discovery I* and *II* projects

"I first met Lee in Seattle in January 1968, and he'd just gotten the record and had the boat there on display. Clark Marshall had a big speed show in those days and Lee had come up with the boat. I did a television piece with him and we sort of became friends. Somehow it really clicked, and we stayed in touch. He invited me to come down and see what he was doing. I went to LA, spent a few days with him, and the more time we spent together the closer we became. I'd say within a year I became his business adviser.

"He was having some difficulties. He was totally broke, having lost virtually everything while in the hospital. He worked very closely with his manager and had put everything in her name as his first wife, Gloria, was divorcing him while he was in hospital. When he finally came to she'd just walked in and told him she wanted a divorce, so that was it. This other lady had spent a lot of time helping Lee recuperate. You know, he was a little bit like a child after his accident. He really had tremendous reliance on people because he'd been through such a terrible beating. People had really had to work with him to get him back functioning as a human being again. They actually had to teach him again how to walk and talk, and do everything all over again, so it was just like growing up again.

"I think that always engendered a certain dependency on this gal. So after the record there were a lot of things up in the air, who was doing what, who was entitled to what. Prestone was his major sponsor at the time, and there was a question whether they were going to put him on a major tour at the time. If so, what would he get paid? He was just sort of being directed, I think, what he did and where he went. His business was sharpening knives. He had an old green truck, and it just was a miracle that thing ran. He drove all over LA, had a very dedicated following, and people were fairly tolerant of him not coming round once in a while, but he always stuck with that and kept it alive, and went back to it after the record.

"Beaudoin was a pretty difficult guy. Lee hated him. A lot of that preceded me, and it was such a bad subject for Lee that it was frequently better to leave it undiscussed. When Lee would get his blood boiling he really got hot, and there was nothing gonna be accomplished by talking about it. He told me some of the background over the years. I met Beaudoin once after he'd taken the boat over. The thing with Beaudoin was that when Lee lost the *Hustler* that was like cutting off both his arms, and I think at one time Beaudoin had fancy ideas himself. Seems to me he may have had it out and running once. The boat had more left in it, I think. Lee did 315 on his first run on the 30th, and he really believed it could have run 330, 340.

"His manager then got very nervous as maybe she felt Lee and I started getting close, and he started making me privy more and more to everything that was going on. She was in the cosmetic business or something, had a big artichoke farm. She was quite a successful lady. She called me up, and I think she wanted everything to seem it was OK and was working in his best interests, but they had a big tiff and she took *everything*. His cars, most of the clothes on his back. I don't know if she *sold* the boat to Beaudoin. I think that was kind of the ultimate vindictive blow, that she gave the boat to Beaudoin. When Lee really started pushing to build a new boat, I think that's when she really started to put her foot down.

"I think after what he'd been through, anything was going to be challenging. Just like learning how to drive a car. He didn't know how to after the accident. For a long time he was apprehensive about it. Not because he ever worried about getting hurt, but he never liked doing anything other than perfectly. He couldn't tolerate being clumsy with something. He was very frustrated, and he fought so hard. In all the years I knew him he had a pretty good temper, particularly in the early years. A lot of it I think was both frustration with himself, just trying to do better or get a new command of the English language and being able to really talk the way he wanted to. He worked so hard at that. Spelling was a frustration, but every single time he would always try and do that much better. He was an absolute perfectionist in everything he did. He was just so determined to get himself back to being the person he had been and the person he wanted to be.

"We used to laugh a lot because he couldn't drink worth a damn. Lee was the cheapest drunk around. One of the first nights I'd met him we'd driven out to a friend's house after a party. Lee had probably just had a beer or something at the most, but I was having a great time. He was trying to get me to walk across the swimming pool, which had a half-inch of ice on it, baiting me. I knew damn well I wasn't going to walk across that pool! Later that night, three or four in the morning, Lee took off. He was seeing a *Playboy* bunny from Seattle, a real nice lady, but he couldn't get up this driveway. He couldn't get that car 10ft. We had a friendly bet of a dollar I could get it to the top. Well, I did, but I damned near killed myself walking down again. I've still got that dollar, because he autographed it for me. It was a great evening.

"He was fun when you got him loosened up and got his mind off things, because with his intensity, well, he just wouldn't stop. He'd drive a lot of people nuts around him because he'd never stop. A lot of people think he was the kind you either liked or walked away from, but you had to know him well, to understand where he was coming from. If you were trying to work with him on a regular basis, I think you just had to understand the determination and drive this guy had. I've never seen anything like it. He would just push for everything, but not obnoxiously. If he went in to see a sponsor and couldn't get anywhere, he'd really try to understand why it didn't work, and what it would take to make a successful programme."

■ ■ ■

The fire and gasoline well and truly exploded with Beaudoin, but Taylor contended all along that it was Beaudoin who had behaved badly when he acquired control of *Hustler* after the record run. Beaudoin himself had no interest in seeing Taylor succeed with a new boat since he claimed to have achieved speeds of 296 and 311mph on Lake Isabella in the summer of 1970. According to his story, the boat was then systematically sabotaged; he claimed wires under the dash were cut, and that fresh-sawn logs were floated on to the lake before one run. You didn't need to be Einstein to figure out whom he suspected. Unlike Taylor, though, Beaudoin never did get round to running under official conditions.

Lee's third wife, Dorothy, met Beaudoin once at the Los Angeles Boat Show. She remembered the meeting well. "Lee was a celebrity there, and had a model of *US Discovery II*. It was only our second date, and the first and only meeting I had with John Beaudoin. It was really an experience for me. I didn't even know who he was, I didn't know much about Lee at that time. But this person came to our booth and he began harrassing Lee. It was really terrible. I understood what was happening. Lee was so angry he left, but then Beaudoin began harrassing me. He was a really weird, strange, unusual person. I was able to successfully insult him so that he finally left."

The critics generally had a field day when *US Discovery I* foundered, but in 1976 Taylor merely switched lanes. *US Discovery II* would be a very different proposition, a rocket boat that really could be capable of outrunning its own noise.

"I used to dream about owning a big, black, shiny boat", he said when describing his nascent interest in water speed. The first dream had cost him two marriages and damn near his life, but nothing could curb the obsession. It might take him a while longer, but Lee Taylor was going on, come hell or high water.

It was that aspect which fascinated me the most. It's one thing to be brave because you lack imagination. Another to quell such imagination. But when you have suffered serious physical and mental injury, gone as close to the black pit, peered in and yet drawn back just in time to survive, it takes an abnormal kind of courage to continue on a path that you know is almost certain to lead you back to the edge again. And maybe, this time, even push you over. Like Campbell, Taylor knew all about fear, but he took it by the hand as he marched forward, rather than letting it hold him back. "I guess I chased it down the street a long time ago", he shrugged.

Early in 1980 *US Discovery II* was ready, all 40 sleek aluminium feet of it. A senior Lockheed designer, Art Williams, had drawn it, based on data Taylor supplied. It looked like a Bonneville car without wheels, sat on the water like some great blue-and-white hunched pterodactyl. US Marines had helped him build it, along with a crew from McDonnell Douglas.

"I don't like the angle of the rear planing surfaces", said Warby, by then the holder of the record at 317mph. "He'll have trouble slowing down." There was little love lost between the two rivals after Taylor had been reluctant to hand over the Royal Motor Yacht Club's Challenge Cup when Warby's first success, at 288mph, had just scraped past *Hustler*'s 10-year-old mark.

Hallett, too, was uneasy about them. "When I first saw the boat I told Lee it was so beautiful it's hard to believe anyone designed it. But I didn't like the shape of the sponsons with their sharp planing angles. I told him he'd get up on the plane real fast, but he'd better watch out when he got off the throttle. I figured the steep angles would get it going OK, but would make it real unstable slowing down. That's just the way it worked out, but Lee just laughed and told me not to worry. He said, 'Don't worry, Rich, it's been designed by a guy who works for North American Rockwell'."

Hallett had been involved with the new project at one time, but he and Lee drifted together and apart a couple of times. They were so close that sometimes, if Rich didn't say the right things, Lee would feel he was being abandoned. He'd get like that with people who were close to him, if he didn't feel they were 100% behind him, especially in the early stages. He was still fairly fragile from all he'd been through.

"Art Williams got a lot more credit than he was ever due for the boat", said McCaw. "Frankly, we got into some litigation with it, where we really didn't have the money to defend a lawsuit. Art picked up all the ideas that were around. There were things in there that were my ideas. He was a difficult guy to work with, but everything that he did became his idea forever after, and one day he laid this patent application on us. We had done a lot of design, but as the ultimate design became refined, Art laid claim to most of it. I personally don't believe he deserved even half of it. Part of our understanding with him was that we had to recognize him as the designer. Lee sort of compiled the ideas. In the end we agreed; there was no reason to get the project sideways over that."

Taylor went to the tranquil Walker Lake, near Hawthorne, Nevada, in the middle of 1980. It was an ideal location for test runs, but there were plenty of problems. At one stage he applied the power too sharply and the lengthy nose

After years of painstaking effort and determination, Taylor put his rocket-powered US Discovery II on the water early in 1980 in readiness for his attack on Ken Warby's record. In 1977 the Australian had first erased Taylor's old mark, squeaking by it with 288mph.

submarined before its buoyancy bobbed it back to the surface.

The enduring problem was trying to get it up on the plane. McCaw: "What would happen was that one sponson would start to fly before the other one, and the thing would get going with a 15-degree banking and start turning. I looked it right in the eye one time and it was like looking down the barrel of a loaded Howitzer coming right at you. Then it would flop to one side. It was like a baby duck trying to deal with water for the first time, real awkward. Finally, we decided to bring it up with a lot more power, and once he got through that he started getting some really good runs.

Stories began circulating of dramatic speeds, and one run at 333mph. "I had a guy timing all his runs", said Warby, "and he never saw anything like that. I reckon Taylor should get himself another air speed indicator." "As near as we could tell, on the 330mph run, all the numbers seemed to indicate the speed was correct. He finally got that thing working, you could just feel it", countered McCaw.

"He was fine when he ran the boat. He was getting agitated with it early on, when it was like trying to tame a wild bronco. It looked awful, so ungainly. Lee still had some shortcomings in lapses of detailed memory; he'd forget names, but he'd become more comfortable with himself, and he started recognizing that people weren't holding that against him. He worked out two, three hours a day, even when we were years from putting the boat in the water. He always trained like he was ready to run the next day."

In November, Taylor transferred to Lake Tahoe. It was a move he was quite happy to make, but which was also forced on him by financial and promotional considerations. One of his sponsors owned the Sahara Tahoe hotel, and the venue was a lot better suited to accommodating finicky city slicker television and media crews, even if its geographical location made the water itself inferior. November was a bad time of year to run at Tahoe, as snow showers cooled spirits and the winds created rollers and swells that never really abated. He knew it was a mistake after his first run, when impacts sustained at an average of only 186mph crinkled part of the fuselage. But more than anything he was conscious that a record-breaker must deliver, that hundreds of important new people in town were expecting him to justify their visit so they could be important new people in another town just as soon as possible.

"When we first put *Discovery* into the water we'll look like a bush league operation", he said. "But when we get to Tahoe we want to look like a major league operation. We want everything down pat."

He was too far into it to pull back. Walker Lake lay temptingly to the east, would have been far, far safer, but it could not have begun to accommodate all of the interested parties. In a way, he was trapped by the very success of his quest for backing. The seeds of disaster were ripening.

OTHER VOICES

Bruce McCaw

"Tahoe was where Lee wanted to run. We'd spent a lot of time over the years looking at sites, and we felt pretty good about it. Walker is in the middle of nowhere, and he really felt it was important for the sponsors to be at Tahoe. I wouldn't say he was locked into it, but there was a lot pushing that way. One time we flew over it in a Learjet, with Lee kneeling in the cockpit as we hit 400mph 10ft above the water. It was as much like running the boat as he could imagine, and with the beauty of the surrounding area it all seemed right.

"He felt a lot of pressure to run the boat at Tahoe, and he and I had had quite a lot of discussions about it. Gary Gabelich and I had been pretty emphatic with him, that if he didn't feel good about it, not to run. It was clear he was going to get plenty of support for whatever decision he felt was right.

"But I think, frankly, the biggest problem was everyone's lack of real understanding about how much movement you could get in that body of water. Just looking at the surface was not enough to tell you what was really going on. He just drove into a hole. You could see it. It had swells and movements of water that were simply too big to see. The real problem, too, was the depth. See, Walker was only 10 or 12ft deep. We could be there, the wind would kick up and blow up the water, and two hours later it would be flat as a millpond. There's not much there, though; we pretty much took over the whole town in Hawthorne.

"Clearly, in retrospect, that would have been the spot. We should have stayed at Walker. But Lee was so emphatic about Tahoe. He just loved Tahoe, too. There was something about it just was in his blood. He loved the area, he loved to ski there, loved to water ski there, loved everything about it. He really felt good about it.

"At the time I think the water was worse than everyone realized, and he took a couple of good dents the day before the accident.

"He was pretty serious about pushing up to 750 if that first attempt had been successful. His idea was to do it and maybe over several years make several attempts around the world and start increasing his own record.

"For a while afterwards we wanted to carry the project on, but the whole effort got really fragmented because there was a lot of bickering as to who owned what. One of the really unfortunate things is that nobody really got to see the cockpit footage because the Sheriff's Department impounded it. I think we would have learned so much about the boat from those films, and maybe gotten an idea of what really did upset it. It appeared as though one sponson just fell into a hole, and that was it. I think he was reluctant to come off the power in a hurry, and that was one of the things Gary had said, don't come off too soon because it's very destabilizing. Gary felt that when the engine was producing power it effectively doubled the length of the boat, so if you suddenly chopped that it could be very destabilizing.

"Lee and I had dinner the night before the accident, just the two of us, and he was the calmest I'd ever seen him. He really felt good about the record, very confident about everything. We just had a really neat evening. Now it's one of those moments I just treasure. Dorothy didn't get up there until early the next day. Gloria was his first wife, Kathy his second. Dorothy was his third. She made such a difference in his life, she was so good for him. She was such a trooper. She couldn't always get off work when Lee was ready to run so she would sometimes drive all night after work from L.A., frequently alone, just to be there. She was just a real honest, sincere gal, and you could tell going in that she looked out for him and took care of him, and she had no expectations about anything. They just enjoyed each other. She does a lot with his daughters, which is kind of nice, because he really loved those kids.

"He was a really well-meaning guy, and anything but greedy. He'd keep whatever the bare minimum was to keep himself going, and everything else went into the project. He had money coming in from his cousin Roy Seikel, who started as a plumber, but then owned 16 Hilton Hotels and 10 or so banks, and who put up the money which pushed the project over the top, but he was still grinding knives right up to the end, going out to keep some old customers happy.

"The interesting thing was, I never felt Lee was just doing it for Lee. He had a genuine belief that the United States should hold the record, and he always felt very strongly about it. When it went to Australia it really bothered him. He didn't feel much about Warby's boat, and felt like Warby had stolen a bunch of ideas from him. He said he wouldn't have taken Warby's boat waterskiing!

"Lee's helmet was ripped off in the accident, and it looks as though he drowned, but apparently he was unconscious. We talked a lot about safety equipment, but worrying about himself was the last thing on his mind."

■ ■ ■

Gary Gabelich was there for the attempt. He was a close friend of Taylor, and had advised him about rockets. He knew a little bit about them, having used one back in 1970 to break the Land Speed Record with the *Blue Flame*. "Lee was very conscious he had a role to play, that he had to perform for people. He knew he couldn't afford to wait around for long. But there's no way he took risks. He was too smart for that. He wanted to live just as much as the next man, but he also felt he had a duty to the sponsors and the spectators." Gary, following in the helicopter that filmed the final run, would be a close witness of the last moments.

Just after 11am on the 13th Taylor went through his cockpit routine, strapped into his seat way back down towards the rear of the pencil-slim fuselage. Once, twice he purged the rocket motor, letting the hydrogen peroxide course hungrily over its catalyst pack to pre-heat it in readiness. Around the shore onlookers craned their necks to catch a glimpse of the spectacular new joust with the unknown. Television cameramen's fingers twitched on their equipment, just in case.

"There's no way this is record-breaking water", Taylor told his crew. "I'll take it easy, just check it out." To Gabelich, the night before, he'd expressed his private hopes. "Dear God, if anything's gonna happen to me, if you're gonna do something, do it good. Either let me set the record, or let me check out with dignity."

Chased by the scream of the rocket, he went through the traps at 269.235mph, that last day of his life, as he played his last game of the Russian Roulette that is seeking records on the water. Right at the end of the run *Discovery* began veering to one side before it danced from one sponson to the other with a horrible frequency. By then his speed was well over 300. Williams had always warned him not to quarter swells, but at that velocity he had no choice when he ran into an ugly series of them exiting the measured kilometre. When the left sponson finally dug far enough into the concrete-hard water it peeled open like a rotten banana and exploded in a shower of buoyancy foam. The long blue-and-white 'piloted water missile' – which Taylor had described so enthusiastically as a 'zero defect design' – was thrown into its fatal corkscrew.

OTHER VOICES

Dorothy Taylor Arevalos

"Lee and I married on March 3, 1974. I met him at girlfriend Jane Arden's house on Halloween, October 31, 1973. He'd come to get her stepson so he could see *US Discovery 1*. The first thing I felt was that he was totally dedicated to the project. He said then that he lived, breathed and ate it, 24 hours a day, seven days a week. Scott Arden worshipped Lee, and would do anything for him.

"Lee and I talked a lot, he got my phone number, took me out to dinner, and took me down to the site at Cerritos to introduce me to his love – I guess it was his second love. I think I became his first, although sometimes I really doubted it! He really was in love with that boat!

"He had four daughters, Debbi, Lori, Kristi and Teri, who were teenagers when we met. When he died he had three granddaughters. Lee thought the world of his four girls. Debbie used to sing at press conferences, and he was real proud of that.

"He had a love of animals, too, especially his kitty, Misty Lou. One time she got lost at the site, it was so huge. She hid in the boat. Later on he got me a teacup poodle, and we called her Cindy Sue, so we had Cindy Sue and Misty Lou,

On November 13, 1980 Lee Taylor piloted US Discovery II through the measured mile on Lake Tahoe at an average speed of 269.235mph despite water conditions unsuited to record breaking. At the end of the run the needle-shaped missile danced from sponson to sponson before rolling over, killing him as thousands watched in horror from the shores.

and Cindy Sue went everywhere with us, in a purse, and she was at every press conference with us, no matter where we went. Every dinner, everything. She only weighed three pounds, and flew with us on airplanes.

"Lee ran several miles every day, and was an avid skier. He worked out every day and never let his injuries bother him at all. His foot was a bit stiff, but his vision was perfect. I thought he was an excellent promoter, getting sponsorship and support. It was unbelievable how he could come up with these things. He got involved with several con artists, though; he was so vulnerable to them.

"He was very patriotic. He said it was more of a challenge to let Ken Warby have the record for a short time. The Stars & Stripes was his idol, and he wanted to have that cup back over here. He really did love the idea of being the number one in the world on water.

"There was always a large crowd of friends and sponsors at the Irvine base. Lee made a lot of friends that way, personal friends that I have to this day. We went to the Colorado River with friends, and Lee was swimming across it, a

251

mile. Cindy Sue ran into this vacant lot where these people had this little tiny black dog. I walked over to meet them. We helped them move in and went out to dinner together afterwards. This was Ron Woodruff, and it turned out he had a major interest in boats, and just happened to have a facility that could help Lee by making the rocket engine. I thought it was kinda cute that it was Cindy Sue who introduced him to the person who ended up building the rocket engine. Lee mixed well. One trip in Oregon he got a couple to tow him all over the lake on water skis, once they realized who he was.

"Lee is buried up at Lake Tahoe. His friends and sponsors helped that happen for him and for me. His daughters and I felt that he loved the place, he loved what he did, he died doing what he wanted to do, and we were going to make sure he was where he really loved it best, and that was Tahoe."

■ ■ ■

I can still hear the words as they woke me on my bedside radio alarm clock. 'An attempt on the World Water Speed Record has ended in tragedy.' Radio One, the early bulletin. 6.30am on Friday, November 14, English time. Suddenly I was wide awake, blood racing, heart pumping. And I *knew*, without having to hear the rest. Nobody else was currently active. It had to be Taylor. It wasn't until I was driving to the newsagents to buy a copy of every national daily that it even began to strike me what an unusual lead story it had been.

The papers told me little. Instead, I would piece together the full life and times of my dead hero through a series of retrospective interviews over the coming years.

On that crisp winter morning I knew only that Lee Allen Taylor had died as he had lived, chasing a speed record in a boat he had spent his waking hours creating and perfecting. As he stretched its outer edge to its limit, he had burst through the envelope into the oblivion that had finally snuffed out a spirit that life itself had never been able to crush.

23

GILLES VILLENEUVE

A rage to win

"I don't want to wait much longer for my 'Lotus 79' to turn up."

One of my enduring memories from motor racing is standing in a forest in the pitch dark, listening to the sound of a racing car running flat-out down the Mulsanne Straight at Le Mans. An eerie feeling, as the exhaust note changes not at all for mile after mile. Somewhere like Bonneville you at least know that the course goes on forever. At Le Mans you know there are corners, and you keep urging the driver to lift off, for God's sake, lift off.

In 1978 I stood in the trees round the back of Brands Hatch. It was a test session in June prior to the British GP. I got used to the sound of the quick lift before a driver would get back on the throttle, but then suddenly there was one engine note that remained the same. Incredible! How could that be? The driver was having to come through Dingle Dell, through the right-handed Dingle Dell Corner and then through the tighter left-hander at Stirling's Bend. Without lifting?

We ran to the fence and kept watching. It was Ferrari number 12. Villeneuve. Later, Ronnie Peterson and Emerson Fittipaldi managed it, too, but neither was as fluid nor as regular as Gilles. That day left a lasting impression. The guy wasn't just quick, he was incredibly smooth and precise when the car was working for him, as the 312T3 was then.

Every era, every race, should have its Gilles Villeneuve. A man who, by his sheer talent and application, could throw out the form book, turn back the clock to the days when the cars didn't greedily covet so much of the success equation.

Gilles was a *racer*, a throwback to uncomplicated days when the size of a driver's heart counted for more than the grip his car might generate in a corner. A giant whose talent allowed him to escape the fetters imposed by the inadequacies of his machinery. He was a virtuoso, and motor racing his stage. Those who saw all of his races thanked God for him, hailed him as the saviour of the modern, suspensionless ground-effect cars which appeared to corner on rails, yet did such unpleasant things to the men in the cockpits. He was the only man who could make even that breed of mechanical monster do things it didn't want, or had no right, to do.

Who could ever forget that 1979 French GP battle with Arnoux? The Ferrari was hopelessly outclassed, Villeneuve's task made all the more impossible by the state of his tyres. Yet corner after corner Gilles just refused to give up. The

253

tyres were gone, so what did it matter if he took a few more yards off their life by locking them wildly as he outbraked the Renault? Time and again the T4's waywardness lost him a corner, and Arnoux appeared safe, yet somehow that information was never transmitted to Gilles. Each time he pushed a little bit harder, longer, deeper, got the corner back at the last second, or so refused to concede it that he won the next. They touched several times, yawed frantically as both drivers fought each other and their cars. Afterwards they laughed and congratulated one another. There was no animosity, not from Arnoux, nor from the crowd, when the inevitable happened and Gilles finished runner-up to Jean-Pierre Jabouille. The French veteran had just won his first GP and the first for Renault's turbocharged car, and in France, yet Gilles' sheer bravado had stolen the day. If any race encapsulated everything that he stood for, that was it.

Afterwards, the wiser heads of Formula One chastised the new boys, and spoke angrily of the risks they had taken. One veteran, though, saw the sense in it, but then he had been brought up in a far, far tougher arena. "It's just a coupla young lions clawin' themselves", said Mario Andretti.

Paradoxically, that was one of the few races of 1979 where the T4 was really bad, where its shortcomings left him on the very ragged edge. But he was well versed in walking that sort of tightrope. Some build their background racing karts on tarmacadam surfaces, but Gilles' nursery medium was ice. Perhaps that explained a lot, accounted for his uncanny ability to keep a car on or just over its limit without losing control. In snowmobile racing he honed his acute sense of balance and learned a surprising amount about handling characteristics that would later have direct benefit to his motor racing. In 1971 he won the 440cc World Series in New York State.

Then, as ever, he followed a simple credo: win as much as you can. He applied it successfully in Formula Ford and Formula Atlantic. By 1976 he was The Man. He took pole position for every one of his Formula Atlantic races in the Ecurie Canada March 76B, and won four races out of five to win the Canadian Players series. In the American IMSA series he won all four that he entered. The only retirement came at Westwood when his engine cut out and he spun into a bank. The following season his battles with Keke Rosberg and Bobby Rahal were to become legend.

OTHER VOICES

Keke Rosberg

"Gilles was probably the maddest bastard I ever met. He was a very different type of driver to Alain and Niki. Winning was everything to him, but the way he won was important, too. He treated every race like a personal challenge.

"He was a hard racer, very hard, but always fair. In some of our races in 1977 we were rubbing wheels, touching bodywork, and even I thought it was getting a bit too much after a while, but he was always fair. To him it was a sport, that's why you knew he would never shut you out. He would always give you room to race.

"Of course he was very brave, abnormally so. We always got on because we played by the same rules. But I did begin to worry about him in later years because he just took so many chances."

■   ■   ■

When he'd first watched a motor race Gilles had been unimpressed with most of the drivers, but had felt that such a sport was well beyond his reach. Now that he had got this far he had one aim in mind. "I'll win enough races so that they'll have to notice me." Already, Jim Clark had assumed the role of a guiding light. Already, he was planning to race in Europe.

After the 1976 whirlwind had hit North American Atlantic, Villeneuve left a trail of destruction as far as lap records were concerned. He had also made an impressive debut in Europe when Ron Dennis (shrewd even then) had invited him to drive one of his March 762s at Pau's annual Formula Two race. Pau is not an easy circuit, and though at the time it might not have created much of a storm, in retrospect Gilles' 10th place on the grid was a fantastic achievement in a highly competitive formula. In the race he was pushing the top six, which included winner Arnoux, Laffite, Tambay and Cheever, when his engine overheated.

He even came to London shortly afterwards to discuss possible terms with entrant Walter Wolf, and thence to visit McLaren's Teddy Mayer at Colnbrook, but there was little serious business to be done. "It was more a chance to put a face with a name", he said.

The thing he was really relying on was the Trois Rivieres street race, where many of the top Europeans such as James Hunt, Alan Jones and Patrick Depailler would be competing. Hunt, close to winning his World Championship, would have this unknown guy Villeneuve as his team-mate. But only just... Gilles' plans to take them all on came so close to crumbling when Skiroule, his sponsor, pulled out. At the last moment, Direct Film stepped in, and the man who would become his manager, Gaston Parent, arranged a system of public subscription. Gilles could barely wait for the race, his one big chance to race with equal equipment against the best from Europe. "This is the only race anyone cares about over there", he declared, and Europe was where he desperately wanted to be.

The previous year he had embarrassed the likes of Jarier and Depailler by qualifying third and running second until his brakes failed. This time he sat the March on pole, but only after several spins. Even then, however, it was notable just how he could place the March when it was so apparently out of control. All through each spin he was able to keep full orientation. Back at Snetterton, while testing the Lotus Indycar in 1965, Clark had staggered the likes of Maurice Phillippe with his ability to spin it between two banks, not once but twice. The first time he had chosen the gap in extremis, the second time he had deliberately aimed for it when the same attempted manoeuvre had gone wrong... They shared that rare skill of remaining in control even when they were out of it.

The dominance of Gilles' victory over the stars brought him back to McLaren later that year, and was instrumental in inking his signature on an agreement that he would contest 'selected' races with the team in 1977. He was on his way.

OTHER VOICES

Chris Amon

"Gilles took over the CanAm Wolf from me, and he always struck me as having enormous talent. I felt that he was somebody who just had to go places. At that point he was wild, hard on the gear, but he seemed to have huge talent and a lot of determination, too.

"I think he enjoyed driving that car. I just wish we could have given him something better. He did a very good job. He was hard on it, especially the brakes, and you couldn't get him to take anything easier. You could tell him the car had a weakness, and know as you were telling him that he was taking no notice. Not that he should have!

"He was one of the greatest talents I saw in my time, although I never really saw him at his best to compare him fairly with, say, Jimmy, who had great attributes, such as his ability to nurse something through. I'm not sure Gilles would ever have achieved that! I suspect that in terms of sheer speed, though, there was little in it."

■ ■ ■

In a racing car Gilles knew no fear, but his bravery was based on calm acceptance of risk rather than being a product of ignorance or lack of imagination. He knew how it felt to get hurt, but he accepted it. Early in his career, in 1974, he broke a leg after crashing his Formula Atlantic car at Mosport as he lapped a backmarker. He refused to believe he was injured at first, not because of delayed shock or anything so mundane, but simply because he could not believe it could have happened. When he accepted it, he also accepted the risk. "I've hit a guardrail, so what? Now I know what it feels like, it's not so bad", was his reaction. Five weeks later he was back, driving with the injured leg in a cast.

Looking back at him as a racer, I find so little to criticize. Oh, he could be hard on his cars, and yes, he did do some crazy things, but there was only one season in which he had what might be described as a truly competitive car, the Ferrari 312T2 in 1979, and even that was barely a match for a decent ground-effect machine. He had much to be thankful for in Mauro Forghieri's powerful flat-12 engine, even if his chassis wasn't up to much, but many of his manoeuvres were simply born of the desperation to be competitive, of running his machinery way faster than he had any right to expect it to run. His starts were brilliant, none more so than that at Interlagos in 1980 in the awful T5. Pironi and Jabouille shared the front row, but there between them, like a

Gilles learned the art of high-speed vehicle control in the most unusual manner, via snowmobiles in Canada.

rocket, went the Ferrari at the start. It was outclassed, but he led for two laps. At Zandvoort, in 1981, it wasn't quite so effective. Ferrari was trying a revised engine on which it desperately needed to put race mileage. "Gilles, please, please don't do anything rash", pleaded Forghieri. Gilles promised faithfully not to, but lasted only as far as Tarzan, the first corner, when the gap he'd aimed for between Patrese and Giacomelli had narrowed by the time he reached it...

There were those who branded him nothing more than a hothead, who could never see beyond all those spins he had in the McLaren M23 on his debut at Silverstone, or the shunts of 1977 in the difficult, unforgiving Ferrari T2. At the time he was criticized as a rookie. Only later would observers come to realize just how bad that car must have been if *Villeneuve* couldn't control it.

His philosophy with the McLaren had been simple: "I have little time to make an impression, and I don't want to be sent home to Atlantic. How else will I know where the limits are if I don't go over them?". He spun at each corner at least once as he embarked on his crash learning course, but once he'd found each limit, he stopped spinning... They didn't notice that.

What some did notice then was a phenomenon. "When I drove that McLaren M23 it was just like a big-engined Atlantic car", he said nonchalantly. "The transition was easy. A bit more power, a bit stiffer. In honesty, that was probably the most delightful car situation I've ever encountered. It was a super chassis." They noticed how he could throw it around with complete confidence, how he ran rings round Jochen Mass in the works McLaren M26, qualifying the old M23 ninth. He was up to seventh in the race, well in touch with the group ahead, when caution dictated a pit stop to report overheating. The gauge was faulty. He went back into the race in a fury and set the fifth fastest lap. Even the sceptics sat up and took notice.

All but Teddy Mayer. He'd put a face with a name, alright, but the name he preferred was Patrick Tambay's. Edward Everett Mayer has done a lot of things that others in motor racing have considered, shall we say, unusual, but throwing Villeneuve away was surely the oddest. Enzo Ferrari certainly thought so. He believed he could see something in the young French-Canadian who gabbled happily in his odd accent. He still thought so after Gilles had crashed the T2 during qualifying in Canada, and again in Japan, where two spectators were killed and 10 injured after he'd ridden over the back of Peterson's Tyrrell and cartwheeled into the prohibited area where they had gathered. That, despite Ferrari's dislike of drivers who damaged his beloved cars. Even at that stage they shared something special.

There are some who still draw comfort from denigrating his every effort, even though the drivers they lionized were the first to pay Gilles tribute. How often did we hear that he crashed too much, took too much out of his machinery, took too many risks? But when did he ever have a chassis and engine package equal to his phenomenal talent? Senna is the closest of the current drivers in terms of talent and commitment, if not in mien and personality, yet if the Lotus 99T was the one car with which Ayrton really had to struggle, most of Gilles' were dogs. By the standards of some of Ferrari's offerings, the Lotus was like a McLaren compared to a Coloni. What might Gilles have achieved in a Williams FW11, or a McLaren MP4/5?

His astonishing displays continued. In 1978 the Lotus 79 was the king, glueing Mario Andretti and Ronnie Peterson to the ground as they flew round the corners. "If it hugged the road any more it would be a white line", quipped the laconic American. And yet there was Gilles, oh so confidently heading them all at Long Beach from the sixth lap to the 38th. It was only his sixth Grand Prix, yet he exhibited all the confidence in the world until he tripped over Regazzoni's Shadow. He staggered onlookers with his determination at Zolder, where he alone gave Andretti a run for his money until a puncture dropped him from second place; fourth was a poor reward that day. He stepped on to a Grand Prix podium for the first time in Austria, with third place, and then at Monza

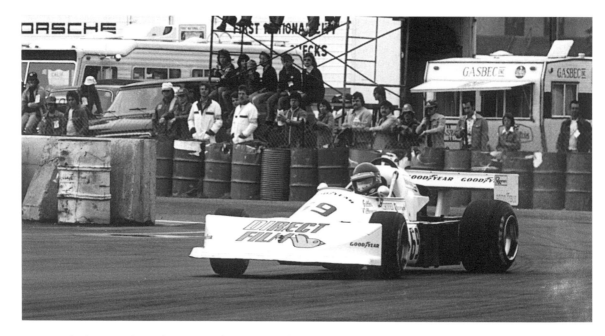

once again he was the only man to keep Mario honest, although both were relegated by penalties for anticipating a screwed-up start. By Montreal he was ready to win, and he took his first Grand Prix victory in front of his adoring home crowd. Typically, Gilles was unhappy that he'd been unable to catch Jarier in the second Lotus 79 while the Frenchman kept running.

1979 was to bring him his greatest year; he led seven of the 15 races, won three of them, and spent more time in the lead than anyone else. It also brought the greatest test of his integrity. The T4 wasn't bad to begin with, thanks mainly to its power. In the South African GP he dominated the damp early going and ran out an easy winner, following up with his third triumph when he took revenge at Long Beach. He added the Race of Champions almost immediately, but then came Monaco. Jody led all the way from pole there, and it was said within Maranello that whomsoever won in the Principality would be the heir apparent should they be in contention for the World Championship. It was a situation that could have gone either way. Scheckter, the reformed *enfant terrible* of Formula One, had matured into a canny racer. Gilles was the first to admit he was still climbing a steep learning curve. The cards happened to fall for Jody, and Gilles was content to honour that.

"The Championship means little to me", he would say. "Moss didn't win it, neither did Ronnie. Who is to say they weren't Champions? I race the way I always have, to win races. If I win enough, the Championship will come."

It was not enough for him to finish a race, no matter how well up, if he didn't feel he had driven to his absolute limit. The idea of driving in calculating style, garnering championship points, was utter anathema. Scheckter simply couldn't understand it. "To me the reason to go racing is to win the World Championship", he said. "Why else would we do it?"

If the car was only good enough for eighth place, and he managed to take seventh, Gilles would treat it as a victory and derive just as much satisfaction from his day. "Jochen Rindt loved motor racing, but he wasn't in love with it", said Jackie Stewart. "Gilles was."

That year at Monza all he had to do was pass Scheckter and win in order to keep open his chances of taking the title. How many times must that thought have occurred to him as he watched his team-mate's tail right in front of him? Yet he had given his word, and that was what the team had decreed. He was a

James Hunt and Motoring News *journalist Murray Taylor raved about the performances of the young Villeneuve after witnessing his brio during the Trois Rivieres Formula Atlantic race in 1976. Soon the sight of the French-Canadian on opposite lock would become familiar all over Europe.*

big enough man, sufficiently confident in his own towering ability, to sit there without cheating at the last moment. It is telling that Jody himself never once seriously believed that Gilles would play him false. They finished 0.46s apart. The two enjoyed a close bond, and Mauro Forghieri maintains to this day that the years working with the two of them were the happiest of his long career at Ferrari.

The turning point for Gilles that year had come at Zandvoort, that famous race where he had tried three-wheeling back to the pits. Jones had led in the Williams, which had far greater ground-effect than the Ferrari, but Gilles had passed the Australian in a devastating move round the *outside* at Tarzan and was ahead when a slow puncture spun him off course. As he restarted, the rubber from the tattered left rear Michelin flailed wildly. "As long as the car moves, I will drive it", was his maxim, and at the time he couldn't see the full extent of the damage. By the time he got back to the pits the entire left rear suspension was history and the wheel and the remains of the tyre hung by mere links. Some pilloried him for his lack of concern for the safety of others, but the rest gasped in awe and admiration for his refusal to accept defeat until the last bitter moment. Truly, he was Nuvolari incarnate, they said. It was the failure to finish there that doomed his title chances.

He dominated the last two races, finally finishing second to Jones in Canada, but only after a monumental scrap. The Australian was the first to admit how inferior the Ferrari was, and was generous in his praise after following it for 50 of the 72 laps. "With him you hardly even dared to breathe. Take a deep breath just when you think you'd got away, and that bloody red shitbox would be filling your mirrors again!"

In Watkins Glen it was Gilles all the way for the fourth win of his career. When it had rained at one stage during qualifying he had gone out for the sheer pleasure it gave him, lapping 11 seconds faster than anyone else.

If the breaks went Jody's way in 1979, they didn't go anywhere near Ferrari in 1980. It was a year of total disaster, the depth of which can be gauged by the fact that Gilles won nothing, and garnered merely two fifths and two sixths for a season of unstinting effort that threw Scheckter's effort into harsh relief. The T5 was simply an update of the T4 in a season that demanded super-efficient skirts and pounds of downforce. The T5 had neither. To make matters worse, turbo power more and more was becoming *de rigeur*. Ferrari had its 126CK in the pipeline, but it wouldn't come soon enough, and when it did, it would flatter only to deceive.

As Jody's motivation all but disappeared, victim of the car and a huge accident in practice at Imola, Gilles' simply burned brighter than ever. No matter how many times he had to stop his sliding car for fresh Michelins, he would come piling back out, charging all the while for one or two points. It was a cruel waste of an awesome talent, but so long as he had the inner satisfaction of knowing he had done the best job anyone could have done in the car, he could keep up his commitment.

When it arrived for the 1981 season the 126CK was a bulky old box, an ill-handling device whose only saving grace was the power its new turbocharged V6 produced. It yielded him only two wins, but both were great. He ran second to Piquet at Monaco before revealing yet another startling facet of his honourable character. Realizing that he was holding up Jones as the Australian thirsted after Piquet, with whom he had had angry words at the previous race, Gilles gave him *just* enough room to overtake. Later that chivalry was rewarded as Jones' Williams began to misfire, and he in turn left Gilles just enough room to pass. It was sporting gamesmanship from two of the world's best drivers, and Gilles romped on to victory.

His last followed immediately, on the twisting and undulating Jarama circuit in Spain, where he led that five-car train home after withstanding sustained pressure throughout the race.

"In terms of results, I preferred to win at Monaco", he smiled. "But from a driving point of view I got far more satisfaction out of Jarama. When I got ahead on lap 15 there were some 65 laps left to run. Early in the race I thought to myself, 'OK, they're going to pass me for sure, but let's hang in there and see what happens'. So I led for 30 laps, and nothing happened. Then we were at 40 laps, and they were still behind. Then there were suddenly only 20 laps to go, and they still hadn't passed me. So I thought, 'Well, they haven't passed you for 50 laps, just don't make a mistake and let them through so close to the finish!'.

"The car felt really awful on the infield, and I thought I was braking pretty early there, because there was so little grip. All the time I was thinking that they could run rings round me if they wanted to. Then it was the last lap and I was still ahead..."

It was a stunning demonstration of cleanliness as he led home Laffite, Watson, Reutemann and de Angelis with a mere 1.24s separating all five.

Again, there were irrepressible moments, such as his spin exiting the chicane at Silverstone, which also accounted for Jones' Williams. Typically, in amongst all the catchfencing the Ferrari began to move as the dust settled, but he made it only as far as Stowe before stopping with a puncture.

"I'd hit the chicane kerbing a few times in practice and it upset the car", he admitted, "but I always managed to control it. In the race I hit it that little bit harder, I guess. I bounced over and clipped the kerb on the opposite side and just didn't have quite enough lock to get away with it. I kept the boot in to keep it away from the catchfencing.

"There were still four wheels on the car, the wing was there, but obviously a bit bent, so I thought, 'Let's give it a go'. But there was a puncture, so that was that!" Typically, he admitted with a grin that the temptation had been very high to try to limp back to the pits.

I saw a slow-motion replay of the 126CK's behaviour on the fastest part of the course, now named after him, during the Canadian GP that year. It was awful, a truly appalling bronco of a car that took every ounce of skill he had to cajole round in a decent lap time. Gilles himself was beginning ever so slightly to despair that he would ever get his hands on a car that would finally allow him to unlock that potential for smooth driving we had seen at Brands Hatch in 1978. He knew he could not afford any more years like 1980 or '81, even if it meant considering leaving Ferrari.

"I really hope that Ferrari has quite a good chassis in 1981", he said quietly, with a serious note to his voice. "We've proved that we have the engine, and with less weight and better aerodynamics we'll be competitive all the time.

"I know what they'll start saying, so I don't want to spend all my years fighting an uncompetitive car. OK, so everybody knows that I'm very quick, but another season like this and I'll have the same problems that faced Ronnie Peterson when he was driving a bad car. They said he was quick but too erratic. Then Ronnie got into the Lotus 79 and showed them that they were all wrong. I don't want to wait much longer for my 'Lotus 79' to turn up. You can't imagine how irritating and frustrating it can be when you have a car which is 15mph quicker on the straight at some circuits and you wind up qualifying it in 16th place on the grid."

As the season went on he considered a change, and certainly there were offers from just about every serious team, but like Tom Pryce, Gilles was an intensely loyal character. He signed again for 1982, and outlined why. "I signed my contract and decided to abide by that commitment. I realize that if I'd said that I didn't want to drive, then they couldn't force me. There is always a way out of a contract if you really want to leave. But I think we're on the verge of making real progress with the turbo. Let's just say that the other teams were talking to me more than I was talking to them!"

The two victories apart, his best result in 1981 was third in the rain at Montreal, and again it was a controversial result as he drove for much of the event peeping round a collision-damaged front aerofoil which had been bent to the vertical. Brutally honest with everyone, himself most of all, he said of that race, "The car was going well in the heavy rain, and I think some of the other guys slowed down a bit more than I did. In fact, if it hadn't been for a misfire I reckon I could have led, although I don't think I'd have been in the lead by the finish.

"OK, the wing might have caused me to crash, and everybody would have called me an idiot. But it didn't. Visibility wasn't much of a problem. The real danger was if the wing had flown off; it might have hurt somebody else or myself. But while it was still attached it wasn't really much of a problem. The visibility on the straight was alright, just, if I tilted my head. But I couldn't really see on the left-hand corners, which made life particularly difficult on the second part of the S-bend beyond the pits." What he meant was the fastest corner on the circuit.

"All I could do", he continued with unaffected nonchalance, "was watch my right front wheel to see whether it was on the dry or wet patch. I was keeping the right-hand side of the car on the verge of the wet patch thinking that if it was there then it must be clear of the barrier on the left-hand side. I suppose I was lucky it was a wet day so that I could work out where I was from the dry patches on the track. It wasn't too bad. I must say that I wasn't aware that I ran over the wing when it finally flew off, although the car went all over the place. I got everything under control, luckily..."

The following season's 126C2, designed by Harvey Postlethwaite, looked like giving Ferrari and Villeneuve their first serious crack at the title since 1979, and as ever he grasped the challenge with both hands.

The San Marino GP at Imola set the stage for the final conflict of Gilles' career. (This was the race boycotted by many of the FOCA teams in the aftermath of the 'water bottles' scandal, which had been provoked by the ingenious use of a loophole in the regulations allowing fluid reservoirs to be topped-up after a race prior to a car being weighed; suddenly, cars whose normally aspirated engines were no longer a match for the turbos were appearing with so-called water-cooled brakes!)

The agreement within Ferrari for the Imola race was that whichever driver was leading if and when the opposition retired, would win the San Marino GP.

He spun a great deal when he first tried the McLaren M23 at Silverstone before the 1977 British GP, but the alert noticed that the spinning stopped after a while, once he had assessed its limits. "I don't want to be sent back to Atlantic..." he said, in explanation of his apparent wildness.

When Arnoux's Renault retired Gilles was in front, having tackled both French cars fair and square as Pironi sat back and watched. Now all they had to worry about was getting their cars home on the circuit that exacts the highest toll of them all in terms of fuel consumption. What happened next is history as Pironi ignored conventions and, in Gilles' mind, stole his race from him right at the end. On the rostrum he scowled as the Frenchman sprayed champagne. Immediately afterwards he left, their friendship broken forever. Not long before he had counselled Nigel Roebuck to be easy on Didier after he had had a 180mph shunt at Ricard. Now he resolved never again to speak to the man who had betrayed his trust. Others thought back to Monza in 1979, and could appreciate how hurt he felt.

He was literally stunned by his team-mate's duplicity, totally unable to accept losing a race in such a fashion, particularly as he had desperately been trying to slow the pace to ensure they would both get home without running dry. "When I want someone to stay behind... well, I think he stays behind", he fumed later that week to Roebuck. "No *way* would he have passed me, nor would anyone else. Not on the last lap... Finishing second is one thing... I would have been mad at myself for not being quick enough if he'd beaten me. But finishing second because the bastard steals it... Jesus, that's why I'm mad. Everyone seems to think we had the fight of our lives, which is a *joke*!"

Alain Prost, a close friend, also spoke with him that week. "I remember well the story of Didier and Gilles", he said after his own anger with Ayrton Senna at the same race seven years later. "I remember very well. He was calling me maybe once or twice a day, and every time he was calling me about Didier and he was very, very angry. I couldn't believe it. When he had his accident, I was absolutely sure what had happened. It was unbelievable."

At 13.51pm on Friday, May 8, 1982 at Zolder, trying to beat Pironi's time in practice for the Belgian GP, Gilles crashed to his death when he tripped over Jochen Mass' sluggish March as the German trailed back to the pits. He became a victim of the very accident he had predicted to Roebuck only weeks before.

OTHER VOICES

Patrick Tambay – his replacement at Ferrari

"You know, my last Grand Prix victory came at Imola in 1983, and that was very, very emotional for me. That race was just so extraordinary for me.

"In Germany in 1982 I had felt very keenly the responsibility that rested on my shoulders, but Imola was much, much more.

"I qualified third on the grid, but my car had given me plenty of trouble. I ended up just three-thousandths of a second slower than Nelson Piquet's Brabham, but by coincidence that meant that I lined up in the same position that Gilles had had in the previous year's race when Didier Pironi had won. Poor Gilles, he never, ever got over that. He felt so cheated!

"Right ahead of me on the grid was a Canadian Maple Leaf that the tifosi had painted on the track where Gilles had lined his car up. I felt very, very emotional thinking about him before the start. I was sitting in my car on the grid with 20 minutes to go, and I just broke down, you know?

"I was just sitting there, crying my eyes out. I was completely broken up. My mechanics, my friends who came to the car to wish me luck, just walked away. They were embarrassed for me, and didn't know what to do or what to say. There was nothing any of them could have done or said.

"I felt better when the race started, and I ran second in the opening stages to my team-mate Rene Arnoux, who had started from the pole position. Then Riccardo Patrese passed me in the Brabham. I took over the lead when Riccardo was delayed during his stop for tyres.

A lesser driver could never have contained Jacques Laffite, John Watson, Carlos Reutemann and Elio de Angelis for so long during the 1981 Spanish GP at Jarama, but Gilles remained in control throughout in the evil-handling Ferrari 126CK. It would be his last F1 victory.

"I drove that race in a dream. I don't know if you believe in metaphysics or whatever, but I swear it wasn't me driving that car that day. It felt as if Gilles was there with me, as if he was doing the work. All round the track there were banners saying things like 'Gilles and Patrick – two hearts, one number!', but I knew they were for him, not me.

"I was just driving his car, and after what had happened the previous year, I desperately wanted to win this one.

"The car was beautiful that day, apart from a problem through Tamburello. In the closing stages, after Patrese had crashed and I was leading again, it kept cutting out as I went through there, and my heart was in my mouth. I was thinking, 'Please don't let it stop now!', and I was so relieved that it kept going. But then it stopped altogether, out of fuel, on the slowing-down lap. The crowd went crazy!"

■ ■ ■

It was one of the most emotional wins of the decade as the Ferrari sped beneath the chequered flag, but by then Patrick was back in control of himself. On the victory rostrum he quietly dedicated his success, "To the memory of the car number 27 which didn't win last year".

One of the most moving film moments I have watched is in Terence Rattigan's Fifties picture *The Sound Barrier*, produced and directed by David Lean. Tony (Nigel Patrick) has been killed trying to fly faster than sound, and later his best friend Philip, admirably played by John Justin, becomes the first man to do so. In the cockpit in the immediate aftermath he croons, "I did it. I *did* it!".

He returns to base exhilarated. "I say, chap called Sound just looked in", says the controller, poking his head through an adjoining hatch. "He's absolutely livid with you, old boy. Says he's going to bump the speed up next time."

Just then Philip's wife bustles in, too concerned with getting his approval of a dress before the shop she bought it from closes, to notice his excitement. Assured he likes it, she hurries off before he can tell her the good news, and leaves him alone, laughing to himself. Suddenly, as the enormity – and the price – of his achievement hits him, his laughter turns to hysterical, wrenching sobs...

I often think of Patrick, bless him, when I replay that film, and of the day he drove for Gilles, and Gilles drove for him. The two were such close friends, and had so much in common.

Gilles Villeneuve could inspire that sort of emotion in people, as the letters that flooded into Maranello after his death testified. That pressday at *Motoring News* was the worst I personally can recall. I can remember exactly what I was doing the day I heard the news, who told me, how he said it. What I felt at the time, what I felt afterwards. How my first thoughts were for those friends in Belgium who had to cope with their personal grief while doing their jobs as well.

I had a Jaguar XJ-S on test that weekend, and I drove it quickly. Just as, for some inexplicable reason, I had had that urge to pedal the hell out of my pushbike the day that Jim Clark was killed. As if violent exercise could in some way be cathartic.

We went out to a local restaurant that night with my friend Nick Young, another racing enthusiast. We had often argued about Gilles. We were all quiet, and I must have been pretty rotten company. I remember on the way back he put on a tape in the car. Quite unconsciously he had chosen Kate and Anna McGarrigal, the French-Canadian sisters...

When Gerry Donaldson's biography of Gilles was published in 1989 I took it out on the plane with me to Mexico. I'd taken one of Roebuck's 'double-dose' sleeping tablets, but I didn't sleep. The story was far too stimulating. I read it in a sitting, and when I came to the climax I was relieved that the cabin was dark as my fellow passengers slept. I later tried reading Jacques Villeneuve's tribute to his brother aloud to my wife, but I didn't finish it.

What I truly loved about Gilles was his utter disdain for defeat. You'd look in the daily papers for a Grand Prix's qualifying times and, no matter how far down he might be, you just knew he would be near the front while he lasted in the race. And he always was. He never drove a race that one could point to and say, 'He was stroking it there'. He believed that racing should be a spectacle, that the spectators should be entertained.

By the late Seventies and early Eighties, the car mattered so much more than the driver. Long gone were the days when a star could overcome the deficiencies of poor machinery; you either had ground-effect, and grip, or you didn't. Except when that star was Gilles. It didn't matter where he qualified, what sort of horrors the car produced. You always knew, come race day, that he would charge. That of the modern brigade, he alone could make the impossible become possible. He once described his perfect race as starting from pole, leading, having to make a pit stop, and then tigering back to win. Not for him the comfort of flag-to-flag successes.

OTHER VOICES

Nigel Roebuck – journalist and friend

"The thing that struck me very early was that he was instantly friendly, so remarkably open. He had no fear of journalists. His creed was always to tell the truth, and that way you couldn't get caught out. It was the same way I found Prost, but to a greater degree. He would either say he couldn't say anything, or he'd tell the absolute truth.

"The remarkable thing was that if you called him and you did it from home, he'd insist on calling you back. He once said to me, '*I'll* call *you*. You're not as overpaid as me'. No other driver in my experience would ever think of that. I remember the way he'd chatter. If you called about testing you'd deal with that in five minutes, and he'd be on the phone for another hour, bitching about his

May 8, 1982, and Gilles takes the Ferrari 126C2 out for the last time in an attempt to beat despised team-mate Didier Pironi's time. Out on the track at the same time was Jochen Mass' Rothmans March, and the Ferrari vaulted over its back wheel as the very qualifying accident Gilles himself had predicted unfolded. For many a light went out in motor racing that day.

ice hockey team losing, things like that, everything under the sun.

"He could be unbelievably feisty, especially against Bernie Ecclestone and Balestre. He hated Bernie with a passion. He never held back from saying what he thought about anyone, even if they could harm his career. And you never felt he was telling you things just so he could use you.

"People often forget how very unsophisticated he was in some respects. He wasn't a sophisticated bloke at all with his background. Not like Prost. Stewart says the same thing about Clark, that late in life he was quite sophisticated, but essentially he never changed. Gilles certainly wasn't a hick, but he never changed a jot in his dealings as he became more successful.

"When I think of that conversation we had two days after Imola in 1982; a more conniving bloke would have weighed things up very carefully in what he said, but Gilles just poured his heart out. That was him, so open; if he felt something, he wouldn't keep it bottled up."

■   ■   ■

Comparisons with Nuvolari and Rosemeyer were as inevitable as they were apposite, particularly as the first were drawn by Enzo Ferrari himself. Gilles reminded Il Commendatore of Nuvolari, and the Old Man loved him for that. Villeneuve, he could forgive anything. He was the only driver he would embrace. "He is like an actor who is always looking for applause", Ferrari once said of his penchant for playing to the gallery. "He taught us what we needed to do for our drivers to defend themselves on the track. He was a combative champion and made Ferrari even more famous. I liked him." Of no other driver did he ever speak so warmly.

Gilles burst into Formula One like a meteor. And like a meteor, his end was, perhaps, inevitable. He loved racing for the pure thrill it gave him, not for the financial rewards, sweet though they doubtless were. The tragedy is that in Harvey Postlethwaite's Ferrari 126C2 in 1982 he finally had the weapon for World Championship success.

"I will miss Gilles for two reasons", said Scheckter. "First, he was the fastest driver in the history of motor racing. Second, he was the most genuine man I have ever known. But he has not gone. The memory of what he has done, what he achieved, will always be there."

Senna might have much of Gilles' ability, fire and commitment, but his cold calculating approach is totally at odds with Gilles' relaxed good humour and his easiness outside the cockpit. He had none of Senna's aloofness; he enjoyed what he did, and if others wished to enjoy it with him, so much the better. It was such openness that deified him, made him a champion for the people, the man they loved to have carry their hopes into battle. He was completely honest, blunt when he had to be. There was no side to him. His wife Joann and young children Jacques and Melanie were an essential part of his racing as they all lived in the paddock in their own motorhome.

His critics said he was reckless. Those who could see the deeper significance in his achievements and manner believed that he redefined the parameters for racing drivers of his era. No other driver in modern times has so epitomized the romance of motor racing. Just as surely as Nuvolari and Rosemeyer have passed into legend, so now, less than a decade after his death, has Gilles Villeneuve.

24

DEREK WARWICK

The last hero

"Everyone said I was brave to do it, but I think the reverse. A brave man wouldn't have gone out that day."

It is a curious world in which the Grand Prix writer walks. It can be exhilarating, frustrating and tedious, all at the same time, but more than anything it can be hurtful if you are not of the variety of man whose hide is thick enough to be fashioned into ladies' handbags or shoes.

It is unlike any other sphere of motor racing, for in the lower echelons the sportswriter is often king, a means whereby some seek to elevate themselves in what they believe will be their climb to the top. Often, too often for comfort, those that climb successfully become forgetful of those who once stood alongside them, who perhaps acted as sounding boards, influencers or, sometimes, quasi-psychologists. Who, invariably, had the time, the inclination and, on occasions, the old-fashioned faith, to share their dream. Who, in their way, helped them realize it. It is not a pleasant experience, but it reflects the pressures of the modern-day Formula One, where the money is beyond the ken of most normal people such as you or I, yet where nothing is more easily taken for granted by its recipients. It is sobering when you see how some journeymen are paid 10 times more than a prime minister.

This is the world of ego and expedience, of manipulation and exploitation, a world where the media is generally tolerated at best, more frequently detested. Where objectivity is derided by those as unable to pronounce it as they are to understand its concept, and many expect the writer to act as little more than an unpaid public relations machine espousing their cause. The truth? What's that?

It is all too easy to become disillusioned or cynical, let down by those one once liked, admired, sometimes even revered. Formula One is a great magnifier of personality shortcomings, and rather a sad thing because of it.

I can truly think of only one man I have known within it who has never once betrayed my estimation of his character. His name is Derek Warwick. A man to whom the passion of driving race cars counts for far more than the remuneration he derives from it, bountiful though that may be. Surely, after Chris Amon, he was the driver to whom Fate was most unkind in denying his efforts the reward of even one Grand Prix victory. And even Christopher Arthur enjoyed the fruits of success on two non-championship occasions.

The majority of Formula One people can seem shallow to the press, although that is a harsh criticism, perhaps. We writers tend to hunt in packs, and we spend a lot of time together. The talk, more often than not, is about racing.

Mostly it is about the people within it. Anecdotes are swapped, heroes praised, the shallow or mendacious condemned as we chomp our pizzas in Cascais, munch our tortellini alla panna in Imola, sip our Cabernet Sauvignon in Sydney, or avoid drinking the water in Brazil or Mexico. Hell, sometimes we even enjoy ourselves, too.

We gossip like fishwives, and we frequently assassinate characters verbally because the laws of libel prevent us venting some of our spleen in print. We ourselves are far from blameless. We are cynical, because very often cynicism is our way of protecting ourselves against disappointment, or denying those who dislike us the satisfaction of seeing how much they can hurt.

We play a little game from time to time, trying to identify which drivers would take the trouble to come and visit us in the hospital if we should ever suffer a serious accident while abroad at a race. Mostly we have many fingers left when the counting is done, but one name unfailingly springs to mind: Warwick's.

So far, the acid test has yet to be made, but I know from personal experience that our man would not disappoint. In November 1989 I spun off while indulging in the mundane domestic task of putting out milk bottles on my front doorstep, and found myself lying in a damp flowerbed gazing at the cold night sky, swearing at the mocking moon and telling my wife I used to like it better when my right ankle wasn't broken 120 degrees out of the orientation that had seemed so satisfactory for the last 36 years. While I was in hospital, she and my brother-in-law each received a call from a man demanding two pints, please, and enquiring after my welfare. Warwick.

Five days before that incident my father had died suddenly. Derek will never know just how much that moment of consideration was appreciated, nor how much it helped.

The Jersey-based Hampshireman has always had a strong sense of loyalty, whether to his friends or to his family. In the early days of his career 'Delboy' was encouraged by father Derry (after initial misgivings) and Uncle Stan, characters both, whose exploits could fill a book of their own. As the wheel turned further, Derek was the staunchest supporter of brother Paul as he fought to find his level in Formula 3000 before his tragic death in the 1991 Gold Cup at Oulton Park. With five victories in five races, Paul was maturing into one of Britain's brightest hopes.

Derek is devoted to his wife Rhonda and children Kelly and Marie, and one of the few times I have ever seen him really angry was when he heard of the remarks made against Rosanne Mansell by Nelson Piquet in an interview in Brazilian *Playboy*. "A guy can say what he likes about other drivers', he growled, "but as far as I'm concerned, families are off limits." Warwick knew Piquet of old.

His own racing upbringing began in the tough school of stock cars where, as a teenager, he cut his teeth. No quarter was asked or given on the dirt ovals, no matter what your age, and he gained the closest grounding a European can ever get to the American sprintcar racing which had sired legends such as Mario Andretti and A J Foyt. By contrast, Formula Ford and Formula Three were tame. Even now, winning the 1972 Stock Car World Championship means a great deal to him, and he has never forgotten his roots.

He came up against Piquet in Formula Three in 1978, and as Martin Brundle would against Ayrton Senna five years later, he provided the only consistent opposition to a man obviously destined for greatness. They ended by splitting the title winnings, Piquet taking the BP Championship, Warwick the Vandervell. "Derek was the hardest man out there to beat", admits Gregg Siddle, the amiable Australian who oversaw Piquet's effort.

He won races in Formula Two as well when he drove for Toleman, after a disastrous graduation year in 1979 with a private March, and the Witney-based team finally provided his passport to Formula One the following season. That

Derek worshipped his younger brother Paul, and was devastated by his death at Oulton Park on July 21, 1991. Despite his grief, he acted as a tower of strength to carry his family through the ordeal, and when he next met up with his racing friends exhibited tremendous sensitivity in relaxing them in his company. If a finer man has graced motorsport, he has yet to be identified.

long-held dream proved to have rather more of a nightmare quality, however, as he and Brian Henton struggled to qualify the baulky cars, which were little more than updated versions of the Formula Two machines fitted with Brian Hart's powerful but underfinanced four-cylinder turbocharged engines. Time and again Warwick's car was the wrong side of the 26-car cut-off point, but his persistence never wavered. Like Nigel Mansell, whom he so resembles physically, he believed completely in his own ability, and he finally made his Grand Prix debut in the last race of the season at Las Vegas.

1982 offered better opportunities. Years later, enthusiasts still wax lyrical about the oh-so confident overtaking manoeuvre he pulled in that year's British GP at Brands Hatch, when he slipped his Toleman past Didier Pironi's Ferrari at Paddock Bend. There was the British bulldog up against the car-and-driver combination that was putting a firm stamp on the World Championship, and making the Frenchman look sluggish.

That sunny day the Toleman was running only half a fuel load, hence its unexpected speed. Everyone suspected it, but it was years before there was any official confirmation. Derek would still rather the truth did not emerge. Not because it might take something away from his own performance (nothing could), but because he would rather not take something away from the pleasure

269

enthusiasts got from the move.

When he left Toleman at the end of 1983 it was not without a measure of soul-searching unusual in Formula One, for to him it was like leaving his family. It was, however, an entirely logical move, for with the might of its state backing, Renault surely was knocking on the door. Victory seemed only a race or two away. Indeed, had he not brushed wheels briefly with Niki Lauda during the opening 1984 round in Brazil, he *would* have won. He was well ahead of eventual winner Alain Prost when his suspension broke as a result of Lauda's touch.

The Renault years made him wealthy, and there were some strong performances, but they flattered only to deceive and brought him no nearer that elusive first victory. Gerard Larrousse and Michel Tetu, architects of Prost's victories with the team, left. Morale slumped under the leadership of Gerard Toth. When the Regie pulled out of racing at the end of 1985 it was almost a relief.

Derek then tested a Renault-engined Lotus 95T at Brands Hatch, and was quick. Lotus wanted him, and Renault was happy to have him carry on their association, but Ayrton Senna didn't want him aboard. The Brazilian vetoed his inclusion in the Lotus team for 1986 amid uproar from the British press, and Warwick suddenly realized that he had missed the boat. He was out of Formula One, and that point in retrospect marked the decline of his career. He would come back, but the spotlight would be trained on others. He would no longer be the coming man. From then on his Formula One career would be conducted with second-rate equipment.

"The deal was all signed and sealed, to all intents and purposes, and because of that I'd put all my eggs in the Lotus basket. They got trodden on when Senna vetoed the whole thing, and that was it. He didn't think Lotus could run two cars to the same standard. Looking back he was probably right. But at the time I was angry. I'd literally lost everything I'd worked for in Formula One. Because I'd put everything into the Lotus seat I had nothing else.

"The incredible thing is that I got a Christmas card from Ayrton that year..."

With his Formula One career dead in the water he washed up on Tom Walkinshaw Racing's shore, sharing a Jaguar with Eddie Cheever in the World Sports Prototype Championship. The two drivers had never hit it off in Formula

On that great day at Brands Hatch in 1982, Warwick in the 'Belgrano' Toleman TG181B prepares to overtake Didier Pironi's Ferrari at Paddock Bend. Years later, he hated to reveal the truth of the Toleman's speed for fear of disappointing the fans.

One up until then, but they loosened up with pranks during a St Moritz training session. "We were having a sauna, and I told Eddie I was surprised he'd signed as number two. He said he'd signed as number one, and we realized that Tom had signed us both on that basis. It broke the ice a bit.

"Then we went to Monza for the first race, the two superstars from Formula One. Eddie started the race and then came in for me to take over, but we had forgotten to practice our stops. I'm eager to get in, and Eddie seems to be taking hours to get out. He's lolloping around, maybe woozy. I get hold of him by the back of the neck to drag him out, but he's done a roll and is in among all the oxygen bottles, flat out, and I'm calling him all the names under the sun. He regains his composure, sees me getting in the car and beats on the roof, hits me on the head; I didn't have my seat! I have the belts done up, and he's trying to jam it in, this way, that way, upside-down, and I'm pushing him out the way. I hit him a couple of times and he says, 'You hit me again and I'll punch you!'. In all the confusion he shuts the door down and everyone's waiting for us, wondering why we've taken so long, and nothing happens when I try to start. There's an ignition cut-off by the door, and when I pulled Eddie out I've knocked it off. I look across the pit and Tom's going berserk!

"At Silverstone we had the use of his motorhome, his pride and joy, because he was away racing in Brno. You weren't allowed to get it dirty, or to get undressed in it. We had sandwiches everywhere, clothes all over, it was all *filthy*. Then somebody looked out a window and said, 'Isn't that Tom coming?'. And we all said, 'Rubbish, he's racing in Czechoslovakia'. The door opened, and Tom came up one step. All of us stood to attention like we were in the Army. Tom looked one way, then the other, and said, 'I'll be back in two minutes'. We all sat like little schoolboys until he'd gone, then raced round tidying up like lunatics!"

When Elio de Angelis was killed testing at Ricard in May 1986, Warwick's sportscar interlude was over and he got his second Formula One chance with Brabham. In the aftermath of the likeable Italian's death the team was inundated with telephone calls from hopeful replacements. Warwick was not among them, refusing point blank to demean either himself or de Angelis' memory with such a callous action. That counted for much with Bernie Ecclestone.

Brabham's laydown BT55 was a disaster, but Derek was back in play as a Formula One driver and he switched in 1987 for a three-year spell with Arrows. As usual, the luck ran against him. Seasons would start well, only to falter as development lagged. Yet each time he would find himself panting at the leash for the first race to come round. "All I have to do even now is go to a race circuit, hear a car start up", he would explain. "That's where my motivation comes from. All the time I'm motivated to brake at the 99-metre board instead of the 100, I'll be happy. When I start to brake at 101 I'll know it's time to stop."

And that motivation still came, even in the worst moments. In Canada in 1988 he had a huge shunt in qualifying, backwards into the wall on the start/finish straight, when Philippe Streiff's AGS had thrown dust on to the kink just by the pit road entry. Despite severe back pains Derek raced the following day and dragged his car home a gritty seventh. Twelve months on he finally seemed on course for a top result at the same circuit, even though Senna had repassed his Arrows to take the lead. Had Derek kept going, he would have benefited from the Brazilian's engine failure; instead, he succumbed to one of his own. "I just felt cheated that time," he admitted. "I was expecting to finish second because I could see Senna closing very fast on me, and I knew I wouldn't be able to hold him off. But I was stroking ahead of the two Williamses and I had them well under control." With Senna's engine failure, it was Boutsen for Williams who swept through for the slice of luck.

"What made it doubly frustrating was that I'd forgotten until then just how easy it is to lead in a good car. You know, you can scratch round for 10th and it's

271

bloody hard, but leading in a good car – it's so easy."

Shortly afterwards he shunted a kart heavily during a demonstration run at Jersey's Bouley Bay, where daughter Marie was competing. He was thrown under a stationary Ford Transit van with sufficient force to remove its front bumper. He missed the French GP as a result, but was back for the British despite continuing discomfort. It was the sort of thing Mansell would have done, but without Mansell's successes, Warwick's steeliness tended not to receive the recognition it deserved.

"It took me two weeks to get over that shunt", he recalled. "To be honest, they were the hardest I've ever known. Everything I had to do to recover hurt me more, and I was in a lot of pain at Silverstone. But what hurt even more was that the car was so bloody awful there! Eddie didn't qualify, which shows you just how bad it was." The pain didn't affect his performance there, though. "When the old adrenalin is flowing", he laughed, "you could drive with a broken leg!"

OTHER VOICES

Ross Brawn – former Arrows designer

"He is a very good tester. His main quality is that he is very consistent, and he doesn't prejudge what should be done to the car. He doesn't come in and say, 'Change the bars and the springs'. He has an open mind to solutions. He makes an honest assessment, and the majority of the time he gets it right. He complains of a problem, you solve it, and he goes quicker.

"His quickest lap is usually within five into the test. He's on the pace. Not everyone can do that. I traditionally get a driver to do three timed laps then come in. With Derek they're within a tenth. That's unusual. It makes life very easy for you.

"His performances in 1989, especially in qualifying, were very encouraging for us as we were in a period when you needed a real balls-out effort, and he showed he could do that. He could always find that half second to put us in the top 10. The majority of times, give him a good car and he'd score points, and he came so close to winning in Canada in 1989. He should have won Rio that year, too, but we gave him two 30-second pit stops, and despite them he finished only 17 seconds behind Mansell. We lost him that one."

■ ■ ■

Despite the setbacks, he remained cheerful, his confidence in his ability to win races unshaken, his belief that others recognized him as a top talent helping to sustain him. He and Cheever helped pull Arrows from a top 10 team into the top five or six. The move to Lotus for 1990 should have been the Big Step, final consummation after several near-misses, including one for 1989 when he would have had to agree to perform as Nelson Piquet's number two and not to overtake the Brazilian during a race. Predictably, he snorted with derision at that. He knew Piquet well, knew he was driving at that stage of his career like an old woman. He stayed with Arrows. "It might never have come to me overtaking Nelson in a race", he said. "I might always have been so far ahead it wouldn't have come to it... But the principle of driving with both hands tied was ridiculous. Formula One is difficult enough without that."

Who could ever have foreseen just what a disaster the Lotus season would be, even when the car's chassis suffered worrying structural failures in the first two races? Or that it would turn out to be such a public test of his character? In true Warwick style he went into it with unbridled enthusiasm, speaking warmly of his belief that Lotus might genuinely bridge the gap between the top four teams

– McLaren, Ferrari, Benetton and Williams – and the second division. His very presence brought it the vital motivation it had lacked throughout the Piquet years. Yet even that was not enough. The team lacked direction and technical strength, and struggled from crisis to crisis. Then, at Monza, Warwick had the progenitor of all shunts exiting the Parabolica curve on the opening lap of the Italian GP. It set in trend an emotional chain of events whose culmination and true import would not be seen until the Spanish GP at Jerez three weeks later.

The Lotus ran wide, hit the tyres and the safety bank to its left, and then, shedding wheels, rolled and slid inverted down the middle of the road. By a miracle nobody else ran into it, and to cheers Warwick clambered out of the upturned wreckage before walking to the side of the road. His escape was in itself impressive, but all the more so was the manner in which he walked. There was not a trace of rubberiness in his legs, even after a 150mph accident. The tifosi's cheers became screams of admiration as he broke into a run on his return to the Lotus pit, salutations to a brave man. It wasn't bravado on Derek's part; there was an intensely practical reason.

"I wanted to get back before the pit lane exit was closed. All I was thinking about was the spare car. It was only as I ran that I became aware of what was happening around me. The noise was unreal."

He was intensely moved, not only by the fact that the cheers drowned out the noise of the engines, but also because spectators all around the back of the circuit were so vocal and physical in their delight at seeing him back in action. He analyzed the incident carefully in the days that followed, took pride in his equanimity as he took the second start, actually brushed wheels with another car going into the first chicane, and raced as hard as he could before, inevitably, the Lotus let him down. He was pleased that it affected him not a jot, that he had reacted calmly and sensibly, even during the accident, switching off the ignition, keeping his head as far as possible off the road passing rapidly beneath it. I called him the following Tuesday to see how he was feeling, and he said he'd taken some tablets the previous morning, and had felt well enough to play golf in the afternoon...

Derek came so near to Grand Prix victory at Jacarepagua in Brazil at the start of 1984, his first outing for Renault, only for an earlier brush with Niki Lauda to manifest itself in broken suspension.

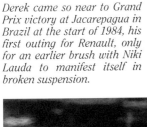

The period after Monza was difficult. "Normally you can rise above the disappointments and the upsets, but that was different. There was a lot of focus on my accident. I had a fantastic week after it, lots of telephone calls and letters

saying how well I'd acted. Camel told me it was proud I was a Camel driver. It was a fairly good time. I had no real reaction, because it wasn't a big accident. Even when I got home. Everyone else thought it was a bigger accident than it was, although it could have been a *massive* accident. I felt nothing really, seeing it on television, because obviously I knew the outcome, knew I walked away, that it could have been big and that the fuel bag was exposed. But it didn't really sink in. I was conscious, aware of what I was doing, pleased with myself about the way I reacted, To my dying day I'll remember the applause when I ran back. I wasn't aware of it for the first 50 yards, then all of sudden... I went through a tunnel of people clapping. It was a nice moment.

"Then by Portugal it all seemed to be slipping away, no matter what I did. It was getting me down. I was pushing as hard as I could, but other than try and tie people up and torture them, there wasn't much more I could do. I was really disappointed not to get the Leyton House drive because I thought it was mine all along, that I just had to bide my time. Maybe I misread it a bit. Then the Tyrrell drive went in Portugal, and I couldn't understand why. I suppose in Formula One that, as good as some drivers are, teams have to survive. They need big budgets, and the difference between some drivers is very small. But it was another big downer."

Just under three weeks later I was sitting behind the barrier at the entry to Jerez's Ferrari curve, the tricky flat-in-fifth right-hander behind the pits where the likes of Gregor Foitek, Luis Sala and Satoru Nakajima had come to grief in previous years. I saw the entire accident that befell Derek's team-mate Martin Donnelly, enough to convince me that, like Derek at Monza, he had suffered some sort of front suspension failure. Martin lay prone on the track, thrown from the shattered mess of his Lotus, which had exploded upon impact with the barrier at the previous corner. Unlike Ferrari, there was no run-off area.

It is hard to say just how much Warwick impressed me that weekend. Here he was, the man who had cried when he was the first on the scene of Gilles Villeneuve's accident at Zolder in 1982, going immediately to the scene of Donnelly's. Who supervised the panicking officials, and carried Lotus onward with a strength he cannot possibly have felt. Camel told him he didn't have to race, and Lotus concurred, yet both left the ultimate decision to him. All that night he agonized, all too aware of the public – and the private – failures the team had already encountered. Aware, too, that the once noble Lotus team was on the brink of collapse, desperately in need of some kind of guidance, some sort of father figure. Others would have taken the safe option and decided not to drive until the full cause could be analyzed back at Hethel, but Derek felt honour-bound not to walk away. Even as late as Saturday morning he was unsure whether he *would* drive, but then there he was in the familiar yellow overalls, and there was Lotus number 11 out on the track.

When he climbed aboard the car he admits he managed to put all fears from his mind. "I had spoken to the team, and they had told me what steps they had taken the previous night to strengthen it", he said quietly. What worried him most, as it had at Monza, was that his own performance should not bear any traces of apprehension.

"My first few laps were slow because of traffic. I was terrified people would think I was deliberately taking it easy."

He proved just how easy he was taking it by qualifying 10th and running strongly until the yellow car's flexing gearbox casing yet again chewed up the transmission's internals. Single-handedly he had dragged Lotus from the depths.

"It hit everyone very hard. I felt much a part of Martin, and tried to react in the right way and calm Diane. I saw Martin in the hospital at the track and it was such a relief. When I left him on the track, as far as I could see he was a goner. It hit me like a sledgehammer. I went to see Diane and I just didn't know what to say to her. I actually told her a bunch of lies that turned out to be the dead truth. Both legs were broken, but I'd seen his eyes open, he was breathing, all was going to be OK. When I got to the hospital at the circuit he was in a lot of pain, but he was there. It was like a miracle. I said some things to him and got a reaction, which was great. A fling of the arm and a flick of the head. I deliberately said some pretty harsh things to him to get him going.

"I spoke to Diane on Saturday evening and she understood that I should race, which lifted me a lot. I felt I'd done a good job. I didn't do it for myself, but because at the end of the day I thought it would be the last straw that broke Lotus' back if I didn't. Everything inside me told me not to do it. Looking back, I think I was very wrong to do it. Everyone said I was very brave, but I think the reverse. A brave person wouldn't have gone out that day. Even now I can't clear that image of Martin lying on the track. It doesn't affect you in the car, but..."

Outside the motorhome he managed to maintain a public mask, even showing two Camel Trophy prizewinners round the cars on Sunday morning. In the circumstances a lesser man might have been forgiven for delegating the task to someone else, but even then Derek appreciated how much the personal touch would mean, and no doubt he made their weekend.

I know how I felt then, with nothing more dangerous to do in the wake of Martin's accident than switch on a word processor, and there was Warwick climbing back on to the tightrope and trying to ignore the holes in the safety net. When a brave man knows fear, yet comes to terms with it and triumphs over it, he moves into the rarefied atmosphere of the Abnormally Brave. Derek Warwick walked there that weekend in Spain. It was the most uplifting thing I have seen in motor racing.

What gave it such a poignant counterpoint was the manner in which things kept going wrong for him. In Portugal he had learned finally that his hopes of joining Leyton House, Tyrrell, or Footwork Arrows had foundered, and in Spain came another closed door as Ligier opted for Thierry Boutsen. Bit by bit he was being squeezed out, and he knew it and hated it. This most pleasant and guileless of drivers finally had to admit to a trace of bitterness as he fought resolutely to avoid feeling sorry for himself. He even investigated the possibility of skipping the final two races of the season, but was contract bound. What made them even harder to bear was the knowledge that he had finally committed himself to a season of sportscar racing with Jaguar the very evening before Sandro Nannini's helicopter accident cut short his career with Benetton. Derek would have been the perfect replacement. In Adelaide, his final scheduled Formula One appearance, it was like racing with a knife twisting in his belly, but as ever he went out fighting.

"As drives slipped away, it was a tough couple of months, really", he recalled, "and I wasn't fun to live with, that's for sure. Rhonda was pleased when it was Thursday and I'd pack my bags. The Monday after Martin's accident I was home and she did say, 'Is now a good time to stop racing?'. She said it once, didn't like the reaction, and has never said it again. Even she's allowed to ask once. It's the only time she's asked in our 18 years together.

"Formula One is my life", he said in Suzuka, like a man unable to believe that a love affair has finally been ended by his partner. "I need to build myself up again for sportscars. I know I've got to leave Formula One, but I don't want to. I can't really understand why I have to. I feel I've given it my full commitment. I've done no wrong. I'm a good racer, still quick. I'm quite good at PR, I have good relationships with the journalists. But somehow it's all turned wrong.

"Many of these guys are very hollow", he said in a rare moment when he was prepared to speak critically of his rivals, "and not that good. Look at Alesi, Modena. Everyone gets in a twist about them, which shows how hyper Formula One can get. With my hand on my heart I can honestly say there are only two drivers out there whom I think are better than me, and that's Senna and Prost. Berger and Mansell and the like? I don't give a tuppence for them."

As he came to terms with the situation, he was bucked by the RAC Rally, on

which he performed impressively in a Subaru. "It was the greatest three weeks I'd had for a long time!", he laughed. His drive attracted a great deal of attention, although one man was steadfastly unmoved. He was the hitchhiker whom Warwick and co-driver Ronan Morgan picked up during their practice. "Do you know who this fella is?", Morgan asked him as he sat stolidly in the back. "This is Derek Warwick. *DEREK WARWICK.* The Grand Prix driver." Their temporary companion remained unmoved. "Unless he's involved with the whippet world up here", he revealed, "it means nowt to me."

In the immediate aftermath of Martin Donnelly's accident in Jerez in 1990 Derek was truly heroic as he held the shattered Lotus team together. Yet at the end of the year a callous F1 turned its back on a man who still clearly possessed the talent of a winner. As he surveyed the paddock in Budapest the following year, Patrick Tambay remarked of him: "He is the best person I've ever met in motor racing. Without him, Formula One, all of this, means nothing..."

OTHER VOICES

Ronan Morgan – RAC Rally co-driver

"I was committed to helping Prodrive on the RAC, on the service side, as they usually had a deal with Lancia. But that wasn't happening after all because of Prodrive's Subaru deal. I was supposed to have been in Kuwait for a rally, but that was cancelled, and I was just preparing to help the team get ready for scrutineering and all that when Dave Richards called me and asked me if I wanted to co-drive for a celebrity. They wouldn't tell me who it was, and I said 'No', because I had visions of being with a bloke who'd never driven before. They'd told me he'd never done a rally, and that I'd be sorry. Eventually I made them tell me, and I said 'Yes' when I knew it was Derek. I hadn't met him, but they all reckoned we'd get on like a house on fire. We did. And we became good friends after the event.

"We had lots of funny incidents during our practice. Derek knew *nothing* about rallying. After our eighth and final day we were driving down the motorway and I said, 'Remember this. This is the route we'll be taking on the

276

rally, and we have to cover it in a certain time.' He thought about that for a bit, and then said, 'You mean to tell me we'll actually be driving the race car on this motorway?'. He went quiet for a bit. Then he said, 'You mean to tell me we'll actually be driving the race car' – that's what he kept calling it – 'on all these roads we've been driving over?'. And I said, 'What did you think was going to happen?'. He said, 'I expected to go to the start of each stage and the car would be warmed-up and all ready to go. I thought it would be moved around on a transporter.' 'And how did you expect to get from place to place?', I asked. 'I thought we'd go by helicopter', he said! After eight days of practice. I mean, he really knew *nothing* about rallying!

"But he was totally enthralled, and he came away with a big respect for the sport, all the logistics and everything. And he said some of the teams were more professional than in Formula One.

"We've kept in touch since, and he's threatened to get his revenge by taking me out in one of his sportscars. I'd love to. He obviously has lots of ability, and he's a super guy, isn't he?"

■　■　■

How will history remember Derek Warwick? As a man with so little rancour for his past disappointments, nor for new British drivers who have moved into the limelight. As a man with no time to fret about opportunities lost, even though he could have taken the Williams ride that eventually launched Mansell to stardom. "That was probably the biggest mistake of my career", he admits. "It launched Nigel, but to be perfectly honest I didn't think the team could do it. My gut feeling was to stay with a manufacturer like Renault, and I was offered a good deal to do just that. Honda and Williams were struggling at the time and I decided against a move. It was a *MISTAKE!*"

It will also remember him for the manner in which he sportingly played his game, as the man who once said, "I like people, and I find it comes easily to talk to them, whoever they are. I can get on with the Lord Mayor, or just as easily with the local refuse mover". As a man of unfailing good humour and optimism, who wore his enthusiasm like a badge of honour. As a rare example of a star unspoiled by his achievements, and unembittered by the way Fate mapped out his career. As one of the few in Formula One for whom nobody has a bad word. As a man who drove his last Grand Prix with fire in his heart and a smile on his lips. As a hard man who yet had shakily to leave the bedside of his fallen team-mate on two occasions.

Most of all it will remember him as a gentle man with time for others, and one hell of an underrated race driver.

25

ROGER WILLIAMSON

Heroes and cowards

"After Roger it weren't fair on any driver because he was so superior, nobody could take his place in my heart. He asked me for nothing in life." – Tom Wheatcroft

I still have the front cover of the now defunct monthly *Competition Car*, No 4, 1972. It made a lasting impression on me because it captured the very essence of Roger Williamson. It showed him in his Formula Three GRD at Monaco that year, with an overhead shot into the cockpit. His left hand is atop the wheel, the right reaching to shift gear. His head, as ever, is cocked in the unmistakable manner he adopted. It looked uncomfortable, but it was the Williamson crouch. It said, 'Watch out, I'm coming'.

Roger Williamson was a brilliant talent. Even then, in only his second year of serious racing in the big league after seasons in karts, Minis and terrorizing the British club scene in his famous Ford Anglia, that much was obvious.

He never gave up. No matter what the odds, Roger never gave up. That made the biggest impression. When I have something that means something to me, I don't give up. Roger is the reason why. I was inspired by what he stood for. I never met him, but he was one of the single greatest influences I've known. *Never* give up. It's what I try to teach my children, what I learned from watching a cheerful little guy from Leicester who just loved racing cars.

The first Formula Three race I ever saw was the International Trophy at Silverstone in 1972. Roger just murdered them. There was something like a 13-car scrap between drivers such as David Purley and Conny Andersson, but right up in front, just in a different class, was Roger, first time out in the new GRD. He won by nearly 14 seconds.

Roger was an extremely straightforward guy. He worked in the family business, and they had an old converted coach that they all lived in at races. His father, Dodge, was razor-sharp, a real character who was once the speedway king of Leicester. He was living his life all over again through Roger, in a way. Dodge would think nothing of laying people out, and though he was only a little guy he was as tough as granite. Roger was a sophisticated version of him, non-aggressive, reserved, but possessed of the same grim determination. With him, it merited a capital D.

Together they ran Northend Motors, a garage and secondhand car business. But though they might have seemed to some like country boys from Leicester, there weren't any flies on either of them. There wasn't much that went on in the town that they didn't know about.

Ian Phillips, now working for Jordan Grand Prix in Formula One, was a

There are few motor racing photographs in which Roger Williamson was not smiling. A cheerful, no-nonsense car dealer, he lived for racing yet expected nothing of anyone else as he worked up the ladder.

rookie journalist working for *Autosport* in the late Sixties. He would come to know Roger better than almost anyone else. "When I first met them at a race, which was a long, long way away from home, they were just amazed that somebody wanted to talk to them. I think that must have been 1969 or '70 with the Anglia, and it just sort of struck a vein somewhere. Then, when they came into Formula Three, it was a whole new world to me."

He hitched around covering the races, and a friendship blossomed, even if Dodge did his best to discourage it, as Tom Wheatcroft, the owner of Donington Park and the man who played the key role in Roger's career, recalled. "It were ever so funny. Ian was hitch-hiking round Europe. Dodge wouldn't let people in the bus, but I'd invite Ian in. Then Dodge would say, 'There's no food, there's only enough for us', and I'd say, 'I'm not hungry, Dodge, let him have mine', and suddenly there'd be enough for us all, 'cause Dodge did the cooking!"

"I never really worked out whether Tom or Dodge bought the new transporter", said Ian. "Tom always said he did, but Dodge wouldn't let anybody in it. He'd say, 'I spent all this money and I'm not having you and your fag ash all over it. Get out!'. I used to live in my car and ask if I could leave some milk in their fridge. He always moaned about me 'cluttering up my motor'. They had this lovely transporter – it was nice for the time, almost so good you couldn't use it. It was built with six beds in it, and they took the view that they didn't really need hotels. When they got to Formula Two, hotels were a bit easier. There was a bit more pressure, it was a bit more intense. But right to the end, there was no way he lost his grass roots, and to be honest, I don't think he ever would have done. He was always, like, growing up from being a secondhand car dealer in Minis to secondhand BMWs, in a way. The thought process was still the same, and I can't ever see that the money that might have been involved ultimately would have made any difference to him."

Wheatcroft later calculated that Dodge's stake in the transporter amounted to the sink unit...

Phillips liked Williamson's driving style. "I think the most distinctive thing about it was how he actually sat in the cockpit. It wasn't exactly a classic style! I wouldn't have said that he was by any means a *style* driver. He just wanted to get stuck in, and he did it the way he knew best, which compromised in a way, but some people have natural style and grace, and I don't think you could ever say that about the way he drove. It was just a case of, 'I'm going to get in there and show these bastards'..."

Wheatcroft, the colourful Leicestershire builder who had begun his own impressive collection of historic racing cars, had bought Donington Park, and would reintroduce racing to it in the late Seventies, is a fanatically enthusiastic motor racing follower. At Monaco in 1971 he, too, was attracted by the Williamson crouch as he watched the Formula Three qualifying. He also saw smoke pouring from the engine, and upon inquiry discovered that the piston rings were worn. The unit was tired. Roger and Dodge had bought it on hire purchase at the beginning of the season, their first in the category, and had yet to make the first payment to Holbay. Tom eventually paid for that one, and bought him a new one. The seeds of friendship took instant root.

"I thought I'd never see the boy again, but I admired how he drove there. I think he finished up seventh, and I think he started about 12th." Wheatcroft is not the type to ask anything of anyone. He was soon to find that Roger came from the same mould. Days later, Williamson turned up late on his doorstep, just before midnight, black as the ace of spades. He'd just been changing a back axle on his Dad's bus and was about to head for Silverstone once he'd cleaned up. But first he had a debt to repay, and he had come straight round the moment he'd knocked off with a couple of tickets for the British race as a 'Thank you' for Monaco.

Tom thought twice about taking up the offer, but was nevertheless touched. Eventually he went. "The first thing I found myself thinking when I woke up that morning was, 'I wonder how the boy's getting on?'." He arrived to see the car on a tow rope after a big shunt and Roger saying, 'That's my career finished'. The previous late night in the garage had taken its toll.

Tom was instrumental in getting the 713M rebuilt at the March factory overnight, giving Max Mosley an undertaking to pay for anything that went missing while 'his' boys were working at Bicester.

That was the year in which the experienced Australian Dave Walker trounced the opposition in a full works Lotus 59 run in Gold Leaf colours and tended by two fully professional mechanics. Roger was his greatest threat. Behind him at that time he had that National Championship-winning season with the Anglia, but it had been run on a shoestring. The shoestring had snapped so many times it was very short until that meeting with Wheatcroft. From then on, the challenge grew until he beat Walker fair and square on Gold Cup day at Oulton Park, a real driver's circuit.

Roger's credo of asking nothing from anyone meant that what kindnesses he received were always reciprocated. As Wheatcroft would edge away to take up his position for a race, Roger would always quietly nudge him in the ribs with an elbow and say, "Thanks, Tom". "Some people, that means nothing with, but that were 100% his heart. You'd know be 'is eyes. He were such a nice lad, and a racer. Absolutely. A Villeneuve type.

"One day he came in and sat on the pit counter, very quiet, and I said, 'Are you all right?'. And he said, 'Well, Tom, I can't understand it, I really pushed it them last four laps, and I'm on the *second* row'. I sez, 'Well, you've got violent understeer'. He were feathering the inside edge of the tyres, and so they fiddled with it and he went out, and when he came in he said, 'It felt like I never tried', and he were on the pole! He never came in and said it was the car, *never* blamed the car. If anything weren't right, he thought it were him off. He were like Jimmy, he didn't bother about an anti-roll bar's thickness or whatever, if he'd got a handling problem he'd let the back go more, go in a bit quicker and let the back go and cut the understeer. He was so natural it was beyond believing. He were just like Jimmy was in that respect. But I always used to think of Roger and Fangio, they were the same height and both had the same sort of determination just to get that time."

Trevor Foster, who worked as a mechanic with Roger in 1972 and '73, went on to work for Shadow and Tyrrell and thence became team manager at Eddie Jordan Racing and Jordan Grand Prix. He remembers Roger fondly. "He used to smile a lot, but never showed much emotion. He would just say, 'Thanks a lot, Tom'. He was just straight talking. He didn't like bullshitters. He didn't have time for the high fallutin'. If he wanted to know you he wanted to know you, you were a friend, and that was it. If you tried to flannel him or tried to impress him or whatever, then he wasn't interested at all, end of story.

"He'd do anything. He'd drive the coach, do whatever he had to do. He'd get up in the morning and do a full day's work. Not a problem. He never used to sit around the garage watching you working on the car. There were always too many other things to do. He had to earn a living. I think that helped to keep him hungry. And anything he did, he had to be competitive. Anything, whatever game it was, he always had to be competitive.

"He was very likeable, very down-to-earth, matter-of-fact, straightforward. Never any bullshit. If he thought the car wasn't right then it was down to the car. If he wasn't driving right, he'd be the first to stand up and say, 'Don't worry about it, it's down to me'. I've even known him in qualifying actually to stop, get out of the car, and walk around, sit down, sort himself out. He'd tell you to leave the car, then he'd go out and do the business. He was a real thinker. He was a very friendly guy, always very happy to speak to anyone, all the old guys he knew, even when he was on the brink of Formula One and winning in Formula Two."

In 1971 Formula Three had just switched to 1,600cc engines, and to begin

This is the lead he opened at the Silverstone International Trophy's F3 race in 1972, his first time out in the Wheatcroft GRD that would take him to that year's national title. Within the cockpit, the head is cocked in the famous Williamson crouch.

with the grids were small, confined to the likes of Walker, Williamson and the Lotuses of Andy Sutcliffe and James Hunt. If you finished, you tended to finish well. Roger finished most of them, with some good results. Perhaps they seemed to come by default, but as the grids started to fill up, with the AIRO team with Alan Jones and Alan McCully and Brian Maguire, and suddenly cars and engines becoming available, the guy who had come out of saloon cars was still up there with the best of them.

Despite the financial help he received from Tom, Roger knew the value of money, and not a penny would be wasted. They employed some more qualified people to look after the car, and they just built their team up slowly. By the end of the year there was nothing to choose between Roger and Walker. Frequently, Roger would refuse to buy new tyres, even when Tom begged him. "We don't need them, Tom", he would say. "I can make up the time." Often, he did. Tom loved that, loved the way that his patronage and support was never taken for granted.

After starting with a March 723 they switched to the GRD 372 for 1972 and there was no stopping him. He won nine races and took the Shell British Championship to add to his Lombard title from 1971. He had nearly twice as many points as runner-up Colin Vandervell. He won the race supporting the French GP at Clermont-Ferrand, and had staged a dramatic comeback drive before crashing at a wet Monaco, having made a poor start from pole position after winning his heat. Even in adversity, he would not give up. In the final British round at Brands Hatch, he tiptoed to a brilliant second place on slicks in the wet behind the wet-shod Jacques Coulon. At Paul Ricard in August he had beaten the cream of the French Championship, only to be disqualified when his engine wouldn't hold a vacuum. "He'd had a puncture in the heat and qualified at back of grid", recalled Tom. "On the second lap he passed the two Frenchmen in front of the pits, and afterwards they pulled the engine down and said it wouldn't hold a vacuum, but it were because a valve weren't shutting properly. The cam were too hot, so therefore we should have had less power. It were only a fraction, but they disqualified us. But the other drivers all took us out. It were in all the French papers that Roger had won!"

Formula Two beckoned, after a brief debut at Pau that year, and for 1973 he and Wheatcroft embarked on their campaign with the GRD 273. It was a heavy, cumbersome car, but Roger tackled it with his inimitable enthusiasm, even though Jean-Pierre Jarier was pulverizing everyone in his works March-BMW. He struggled with eighths and ninths, but starred at Thruxton, where he won his heat and led the final, only to be delayed by a puncture. Despite all the disappointments, he never once suggested a change of chassis to Wheatcroft, and it was only when he crashed the 273 at Nivelles after brake failure that the programme changed course. Tom had begun to play games with GRD's Mike Warner after the latter had boasted to him that he could read people's minds. "He told me he thought I'd bought two Marches for Roger. Up until then it hadn't even dawned on me, but after that I thought, 'Bugger it, we've had enough of struggling'."

He told Roger that on their way back round the pits they had to pass Max Mosley, "So we might as well do a deal with him". They did. The GRDs went back, and at Rouen he was walking his heat first time out in the March until the BMW engine broke. Roger had never seen Rouen before, nor the car, but he was smack on the pace. At the Monza Lottery his winning drive went down into history.

The team arrived late after the coach broke down on the way, and when they finally made it they couldn't get it under the tunnel, so they had to unload the car and push it across to the pits. Then they had to race through in the estate car with a few bits thrown in while Roger got changed. Official qualifying was already well under way, and he had never seen the place before. He was strapped in the car and sent out to find his way round, and within half an hour he was second quickest. "Literally", said Foster, "he warmed the car up and Boom!, he was straight into it. He would come in all through qualifying and say, 'I just can't believe these chicanes. I'm going to drive straight across one because I keep coming up to them thinking I'm not going to brake yet, not yet, not yet, NOW!' And the next lap he'd do the same thing and go a little bit further."

He started from pole position, a tenth ahead of local ace Vittorio Brambilla, and he won the first 20-lap heat by an easy 11 seconds from Patrick Depailler's Elf-Ford Hart and the Italian. In the second heat he and the Frenchman were side-by-side into the first chicane when the Monza Gorilla barged into him and sent them both down the escape road, where they had to wait for the entire field to go by. As he rejoined, Brambilla did his utmost to delay Roger further, but as he swung out wide Roger saw his chance and pounced through. He had 19 laps to close to within those 11 seconds of Depailler, and thus began the Formula Two equivalent of Jim Clark's 1967 Italian GP performance. Later that year Stewart would do something similar, and in 1988 Johnny Herbert would stage such a blinding drive in the F3000 race after an early barge from a backmarker. Each was a classic.

After winning a dramatic Monza Lottery in Wheatcroft's new F2 March in 1973, Roger led easily at Misano Adriatico until electrical failure. By then, Formula One was already beckoning and the future could not have looked brighter...

If any race epitomized Roger's refusal to accept defeat, that was the one. He was up to seventh by the end of that first lap. Four laps later he was 10 seconds behind second-placed Coulon in his March-BMW, and then by lap seven only Depailler remained in front. He got the gap to the Elf down to less than 11 seconds two laps later, but he wasn't prepared to leave it at that. Roger wanted to win outright. By lap 15 he was alongside Depailler, but spun as he tried to take the outside line into the first chicane. He just avoided the escape road barrier and then spun the March back in the right direction and regained the track before Coulon could profit. With only three laps left he repeated the move, this time without drama, and romped home to a staggering triumph.

"I got that drunk after the management took us out for a lovely meal that night", recalled Wheatcroft fondly.

OTHER VOICES

Trevor Foster – Wheatcroft mechanic

"I would have to say, looking back now, that he wasn't one of the most technical guys, but he knew the basic things that he wanted, and if you gave him that then he was what you'd just call naturally quick. As far as engineering was concerned, he wasn't actually that strong. But he would drive round a problem. When he went out, he'd often come back in and say, 'That's as quick as it'll go. That's it'. You knew then that if you said, 'No, that isn't quick enough', he could go out and do another 10 laps, but he wasn't going to go any quicker. Whatever he got to, he was always straight on to it.

"We just loved him, we thought he was brilliant. He was that sort of driver. To me, Johnny Herbert seems a lot like him. You never knew what Johnny could do, you couldn't believe it. He just used to raise his standards all the time, too. Roger never used to give up. *Never* used to give up. Just look at that Monza Lottery.

"I never saw him depressed, even in the days when we struggled with the GRD, which really was a bit of a boat compared to the March. The Ford BDG engines were no match for the BMWs, either. He never badgered Tom, he was never constantly on to him saying, 'I've got to have a March'.

"Racing has changed over the last 18 or so years, and it's hard to say whether Roger would have had the same mental approach outside the car now. In those days he just used to be buying and selling cars when he wasn't racing. He was washing cars, doing this, that and the other. No matter where he went, what he did, next day, bomp, he was back in at work. 'Right, what're we going to do?', and this, that and the other.

"His mother was unbelievable. She had all these trophies. I've never seen a room like it in my life. From all his years karting, and she used to be up at 5 o'clock every morning – she doted on him – and she systematically used to polish these trophies. Every day. Not all of them every day, but you know, she'd do so many trophies each morning. And at 6.30 or whatever, she'd know that Roger'd get up for breakfast. She never used to go to the races. She was very nervous about it. They might as well have been cleaned once a fortnight, but there was always this thing, she did them religiously."

■ ■ ■

His fresh successes didn't change Roger Williamson at all. He led at Misano Adriatico before electrical trouble sidelined him, and finally he made his overdue Formula One debut at Silverstone. It ended with Jody Scheckter's first-lap shunt into the pit wall exiting Woodcote. At Zandvoort Roger was killed.

He and David Purley were running their similar March 731Gs in close company when the left front tyre on Roger's car exploded on their eighth lap at the section of the track where Piers Courage had crashed three years earlier. They had just negotiated the left-right flick called Hondenvlak and were in the first of two fast fifth-gear right-handers when the incident occurred. The March struck the outer guardrail, the supports of which, incredibly, had only been set in the soft sand that is such a feature of the seaside track. It bent back with the weight of the car, before flipping it back on to the track, where it landed upside-down, right on the apex of the second right-hander. The left-hand fuel tank had been damaged, and a small fire started.

Purley immediately stopped his car and abandoned his own race in a selfless act of heroism harrowingly captured on BBC television. Only yards away stood a fire tender, but no order was given to stop the race and its driver refused, perhaps rightly, to drive against the direction of the traffic. Worse, marshals with fire extinguishers merely watched as Purley fought a lone battle to right the upturned March. He could hear Williamson inside it. Roger pleaded with him to get him out. Time and again Purley tried to lift the car, but each time he failed. For two laps – at least 2m 47s –the fire was minimal, but then it grew dramatically in intensity. David tried to fight it after grabbing an extinguisher from one marshal, but by then the fire had too strong a hold.

As the marshals still remained immobile, appalled spectators began to try and help, unable to believe what they were seeing. Only then were marshals with police dogs galvanized into action, to keep them back. Finally, in the most callous act of cowardice ever seen in motor racing, they moved at last and tried to drag the desolate Purley away. He shrugged them off angrily.

Roger was uninjured in the cockpit, but they left him to die of asphyxiation. When they finally arrived, the fire trucks were far, far too late.

White smoke had plumed across the track, and many drivers later reported feeling their throttles tightening each time they drove through, yet no order was ever given to stop the race. Incredibly, Zandvoort, the circuit that will forever live in infamy, was granted further races until 1985.

OTHER VOICES

Ian Phillips – journalist and friend

"Ironically, Roger had asked me if I would be prepared to go and work for them in setting up their Formula One plans for 1974. I had decided I was going to leave *Autosport*. Actually, the Monday after he was killed I was expecting to hear the news that he was going ahead. As it happened I got a call at 9 o'clock that morning. I had been at a Formula Two race in Mantorp Park when he was killed, and I hadn't got back until about 5 o'clock in the morning. When the phone rang I said to my girlfriend, 'Oh, I don't want to talk to anybody'. It was Richard Feast, who was then the editor of *Autosport*. He told me what had happened, and that while I'd been away I'd been made the editor, so it was a bit of a mixed emotion day one way and another.

"Purley actually had a conversation with him. David was trying to turn him over and told me afterwards how Roger had said to him, 'For God's sake, David, get me out of here', and he just couldn't get him out. The circumstances were just appalling. Berger's thing at Imola in 1989 proved just how much things have changed over the years.

"It changed my outlook on racing. It was the first time anybody had been killed in racing that I knew well, and yes, for a time – probably only a short time – I wondered was it really all worth it? I wasn't sure whether I wanted to be involved, but I think that's a natural reaction when you're young and you've never actually been touched by a tragedy. It was the first time for me. You know what it's like, you've been in it long enough.

"Unfortunately, it's a thing you have to become hardened to, and to accept that it's part of life and that all those participating know that it can happen. Thankfully, these days the risks are being minimized. Certainly, from my point of view, I had to question if it was really all worth it, when a young life could be just wiped out like that. Being only 22 I couldn't comprehend it all, and I suppose in a way you are always slightly reticent in relationships from then on. You can be close to people, but not that close. I mean, be good friends, talk whatever, but keep your distance."

■　■　■

The bright little guy was gone. Outside of the car he was an ordinary bloke who happened to love motor racing. "The whole thing with Roger was that he used to come back and go down the pub or something with his mates", said Trevor. Phillips would recall another side of him. "On a number of occasions when I was travelling with him, his ability to talk the police around to his way of thinking was quite amazing. It was either for speeding, or when he sold me this coach for £200, or something like that. He drove it down from Leicester, with no lights, no MOT, and he got caught bringing it into London. We were really getting taken to the cleaners, but he talked his way out of it. I really don't know how he did it!"

On another occasion he went speeding into a local village with Tom aboard. "I said, 'You'd better slow down, lad, that were a copper we just passed'. 'No', he said, 'it were a bus conductor. Don't worry'. And I said, 'Well, that bus conductor wants you to pull over...'."

His two Formula One races told us precious little, and did nothing to allow him to display his ability, although outings in a Kitchmac (Tony Kitchener's modified F5000 McLaren M10B) showed he could handle power. That year's works March, the cobbled together 731G, was a dog. March was concentrating more on its customer market in Formula Two, and there, mercifully, Roger was able to show his true mettle.

"I don't believe he actually did a test before the British GP", said Foster. "And of course he didn't get a chance to prove anything in the race because he was caught up in that Scheckter accident on the first lap.

"What happened was he came back to the UK for that race and he had the big shunt, and as there was no spare car he didn't restart. March wasn't sure if it could repair the car in time, so Roger told us to drive up through Holland on the way to Sweden because the Mantorp Formula Two race was that weekend, and he said to ring in on the Wednesday and he'd be able to tell us either if we were doing the Swedish round, or whether to divert and come to Zandvoort. We were actually there, watching the race, with his father."

In February 1973 he had tested for BRM, and there was able to give a more meaningful indication of what he might have done in a Formula One car. Louis Stanley was still looking for a partner for Clay Regazzoni and Jean-Pierre Beltoise, and one day he called Wheatcroft and asked him if Roger could test at Silverstone.

It was quite a cold day, and his first time in a Formula One car. He passed the test brilliantly. In consideration of his status, Stanley made him drive the unloved P180 first, Tony Southgate's dragster with rearward weight bias. The lap record then was 1m 18.2s, and after a handful of laps Roger equalled it before an upright broke. He was unharmed, but it was a very hairy moment. It troubled him not at all, and by now BRM's management was getting very interested.

Stanley plugged him into a P160, and this time he recorded 1m 18.0s. They tried him on other tyres and he broke the lap record again, dipping into the 1m 17s. Every time he went out in it he went below the existing record.

After that Stanley wanted to sign him up, and invited Tom and Roger down for traditional tea at the Dorchester. "But I wouldn't let him sign. BRM was on the way down, and if he were going in a car he were going in a V8, a Cosworth. It was a day I were conned, really, 'cause they told me Clay Regazzoni were fogbound in Switzerland, and it were no such thing. It were just a try on. Then Louis brings a contract out, wants me in the Dorchester, wants him to sign it, but no way.

"Derek Bell were there that day, and he came down and he said, 'By God, Tom, you've got a fast lad there', which I always remember. It was very nice of him. Drivers very rarely compliment another driver, and I appreciated that."

Team manager Tim Parnell was also highly impressed. "He was terrific. Roger Williamson without a doubt was a future World Champion. That day we came here (we were talking at Silverstone) he broke the lap record, and that was the fastest a BRM had ever been round here. He was very fast. He'd have been a top driver, there was real Championship material there. A tragedy, an absolute tragedy, that."

Stanley predicted Williamson would be equal to Stewart within two years, but by April that year, when Roger had rejected the BRM offer, he was quoted in an interview as saying, "In spite of breaking lap records, he is not ready for Formula One racing for another year. To put him in a works team at the outset would be foolish, irresponsible and bad judgment...". It was, of course, exactly what BRM had done with Stewart in 1965...

"We got to the British Grand Prix, and *nobody* knew that Ken Tyrrell had been in touch", said Wheatcroft. "He wanted Roger. He'd come to races and watched him. Jackie Stewart was going to retire, of course, and Ken knew that early on."

Just as, years later, Johnny Herbert, who resembled Roger in so many ways, was on the verge of signing for Benetton when he broke his ankles in that F3000 shunt at Brands Hatch in 1988, so, just before he died, Roger had been discussing a contract with Tyrrell for 1974 as partner to Francois Cevert.

OTHER VOICES

Tom Wheatcroft

"The truth was we had a contract to sign with Ken, but we had to keep altering it. Then Roger come up the office one morning, and he were in my office all day and then he come home and had a meal with me. It were just after the 9 o'clock news, and after being with me all day from about 9 o'clock in the morning, he finally said to me, 'Oh, Tom, I'm worried. I'd like to stay with you, and drive for you.'

"And I said, 'Well, Roger, we'd only hold you up. Ken's forgot more than we'll ever know'. And we had a chat, and we rang Pat McLaren up and ordered two M23s. Still in my workshop I've got all the stuff that we bought, never been unwrapped, to make a car for ourselves as well. We were going to make a Formula Two car and run it during that season in odd races, as well as do Formula One, and we were going to do that, and then we'd learn how to make a car off the Formula Two.

"The McLarens would have been private, for myself, and Pat would have sold them to us, it was all laid on. Course, I knew her well 'cause I'd done quite a few deals when Bruce were alive, so we weren't like strangers, you know. I knew her like I know Ken.

"Roger were very loyal. Never lied, never did anything like that. Never asked me for anything. One of the nicest times of my life were at Kyalami, in South Africa, when Roger and I went out there for six weeks testing a Formula Two car for March. Then the Formula Ones come down to test for the Grand Prix. They'd flash past him, but they still let us run, then when they went round the

In the early stages of the 1973 Dutch GP, Roger leads David Purley past Jack Oliver's Shadow after the Englishman had hit the barriers at Gerlachbocht. Laps later the STP March's left front tyre burst and threw it into the barriers, which launched it across the road. Despite Purley's bold efforts, cowardly Dutch marshals left Roger to die in his car, rather than help Purley to turn it back on its wheels before the fire really took hold.

back he'd pass them again! Niki Lauda were out for his first Formula One drive, and that's how I met him and Ronnie Peterson.

"I were ill for weeks after Roger was killed. Just the smell of burning. I were a bit ashamed of myself, sometimes, when I look back on how I was then."

■ ■ ■

Tom had nothing to be ashamed of, for Roger had been like another son. It is still painful, nearly 20 years on, to ponder too much just what Roger Williamson might have achieved in 1974 in a Wheatcroft McLaren M23, a car identical to the one in which Emerson Fittipaldi would win that year's World Championship, and the forerunner of the model James Hunt would use to the same purpose two years later. To be reminded again of that awful loss of talent and the circumstances in which it was so callously wasted.

He didn't want money or fame. All he asked of life was the chance to race cars with Tom Wheatcroft. Those craven marshals who plunged Dutch motorsport to such disgusting depths that day in July 1973 denied him even that simple wish.

INDEX OF PERSONALITIES